FONDAZIONE
BANCO DI SICILIA

Museo d'Arte
e Archeologia
I. Mormino

The Ignazio Mormino Museum of the Banco di Sicilia Foundation is located in Villa Zito, an early 18th century Neo-Classical style building. The museum showcases collections of majolica artefacts, stamps, etchings and drawings, coins, paintings, as well as an important archeological section. Another important area of the museum consists in an extensive library of over sixty thousand books concerning the special topics of archeology, numismatics and the history of Sicily. Of the 4,751 archeological findings property of the museum today, 3,800 come from the Selinunte necropolis in the province of Trapani, witness to the importance of this most important of Greek colonies on the shores of the Western Mediterranean sea. Other excavation project fundings have involved, in the Sixties, the archeological sites of Himera, Terravecchia di Cuti and Solunto, all located in the province of Palermo.

The considerable iconographic material from the picture gallery and from the collections of etchings and drawings is an excellent historical source of representation of Sicily's landscape.

VILLA ZITO
Via della Libertà No. 52
90143 Palermo
Phone ++39 091 6085974/77
Fax ++39 091 6085978
info@fondazionebancodisicilia.it
www. fondazionebancodisicilia.it

ADMISSION:
EUR 4.00 - regular ticket
EUR 2.00 - reduced ticket
(visitors under 18 and over 65,
students, groups)
Free admission for school groups
Booking required for groups
(max. 30 people) and guided
tours (only for groups).

OPENING HOURS:
Mondays to Fridays:
from 9.00 a.m. to 1.00 p.m.
and from 3.00 to 5.00 p.m.
Museum, Museum Shop
and Library
Saturdays:
from 9.00 a.m. to 1.00 p.m.
Museum and Museum Shop

CLOSED:
On Sundays and holidays

Catania University Botanical Garden

One of the few green areas in Catania's old town, the Botanical Garden, created in 1858 by Francesco Tornabene, is a veritable living museum, still to this day with the original structure, as shown by the neoclassical building with a double colonnade front, and the near geometric layout of the garden.

The thick tangle of exotic plants makes it look like a tropical garden, a cool oasis in the heart of the city, offering a number of remarkable collections. Surely the richest one (with about 2,000 species) is the succulent plants collection, one of the garden's main attractions thanks to the original forms and structures on display. Just as interesting is the palms collection, numbering about a hundred trees.

In the Sicilian Garden are kept plants growing spontaneously all over Sicily.

Entry: via A. Longo, 19 95125 Catania
Telephone +39 095 430901 - Fax +39 095 441209
e-mail: dipbot@mbox.dipbot.unict.it
Internet: http://www.dipbot.unict.it
Opening times: weekdays from 9.00 a.m. to 1.00 p.m.

Syracuse
Italy - Sicily

a masterpiece.

i-white carlo coniglio - foto archivio apt

Azienda Autonoma
per l'Incremento Turistico
di Siracusa

cultural events
Classical performances - Greek Theatre
Ortigia festival

www.apt-siracusa.it
info: 0039 (0)931 481232

AUTHENTIC
Sicily

TOURING CLUB OF ITALY

Touring Club Italiano
President and Chairman: *Roberto Ruozi*
General Manager: *Guido Venturini*

Touring Editore
Managing Director: *Alfieri Lorenzon*
Editorial Director: *Michele D'Innella*

International Department
Fabio Pittella
fabio.pittella@touringclub.it

Senior Editor: *Luciana Senna*
Editor: *Monica Maraschi*
Writer and Researcher: *Banca Dati Turistica*
Translation: *Timothy Dass, Judith Mundell, Elisabeth Poore, Jennifer Robson*
Maps: *Touring Club Italiano*
Design and layout: *Studio Gatelli, Milano*
Cover photo: *Temple E, Selinunte (Regione Siciliana, Assessorato al Turismo)*

Advertising Manager: *Claudio Bettinelli*
Local Advertising: *Progetto*
www.progettosrl.it - info@progettosrl.it

Prepress: *Emmegi Multimedia, Milano*
Printing and Binding: *CPM, Casarile*

Distribution
USA/CAN – *Publishers Group West*
UK/Ireland – *Portfolio Books*

Touring Club Italiano, corso Italia 10, 20122 Milano
www.touringclub.it
© 2005 Touring Editore, Milan

Code K7M
ISBN 88 – 365 – 3403 – 1

Printed in April 2005

SUMMARY

WHAT IS THE TOURING CLUB OF ITALY?

Long Tradition, Great Prestige

For over 110 years, the Touring Club of Italy (TCI) has offered travelers the most detailed and comprehensive source of travel information available on Italy. The Touring Club of Italy was founded in 1894 with the aim of developing the social and cultural values of tourism and promoting the conservation and enjoyment of the country's national heritage, landscape and environment.

Advantages of Membership

Today, TCI offers a wide rage of travel services to assist and support members with the highest level of convenience and quality. Now you can discover the unique charms of Italy with a distinct insider's advantage.

Enjoy exclusive money saving offers with a TCI membership. Use your membership card for discounts in thousands of restaurants, hotels, spas, campgrounds, museums, shops and markets.

These Hotel Chains offer preferred rates and discounts to TCI members!

4

How to Join

It's quick and easy to join.
Apply for your membership online at
www.touringclub.it
Your membership card will arrive within
three weeks and is valid for discounts
across Italy for the entire year.
Get your card before you go and start
saving as soon as you arrive.
Euro 25 annual membership fee
includes priority mail postage for
membership card and materials.
Just one use of the card will more than
cover the cost of membership.

Benefits

• Exclusive car rental rates with Hertz
• Discounts at select Esso gas stations
• 20% discount on TCI guidebooks
and maps purchased in TCI bookstores
or directly online at
www.touringclub.com
• Preferred rates and discounts available
at thousands of locations in Italy: Hotels -
B&B's - Villa Rentals - Campgrounds -TCI
Resorts - Spas - Restaurants - Wineries -
Museums - Cinemas - Theaters - Music
Festivals - Shops - Craft Markets - Ferries -
Cruises - Theme Parks - Botanical Gardens

Italy is known throughout the world for the quantity and quality of its art treasures and for its natural beauty, but it is also famous for its inimitable lifestyle and fabulous cuisine and wines. Although it is a relatively small country, Italy boasts an extremely varied culture and multifarious traditions and customs. The information and suggestions in this brief section will help foreign tourists not only to understand certain aspects of Italian life, but also to solve the everyday difficulties and the problems of a practical nature that inevitably crop up during any trip.

This practical information is included in brief descriptions of various topics: public transport and how to purchase tickets; suggestions on how to drive in this country; the different types of rooms and accommodation in hotels; hints on how to use mobile phones and communication in general. This is followed by useful advice on how to meet your everyday needs and on shopping, as well as information concerning the cultural differences in the various regions. Lastly, there is a section describing the vast range of restaurants, bars, wine bars and pizza parlors.

TRANSPORTATION

From the airport to the city

Public transportation in major cities is easily accessible and simple to use. Both Malpensa Airport in Milan and Fiumicino Airport in Rome have trains and buses linking them to the city centers. At Malpensa, you can take a bus to the main train station or a train to Cadorna train station and subway stop.

Subways, buses, and trams

Access to the subways, buses, and trams requires a ticket (tickets are not sold on board but can be purchased at most newsstands and tobacco shops). The ticket is good for one ride and sometimes has a time limit (in the case of buses and trams). When you board a bus or tram, you are required to stamp your previously-acquired ticket in the time-stamping machine. Occasionally, a conductor will board the bus or tram and check everyone's ticket. If you haven't got one, or if it has not been time-stamped, you will have to pay a steep fine.

Trains

The Ferrovie dello Stato (Italian Railways) is among the best and most modern railway systems in Europe. Timetables and routes can be consulted and reservations can be made online at www.trenitalia.com. Many travel agents can also dispense

The 14th-century Santuario della Madonna at Custonaci, in the Province of Trapani

tickets and help you plan your journey. Hard-copy schedules can be purchased at all newsstands and most bookstores. Automated ticket machines, which include easy-to-use instructions in English, are available in nearly all stations. They can be used to check schedules, make reservations, and purchase tickets. There are different types of train, according to the requirements:

Eurostar Italia _ES★_ trains: Fast connections between Italy's most important cities. The ticket includes seat booking charge.

Intercity _IC_ and **Espresso** _E_ trains: Local connections among Italy's towns and cities. Sometimes _IC_ and _E_ trains require seat booking. You can book your seat up to 3 hours before the train departure. The seat booking charge is of 3 euro.

Interregionale _iR_ trains move beyond regional boundaries. Among the combined local-transport services, the _iR_ trains are the fastest ones with the fewest number of stops. No seat booking available.

Diretto _D_ and **Regionale** _R_ trains can circulate both within the regions and their bordering regions. No seat booking available.

Do not forget: You can only board trains in Italy with a valid ticket, which must be time-stamped before boarding; there are numerous time-stamping machines in every station. You cannot buy or stamp tickets on board.

If you don't have a ticket - or did not stamp before boarding - you will be liable to pay the full ticket price plus a 25 euro fine. If you produce a ticket that is not valid for the train or service you're using (i.e. one issued for a different train category at a different price, etc.) you will be asked to pay the difference with respect to the full ticket price, plus an 8 euro surcharge.

Taxis

Taxis are a convenient but expensive way to travel in Italian cities. There are taxi stands scattered throughout major cities. You cannot hail taxis on the street in Italy, but you can reserve taxis, in advance or immediately, by phone: consult the yellow pages for the number or ask your hotel reception desk or maitre d'hotel to call for you.

Taxi drivers have the right to charge you a supplementary fee for every piece of luggage they transport, as well as evening surcharges.

Driving

Especially when staying in the countryside, driving is a safe and convenient way to travel through Italy and its major cities. And while it is best avoided for obvious reasons, driving in the cities is not as difficult as it may seem or may have been reported to be. It is important to be aware of street signs and speed limits, and many cities have zones where only limited traffic is allowed in order to accommodate pedestrians. Although an international driver's license is not required in Italy, it is advisable. ACI and similar associations provide this service to members.

The fuel distribution network is reasonably distributed all over the territory. All service stations have unleaded gasoline ("benzina verde") and diesel fuel ("gasolio"). Opening time is 7am to12:30 and 15 to 19:30; on motorways the service is 24 hours a day.

Type of roads in Italy: The *Autostrada* (for example A14) is the main highway system in Italy and is similar to the Interstate highway system in the US and the motorway system in the UK. Shown on our Touring Club Italiano 1:200,000 road maps as black. The Autostrada are toll highways; you pay to use them. The *Strada Statale* (for example SS54) is a fast moving road that may have one or more lanes in each direction. Shown on our Touring Club Italiano 1:200,000 road maps as red. *Strada Provinciale* (for example SP358) can be narrow, slow and winding roads. They are usually one lane in each direction. Shown on our Touring Club Italiano 1:200,000 road maps as yellow. *Strada Comunale* (for example SC652) is a local road connecting the main town with its sorrounding. Note: In our guide you will sometime find an address of a place in the countryside listed, for example, as "25 Km along the SS54". This means that the you have to drive along the Strada Statale 54 until you reach the 25-km road sign. Speed limits: 130 kmph on the

Autostrada, 110 kmph on main highways, 90 kmph outside of towns, 50 kmph in towns.

The town streets are patrolled by the Polizia Municipale while the roads outside cities and the Autostrada are patrolled by the Carabinieri or the Polizia Stradale. They may set up road blocks where they may ask you to stop by holding out a small red sign.

Do not forget:
- Wear your seat belt at all times;
- Do not use the cellular phone while driving;
- Have your headlights on at all times when driving outside of cities;
- The drunk driving laws are strict - do not drink and drive;
- In case of an accident you are not allowed to get out of your car unless you are wearing a special, high-visibility, reflective jacket.

ACCOMMODATION

Hotels

In Italy it is common practice for the reception desk to register your passport, and only registered guests are allowed to use the rooms. This is mere routine, done for security reasons, and there is no need for concern.

All hotels use the official star classification system, from 5-star luxury hotel to 1 star accommodation.

Room rates are based on whether they are for single ("camera singola") or double ("camera doppia") occupancy. In every room you will find a list of the hotel rates (generally on the back of the door). While 4- and 5-star hotels have double beds, most hotels have only single beds. Should you want a double bed, you have to ask for a "letto matrimoniale". All hotels have rooms with bathrooms; only 1-star establishments usually have only shared bathrooms.

Most hotel rates include breakfast ("prima colazione"), but you can request to do without it, thus reducing the rate. Breakfast is generally served in a communal room and comprises a buffet with pastries, bread with butter and jam, cold cereals, fruit, yoghurt, coffee, and fruit juice. Some hotels regularly frequented by foreign tourists will also serve other items such as eggs for their American and British guests.

The hotels for families and in tourist localities also offer "mezza pensione", or half board, in which breakfast and dinner are included in the price.

It's always a good idea to check when a hotel's annual closing period is, especially if you are planning a holiday by the sea.

Farm stays

Located only in the countryside, and generally on a farm, "agriturismo" – a network of farm holiday establishments – is part of a growing trend in Italy to honor local gastronomic and wine traditions, as well as countryside traditions. These farms offer meals prepared with ingredients cultivated exclusively on site: garden-grown vegetables, homemade cheese and local recipes. Many of these places also provide lodging, one of the best ways to experience the "genuine" Italian lifestyle.

Bed & Breakfast

This form of accommodation provides bed and breakfast in a private house, and in the last few years has become much more widespread in Italy. There are over 5,000 b&bs, classified in 3 categories, and situated both in historic town centers, as well as in the outskirts and the countryside. Rooms for guests are always well-furnished, but not all of them have en suite bathrooms.

It is well-recommended to check the closing of the open-all-year accommodation services and restaurants, because they could have a short break during the year (usually no longer than a fortnight).

COMMUNICATIONS

Nearly everyone in Italy owns a cellular phone. Although public phones are still available, they seem to be ever fewer and farther between. If you wish to use public phones, you will find them in subway stops, bars, along the street, and phone centers generally located in the city center. Phone cards and pre-paid phone cards can be purchased at most newsstands and tobacco shops, and can also be acquired at automated tellers. For European travelers, activating personal cellular coverage is relatively simple, as it is in most cases for American and Australian travelers as well. Contact your mobile service provider for details. Cellular phones can also be rented in Italy from TIM, the Italian national phone company. For information, visit its website at www.tim.it. When traveling by car through the countryside, a cellular phone can really come in handy.

Note that when dialing in Italy, you must always dial the prefix (e.g., 02 for Milan, 06 for Rome) even when making a local call. For cellular phones, however, the initial zero is always dropped.

Freephone numbers always start with "800". For calls abroad from Italy, it's a good idea to buy a special pre-paid international phone card, which is used with a PIN code.

Internet access

Cyber cafés have sprung up all over Italy and today you can find one on nearly every city block. The Italian national phone company, TIM, has also begun providing internet access at many of its public phone centers.

EATING AND DRINKING

The bar

The Italian "bar" is a multi-faceted, all-purpose establishment for drinking, eating and socializing, where you can order an espresso, have breakfast, and enjoy a quick sandwich for lunch or even a hot meal. You can often buy various items here (sometimes even stamps, cigarettes, phone cards, etc.). Bear in mind that table service ("servizio a tavola") includes a surcharge. At most bars, if you choose to sit, a waiter will take your order. Every bar should have a list of prices posted behind or near the counter; if the bar offers table service, the price list should also include the extra fee for this.

Lunch at bars will include, but is not limited to, "panini," sandwiches with crusty bread, usually with cured meats such as "prosciutto" (salt-cured ham), "prosciutto cotto" (cooked ham), and cheeses such as mozzarella topped with tomato and basil. Then there are "tramezzini" (finger sandwiches) with tuna, cheese, or vegetables, etc. Often the "panini" and other savory sandwiches (like stuffed flatbread or "focaccia") are heated before being served. Naturally, the menu at bars varies according to the region: in Bologna you will find "piadine" (flatbread similar to pita) with Swiss chard; in Palermo there are "arancini" (fried rice balls stuffed

with ground meat); in Genoa you will find that even the most unassuming bar serves some of the best "focaccia" in all Italy. Some bars also include a "tavola calda". If you see this sign in a bar window, it means that hot dishes like pasta and even entrées are served.

A brief comment on coffee and cappuccino: Italians never serve coffee with savory dishes or sandwiches, and they seldom drink cappuccino outside of breakfast (although they are happy to serve it at any time).

While English- and Irish-type pubs are frequented by beer lovers and young people in Italy, there are also American bars where long drinks and American cocktails are served.

Breakfast at the bar

Breakfast in Italy generally consists of some type of pastry, most commonly a "brioche" – a croissant either filled with cream or jam, or plain – and a cappuccino or espresso. Although most bars do not offer American coffee, you can ask for a "caffè lungo" or "caffè americano", both of which resemble the American coffee preferred by the British and Americans. Most bars have a juicer to make a "spremuta", freshly squeezed orange or grapefruit juice.

Lunch and Dinner

As with all daily rituals in Italy, food is prepared and meals are served according to local customs (e.g., in the North they prefer rice and butter, in South and Central Italy they favor pasta and olive oil).

Wine is generally served at mealtime, and while finer restaurants have excellent wine lists (some including vintage wines), ordering the house table wine generally brings good results (a house Chianti to accompany your Florentine steak in Tuscany, a sparkling

Prosecco paired with your creamed stockfish and polenta in Venice, a dry white wine with pasta dressed with sardines and wild fennel fronds in Sicily). Mineral water is also commonly served at meals and can be "gassata" (sparkling) or "naturale" (still).

The most sublime culinary experience in Italy is achieved by matching the local foods with the appropriate local wines: wisdom dictates that a friendly waiter will be flattered by your request for his recommendation on what to eat and drink. Whether at an "osteria" (a tavern), a "trattoria" (a home-style restaurant), or a "ristorante" (a proper restaurant), the service of lunch and dinner generally consists of – but is not limited to – the following: "antipasti" or appetizers; "primo piatto" or first course, i.e., pasta, rice, or soup; "secondo piatto" or main course, i.e., meat or seafood; "contorno" or side-dish, served with the main course, i.e., vegetables or salad; "formaggi", "frutta", and "dolci", i.e., cheeses, fruit, and dessert; caffè or espresso coffee, perhaps spiked with a shot of grappa.

The pizzeria

The pizzeria is in general one of the most economical, democratic, and satisfying culinary experiences in Italy. Everyone eats at the pizzeria: young people, families, couples, locals and tourists alike. Generally, each person orders her/his own pizza, and while the styles of crust and toppings will vary from region to region (some of the best pizzas are served in Naples and Rome), the acid test of any pizzeria is the Margherita, topped simply with cheese and tomato sauce. Beer, sparkling or still water, and Coca Cola are the beverages commonly served with pizza. Some restaurants include a pizza menu, but most establishments do not serve pizza at lunchtime.

The wine bar (enoteca)

More than one English-speaking tourist in Italy has wondered why the wine bar is called an enoteca in other countries and the English term is used in Italy: the answer lies somewhere in the mutual fondness that Italians and English speakers have for one another. Wine bars have become popular in recent years in the major cities (especially in Rome, where you can find some of the best). The wine bar is a great place to sample different local wines and eat a light, tapas-style dinner.

CULTURAL DIVERSITY

Whenever you travel, not only are you a guest of your host country, but you are also a representative of your home country. As a general rule, courtesy, consideration, and respect are always appreciated by guests and their hosts alike. Italians are famous for their hospitality and experience will verify this felicitous stereotype: perhaps nowhere else in Europe are tourists and visitors received more warmly. Italy is a relatively "new" country. Its borders, as we know them today, were established only in 1861 when it became a monarchy under the House of Savoy. After WWII, Italy became a Republic and now it is one of the member states of the European Union. One of the most fascinating aspects of Italian culture is that, even as a unified country, local tradition still prevails over a universally Italian national identity. Some jokingly say that the only time that Venetians, Milanese, Florentines, Neapolitans, and Sicilians feel like Italians is when the national football team plays in international competitions. From their highly localized dialects to the foods they eat, from their religious celebration to their politics, Italians proudly maintain their local heritage. This is one of the reasons why the Piedmontese continue to prefer their beloved Barolo wine and their white truffles, the Umbrians their rich Sagrantino wine and black truffles, the Milanese their risotto and panettone, the Venetians their stockfish and polenta, the Bolognese their lasagne and pumpkin ravioli, the Florentines their bread soups and steaks cooked rare, the Abruzzese their excellent fish broth and seafood, the Neapolitans their mozzarella, basil, pizza, and pasta. As a result of its rich cultural diversity, the country's population also varies greatly in its customs from region to region, city to city, town to town. As you visit different cities and regions throughout Italy, you will see how the local personality and character of the Italians change as rapidly as the landscape does. Having lived for millennia with their great diversity and rich, highly heterogeneous culture, the Italians have taught us many things, foremost among them the age-old expression, "When in Rome, do as the Romans do."

NATIONAL HOLIDAYS

New Year's Day (1st January), Epiphany (6th January), Easter Monday (day after Easter Sunday), Liberation Day (25th April), Labour Day (1st May), Italian Republic Day (2nd June), Assumption (15th August), All Saints' Day (1st November), Immaculate Conception (8th December), Christmas Day and Boxing Day (25th-26th December).

In addition to these holidays, each city also has a holiday to celebrate its patron saint's feast day, usually with lively, local celebrations. Shops and services in large cities close on national holidays and for the week of the 15th of August.

EVERYDAY NEEDS

State tobacco shops and pharmacies

Tobacco is available in Italy only at state licensed tobacco shops. These vendors ("tabaccheria"), often incorporated in a bar, also sell stamps.

Since 11 January 2005 smoking is forbidden in all so-called public places - unless a separately ventilated space is constructed - meaning over 90% of the country's restaurants and bars.

Medicines can be purchased only in pharmacies ("farmacia") in Italy. Pharmacists are very knowledgeable about common ailments and can generally prescribe a treatment for you on the spot. Opening time is 8:30-12:30 and 15:30-19:30 but in any case there is always a pharmacy open 24 hours and during holidays.

Shopping

Every locality in Italy offers tourists characteristic shops, markets with good bargains, and even boutiques featuring leading Italian fashion designers. Opening hours vary from region to region and from season to season. In general, shops are open from 9 to 13 and from 15/16 to 19/20, but in large cities they usually have no lunchtime break.

Tax Free

Non-EU citizens can obtain a reimbursement for IVA (goods and services tax) paid on purchases over €155, for goods which are exported within 90 days, in shops which display the relevant sign. IVA is always automatically included in the price of any purchase, and ranges from 20% to 4% depending on the item. The shop issues a reimbursement voucher to present when you leave the country (at a frontier or airport). For purchases in shops affiliated to 'Tax Free Shopping', IVA may be reimbursed directly at international airports.

Banks and post offices

Italian banks are open Monday to Friday, from 8:30 to 13:30 and then from 15 to 16. However, the afternoon business hours may vary.

Post offices are open from Monday to Saturday, from 8:30 to 13:30 (12:30 on Saturday). In the larger towns there are also some offices open in the afternoon.

Currency

Effective 1 January 2002, the currency used in many European Union countries is the euro. Coins are in denominations of 1, 2, 5, 10, 20 and 50 cents and 1 and 2 euros; banknotes are in denominations of 5, 10, 20, 50, 100, 200 and 500 euros, each with a different color.

Credit cards

All the main credit cards are generally accepted, but some smaller enterprises (arts and crafts shops, small hotels, bed & breakfasts, or farm stays) do not provide this service. Foreign tourists can obtain cash using credit cards at automatic teller machines.

Time

All Italy is in the same time zone, which is six hours ahead of Eastern Standard Time in the USA. Daylight saving time is used from March to October, when watches and clocks are set an hour ahead of standard time.

Passports and vaccinations

Citizens of EU countries can enter Italy without frontier checks. Citizens of Australia, Canada, New Zealand, and the United States can enter Italy with a valid passport and need not have a visa for a stay of less than 90 days.

No vaccinations are necessary.

Payment and tipping

When you sit down at a restaurant you are generally charged a "coperto" or cover charge ranging from 1.5 to 3 euros, for service and the bread. Tipping is not customary in Italy. Beware of unscrupulous restaurateurs who add a space on their clients' credit card receipt for a tip, while it has already been included in the cover charge.

Foreign Embassies in Italy

Australia
Via A. Bosio, 5 - 00161 Rome
Tel. +39 06 852721
Fax +39 06 85272300
www.italy.embassy.gov.au.
info-rome@dfat.gov.au

Canada
Via G.B. de Rossi, 27 - 00161 Rome
Tel. +39 06 445981
Fax +39 06 445983760
www.canada.it
rome@dfait-maeci.gc.ca

Great Britain
Via XX Settembre, 80/a - 00187
Rome
Tel. +39 06 42200001
Fax +39 06 42202334
www.britian.it
consularenquiries@rome.
mail.fco.gov.uk

Ireland
Piazza di Campitelli, 3 - 00186
Rome
Tel. +39 06 6979121
Fax +39 06 6792354
irish.embassy@esteri.it

New Zealand
Via Zara, 28 - 00198 Rome
Tel. +39 06 4417171
Fax +39 06 4402984
nzemb.rom@flashnet.it

South Africa
Via Tanaro, 14 - 00198 Rome
Tel. +39 06 852541
Fax +39 06 85254300
www.sudafrica.it
sae@flashnet.it

United States of America
Via Vittorio Veneto, 121 - 00187
Rome
Tel. +39 06 46741
Fax +39 06 4882672
www.usis.it

Foreign Consulates in Italy

Australia
2 Via Borgogna
20122 Milan
Tel. +39 02 77704217
Fax +39 02 77704242

Canada
Via Vittor Pisani, 19
20124 Milan
Tel. +39 02 67581
Fax +39 02 67583900
milan@international.gc.ca

Great Britain
via S. Paolo 7
20121 Milan
Tel. +39 02 723001
Fax +39 02 86465081
ConsularMilan@fco.gov.uk

Lungarno Corsini 2
50123 Florence
Tel. +39 055 284133
Consular.Florence@fco.gov.uk

Via dei Mille 40
80121 Naples
Tel. +39 081 4238911

Fax +39 081 422434
Info.Naples@fco.gov.uk

Ireland
Piazza San Pietro in Gessate 2 -
20122 Milan
Tel. +39 02 55187569/02 55187641
Fax +39 02 55187570

New Zealand
Via Guido d'Arezzo 6,
20145 Milan
Tel. +39 02 48012544
Fax +39 02 48012577

South Africa
Vicolo San Giovanni Sul Muro 4
20121 Milan
Tel. +39 02 8858581
Fax +39 02 72011063
saconsulate@iol.it

United States of America
Via Principe Amedeo, 2/10
20121 Milan
Tel. +39 02 290351
Fax +39 02 29001165

Lungarno Vespucci, 38
50123 Florence
Tel. +39 055 266951
Fax +39 055 284088

Piazza della Repubblica
80122 Naples
Tel. +39 081 5838111
Fax +39 081 7611869

Italian Embassies and Consulates Around the World

Australia
12, Grey Street - Deakin, A.C.T.
2600 - Canberra
Tel. 02 62733333, 62733398,
62733198
Fax 02 62734223
www.ambitalia.org.au
embassy@ambitalia.org.au
Consulates at: Brisbane, Glynde,
Melbourne, Perth , Sydney

Canada
275, Slater Street, 21st floor -
Ottawa (Ontario) K1P 5H9
Tel. (613) 232 2401/2/3
Fax (613) 233 1484 234 8424
www.italyincanada.com
ambital@italyincanada.com
Consulates at: Edmonton,
Montreal, Toronto, Vancouver,

Great Britain
14, Three Kings Yard, London
W1K 4EH
Tel. 020 73122200
Fax 020 73122230
www.embitaly.org.uk
ambasciata.londra@esteri.it
Consulates at: London, Bedford,
Edinburgh, Manchester

Ireland
63/65, Northumberland Road -
Dublin 4
Tel. 01 6601744
Fax 01 6682759
www.italianembassy.ie
info@italianembassy.ie

New Zealand
34-38 Grant Road, Thorndon,

(PO Box 463, Wellington)
Tel. 04 473 5339
Fax 04 472 7255
www.italy-embassy.org.nz
ambwell@xtra.co.nz

South Africa
796 George Avenue, 0083 Arcadia
Tel. 012 4305541/2/3
Fax 012 4305547
www.ambital.org.za
ambital@iafrica.com
Consulates at: Johannesburg,
Capetown, Durban

United States of America
3000 Whitehaven Street, NW
Washington DC 20008
Tel. (202) 612-4400
Fax (202) 518-2154
www.italyemb.org
stampa@itwash.org
Consulates at: Boston, MA -
Chicago, IL - Detroit, MI - Houston,
TX - Los Angeles, CA - Miami, FL -
Newark, NJ - New York, NY -
Philadelphia, PA - San Francisco, CA

ENIT (Italian State Tourist Board)

Australia
Level 4, 46 Market Street
NSW 2000 Sidney
PO Box Q802 - QVB NSW 1230
Tel. 00612 92 621666
Fax 00612 92 621677
italia@italiantourism.com.au

Canada
175 Bloor Street E. Suite 907 –
South Tower
M4W3R8 Toronto (Ontario)
Tel. (416) 925 4882
Fax (416) 925 4799
www.italiantourism.com
enit.canada@on.aibn.com

Great Britain
1, Princes Street
W1B 2AY London
Tel. 020 7408 1254
Tel. 800 00482542 FREE from
United Kingdom and Ireland
italy@italiantouristboard.co.uk

United States of America
500, North Michigan Avenue
Suite 2240
60611 Chicago 1, Illinois
Tel. (312) 644 0996 / 644 0990
Fax (312) 644 3019
www.italiantourism.com
enitch@italiantourism.com

12400, Wilshire Blvd. – Suite 550
CA 90025 Los Angeles
Tel. (310) 820 1898 - 820 9807
Fax (310) 820 6357
www.italiantourism.com
enitla@italiantourism.com

630, Fifth Avenue – Suite 1565
NY – 10111 New York
Tel. (212) 245 4822 – 245 5618
Fax (212) 586 9249
www.italiantourism.com
enitny@italiantourism.com

There is no other place quite like Sicily. located just off the southern tip of Italy in the center of the Mediterranean, Sicily is an island forged by many cultures.

Through the ages a steady stream of peoples have left their mark including the Greeks, Romans, Arabs and Normans. Yet Sicily remains an island unique unto itself—a beautiful collision of the past and present— a melting pot of great Mediterranean traditions full of magnificent artwork, architecture, and folklore, plus an amazing bounty of archeological remains including two of the best-preserved Greek temples in the world.

The many facets of Sicily's rich cultural heritage can be discovered in the style and design of the ancient amphitheaters, breathtaking cathedrals, intricate mosaics, baroque palaces and dramatic churches.

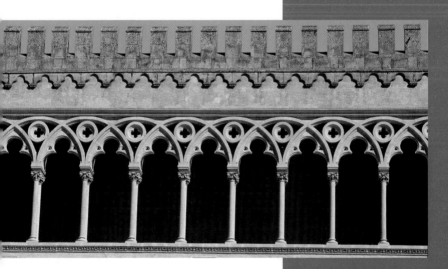

Highlights

- Valley of the Temples at Agrigento
- The Cappella Palatina in Palermo
- The splendid gold mosaics of the Duomo at Monreale
- Villa del Casale at Piazza Armerina

Bold, stars and italics are used in the text to emphasize the importance of places and works of art:

bold type **** → not to be missed
bold type *** → very important
bold type → important
italic type → interesting

AGRIGENTO

From the hills, you can see the sea that lies between Sicily and Africa; all is green in winter, then almond blossom heralds the beginning of spring, and in summer the land is burnt golden by the sun. The light is always bright, and there are very rarely clouds in the sky. Agrigento stands on a hill and overlooks the extensive ruins of the Greek town of *Akragas*, and the Valley of the Temples: some of the temples, with their Doric columns in tufa, have remained standing, and some have been re-erected. Here lies what remains of the ancient town where the philosopher, physician, and naturalist, Empedocles, once walked dressed in purple, and which the poet Pindar described as "the most beautiful city of mortals". Agrigento was at its most magnificent in the 5th century BC, when democracy was introduced, when the town's territories extended to the Tyrrhenian sea, and when the Temples and the Acropolis were built. The modern-day town on the hill has become known for its cultural stagnation and widespread illegal construction; these two aspects of Agrigento were described with dismay by Luigi Pirandello, and denounced with vehemence by Leonardo Sciascia, two 20th-century writers associated with the city. The streets and houses reveal Agrigento's multi-cultural past: the Arab town of Girgenti, with its courtyards and labyrinth of alleyways; the churches and civic palazzi of the Norman city; and the splendid Baroque architecture constructed during the centuries of Spanish domination.

Area archeologica ❶

Agrigento's archeological area is a Unesco World Heritage site. The main attractions are the Museo archeologico (Archeological Museum) and the renowned **Valle dei Templi** (Valley of the Temples). The temples blend perfectly with nature and their surroundings. They are the magnificent remains of the city of *Akragas*, and were built in sandstone tufa, which takes on an amber golden hue in the light of the setting sun. The church of **San Biagio** is situated in the first part of the area. The small church was built under the Normans on the remains of the *Tempio di Demetra e Kore* (Temple of Demeter and Kore); this small structure in antis was built between 480 and 460 BC. The cemetery contains the **santuario rupestre di Demetra** (rock sanctuary of Demeter), the most ancient sacred site in Agrigento, dating back to the 7th century BC, before the Greek city was founded. It is a rectangular structure, which acts as a vestibule to the real sanctuary, which consists of three large tunnels excavated in the rock.

The Valley of the Temples, a UNESCO World Heritage Site

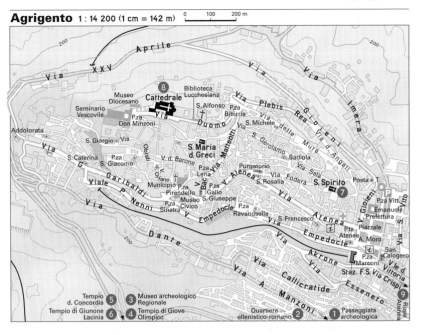

Agrigento 1 : 14 200 (1 cm = 142 m)

Quartiere ellenistico-romano ❷

The Hellenistic-Roman quarter covers an area of around a hectare, and is one of the best-preserved ancient city areas in the whole of Sicily. Archeological work here has uncovered an extremely regular street plan dating from the 4th century BC, in a grid pattern following the rules laid down by Hippodamus of Miletus. The Roman quarter is superimposed on the original Greek town. The mosaic floors, the wall decorations, the water pipes and the heating pipes are all Roman.

Museo Archeologico Regionale ❸

This is one of Sicily's most important archeological museums, and was opened in 1967 in a modern building which incorporates the remains of the ancient church of San Nicola. The museum is organised according to strict chronological criteria, in two sections: one contains finds from *Akragas*, and the other from the provinces of Agrigento and Caltanissetta. There is much prehistoric material from the 2nd and 1st millennia BC, from the area where the city was later founded. A wonderful collection of Greek vases includes 6th- to 5th-century BC red-figure and black-figure Attic vases, and 5th- to 3rd-century BC Greek-Italiot vases. Hall VI is dedicated to the Tempio di Giove Olimpico (Temple of Olympian Zeus), and features one surviving telamon* (7.75m), while the heads of three other telamones are displayed in niches. The Greco-Roman sculpture works include the renowned Ephebus* (470 BC), an original Greek statue with austere lines and finely-sculpted hair; finds from the Hellenistic-Roman quarter include an exquisite mosaic depicting a gazelle at a spring (1st century AD). The excellent numismatic collection includes Greek, Roman, Byzantine, and Arab-Norman coins.

Tempio di Giove Olimpico ❹

The Temple of Olympian Zeus was designed to be one of the great buildings of Greek architecture (112.6m x 56.3m): it was built after 480-470 BC by Carthaginian prisoners from *Himera*, but it was never completed. Destroyed by earthquakes, today it appears as a rectangular space surrounded by

AGRIGENTO IN OTHER COLORS...
■ ITINERARIES: P 109, 120
■ FOOD: P 141, 152
■ SHOPPING: P 177, 179
■ EVENTS: P 184, 189
■ WELLNESS: P 200
■ PRACTICAL INFO: P 207

ruins. It was a hexastyle, pseudo-peripteral temple, meaning that it had six columns on each short side of the rectangle, and half columns set into the walls on the long sides; colossal human figures (telamones) supported the weight of the inner entablature (one has been reconstructed in the Regional Archeological Museum). A number of religious buildings and dwellings for priests have been excavated in the area between the Temple of Olympian Zeus and the sanctuary of Demeter and Kore.

Tempio della Concordia ❺

The Temple of Concord, together with the Theseion in Athens, is one of the best preserved of all Greek temples and one of the most perfect works of Doric architecture. It was built around the middle of the 5th century BC, on a four-step stylobate, and perhaps dedicated to the Dioscuri (its current name derives from a Latin inscription found nearby). It's a hexastyle, peripteral temple with 34 columns around the perimeter, originally covered in brightly coloured stucco, with the cella raised on one step, pronaos and opisthodomos in antis; the roof no longer exists. The arches in the lateral walls of the cella were built in the 4th century AD, when the temple was converted into a Christian basilica with central nave and two side aisles. It remained as such until 1748 when it was deconsecrated and returned to its original form. The *Via dei Templi* (Road of the Temples) continues along the line of the ancient fortifications, running parallel with the edge of the hill; there is one quite long stretch where numerous 4th- to 5th-century Christian tombs are carved out of the living rock.

Tempio di Giunone Lacinia ❻

The Temple of Hera stands alone on the top of the hill, an unforgettable scene combining ancient remains and natural beauty. In front, there is a sacrificial altar. The temple was built in the middle of the 5th

century BC, just before the nearby Temple of Concord, which is similar. It is hexastyle, peripteral and has a four-step stylobate; 25 of the original 34 columns are still standing on the north and east side. The walls of the cella, discolored by a fire in 406 BC, were completely destroyed by an earthquake in medieval times.

Santo Spirito ❼

An abbey church, in rather a sad state, founded in the 13th century; it has a tufa facade with a 14th-century portal and Gothic rose window. The 18th-century interior is ornamented with rich, elaborate stucco work, attributed to Giacomo Serpotta. The adjoining **monastery** is one of the oldest and best-preserved in Sicily: the large *cloister* leads to the *chapter-house* with pointed arches, and the old *refectory*. The *Ethno-anthropological Section* of the Archeological Museum on the first floor, contains traditional objects and furnishings, ceramics, local terracotta ware, ex votos, and various tools.

Cattedrale ❽

The cathedral was founded by the Normans at the end of the 11th century (surviving remains on the right flank); it

The cathedral dominated by the massive unfinished bell-tower

The beautiful theater at Eraclea Minoa with the *proscenium* (stage) framed by the sea

was enlarged in the 14th century, and significantly modified in the 16th and 17th centuries. Beside it, there is a solid 15th-century campanile which was never completed. The *interior* has a central nave and side aisles on polygonal pilasters; the open-beam roof is painted with figures of saints and bishops, and aristocratic 16th-century coats-of-arms. The first half of the nave has an opulent wood lacunar ceiling (1682). The presbytery, decorated with Baroque stuccoes and frescoes, features an unusual acoustic phenomenon: from the apse cornice, the slightest whisper made at the entrance to the church can be heard. In the left aisle, a fine Gothic arch marks the entrance to the chapel (now baptistery) which contains the tomb of Gaspare De Marinis, by Andrea Mancino and Giovanni Gagini (1492).

Rupe Atenea ❾

This rocky outcrop, with a fantastic view, is found on the north side of the town walls, where the acropolis was probably situated; on the southern slope, remains have been uncovered of part of the town walls, of a watchtower, and of an oil mill dating from the 4th century BC.

The Baroque facade of San Francesco at Naro, originally 13th-century but re-built in the 17th century

DAY TRIPS

ERACLEA MINOA [13 km]

One of Sicily's most beautiful archeological sites, in a superb location overlooking the sea; it contains the ruins of an ancient settlement which was originally Phoenician and later Spartan, and which was most famous in Hellenistic times. The **theater** is magnificent, with the stage opening towards the sea, interesting stratifications of residential areas and the remains of the town walls; artifacts found here may be seen in the *Antiquarium*.

MONTEVAGO [90 km]

This ancient town was founded under the Arabs, around a castle and a small church, and developed in an orthogonal shape, around the main square. It was destroyed by an earthquake in 1968; the center was rebuilt near the ruins of the old town, in line with modern practice. Today it is a popular spa town.

NARO [28 km]

Naro, one of the highest towns in the area, has very successfully preserved its magnificent Baroque heritage.
In Greek times, the town was under the dominion of Agrigento; late-medieval

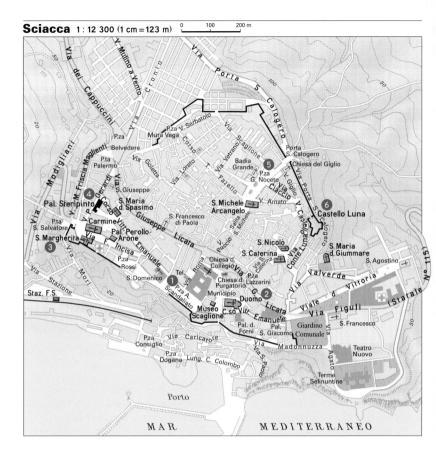

construction replaced Norman architecture around the Castello Chiaramontano. Between 1400 and 1600 the town layout was influenced by building carried out by the Carmelite, Dominican and Jesuit orders. Today the town has a late Baroque, 18th-century appearance, which is very evident in the central **Via Dante**; this street separates the upper part of town from the lower, and features 17th- and 18th- century buildings, such as the church of *San Salvatore*, *Palazzo Destro* and the *Chiesa Madre* (Mother Church). The Palazzo Municipale (Municipality) houses the *Biblioteca Feliciana* (Felician Library) and a small *Museo* (Museum) with local archeological finds, and furnishings and paintings from the Duomo.

The **Castello** (594m) towers over the houses in the oldest part of the town; this solid castle was built in the 14th century over earlier Norman fortifications. The massive square tower on the eastern corner is said to have been built by Frederick II of Aragon. Nearby is the late 12th-century *Duomo vecchio* (Old Duomo).

SCIACCA [62 km]

Encircled by 16th-century walls, Sciacca is located on a plateau on the southern coast of Sicily, between Agrigento and Mazara del Vallo. It's a popular seaside resort, and it's also the oldest spa town in the island. In Roman times, it was called *Thermae Selinuntinae*, since it was originally an outpost of Selinunte towards Agrigento.

Sciacca is fascinating as a place where Arab, Norman and Greek cultures co-existed and alternated with each other, in medieval times: this multi-cultural past can still be seen today in the three main areas of the town.

Piazza Scandaliato ❶ is the square which looks out over the harbour and the sea; on one side is the long facade of the 17th- to 18th- century *Collegio dei Gesuiti* (Jesuit College), which today is the town hall, and the adjoining *Chiesa del Collegio* (College Church). Nearby is the **Duomo** ❷, rebuilt in 1656 and dedicated to Santa Maria Assunta; the original Norman building (1108) can still be seen on the outside of the three apses. The Baroque facade is unfinished and decorated with statues by Antonino and Giandomenico Gagini (16th century) from the old church. The 14th-century church of **Santa Margherita** ❸ in the western part of the town preserves its original front doorway; the *side doorway** is Gothic-Renaissance, and decorated with reliefs. One of the most interesting palazzi in this area is the 16th-century **Palazzo Steripinto** ❹ situated at the end of *Corso Vittorio Emanuele* and known as the "Testa della Corsa" (Race Head) because it was the finishing line for Berber

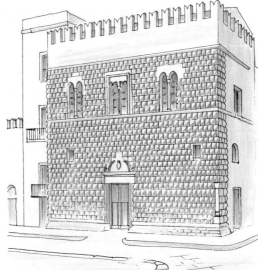

Sciacca, Palazzo Steripinto is an unusual building in the Sicilian Catalan style

horse races. The palazzo was built in 1501 and its name derives from the words *Hosterium pictum*, meaning decorated fortress. It is in Siculo-Catalan style, with a diamond-point ashlar facade, divided windows and battlements.

The high part of the town includes the impressive **Piazza G. Noceto** ❺, with the 14th-century church of *San Michele Arcangelo*, rebuilt in 1632-35, and the Renaissance church of *Santa Maria del Giglio*. On one of the bastions of the town walls are the remains of **Castello Luna** ❻

(Moon Castle); from here the road leads down to the medieval area of *Terravecchia*, with its winding lanes and stepped alleys.

SICULIANA [18 km]

The town grew up behind the eastern flank of a hill, above the road. It was originally an Arab settlement, although historic sources document its existence only from the 15th century, when it developed around the medieval castle. The town of *Siculiana Marina*, situated on the coast, has grown up in recent times.

Fishing-boats moored in Sciacca harbor

CALTANISSETTA

The town lies on a hill terrace on the southern slopes of Monte San Giuliano. Of Arab origin, Caltanissetta began to develop in the 11th century, between the abbey of Santo Spirito and the fortress of Pietrarossa, whose walls encircle the old town around the Cathedral, with its narrow winding alleys. In the 17th century, the town expanded beyond the walls, and developed into four quarters, in an urban layout which can still be seen today. In the 19th century it became very prosperous as a result of the sulfur mines in the area.

Cattedrale ①

The cathedral was begun in 1539, the main structure was completed in 1622, and it was modified in the 19th century. It looks onto *Piazza Garibaldi*, the square which is the center of the town's life. Inside, the nave is lavishly decorated with stucco work; the frescoed vault, the altar-piece and the wood statue of the Immaculate Virgin date from the 18th century.

Corso Umberto I ②

The town's main thoroughfare is flanked by small palazzi which were rebuilt or restored in the 19th century. Most worthy of note are the *Municipio* (Municipality), the Baroque facade of the church of **Sant'Agata** (St Agatha), and the impressive *Palazzo Moncada*, a 17th century building which was never completed.

> ### CALTANISSETTA IN OTHER COLORS...
> **Food:** P 137, 162
> **Shopping:** P 174
> **Events:** P 184, 190
> **Practical info:** P 211

Museo Archeologico ③

The Archeological Museum was recently reorganized with material from the Museo Civico, and houses finds from excavations carried out from the fifties onwards in various places around Caltanissetta, Gibil Habil, Sabucina, and Capodarso. They include artifacts from prehistoric times (pots and tools from late Bronze Age dwellings), objects from local necropolises of the 7th century BC, and Greek necropolises of the 6th and 5th centuries BC, decorated terracotta pots from the 7th- to 6th-century BC Archaic town, and Greek and Siceliot pottery.

Museo Mineralogico, Paleontologico della Zolfara ④

The museum houses a rich collection of gypsiferous and sulfur-bearing minerals from the area; one section features old machinery used to mine and process sulfur, with

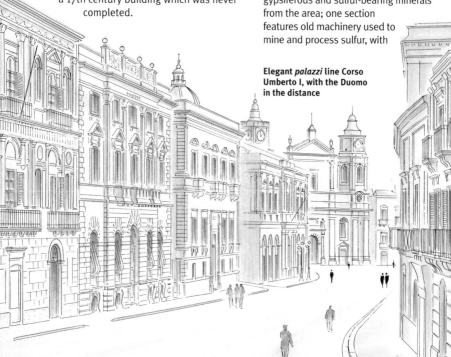

Elegant *palazzi* line Corso Umberto I, with the Duomo in the distance

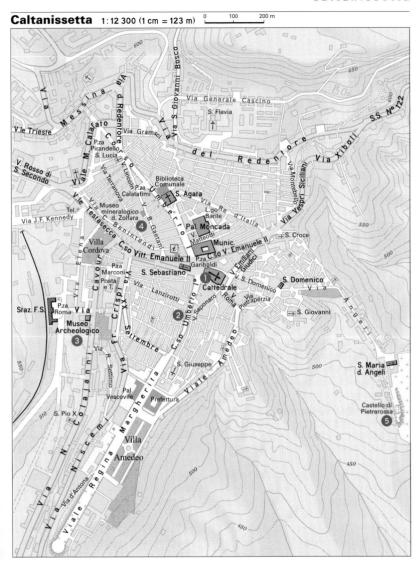

Caltanissetta 1:12 300 (1 cm = 123 m)

DAY TRIPS

old photographs and maps of the mining areas. The museum's *fossil collection* is also important, including fossils from the Silurian to the Quaternary ages.

Castello di Pietrarossa ⑤

The remains of this castle stand on a rocky spur, to the east of the town; possibly of Arab origin, it was rebuilt in Norman times and destroyed by an earthquake in 1567. The site provides a view over the town and the whole area. The former church of *Santa Maria degli Angeli*, beside the rock and castle ruins, preserves its original richly-decorated 14th-century Gothic doorway.

GELA [75 km]

A long terrace overlooks the beach west of the mouth of the Gela river, on the south coast of Sicily. This was the site of the Doric colony founded by settlers from Crete and Rhodes in 668 BC. Today's modern town has some important archeological remains and occupies the site of the ancient town, which was destroyed a number of times. The town's recent growth has been characterized by widespread unauthorized construction, which has

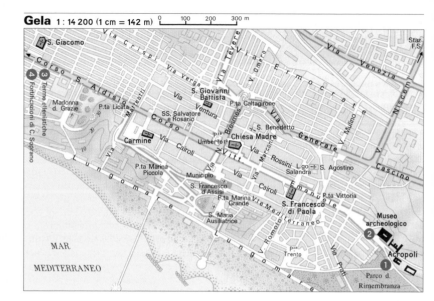

Gela 1 : 14 200 (1 cm = 142 m)

buried the underlying layers of the past in modern chaotic urban development. In addition, a large oil refinery was built in 1961, beyond the acropolis and beside the town.

The archeological area of the **Acropoli** ❶ (Acropolis) occupies an area east of the town; excavations have revealed a *quarter* dating from the 4th century BC, with private houses, shops and two temples dedicated to the goddess Athena.

The **Museo Archeologico Regionale** ❷ (Regional Archeological Museum) built nearby consists of two sections, with a wealth of material: on the ground floor are finds from the ancient town (grave goods, pottery, ornaments, clay

decorations); the upper floor contains objects from sanctuaries outside the town, Greek necropolises and outlying domains of Gela, which was one of the main Greek colonies in Sicily.

On the edge of the town, there are the **Terme ellenistiche** ❸ (Hellenistic Baths) dating from the late 4th century BC, and the **Fortificazioni di Capo Soprano** ❹ (Capo Soprano Fortifications), built during the colony's greatest period of expansion; the walls are 13 meters high in places. The old town center is dissected in two by **Corso Vittorio Emanuele**, the main street where the town's inhabitants like to walk. It has many Baroque buildings, and some interesting churches; one is the 18th-century Chiesa Madre (Mother Church), which houses some important artworks.

SULFUR-MINING AREA [57 km]

This old sulfur-mining area between Caltanissetta and the hills of Agrigento is full of abandoned sulfur mines, with desolate, bare hills riddled with tunnels and shafts. Some of the mines can be visited. In the 1800s and 1900s the mines appeared to bring prosperity to various towns in the area, but today many have bitter memories of this time. Some towns, such as Milena and **Mussomeli** have managed to survive as real farming and market towns.

Mediterranean vegetation and ancient ruins on the Acropolis at Gela

CATANIA

For better or for worse, the development of the city of Catania has been conditioned by its close proximity to Mount Etna. It has benefited from the fertile soil on its slopes, succumbed to the lava flows and turned lava into material for building houses. The people here have never wanted to leave their land and have come to terms with living with the daily risk of eruptions and earthquakes. Today, Catania looks like any other large urban complex, with a splendid historic center. It was rebuilt after the 1693 earthquake with all the lavishness of the Baroque style, and is now surrounded by four areas of urban development. To the south is the district that sprang up between the late 18th and early 19th centuries in the area which was covered by the lava in the 1669 eruption. To the north, the city has expanded in the direction of the volcano, and reflects the gradual development of architectural styles from the Baroque to the present day. To the west and east lie the areas built in the 20th century, laid out according to a series of wide streets, the final section of which, over the last few decades, has become the much sought-after and elegant commercial center of the city.

Historically, the city was founded by the earliest colonizers from Ancient Greece (in the 8th century BC). They ruled for three hundred years, until the Romans gained the upper hand. Roman dominion is reflected in numerous buildings, the remains of which are still standing today.

The medieval town plan established by the Norman and Swabian invaders has been almost completely wiped out by earthquakes and eruptions. After the 1669 eruption and the earthquake soon after in 1693, the city was brought to its knees as a result of the destruction of farming land and the influx of large numbers of refugees without any income. When the city was rebuilt, during which time the Benedictine order distinguished itself among the clergy, greater attention was paid to anti-seismic precautions. The streets were built straight and wide, interspersed with broad squares, with the specific aim of enabling the inhabitants to use the open spaces in the event of future earthquakes.

During the course of the 19th and 20th centuries, population growth, the building of the railway and the expansion of the infrastructures of the Italian Navy resulted in haphazard urban development, effectively cutting off the city from its view of the sea.

Aerial view of the city center

Piazza del Duomo ❶

Built after the 1693 earthquake on the site of the medieval *platea magna*, this is the crossroads of the two main arteries of the city. In the center stands the symbol of Catania, the famous **Fontana dell'Elefante** (Elephant Fountain), designed by Giovan Battista Vaccarini in 1736, using ancient treasures: a lava elephant dating from the Roman period (popularly known as "u liotru") and an Egyptian obelisk with hieroglyphics relating to the cult of Isis, surmounted by the symbols of St Agatha, patron saint of Catania.

The east side of the square is adorned by an architectural feast comprising the Duomo and the dome of the church of the Badia di Sant'Agata, now the *Museo diocesano* (Diocesan Museum) which houses sacred objects and gold and silverware dating from the 14th to 18th centuries.

Cattedrale ❷

Built in the second half of the 11th century above the remains of Roman baths (the Terme Achilliane), the cathedral was rebuilt in 1169 and again after the 1693 earthquake. The original fortified parts of the building—part of the upper transept and the three apses—date from Norman times and can be seen from the courtyard of the Archbishop's Palace. The marble balustrade surmounted by statues surrounding the cathedral is a 19th-century addition, as is the bell tower of eclectic taste. **Inside**, the nave and two side-aisles are separated by pilasters. Restoration work in the transept has brought to light features of the Norman building. Several of the funerary monuments are worthy of note: the 19th-century tomb of the composer from Messina, Vincenzo Bellini, a 3rd-century AD Roman sarcophagus containing the remains of the Aragonese monarchs who resided in Catania, and the Gothic tomb of Constance of Aragon (1363), in the *Cappella della Madonna*. A fine 16th-century *marble portal**, with 14 bas-reliefs depicting *scenes from the Life of the Virgin Mary* provides access to the chapel. In the *right-hand apse* is the *Cappella di Sant'Agata** (Chapel of St Agatha). The chapel is accessed through a fine marble portal and contains the relics and part of the treasury of the saint (notice in particular the gold-plated silver reliquary bust dating from 1373-76 and the large *silver-plated reliquary** dating from the 15th to 16th century).

In the 18th-century *sacristy*, there is an interesting fresco attributed to Giacinto Platania (1679) depicting Catania being engulfed by the eruption of Etna in 1669. The grilles in the ground are for ventilating the excavations of the *Terme Achilliane* which extend below the church, the seminary and the square in front of the church.

Castello Ursino ❸

Erected by Frederick II of Swabia in 1239-50, the castle was surrounded by walls and altered in the mid-16th century. It was damaged several times by the lava and earthquakes. In 1837, the castle was converted into a prison and was then insensitively restored in 1934. This massive structure, surrounded by a moat, is built on a square plan and reinforced by round towers at each corner with smaller towers

The statue of St Agatha on the facade of the Duomo

Catania: the Cathedral

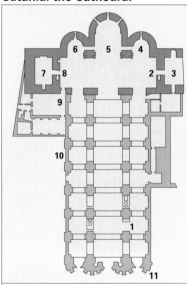

| | Norman structures |
| | 18th century structures |

1 Bellini's tomb
2 Marble portal by G.B. Mazzolo (1545)
3 Chapel of the Madonna
4 Chapel of St Agatha
5 Presbytery
6 Chapel of the Holy Sacrament
7 Chapel of the Holy Crucifix
8 Marble portal by G.B. Mazzola (1563)
9 Entrance to the sacristy
10 Marble portal by G.B. Mazzola (secondary monumental entrance)
11 Entrance to the Terme Achilliane (Roman baths)

Via dei Crociferi in Catania is a triumph of the Baroque style

porcelain, 17th- and 18th-century gold- and silverware and ivory, 18th-century cribs and wax figures by the Neapolitan school, examples of marquetry and inlaid marble, costumes, clothes and examples of embroidery, fans and a fascinating collection of shoes.

Museo Civico Belliniano ❹

The house where the composer Vincenzo Bellini (1801-1835) was born is now a museum. The exhibits include documents, an iconographic collection, opera scores and mementos of the composer. The building also houses the *Museo Emilio Greco* (1913-95), with etchings and lithographs by this artist/sculptor from Catania.

halfway along each side. The castle houses the **Museo civico**, created in 1934 by combining much of the material from the Museo Biscari with collections from the Benedictine monasteries and works donated by Baron Zappalà-Asmundo. Exhibits in the *archeological collection* include Greek sculptures from the 6th-4th (6th to 4th) centuries BC (*young man's head* ∗, Attic sculpture from the early 6th century); Roman statuary, earthenware sarcophagi and burial urns, floor mosaics and architectural fragments, Greek pottery, Greek, Etruscan and Roman bronzes, and an important vase collection. The *sculptures* include fine medieval and Renaissance works, an impressive collection of bronzes from the 15th to 18th centuries and numerous 18th-century busts. The museum collection also includes numerous *paintings*: the Byzantine and Byzantine-style panels, and works by Matthias Stomer, Gherardo delle Notti and Domenico Fetti are particularly worthy of note. There is a very fine *coin collection* as well as a collection of medieval and Renaissance *weapons and armor*. Other interesting collections include 18th-century majolica and

Via dei Crociferi ❺

This is regarded as one of the most magnificent streets in the city, because of the sumptuous Baroque churches and fine 18th-century palazzi ranged along each side. At the top of the street, the *Arco di San Benedetto* (Arch of St Benedict) (1704), which, according to tradition, was built in a single night, links the buildings of the *Badia grande* and the *Badia piccola* (an old Benedictine monastery and a newer Benedictine convent). Immediately beyond it, on the left, the church of **San Benedetto** (1704-13) towers above a majestic flight of steps. It has a carved wooden portal, an elegant entrance-hall decorated with statues and a fine interior bristling with marbles and stucco-work. Nearby is the former *Collegio gesuitico* (Jesuit College), planned around four courtyards. The first is an elegant cloister partly attributed to G.B. Vaccarini (1742). Opposite stands the church of **San Giuliano**, a marvelous example of Catania Baroque attributed to the same architect, Vaccarini (1739-51), with a convex facade and a dome surrounded by a loggia. Inside, above the splendid high altar, hangs a 14th-century wooden crucifix.

Catania

1:14 000 (1 cm = 140 m)

0   100   200   300 m

28

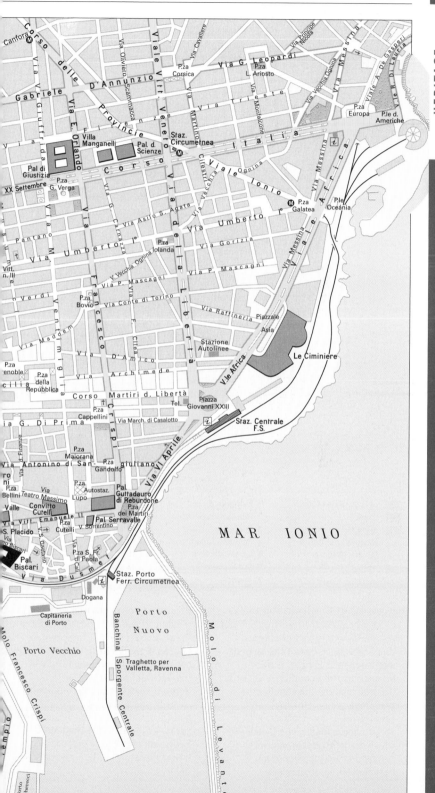

Catania: Monastery of San Nicolò l'Arena

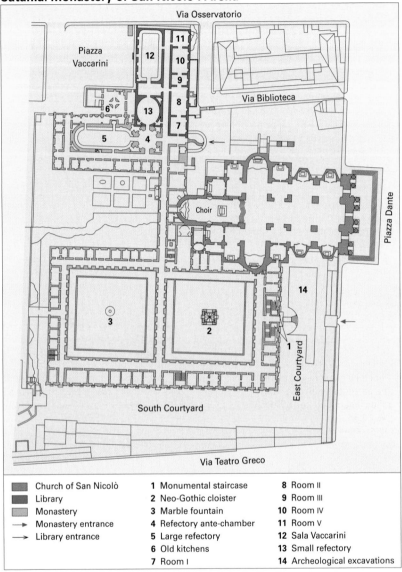

▮ Church of San Nicolò	**1** Monumental staircase	**8** Room II
▮ Library	**2** Neo-Gothic cloister	**9** Room III
▮ Monastery	**3** Marble fountain	**10** Room IV
→ Monastery entrance	**4** Refectory ante-chamber	**11** Room V
→ Library entrance	**5** Large refectory	**12** Sala Vaccarini
	6 Old kitchens	**13** Small refectory
	7 Room I	**14** Archeological excavations

Monastero di S. Nicolò l'Arena ❻

Originally adjoining the church, today, the monastery is part of Catania University. Once one of the largest monasteries in Europe, it was founded by the Benedictine Order in the 16th century and rebuilt on a grandiose scale in the early 18th century. It has two cloisters with a portico and a loggia, the facades of which are richly decorated with splendid inlaid majolica work. In the east cloister, archeological excavations have uncovered the remains of buildings dating from the Greek Archaic period. The complex houses the *Biblioteche riunite*, consisting of the original library of the Benedictines, the collection of Baron Ursino Recupero, containing many precious volumes about the history of Catania and Sicily, and the personal library of the poet Mario Rapisardi, who was professor of Italian literature at the University of Catania from 1870.

Anfiteatro ⑦

Part of the Roman amphitheater, which possibly dates from the 2nd century AD, can be seen from Piazza Stesicoro, with its basic structure of black lava, faced with white marble. The underground passageways running around the bottom of the amphitheater are well preserved, along with part of the vaulting. Not far from the square, graced by a monument to the composer Bellini (1882), is the Baroque church of *Sant'Agata al Carcere*, (St Agatha in Prison) incorporated within the remains of a Spanish bastion. Built above the site of the *Roman prison* where legend has it St Agatha was imprisoned, the lively facade incorporates a fine 13th-century portal from the old cathedral of Catania. The presbytery of the church has retained its original medieval features.

DAY TRIPS

ACIREALE [17 km]

This is the largest of the seven towns deriving from the ancient city of *Akis*, a Phoenician colony destroyed during the earthquake of 1169. Known for its mild climate and hot springs, life here moves at a relaxed pace, focusing on pauses at the tables outside the many ice-cream shops. The town owes its Baroque appearance to the fact that it was rebuilt after the earthquake of 1693. The nearby coast, with its citrus groves and the view of the snowy summit of Mount Etna in the distance, is called the "riviera dei Ciclopi" (Riviera of the Cyclops) in memory of the Homeric myth. According to the legend, it was here that a Cyclops (one-eyed giant) named Polyphemus, out of jealousy for his beloved Galatea, killed a young man called Acis, who was then transformed by the compassionate gods into the river that still bears his name.

The center of the town is **Piazza del Duomo ①**, an elegant "drawing room" surrounded by fine buildings in the flamboyant Baroque style typical of the Catania area. This square is the final destination of the procession of allegorical floats held every year during the carnival.

The **Duomo ②**, built in the early 17th century, has a facade reminiscent of the Gothic style dating from the early 20th century. *Inside*, there are frescoes and paintings by Pietro Paolo Vasta, an

The rocks known as the *faraglioni* off Aci Trezza, south of Acireale

18th-century painter from Acireale, whose works adorn many churches in the town.

Not far away is the **Pinacoteca Zelantea** , with a collection of artworks and archeological material. Adjoining the art gallery is the very interesting *Biblioteca* (Library), founded in 1671, one of the finest in the region.

At **Aci Castello** there is a small Norman fortress, erected in 1076 and built entirely of black lava. Today it houses the **Museo civico**, which has sections devoted to Sicilian archeology and mineralogy and a botanical garden.

A fish market is still held in the little traditional fishing town of **Aci Trezza**.

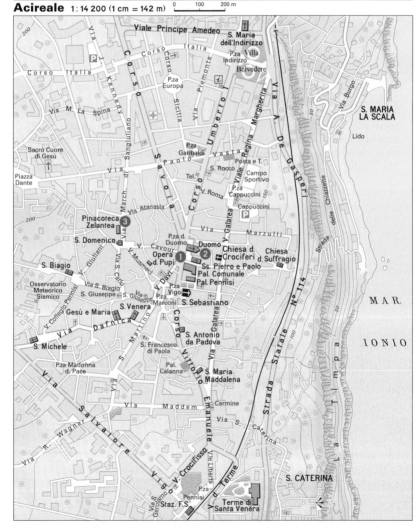

Acireale 1 : 14 200 (1 cm = 142 m) 0 100 200 m

The historic center of Caltagirone is laid out on three hills

CALTAGIRONE [68 km]

The town, laid out on three hills, is particularly famous for the flight of 142 steps decorated entirely in enameled ceramic tiles, a monument to the local craft industry. This has been a center for high-quality colored enameled ceramics since the Arab period (9th to 11th centuries). Balustrades, vases, decorative features and other ceramic furnishings enhance the streets of this little town, which is mainly Baroque in character, due to the re-building phase that followed the 1693 earthquake. It has remarkable public buildings dating from the Renaissance and Baroque periods.

At the entrance to the town, in the large public garden known as the *Villa*, is the **Museo regionale della ceramica** (Regional Ceramics Museum). One enters the museum through the curious *Teatrino* (Little Theater), a belvedere dating from 1792 with steps and balustrades, decorated with polychrome majolica reliefs. The museum contains examples of Sicilian ceramic ware from prehistoric times to the present day. Particularly worthy of note are the small terracotta figures by Giacomo Bongiovanni (18th century) and Giacomo Bongiovanni Vaccaro (19th century), which depict scenes from everyday life with extraordinary realism.

The town focuses around **Piazza del Municipio**. Here stands the Baroque **Chiesa del Collegio** or **Chiesa del Gesù**, with a rich interior decorated with marble inlay work and carvings. Not far away are two examples of Art Deco buildings: the former headquarters of the *Electrical workshops* and the *Post Office*.

From the square, the long flight of famous **Steps** lined with shops selling ceramic ware on either side leads up to the church of **Santa Maria del Monte** (St Mary of the Mountain). The 18th-century church with its elegant bell tower contains a much revered picture of the Madonna di Conadomini (13th century).

The **Duomo** stands on the central *Piazza Umberto I*. It is a modern re-construction of a building dating from Norman

THE WONDERLAND STAIRCASE OF CALTAGIRONE

Each year, on July 24 and 25, the 142 steps of the famous staircase are illuminated with decorative lanterns to mark two religious festivals. The "coppi", colored-paper cylinders containing slow-burning candles, are placed on the staircase at regular intervals, creating beautiful colored patterns, providing a flickering spectacle of magical charm at night.

times. To the right is the **Corte Capitaniale**, a long, one-storey building by Antonuzzo and Gian Domenico Gagini (16th to 17th centuries).

Turning into Via Luigi Sturzo, we pass the **Museo Civico**, which has an archeological section, an art gallery and historical material: medieval engravings, Swabian, Norman and Aragonese manuscripts, and majolica ware. Next to the museum stands the 18th-century church of *Sant'Agata*, headquarters of the ceramicists' guild. The church of **San Francesco d'Assisi**, rebuilt in the Baroque style above the remains of the original Gothic structure, is accessed by the *Ponte di San Francesco* (Bridge of St Francis), built between 1627 and 1666 and decorated with majolica tiles. From here, on a clear day, you can see the sea.

The western slopes of Mount Etna

ETNA [34 km]

Yellow broom flowers appear in spring against the background of black lava, on the summit it snows for six months of the year, and from the foot of the mountain, you can hear the sound of the waves breaking on the shore. The largest and most active volcano

Small pieces of pumice stone are hurled skywards from the crater of Mount Etna

in Europe - Sicilians refer to it simply as "a muntagna", the mountain - dominates the whole Ionian coast of the island from Catania to Taormina. It is not only a tourist attraction but also a point of reference when probing into the history and traditions of the towns around its perimeter. The lower slopes of the volcano have been inhabited by princes

and kings but, more importantly, this is land that is dearly loved by the people who have farmed here for centuries and who have handed down skills, specialist knowledge and customs.

As we climb up through the surreal landscape on the slopes of the mountain, there are green citrus groves, interspersed with tell-tale traces of lava, vineyards (up to 1,300 m), then woodland and, finally, a bare, harsh rocky landscape, where plants such as juniper and Astragalus aetnesis, an endemic form of milk-vetch, grow. Since 1987, this unique natural habitat has become a protected area, the **Parco dell'Etna**.

The cone of the volcano looks as if it the top was sliced off at 3,323 m. Its slopes are dotted with about 200 craters formed during the course of various eruptions. It was from one of these craters, in March 1669, that the lava flowed down and engulfed Catania, moving the coastline out by a few hundred meters. It was the most violent eruption in the city's history. Splendid descriptions have come down to us of the interminable eruption, which lasted from 1614 until 1624, giving rise to one of the most extraordinary landscapes on Mount Etna, known as the *Sciara dei Dammusi* ("dammusi" being the name given to the houses with flat roof terraces, typical of the Eolian islands) with its famous *grotta del Gelo* (Ice Cave). The last great eruption was between 1991 and 1993.

In all, over the centuries, as many as 135 eruptions have been recorded. However, this has not prevented a large number of small towns from springing up on the lower slopes of the volcano. One town, Belpasso, has been re-located three times.

RANDAZZO [69 km]

This is the nearest town to the main crater of Mount Etna (km 15), yet it has never been directly targeted by the lava flows. Mount Etna dominates the landscape and lava has been used to build dry-stone walls in the countryside and to build and decorate splendid buildings in the city and to pave the roads.

Founded in ancient times, today's town dates back to the Byzantine period and grew in importance during the Swabian period, when it began to acquire the urban layout it still has today. Under the dominion of Peter of Aragon, the town was fortified and defensive walls were built, some sections of which are still standing.

The most important monuments are the churches of the three main districts of Randazzo. These were inhabited by three different ethnic communities who, until the 16th century,

spoke different dialects: Latin in Santa Maria, Greek in San Nicolò and Lombard in San Martino.

The town's most beautiful church, the **Chiesa di Santa Maria*** overlooks Piazza Basilica. Built between 1217 and 1239 in the Norman-Swabian style, it was altered at a later date. The three apses which resemble merloned towers date from the original church, whereas the Renaissance interior, with its nave and two side-aisles supported on lava columns, houses a veritable museum of frescoes, canvases and inlaid marble dating from various periods.

The primitive structure of the **Chiesa di San Nicolò** dates from the 14th century, but the church was rebuilt in the 16th century. Inside are numerous works by the Gagini family, including a striking statue of *San Nicola in cattedra* (St Nicholas enthroned) (1523).

The **Chiesa di San Martino** was founded by the Swabians (in the 13th century), but the magnificent bell tower on the right dates from the 14th century. The 16th-century interior houses statues by the Gagini school and a magnificent polyptych.

Near the church stands the *Swabian castle*, the only part of the eight-towered structure built by Frederick II to survive. Today it houses the *"Paolo Vagliasindi" Archeological Museum**, which contains important archeological exhibits from the area of Mount Etna, and the unusual *Museo dei Pupi siciliani* (Sicilian Puppet Museum).

CATANIA
IN OTHER COLORS...
ITINERARIES: P 109, 112, 125
FOOD: P 141, 146, 162
SHOPPING: P 174, 177, 179
EVENTS: P 184, 186, 190
WELLNESS: P 198
PRACTICAL INFO: P 213

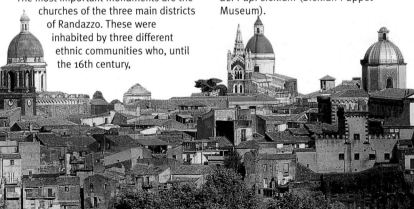

Randazzo, a medieval town built entirely of lava

ENNA

Enna is known as Sicily's "Belvedere" (Lookout Point): it is located on a high hill in the heart of the island, among fertile hills. The town has retained its historic appearance. Its architecture and layout still have a somber medieval feel, only marginally touched by Baroque and 18th-century ornamentation. Traditional local values have probably been safeguarded by the survival of an economy which is essentially based on agriculture. As long ago as Roman times, the area around Enna was devoted to the production of grain and cereals. This continued when the Arabs occupied and fortified the town, which still today preserves its late 14th-century layout.

The clean streets, the well-maintained buildings, the absence of neon and advertising billboards, even the care with which the excellent cakes and pastries are displayed in the windows of the elegant cake shops: these are all signs suggesting how different Enna is not only from the chaotic coastal cities, but also from the towns in more depressed areas.

Enna 1:10 000 (1 cm = 100 m)

Piazza Vittorio Emanuele ❶

This square, at the town's center, is overlooked by **San Francesco d'Assisi**, a rather austere and forbidding church of 14th-century origin; it's built on a rock, beside a solid 15th-century belltower. Inside, a painted wood cross of the 15th century, and a Flemish panel (Epiphany). There is a sweeping view* over the Madonìe and Etna from nearby *Piazza Crispi*.

Duomo ❷

The Duomo was built in the 14th century and rebuilt in the 16th. The polygonal apses and a doorway with

The 17th-century marble pulpit in the Duomo

a pointed arch on the right transept wall were part of the original structure. The lower part (16th-century) of the elegant facade has three arches. The tall campanile was built in the 17th-century. The flank fronting onto Piazza Martini features a 16th-century doorway with a marble bas-relief depicting St Martin and the Beggar. The *interior* has a nave and two side aisles, columns in lava stone, with pointed arches, and 17th-century lacunar ceilings. Various elements come from the medieval church: the two statues of the Annunciation, the two stoups, the pedestals and capitals of the columns and two stylophore lions. The Cappella della Visitazione (Chapel of the Visitation), on the right of the presbytery, is richly lined with

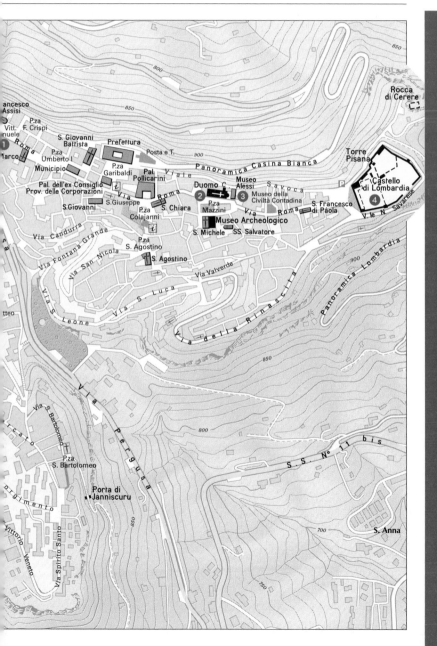

18th-century polychrome marble. The Chapel contains the so-called "Nave d'oro" (Golden Boat), an ornate structure which is used in processions to carry the 15th-century statue of the Madonna of the Visitation, the town's patron saint.

Museo "Alessi" ❸

The "Alessi" Museum in the Palazzetto della Canonica (Rectory) has a number of collections. The *Pinacoteca* includes Byzantine icons, 16th- to 17th-century paintings, and 19th-century works by artists from Enna. The *Tesoro del Duomo* (Duomo Treasury) has goldsmithery, and holy vestments and furnishings, including candlesticks (1595) and a 17th-century crown with enamels and gemstones. The *numismatic collection* features some rare Greek, Roman and Byzantine coins: and the *archeological collection* has pottery from various periods, clay statues and a good number of oil lamps.

Castello di Lombardia ❹

The Castle of Lombardy is one of Sicily's most impressive. It was built by Frederick II on a previous Arab fortification which had been enlarged by the Normans. It was also modified by Frederick III of Aragon who chose to live here. It is irregular in shape, and preserves only six of the twenty original towers. The interior has a complex set of courtyards; the first has been converted into an open-air theater, and the third has the remains of the little church of San Martino. One of the most sweeping views* of Sicily can be seen from the best-preserved tower, the *Torre Pisana* (Pisan Tower).

DAY TRIPS

CENTURIPE [58 km]

The town was once an important Siculian settlement (Kentoripa). From the 5th century BC, it became a Greek colony, and under the Romans it was one of Sicily's most prosperous towns. Neglect during medieval times and rebuilding in the 16th century did not destroy the Greek and Roman remains which today can be seen outside the town. The *Museo archeologico* (Archeological Museum) has over 3000 pieces found during excavations, such as materials and tools related to work and domestic activities. Finds from the necropolis include the large marble head of the emperor *Hadrian* and a collection of delicate clay figurines dating from the 3rd- to 1st-century BC. As you wander around

Enna, view from the top of the Castello di Lombardia

The archeological excavations at Morgantina

the ruins of a settlement which was founded in Hellenistic times (4th- to 3rd-century BC) under the dominion of Siracusa, and which was destroyed fairly early on by the Romans. The **excavations** have revealed the interesting design of the *agorà*, the public square built on two levels. The upper part contains the remains of the *bouleutérion* (council hall) and of the *ginnasio romano* (Roman gymnasium). The area flanked by a long, columned *portico* was the site of the *macellum* (market), and the *quartiere residenziale* (residential quarter) was on the hill. In the lower part of the agorà were the *theater** (4th century BC), a *sanctuary* dedicated to the gods of the underworld, and some *kilns* for making pottery.

among the Greek and Roman ruins, you will see the *Augustales* (2nd century) related to the cult of the emperor, the barrel-vaulted *dogana* (customs) building, and the remains of the *edificio termale* (baths) dating from imperial times.

MORGANTINA [6 km]

In a superb setting, in the middle of a wide flat valley far from any towns, are

Morgantina

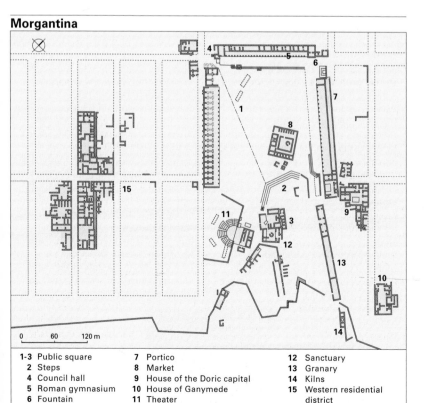

1-3	Public square	7	Portico	12	Sanctuary
2	Steps	8	Market	13	Granary
4	Council hall	9	House of the Doric capital	14	Kilns
5	Roman gymnasium	10	House of Ganymede	15	Western residential
6	Fountain	11	Theater		district

Piazza Armerina 1:13 200 (1 cm = 132 m)

Map labels:
S. Andrea · Viale Sant'Andrea · Via Papa Roncalli · 670 · 630 · 650 · Via S. Giorgio · Via Tasso · Via F. Guccia · Via Generale Ciancio · Via Chiaranda · Via Muscara · 700 · V. G. Lo Giudice · V. G. Lo Giudice · S. Pietro · Giardino Garibaldi · Posta e T. · P.za Gen. Garibaldi · Mon. ad A. Cascino · 650 · Castellina · V. Cozzini · Commenda dell'Ordine di Malta · Teatro Cascino Garibaldi · P.za Umberto I · Monte · Via Cavour · Duomo · i · S. Rocco · V. G. Garibaldi · Chiesa di S. Giovanni Evang. · Monumento a M. Trigona · P.za Duomo · V. Umberto I · Chiesa di S. Stefano · S. Anna · Pal. di Cifra · P.za Garibaldi · Chiesa dei Teatini · Casalotto · Pal. Velardito · Via Emanuele · Via Roma · Via Liberta · S. Ignazio di Loyola · Via Giacomo Matteotti · Giardino Ciancio · P.za A. De Gasperi · Strada Prov. · Biblioteca comunale · Via Principato · Viale · Castello Aragonese · Canali · 630 · P.za Reg. Siciliana · 750 · P

PIAZZA ARMERINA [34 km]

The old town on the slopes of the hill of Armerina is set in one of the greenest areas of central Sicily. This excellent site, inhabited since the 8th- to 7th-century BC, attracted the Romans, the Byzantines and, in the late middle ages, the Arabs. In the 11th century, the Normans built a fortified citadel and founded the first proper town. The town expanded; in the 17th century, its layout was consolidated with the building and restructuring of monasteries by religious orders.

Looking onto Piazza Garibaldi ❶, the central square, are the 18th-century *Palazzo di Città*, with its fine wrought-iron balcony railings, and the Baroque *Chiesa di San Rocco*, with its great doorway in finely carved tufa. The **Duomo** ❷, built in 1604 on a pre-existing church, retains its original structure only in the lower part, in Gothic-Catalan style. The interior houses many artworks, notably a fine *Crucifix** panel, painted on both sides (1485). Towards the south of the town, we find the massive 14th-century *Castello Aragonese* (Aragonese Castle), which is square with solid towers at each corner. The *Chiesa di Sant' Andrea** ❸ (Church of St Andrew), built in 1096, stands on a rise. It houses a 12th- to 13th-century fresco cycle, with connections with Benedictine painting. Outside the town is the archeological area of the **Villa Romana del Casale**, an opulent Roman villa of the late imperial age. It constitutes the most important surviving work created by the Romans in Sicily, and was listed as a *UNESCO World Heritage* site in 1997. It was built between the end of the 3rd century and the beginning of the 4th, as a grand country house and luxury hunting lodge on a prosperous agricultural

ENNA
IN OTHER COLORS...

FOOD: P 146, 156, 163
SHOPPING: P 175
EVENTS: P 191
PRACTICAL INFO: P 215

The Ulysses and Polyphemus mosaic in the entrance-hall of the Roman villa at Casale

interesting, apart from its excellent state of preservation, chiefly because of its **floor mosaics****, which are among the most extensive and beautiful of surviving Roman mosaics. The technique, style and designs are reminiscent of northern African floors and were certainly the work of African masters. The most impressive mosaics are: in the **basilica**, a spacious rectangular hall used for official receptions; along the **Corridoio della Grande Caccia** (Corridor of the Great Hunt), so named because of the hunting theme of the mosaic; in a living room, dedicated to the myth of Orpheus, showing animals spell-bound by his lyre-playing. In the **Sala delle dieci ragazze** (Hall of the Ten Girls) is the famous mosaic of young female athletes wearing what look like modern-day *bikini* is.

estate, and was at its most splendid in the 4th and 5th centuries. Inhabited until the 12th century, it was then buried under mud during floods. It covered an area of around 3,500 square meters, and consisted of a complex of rooms (around 40) arranged on three levels on the slope of a hill and organised in sectors with differing functions: the baths, the large peristyle around which were the living rooms and guest rooms, the basilica and private apartments, and the large dining room with the triclinium. It's

Piazza Armerina: Roman villa of Casale

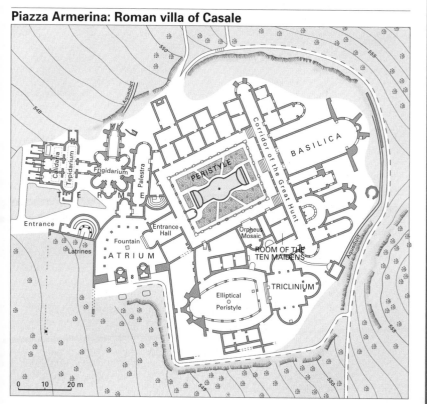

The Roman Villa of Casale

Numerous theories have been put forward as to who the owner of this sumptuous villa, which dates from the first half of the 4th century AD, might have been. Suggestions range from the Emperor himself to a Roman aristocrat who, at that time, held a very prestigious public post, possibly Valerio Proculo Populonio, who came from an important family of African origin. During the 4th century AD, the cream of the Roman aristocracy, who owned vast estates in Sicily, began to become more involved in the administration of their land, which was no longer cultivated by slaves, but by families of free colonists. One sign of this process of transformation is that numerous villas began to be built in the Sicilian countryside, for example, at Piazza Armerina, Tellaro and Patti. Of these, the villa of Casale, which is quite unique because of the richness and beauty of its mosaics, was a place where the owners received and entertained guests and relaxed. However, it was also the administrative center for the villa's vast estate. In the structure of the monumental complex, public and private areas overlap and contrast with each other. The reception rooms, such as the Corridor of the Great Hunt, the basilica, the apartment of the *domus* (master of the house) the elliptical peristyle and the triclinium (dining-room) differ dramatically from the apartment of the *domina* (lady of the house), the guest rooms and the rooms used by the servants.

1 Monumental entrance to the villa
2 Bath complex
3 Rectangular peristyle
4 Mosaics with geometric motifs
5 Guest rooms
6 Corridor of the Great Hunt
7 Apartment of the *domina* (lady of the house)
8 Marble floor
9 Basilica
10 Apartment of the *dominus* (master of the house)
11 Dining-room
12 Elliptical peristyle

Corridor of the Great Hunt. The mosaic depicts the capture and transportation of North African wild animals destined for spectacles held in Roman amphitheaters.

The sandy spur of Capo Peloro to the north and the sickle-shaped natural harbor of Messina to the south form the coastal landscape on the strait dividing Sicily from mainland Italy. According to popular legend, this stretch of sea was dominated by two mythical sea-monsters, Scylla and Charybdis, which used to devour whole ships in their whirlpools. Our visit to this city begins at the sea. From the decks of the ferries, visitors will already be able to catch a glimpse of the modern city, once crossed by broad horizontal channels which have now become roads. There is virtually nothing left of old Messina: the city reborn after the terrible earthquake of 1908 contains very few traces of its former glory. After all, its historical importance lies not in its monuments, but in its strategic position on the straits, a safe haven for passing ships.

When it was founded by the Siculi (a local tribe) before the 8th century BC, it was called Zancle (meaning sickle) and soon became an important stopping-place on international trading routes. The Roman conquest of the island began here and, after the Byzantine and Arab periods, the Normans and the House of Anjou gave the city fortifications and provided infrastructures for the trade in wool, silk and leather.

After the last earthquake, the reconstruction plan of 1911 designed a new city in which left no room for historical nostalgia, with wide streets and strong anti-seismic buildings, organized in blocks according to a strict grid plan.

Piazza del Duomo ❶

In the center of the city, from this broad square there is a view of the hills behind, with the Santuario di Montalto and, over to the right, the votive Chiesa di Cristo Re (Church of Christ the King) with its tall octagonal dome. On the east side of the square stands the broad facade of the Duomo, with its tall, spired *bell tower* (1908). It is famous for its large and extremely complex astronomical clock, with several layers of moving figures, which was inaugurated in 1933. Opposite the bell tower is the **Fontana di Orione*** (Fountain of Orion), executed in 1547 by Giovanni Angelo Montorsoli to celebrate the construction of the city's first aqueduct.

Duomo ❷

Built by Roger II in the first decades of the 12th century and consecrated in 1197, the Duomo was partly destroyed by the earthquake of 1783. Its modern appearance, which follows the general lines of the medieval building, dates from the reconstruction of 1919-20. The lower tier of the *facade* is decorated with mosaics and reliefs depicting pastoral scenes and scenes of everyday life (early 15th century). The three portals have been partly rebuilt, using new pieces to replace the lost originals. On the right-hand side, the portal by Rinaldo Bonanno was possibly executed according to a design by Polidoro da Caravaggio (16th century). The **interior**, much of which has been rebuilt, has a nave and two side-aisles, with painted wooden medieval

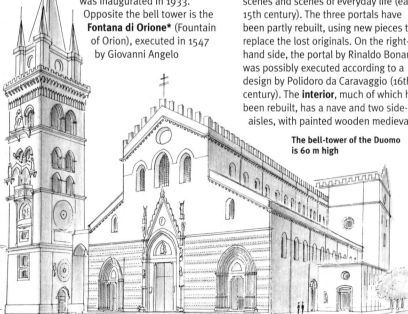

The bell-tower of the Duomo is 60 m high

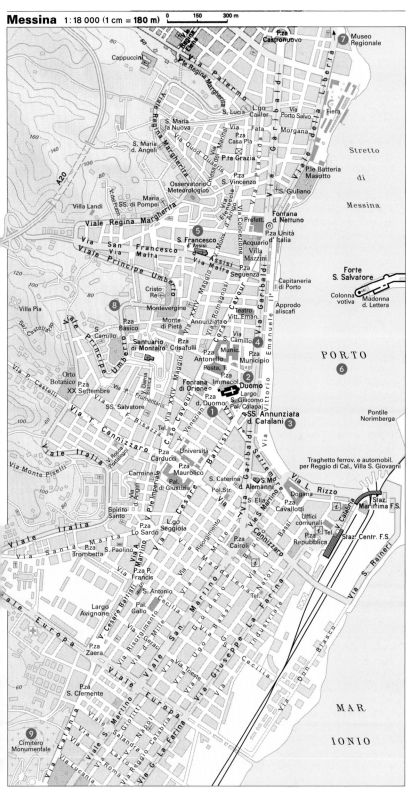

Messina

1:18 000 (1 cm = 180 m)

0   150   300 m

tie-beams. The first altar on the right contains a statue of John the Baptist attributed to Antonello Gagini (1525), the only one to survive the fire of 1943. The right-hand pilaster of the *presbytery* bears the cenotaph of Archbishop Guidotto de Abbiate, a 14th-century work of the Sienese school. The elaborate Baroque canopy over the altar, the wooden choir stalls and the mosaic in the apse are copies of the originals. In the *left-hand apse* is the Cappella del Sacramento (Chapel of the Sacrament), designed in the late 16th century. This is the best-preserved of the chapels, being the one least affected by natural (and un-natural) disasters. The mosaic in the vault of the apse is the only original and dates from the 14th century.

SS. Annunziata dei Catalani ❸

Built under the Normans during the second half of the 12th century, the church dedicated to the Most Holy Virgin Annunciate of the Catalans overlooks a little square graced by a monument to Don Juan of Austria (1572-73), with a bronze statue of the victor of Lèpanto (a crucial sea battle of 1571 in which a joint Christian fleet defeated the Turks) and reliefs depicting the layout of the fleet during the famous battle, the defeat of the Turks and the triumphal return of the ships to Messina harbor. The external decoration of the church shows obvious Arab influence.

Via Garibaldi ❹

Messina's main street is long and straight and runs through the middle of the city near the docks. On the left-hand side is the huge square with the imposing *Municipio* (City Hall) (1934) and the *Teatro Vittorio Emanuele*, inaugurated in 1852, and which was not razed to the ground by the terrible earthquake. In *Piazza Unità d'Italia* stands the **Fontana del Nettuno** (Fountain of Neptune), by Montorsoli (1557), which

MESSINA
IN OTHER COLORS...

■ **ITINERARIES:** P 116
■ **FOOD:** P 138, 153, 156, 164
■ **SHOPPING:** P 175, 177, 180
■ **EVENTS:** P 186, 192
■ **WELLNESS:** P 199, 202, 203
■ **PRACTICAL INFO:** P 222

has been re-constructed in a way not entirely faithful to the original design. The *Prefettura* (Police Headquarters) (1920) overlooks the square, on the south side of which stands **San Giovanni di Malta** (St John of Malta), a small church built in the late 16th century. Inside, there is 17th- and 18th-century silverware, busts and reliquaries and a votive chapel containing the coffins of Holy Martyrs.

S. Francesco d'Assisi ❺

This church dedicated to St Francis, rebuilt after the earthquake using original features, dates from the 13th century. The portal with the pointed arch in the side of the church, dates from the early 16th century. Above the main portal, with its 15th-century pointed arch, is a 16th-century rose-window.

Porto ❻

In terms of size, this is the widest natural harbor on the island, where ships of any tonnage can moor. To the east of the harbor are the remains of the 16th-century *Forte di San Salvatore*, vanguard of the city's fortifications against the Turks. On the round tower is a *votive column* with a statue of the Madonna della Lettera (Madonna of the Letter from 1934), the patron saint of Messina. Set around the huge, curved harbor are shipyards, boat repair workshops and a dry dock. To the north, a broad terrace with palm trees offers beautiful views across the strait to the Calabrian coast.

Forte San Salvatore with the Calabrian coast in the background

Museo Regionale ❼

The museum was set up in a former spinning-mill in 1914. It contains the collections of the Museo Civico of Messina, and numerous works from churches and palaces destroyed in the 1908 earthquake. The vast area around the building, the rooms of the museum and the new part of the museum under construction are full of architectural and decorative features recovered from the rubble of the buildings destroyed by the earthquake and the bombardments of WWII. Works of *Byzantine-Norman culture* include three fragments of tie-beams from the Duomo, painted by local artists and depicting themes from the Old and New Testament. Gothic works include a fine *Madonna degli Storpi** (Madonna of the Lame) and a sculpture by Goro di Gregorio (1333), whereas the large polychrome wooden *Crucifix** by an unknown sculptor of Provençal and Catalan background dates from the *early Renaissance in Messina* . The finest artworks in the museum are the **polyptych of St Gregory**** by Antonello da Messina (1473), and the two large canvases (**Adoration of the Shepherds*** and **Raising of Lazarus***) painted by Caravaggio during his brief sojourn in Messina in 1608 and 1609.

Circonvallazione a monte ❽

This panoramic "ring road" consists of a series of broad streets which curve around the hill above the city with pleasant views of Messina itself and the strait beyond. The most interesting section is *Viale Principe Umberto*, where two important churches are located: the votive church of *Cristo Re* (Christ the King), built in 1937, and the *Santuario di Montalto* (Sanctuary of Montalto), which has a 16th-century Madonna of Victory, painted after the Battle of Lèpanto (1571). Further along, *Viale Italia* provides access to the *Forte Gonzaga* (Gonzaga Fortress), a fine example of 16th-century military architecture.

Cimitero monumentale ❾

This cemetery, built in a panoramic position commanding views of the coast and across the strait, is one of the most beautiful in Italy. Designed in 1872, it has some fine examples of Sicilian Art Deco work.

DAY TRIPS

GOLA DELL'ALCANTARA [5 km]

This deep, picturesque gorge situated below the slopes of Mount Etna, was gouged out of a lava flow from an eruption in prehistoric times by the Alcàntara River. Visitors can wade 150 m along the river bed (rubber boots are available for hire) between the high basalt walls of the gorge, or admire this unique natural environment from the top, which can be reached on foot or by lift.

The deep and highly spectacular Alcantara Gorge

CAPO D'ORLANDO [97 km]

According to tradition, the promontory on which the site was built was named after an officer serving under Charlemagne, who founded the castle. Near the ruins of the 14th-century *castle* is the **Santuario di Maria SS. di Capo d'Orlando** (Sanctuary of the Most Holy Virgin of capo d'Orlando), built in 1598. At Bina, a museum of the famous Sicilian poet Piccolo has been created in the family villa.

GIARDINI NAXOS [51 km]

This vast archeological site on the promontory of Capo Schisò contains the ruins of the earliest Greek colony to be founded in Sicily by the Chalcidians. Its foundation in the 8th century BC started

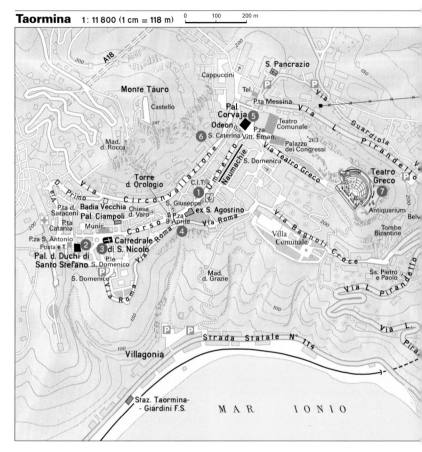

Taormina 1: 11 800 (1 cm = 118 m)

the Greek colonization of the island. Prior to this, they had thought that it was populated by monsters and fierce pirates. The settlement was destroyed in 403 BC by the tyrant Dionysius of Siracusa. Today, visitors can see the *walls* and the *fortifications* built of lava blocks, the residential areas built on a regular grid plan and the walled area used for sacred rites, including the remains of a *temple* dating from the early 5th century BC. Finds from the site are housed in the small *site museum*.

MILAZZO [41 km]

Milazzo is situated on the northern coast of Sicily at the neck of a narrow beach-fringed peninsula jutting out more than 7 km into the Tyrrhenian Sea. Despite modern expansion, this busy port still bears traces of its history, divided, as it is, into the 16th-century walled town, the "borgo" and the lower town. Before becoming an important commercial and tourist port (this is the departure point for

boats to the Eolian Islands), in antiquity, the town was an important possession of Siracusa, a commercial base during the Arab period and one of main strongholds of the Aragonese in Sicily.

The **walled town**, in the highest part of the old town, is surrounded by 16th-century Aragonese walls. This is the site of the **Castello**, an ancient defensive building extended by Frederick II (in the 13th century) and completed by the Spanish (in the 15th century), and the *Duomo vecchio* (Old Duomo), a Baroque building erected in 1608. From here, a flight of steps leads down to the **Borgo**, which grew up in the 16th century as an extension to the Aragonese town. It includes many important Baroque religious and public buildings. A cloister is all that remains of a Dominican monastery that was converted into a courthouse for the Inquisition. The **lower town** was built in recent times, when the development of commercial activities gave a new boost to the harbor area.

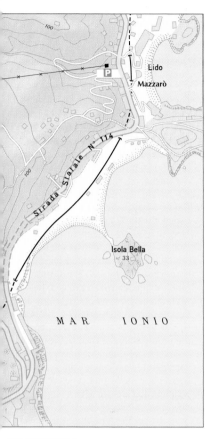

name derives, but with breathtaking views to the south towards Mount Etna's snow-clad summit.

It first became famous in the 18th century, when travelers from northern Europe discovered its particular Mediterranean light, its mild climate, the colors and perfumes of its vegetation, its monuments and architecture. Yet, even back in medieval times, it was described as an "illustrious" town, on account of the archeological remains of ancient *Tauromenium*, founded in 358 BC.

It was in the Middle Ages, first at the hand of the Saracens, then under the Normans, that the town began to expand. The castle was built on the top of Monte Tauro, the town was developed into a thick maze of narrow streets and flights of steps around the cathedral and soon became established as a commercial center on the road between Messina and Siracusa.

Corso Umberto I ❶, the main thoroughfare built along the line of the old Via Consolare, is the "drawing room" of the town ". At the western end of the town stands the **Palazzo dei Duchi di Santo Stefano ❷** (Palace of the Dukes of St Stephen), an elegant building dating from the Swabian-Angevin period, the original structure of which dates from the second half of the 13th century.

Just beyond it is the **Cattedrale ❸**, dedicated to St Nicholas. This somber building dates from the 13th century and

TAORMINA [49 km]

A real gem, and unique in terms of its position and shape, the town is perched on a short terrace high above the sea, protected by Monte Tauro from which its

Giardini Naxos

The facade of the Duomo of Taormina, with two one-light windows and a rose-window

was altered between the 16th and 18th centuries. On either side of the richly decorated 17th-century portal in the facade is a 14th-century single-light window. High above the door is a small 16th-century rose-window. In front of the church is a Baroque *fountain* dating from 1635 with a statue of a female centaur with only two legs, one of the symbols of Taormina. The *interior* of the church is built on a simple basilica plan, with a nave and two side-aisles supported by monolithic marble columns.

About halfway along the street, **Piazza IX Aprile** ❹ has a panoramic terrace with marvelous views. On the left of the square stands the former little Gothic church of *Sant'Agostino*, while, under the 17th-century *Torre dell'Orologio* (Clock Tower) is the *Porta di Mezzo* (Halfway Gate) leading into the

medieval town, where many examples of 15th-century architecture still survive. Passing the so-called **naumachie***, an imposing brick curtain wall which constitutes one of the most important Roman remains in Sicily, we reach Piazza Vittorio Emanuele. **Palazzo Corvaja** ❺ was built in the 11th - 15th centuries and has a 14th-century facade with two-light windows. In the same square, the church of **Santa Caterina d'Alessandria** ❻ (St Catherine of Alexandria) incorporates the remains of the **Odeon**, a small theater dating from the Roman Imperial period.

Not far away is the **Teatro greco** ❼ (Greek theater), a masterpiece of its kind, built in the Hellenistic period (3rd century BC) and almost completely rebuilt in the Roman period (possibly in the 2nd century AD). The *cavea* (auditorium), consisting of nine tiers of seating and crowned at the top by a double portico supported by columns, was achieved by taking advantage of the natural slope of the hill. The *scena* (monumental stage), of which a considerable amount is still standing, had a back wall with a series of columns and niches, with a large device in the center revealing, as if it were the perfect backdrop, the Bay of Schisò and Mount Etna. From the top of the cavea, and the terraces on either side of the stage, visitors can enjoy one of Sicily's most famous **views**** along the coast and across to the

The ancient remains of the Greek theater at Taormina

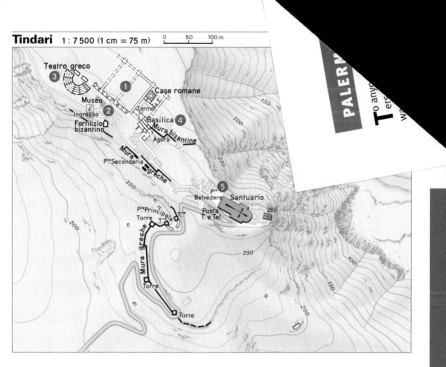

Tindari 1 : 7 500 (1 cm = 75 m)

gigantic massif of Mount Etna.
More breathtaking views can be admired
from *Via Roma*, which drops down to the
gardens of the *Villa comunale*.

TERME VIGLIATORE [50 km]

A pause at San Biagio, a hamlet of
Terme Vigliatore, provides the chance to
visit a **Roman villa** of the 1st century AD,
discovered in 1953. The remains include
part of the *peristyle*, with a small *bath
complex* on the right and, in the center,
the *tablinum* (dining-room) in the form
of a large exedra with an apse. The
black and white mosaics in some of the
rooms and the floor of the tablinum
decorated with hexagonal marble tiles
are in good condition.

TINDARI [10 km]

The ruins of *Tyndaris*, one of the last
Greek colonies founded in Sicily,
overlook the Tyrrhenian Sea from a high
cliff on the promontory of the same
name. The Saracens destroyed the city
in the 9th to 10th centuries, or, at least
what was left of it, after a landslide in
Roman times, described by Pliny (1st
century AD), caused part of it to fall into
the sea. Tyndaris is also famous for its
large sanctuary dedicated to the Virgin
Mary, to which pilgrims flock from all
over Sicily and Calabria.

The **excavations of Tyndaris** ❶
highlight the very regular plan of the
city: three long, straight roads
("decumani"), lined on either side by
"tabernae" (shops), ran perpendicular
to smaller roads ("cardini") running
downhill, forming identical "insulae"
(blocks) with buildings on terraces at
different levels.
Part of the original paving of the **upper
decumanus** ❷ is still in place, whereas,
in the "insula" there is a large *town
house*, with spacious terraces and a
peristyle with 12 columns, dating from
approximately the 1st century AD, with
splendid floor mosaics. The seating and
part of the stage is still visible in the
theater ❸, which is built into the slope
of the hill. In the **Basilica** ❹ of the Late
Imperial period overlooking the *agorà*
(market place), the original first three
floors of the building are still standing.
Piazzale Belvedere ❺, a panoramic
terrace with a view* over Capo Tìndari,
the coast and the Eolian Islands,
provides access to the imposing
Santuario della Madonna del Tìndari
(Sanctuary of the Tyndaris Madonna),
built in the 20th-century. Above the
main altar stands the revered statue of
the "Madonna nera" (Black Madonna),
which, according to tradition, came here
from the East as the result of a miracle.

ne arriving by sea, the city must look much as it would have done to earlier travel-
: a succession of domes and palaces carved out of the tuff stone which reflects the
rm light, patches of green provided by the city's palm trees and gardens. A city of violent
contrasts, where the gradual accumulation of civilization has assimilated fascinating cultural influences but also howls of anger and bitterness, Palermo should be admired for its magnificent combination of urban and natural landscapes. From the top of Monte Pellegrino and
within the intricate maze of alleys and squares of the old city, everything blends in a vortex
of theatrical mirages, fiction and stage scenery, making it impossible to gain an overall view.
A capital that is splendid and shabby at the same time, Palermo has always spread its
splendor and its poverty into the surrounding area, extending the symbols of its dominant
classes, the clergy and the aristocracy.

The city founded by the Phoenicians in the 8th century BC with the name of Panormos
(meaning "all harbor") was the first Punic base in Sicily. The first expansion came with the
Arab conquest (831). Palermo became the seat of an emir, and was described as a mythical city, comparable in terms of importance and splendor with the cities of Córdoba and Cairo at that time.

Subsequently, with the Norman conquest (1072) and the alliance struck between monarchy and the clergy, this city bore witness to a flowering of extraordinary beauty in the architectural synthesis of Arab and Norman styles of which the Cappella Palatina is the maximum expression. Here, the Swabian Emperor Frederick II, a great and extraordinarily cultured man, liked to mingle with men of letters, mathematicians, astronomers and intellectuals.

**Detail of the picturesque Piazza Vigliena,
popularly known as the "Quattro Canti"**

In the Middle Ages, the rise of the great land-owning families led to ambitious programs of
building and urban development. Imposing new fortified palaces were built, the city walls
were reinforced, and the main squares were reorganized. When it became capital of the
vice-royalty under Spanish dominion, in the 16th and 17th centuries, the city underwent pro-
found changes, with the aim of exalting ecclesiastical and feudal power. Palaces, churches,
monasteries and oratories were built in the city, while, all around it, splendid residential villas were erected for the nobility. In the second half of the 19th century, in the climate of the
"belle époque", great industrial activity, together with a carefully planned program of town-
planning brought Palermo to the forefront of the Art Deco movement in Italy.

Quattro Canti ❶

This is the name (meaning Four Corners) given to the little square of *Piazza Vigliena*, also known as the *Ottangolo* (Eight Corners) or the *Teatro del Sole* (Theater of the Sun). Built in the 17th-century, the Baroque decoration of its four corners symbolically reproduced the division of the city into four sectors, defined by a huge cross formed by two perpendicular roads. Built between 1608 and 1620, the three-tiered facades of the four corners are decorated with niches, small balconies and statues. The first tier features four fountains representing the seasons of the year; the second tier depicts the Spanish monarchs, Charles V, Philip II, Philip III and Philip IV; while the third tier depicts St Cristina, St Ninfa, St Oliva and St Agatha, patronesses of Palermo.

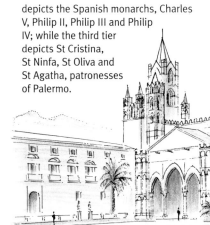

Cattedrale ❷

This important architectural monument embodies the whole history of the city in the stratification of styles resulting from numerous alterations to its fabric over the centuries.

Built by the Normans in 1184 as a re-converted Christian church on the site of a previous basilica that had been converted into a mosque by the Saracens, it was altered many times before the radical transformation of 1781-1801 when the interior was changed and the dome was added. The main *facade* has retained its original appearance dating from the 14th to 15th centuries. Its two towers are decorated with two-light windows and small columns, blind arcading and a Gothic portal surmounted by a two-light window. Two pointed arches connect the facade to the *bell tower*, the solid lower part of which is medieval. Other bell towers were added to the top "in the same style" in the 19th century. On the *left-hand side* of the cathedral is a Gaginesque portico dating from the mid-16th century, subsequently incorporated within a late-18th-century structure. At the beginning of the *right-hand side* of the cathedral, set between two little towers is a broad porch with three high pointed arches, an example of the flamboyant Catalan Gothic style, built in 1429-30. A passage from the Koran is engraved on the first column on the left, which probably belonged to the building during the Arabic period.

PALERMO IN OTHER COLORS...

- **ITINERARIES:** P 117
- **FOOD:** P 142, 146, 153
- **SHOPPING:** P 175, 178, 181
- **EVENTS:** P 186, 187, 193
- **WELLNESS:** P 202
- **PRACTICAL INFO:** P 227

The *triple apse** has retained its 12th-century form, and is decorated by a motif of intersecting arches. The **interior**, transformed in the Neo-classical style, has a nave and two side-aisles supported by pilasters. In the *right-hand aisle*, the first and second chapels contain the famous **royal and imperial tombs***, massive porphyry sarcophagi of majestic simplicity. They contain the remains of Constance of Aragon (died 1222), Henry VI (died 1197), Frederick II (died 1250), the Empress Constance (died 1198) and Roger II (died 1154). The chapel to the right of the presbytery, the *Cappella di Santa Rosalia*, (Chapel of St Rosalia) contains a silver coffer (163) with relics of the city's patron saint. In the *presbytery*, the splendid wooden choir stalls of 1466 are decorated in the Catalan Gothic style. In the *left-hand aisle* there is a *Madonna and Child** by Francesco Laurana and his pupils (1469). A small door in the right transept leads into the hall of the sacristy. From here, turn left into the *Sagrestia dei Canonici,* (Canons' Sacristy) where there is portal dating from 1568. To the right of the hall of the sacristy a door leads into the **Treasury** which contains precious gold, silver and enameled objects, illuminated codices and sacred vestments. The most interesting exhibit is the gold crown of Constance of Aragon, wife of Frederick II, studded with enamel, gems and pearls. In the *crypt*, consisting of two aisles supported by columns (12th century), there are seven small apses containing sarcophagi dating from various periods.

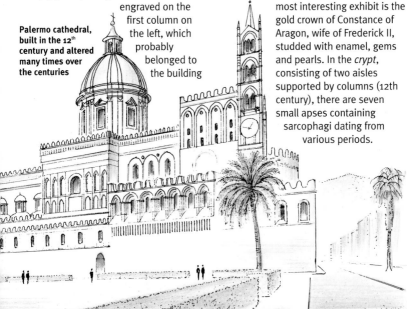

Palermo cathedral, built in the 12th century and altered many times over the centuries

Palermo 1:14 000 (1 cm = 140 m)

0   100   200 m

Fondazione Mormino
Ass. Reg. d. Turismo

16 Parco della Favorita
P.za Gentile
Via Duca V. Verdura

V. G. Sciuti
Via L. Ariosto
Via L. Leopardi
Via E. Notarbartolo
V. Mariarella
della Libertà

Staz. Notarbartolo F.S.
Via L. da Vinci
Via D. Costantino

Giardino Inglese
Villa Gallidoro

Villa Gonzaga
Villa Bordonaro
Villa d. Croci
Via P. Calvi
Via d. Croci

Villa Trabia
P.za F. Crispi
P.za Mordini
Via E. Calvi
Via Archimede
Via Archimede Carini

Via Terra Santa
La Farina
Catania
Princ. Siracusa
Via Messina
della Libertà

P.za D. Siculo
Via G. Marconi
Via Messina
Galleria Arte mod
Politeama

Via G. Cantore
Via G. Cusmano
Via Malaspina
Via G. Martino
Via Villafranca
Via Settembre
Via Dante

P.za Busacca
Via G. Aurispa
Via G. Aurispa

Staz. Lolli F.S.
P.za Virgilio
Via Dante

P.za Rugger Settimo
P.za Castelnuovo
7
Ruggero S.

Villa Malfitano
Via Serradifalco
Via Dante

V. Latini
V. Paternostro
P.za Amendola
P.za S. Oliva
S. Francesco di Paola

Quattro di Camp.
Stabile
V. Ungher
V. Pignatelli D'Aragon

P.za Principe di Camporeale
Via Regina Margherita

V. Cluverio
Via Goethe
Via Carini
S. Francesco di Paola
Villa Filippina
Via N. Turrisi

Teatro Massimo

Cantieri Culturali della Zisa
V. Whitaker
V. Cantù

Corso Finocchiaro Aprile
V. Guglielmo il Buono
V. Venezian
Via Re Federico
C.so Eman. Orlando
P.za Vitt.
Via Volturno
P.ta Carini

Zisa
17
P.za Zisa

V. Contessa Giudritta
Via C. Lascaris
Via Imera
Alberto Amedeo
Pal. di Giustizia
P.za Concezione
P.za d. Aragone
Via S. Agostin

Via Zisa
P.ta Cuccia
P.za Noviziato
V. Bent Paoli
P.

Vicolo Zisa
Via Cipressi
P.za Ingastone
Via d'Ossuna
Via G. Imera
Corso Alberto Amedeo
P.ta d'Ossuna
P.za Beati Paoli

Convento d. Cappuccini
Piazza Danisinni
Via Mosca
P.ta Paranni
P.za Papireto
2
Cattedrale

Via G. Mosca
Via Colonna
Via G. Imera
Pal. Arcivescovile (Museo Diocesano)
Cso Vitt. Emanuele
Villa Bonanno

Via Cappuccini
V. Rotta
P.ta Nuova
3 Pal. d. Normanni
P.za d. Vittoria
P.za del Parlamento

Via Calatafimi
P.za Indipendenza
4 Cappella Palatina
P.ta d. Castro
5 S. Giov. d. Eremiti

Albergo delle Povere
Pal. Orleans (Residenza Regione Siciliana)
Parco d'Orleans
Corso Pisani
Corso Re Ruggero
18
19
Cuba
S. Spirito

54

Palazzo dei Normanni ❸

This palace is one of the key monuments in the city in terms of historical and artistic importance. Built by the Saracens in the 9th century on the site of a Punic and Roman citadel, it was extended by the Normans who transformed the original fortress into a splendid palace, and a center of political power and administration for the State (12th century). Under Frederick II, it also became a cultural center on a European scale. After a period of neglect and degradation, concurrent with the decline of the Swabian dynasty and the decadence of Sicilian political life, the palace was radically transformed at the orders of the Spanish viceroys, who, from 1555 onwards, decided to use it as a residence. On the right of the imposing facade built in the 16th-century style (1616) stands the *Torre Pisana* (Pisan Tower) or *Torre di Santa Ninfa* (Tower of St Ninfa), part of the original Norman palace, its facade decorated with blind arcading. (The so-called "room of the Treasury" was discovered inside the tower: behind the double doors four huge jars were found buried under the floor). The former palace, which is now the seat of the Sicilian Regional Assembly, contains the royal apartments and the Cappella Palatina (Palatine Chapel) and also houses the *Museo di Astronomia* with a collection of instruments dating from the late 18th to 20th centuries. The royal apartments include the *dining-room*, once an open-air atrium, with tall pointed arcades supported by square columns, and the *Sala di Re Ruggero* (King Roger's Hall), where magnificent mosaics of hunting scenes of obvious Persian influence (c. 1170) adorn the walls, the undersides of the arches and the vaults.

Cappella Palatina ❹

This splendid example of Norman art was founded by Roger II in 1130 and consecrated in 1140. On the outside wall is a narrow portico supported by columns, decorated with mosaics executed in 1800 to replace earlier ones. The **interior** of the chapel is extraordinarily beautiful, and is one of the finest examples of integration between architecture and figurative art. The nave and two side-aisles are divided

by a series of pointed arches supported on ancient columns. It ends in the sanctuary, raised and closed off by transennae, with a triple apse and a dome. The floor is decorated with marble mosaic, marble inlay covers the lower part of the walls, while, above the nave, there is a beautiful *wooden ceiling* executed by Arab artisans (c. 1143), with honeycomb and stalactite decoration (*muqarnas*). At the beginning of the nave is the vast Royal Throne, encrusted with mosaics, executed in the 12th century, an exquisite blend of Romanesque, Arab and Byzantine influences. Near the sanctuary, on the right, there is a fine *mosaic ambo* supported by columns and a superb Paschal *candlestick*, with carvings of acanthus leaves, human and animal figures, both dating from the 12th century. All the upper walls are decorated with **mosaics** on a gold background. The earliest mosaics in the sanctuary (1143) reflect most purely the characters of the great Byzantine tradition (Scenes from the Gospels with inscriptions in Greek; Christ Pantocrator surrounded by angels, archangels, prophets and evangelists in the dome). The mosaics in the nave with Latin inscriptions are of a later date (1154-66 c.), and depict stories from the Old Testament. The mosaics in the side-aisles depicting the stories of St Peter and St Paul are of an even later date.

S. Giovanni degli Eremiti ❺

The church takes its name from the monastery dedicated in 581 to St Ermete, subsequently corrupted to "Eremiti", which formerly stood on this site. It is accessed from Via dei

San Giovanni degli Eremiti

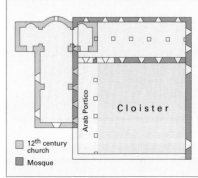

Arab Portico

Cloister

■ 12th century church
■ Mosque

The cloister of San Giovanni degli Eremiti

decoration, with sculptures by Gioacchino Vitagliano against a background of landscapes executed in marble inlay work. To the right of the church is the west facade of the **Casa Professa**, with a fine 17th-century portal and cloister. This building provides access to the *Biblioteca comunale* (Municipal Library) founded in 1760. Nearby, *Via Ballarò* is the setting for a characteristic food market, one of the historic markets of Palermo.

Benedettini, through a gate which leads into a delightful garden full of exotic plants. The deconsecrated church in this enchanting setting is one of the most important Norman monuments in Palermo. It was built by Arab artisans in 1136 at the wishes of Roger II. Above the bare, squarish building, which has a bell tower decorated with one-light windows, are five squat little domes, lending the whole complex an oriental air. *Inside*, the single nave is surmounted by two domes, while the niches in the corners are of clear Arab influence. There is a square room on either side of the presbytery, which has an apse and is surmounted by a dome. The room on the right leads into a rectangular room, possibly part of a former mosque. In the garden are the remains of an Arab *cistern* and a delightful little 13th-century **cloister*** with small paired columns, which once belonged to the original Benedictine monastery.

Chiesa del Gesù ⑥

The interior of this 17th-century church, the first Jesuit church in Sicily, is an extraordinary example of Sicilian Baroque. It contains a profusion of carvings and marble inlay work, stuccoes in relief, sculptures and paintings, adorning every corner of the church like a splendid cloak. During the massive restoration after WWII, almost all the stuccoes and frescoes destroyed by the bombing of 1943 were replaced. The presbytery and the apse have retained their original extremely rich

S. Cataldo ⑦

Built during the Norman period (c. 1160), the church has retained its original forms, with blind arcading on the outside walls of bare stone, Arab crenellations and three semi-spherical domes supported by drums. *Inside*, the nave and two side-aisles are separated by columns from ancient sites. Here, the bareness of the walls, which were never covered with mosaics, is quite striking. The mosaic floor and the altar are original. The church is the main seat of the Order of the Knights of the Holy Sepulchre.

Martorana ⑧

This jewel of Norman architecture, also known as *Santa Maria dell'Ammiraglio* (St Mary of the Admiral), was built in 1143 at the wishes of George of Antioch, who was admiral under Roger II. In 1433 it was presented to the nearby Benedictine convent founded in 1194 by Eloisa Martorana, after whom the church was named. Next to the Baroque facade, added following the transformations during the 16th and 17th centuries, stands the original elegant **bell tower****, decorated with pointed arches and three tiers of large two-light windows. The **interior****, which was originally square and built on a Greek-cross plan with a triple apse, is divided by the four columns supporting the dome. There used to be a porch connecting it to the bell tower, which was altered in the 17th century. On the walls of the original front of the church are two mosaics: on the right, Roger II is crowned by Christ; on the left, George of Antioch kneels at the Virgin Mary's feet. The main part of the church (the upper walls, the undersides of the arches, the arches themselves and the dome) is covered in shining **mosaics****, executed in the pure Byzantine style. Together with those in the Cappella Palatina, these are the oldest mosaic cycles in Sicily. The use of iconography and the way the mosaics are arranged reflect the most orthodox canons of Byzantine art, with the central figure of Christ Pantocrator surrounded by archangels, prophets, the evangelists, apostles and saints. This is also true of the mosaics depicting the Nativity, the Transition of the Virgin, the Annunciation and the Presentation at the Temple. Mosaic transennae precede the apses. The floor, decorated with marble inlay and mosaics, is original. The original apse, destroyed in 1693, has been replaced by a Baroque chapel with marble inlay work and a tabernacle in lapis lazuli.

Palazzo Abatellis ❾

This palace was erected between 1490-95 by Matteo Carnilivari as a residence for Francesco Abatellis, master-pilot of the kingdom and a magistrate of Palermo, on the old *Via Alloro*, a residential street dating from the late medieval period. A compact building of bare stone blocks, the typical forms of the late Catalan Gothic style are toned down by lighter Renaissance motifs. Elegant three-light windows enhance the facade, either end of which is a tower with Gothic decoration and two- and three-light windows with slender columns. The fine portal is decorated with motifs of bundles of sticks held together with ropes. Badly damaged during WWII, since 1954 it has housed the prestigious collection of the Galleria Regionale della Sicilia (Regional Gallery of Sicilian Art).

Galleria Regionale della Sicilia Palazzo Abatellis ❿

The gallery contains paintings and sculptures, especially works from the 14th to 16th centuries, previously housed in the Museo Nazionale. In the atrium, the porticoed courtyard and loggia there are reliefs, sculptures and architectural fragments dating from the pre-Romanesque period to the Renaissance. On the ground floor, there

Antonello da Messina's famous painting of the Annunciation, one of the masterpieces on display at the Galleria Regionale della Sicilia

are wooden sculptures from the 12th to 16th centuries and stone sculptures from the 14th and 15th centuries, statues by Antonello and Domenico Gagini and the **bust of Eleonora of Aragon**** (c. 1471), a masterpiece by Francesco Laurana. The large fresco of the **Triumph of Death****, attributable to the International Gothic style and executed around the mid-15th century, is particularly worthy of note. The Pinacoteca on the first floor contains numerous paintings on wood by Italian masters of the 14th to 15th centuries: Antonio Veneziano (Madonna and Child); Bartolomeo Pellerano; Turino Vanni (Madonna and Saints); Giovanni di Nicola (*Madonna del Latte**); the unknown "Master of the Trapani polyptych" (Coronation of the Virgin and archangels); an unknown Sicilian Master of several Coronations (Annunciation*); Pietro Ruzzolone. A particular gem in this collection is the small panel of the **Virgin Annunciate**** (1473), one of the most interesting works of Antonello da Messina, who also painted the three cusps of a polyptych dated 1473 with figures of *saints**. Works representing the 16th and 17th centuries include paintings by the so-called Master of Pentecost, Vincenzo da Pavia, Palma il Giovane, Mattia Preti (Christ and the Centurion), Pietro Novelli (Madonna and Child with saints) and Corrado Giacquinto. There are also various other works of the Flemish school, including the famous **Malvagna tryptych****, a fine work by Jan Gossaert, known as Mabuse (1510).

S. Francesco d'Assisi ⑪

This church dedicated to St Francis of Assisi, one of the most important in Palermo, is a significant presence of the mendicant order in the commercial district. Built between 1255 and 1277, it has been altered many times over the centuries, with the addition of side-chapels, cross-vaulting in place of the wooden ceiling, 17th-century frescoes and extremely fine stuccoes by Giacomo Serpotta (1723). The restoration which followed the bombing of 1943 restored the church to its original Romanesque forms. In the facade, there is a portal in the flamboyant Gothic style dating from 1302, above which is a beautiful rose-window. The doors in the side of the church date from the 16th century.
Inside, the nave and two side-aisles are supported by round pilasters. In the side-aisles, there are chapels in the Gothic and Renaissance style, many of which contain valuable decoration and sculptures from the 15th and 16th centuries by the Gagini, Pietro di Bonitate and Francesco Laurana (*portal** 4th chapel on the left, 1468).

Museo Archeologico Regionale "Antonino Salinas" ⑫

One of the finest and most interesting archeological museums in Italy, in terms of the vastness and quality of its collection, particularly the series of large sculptures from Selinunte, occupies a 17th-century building of the former monastery of the Padri Filippini. The collections, divided into sections according to the kind of artifacts and where they were found, are displayed in many rooms occupying three floors. The rooms on the *first floor* are devoted to submarine archeology and oriental and classical sculpture. It includes the largest and most complete collection of *anchors** (made of stone, lead and iron) in existence, in addition to finds from submarine archeological excavations conducted off the coast of Sicily, material of eastern influence such as sculptures from the Archaic period (6th century BC) and Egyptian sculptures and inscriptions, including the *Pietra di Palermo*, a fragment of a large black diorite slab engraved with hieroglyphics during the 5th Dynasty.
In the rooms devoted to *classical sculpture* interesting exhibits include some inscriptions, the group of *twin-headed votive stones from Selinunte** (4th-3rd century BC) depicting pairs of gods of the Underworld, architectural fragments from the temples of Selinunte, in stone and painted terracotta, and *lion's head water-spouts*** from the Temple of "Victory" at Himera, which, according to tradition, was built immediately after 480 BC to celebrate the victory of the Greeks over the Carthaginians. A large room contains the collection of **sculptures from the temples at Selinunte****, which are of exceptional importance for scholars of early Sicilian sculpture. Notice in particular: *the three metopes from temple C*** (mid-6th century BC); *the two half metopes from Temple F** (early 5th century BC); *the four metopes from Temple E*** (460-450 BC).
On the *first floor* there are *collections of various material* from diverse locations. The *bronze collection* includes statuettes of Greek, Etruscan and Roman heroes, mirrors and numerous votive objects. Don't miss *two large bronzes* of particular interest depicting a ram, from Siracusa (early 3rd century BC), and *Hercules fighting a stag**, a Roman copy of an original by the Lyssipos school. Two other rooms contain gold and silver ware and a coin collection.

The *second floor* houses *prehistoric exhibits* from western Sicily, from the Palaeolithic, the Bronze Age and the Iron Age: flint tools, vases, stone weapons, a few copper objects and decorated pottery. *Greek pottery* is represented by black- and red-figure proto-Corinthian, Corinthian and Attic vases. The tour of the museum ends with rooms devoted to *mosaics* and *Roman frescoes* (notice the large mosaic from the Imperial period depicting Orpheus and the animals, from Palermo) and *Italiot pottery* from the 4th to3rd centuries BC.

The Oratory of Santa Cita: Giacomo Serpotta's spectacular rendering in stucco of the Battle of Lépanto

S. Domenico ⑬

Erected in 1640 on the site of a former building and founded with the adjoining monastery in the 14th century but rebuilt in 1458, this is one of the most interesting Baroque churches in the city. Its broad facade, flanked by two bell towers, dates from 1726. The vast *interior*, with a nave and two side-aisles supported by heavy columns, constitutes a sort of pantheon of the glories of Palermo, since it contains numerous tombs and cenotaphs of illustrious Sicilians (amongst others, the statesman Francesco Crispi). In the adjoining monastery, some of the rooms off the cloister house the *Museo del Risorgimento* which has exhibits pertaining to Giuseppe Garibaldi's famous expedition known as the "Mille" (Thousand).

Oratorio del Rosario di S. Domenico ⑭

The interior of this small oratory tucked away behind the church of St Dominic is regarded as a masterpiece on account of its beautiful **stucco decoration****, executed by Giacomo Serpotta. On the walls are paintings by Pietro Novelli, Giacomo Lo Verde, Matthias Stomer and Luca Giordano depicting the Mysteries of the Rosary. The fresco on the ceiling by Pietro Novelli depicts the Coronation of the Virgin. At the altar, a Madonna of the Rosary with St Dominic and the patronesses of Palermo* by Anthony Van Dyck (1628).

Oratorio di S. Cita ⑮

The oratory, preceded by a late 16th-century loggia, is famous for the magnificent *stucco work** which adorns the interior. The stuccoes, executed by Giacomo Serpotta between 1688 and 1718, depict allegories, cherubs and the Mysteries of the Rosary. On the entrance wall is a depiction of the Battle of Lèpanto (1571), with cherubs and trophies of arms. Along the walls, the pews reserved for members of the confraternity are inlaid with mother-of-pearl. At the altar is a Madonna of the Rosary by Carlo Maratta and, at each side, Baroque choir stalls with angels by Giacomo Serpotta.

Parco della Favorita ⑯

North-west of the historic center of Palermo, at the foot of Monte Pellegrino, lies a vast park of 400 hectares, created by Ferdinand III of Bourbon in 1799. Now open to the public and host to a number of important sporting facilities, it once played a dual role as a hunting and fishing reserve and as a garden for agricultural experiments, for which the king had a particular passion. The park, which is laid out longitudinally, is crossed by two long avenues, called Viale di Diana and Viale di Ercole. The latter terminates at the *Fountain of Hercules*, where there is an imposing Doric column surmounted by a statue, a copy of the Hercules in the Farnese Collection of the Museo Nazionale in Naples.

Zisa ⑰

A jewel of Fatimid architecture of the Norman period, the palace (from the Arabic word *aziz*, meaning "splendid") was begun by William I and finished by William II in about 1165-67. This was a summer residence for the Norman kings of Sicily. Once immersed in a garden, it is a compact, rectangular building, with two square towers on the shorter sides and three tiers of blind arcading which formerly enclosed two-light windows. When the merlons were added in the 16th century, the cornice with an Arabic inscription was destroyed. Transformed and adapted over the centuries, the interior is complex, with public rooms and private apartments arranged on various floors. On the ground floor is the *Sala della Fontana* (Hall of the Fountain), a reception room built on a cross plan, with stalactite pendant decoration on the ceiling and a mosaic frieze around the walls. Near the palace stand the *Cantieri Culturali alla Zisa* (the former warehouses of the Ducrot furniture workshop, 1900-30), now used as an exhibitions and conference center.

Cuba ⓲

Now incorporated in the courtyard of a barracks, this example of Fatimid architecture was built by William II in 1180. Originally conceived as a pleasure pavilion in the Norman Genoard Park and at one time surrounded by an artificial lake, the building has a rectangular plan, squared, compact spaces, small flat projections at the center of each side and blind arcading covering the entire height of the walls. A band with an Arabic inscription records the name of the king and the date of the building's

foundation. The building, chosen by Giovanni Boccaccio as the setting for one of the stories in his book *The Decameron*, was converted into a lazaretto in the 16th century, had associations with a cavalry barracks during the Bourbon period and was radically restored in 1936.

S. Spirito ⓳

A Norman church within the walls of the *Cimitero di Sant'Orsola* or *di Santo Spirito* (Cemetery of St Ursula or of the Holy Spirit), founded by the viceroy Caracciolo in 1782, which contains fine funerary monuments and chapels from the 19th and 20th centuries. The *church*, built in 1178, is also called the *Chiesa del Vespro* (Church of the Vespers) because it was in front of this church, on March 31, 1282, at the hour of vespers, that the revolt of the people of Palermo began against the Angevins, an event known historically as the *Sicilian Vespers*. The apse of the church is decorated with inlaid lava while the interior is austere with a simple nave and side-aisles.

DAY TRIPS

BAGHERIA [15 km]

The densely populated little town set among expanses of citrus, medlar and olive groves, facing the sea and Monte Catalfano, still has some splendid Baroque villas, which sprang up around the residence of Giuseppe Branciforte, Prince of Butera, now open to the public. The 18th-century **Villa Cattolica** houses the Galleria Comunale d'Arte Moderna (Municipal Gallery of Modern Art), opened in 1973 thanks to a donation from the painter Renato Guttuso, with works by Basaldella, Schifano and Levi. **Villa Palagonia** is a strange oval building erected in 1715 for the Prince of Palagonia. The garden is famous for its grotesque statues of dwarfs, monsters and beggars.

Villa Valguarnera at Bagheria, set in a splendid park

CEFALÙ [66 km]

The high crag with the town nestling at its feet and the arabesque of the arches high in the apse of the Norman cathedral are classic images of Italy, not only of Sicily. This town on the north coast of the island is built on a regular plan, enhanced by small medieval arches which support the rows of houses on either side. It is also a fishing port and a popular seaside resort.

The main square, overlooked by small, late-Baroque buildings, is dominated by the imposing **Cathedral ❶**. Built at the wishes of Roger II in 1131, it is one of the most outstanding examples of Sicilian architecture from the Norman period. The *facade*, dating from 1240, is framed between two massive towers with one- and two-light windows and decorated with two tiers of fake loggias. Below the facade is a 15th-centry porch with three arches over a portal with marble inlay work. On the *right-hand side of the cathedral* the majestic transept is visible with its buttresses and loggias, also the lateral triple apse with the typical motif of intersecting arches. The **Interior**, somber and spacious, has a nave and two side-aisles. Tall columns with carved capitals support pointed arches with double archivolts. The apse and the vault shimmer with beautiful **mosaics**** on a gold background, executed in 1148. The solemn figures, depicted with inscriptions in Greek or Latin, are arranged according to the

Cefalù 1:9 500 (1 cm = 95 m)

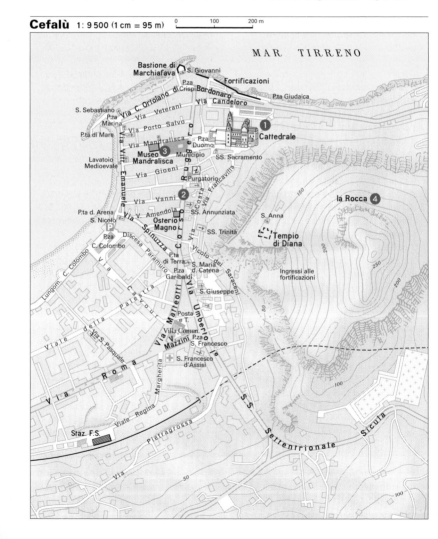

The outline of Cefalù with its Norman cathedral

principles of the heavenly hierarchies: in the apse, Christ Pantocrator, the Virgin Mary and archangels and the Apostles; on the walls, in four superimposed bands, the Saints and Prophets; in the cross-vault, Cherubim and Seraphim. A door at the beginning of the left-hand aisle leads into the *cloister* dating from the 12th century. Partly destroyed by a fire in the 16th century and damaged with the passing of time, it is surrounded on three sides by a portico with small paired columns decorated with carved capitals.

Corso Ruggero ❷ is the town's main street and bisects the town: one half is a maze of narrow streets with steps winding up towards the cliff, while the other has straight, perpendicular roads leading down to the sea. Level with Piazza del Duomo is the *Municipio* (Town Hall), a 16th-century former monastery which has completely transformed. Further on is the *Osterio Magno*, popularly thought to have been the residence of Roger II, built in the 13th to 14th centuries but transformed over the years. The street ends at **Piazza Garibaldi**, where the Porta di Terra (Land Gate), one of the entrances to the town, used to stand. From here remains of the megalithic town walls are visible. Behind the Town Hall is the **Museo Mandralisca ❸** which contains the archeological artifacts, paintings, minerals and shells collected in the 19th century by one of the town's benefactors, Baron Enrico Piraino di Mandralisca. The exhibits include a krater* from the island of Lìpari depicting a tuna fish seller and the famous **Portrait of an Unknown Man**** by Antonello da Messina (1465).

Not far away is the *little harbor*. From the jetty there are good views of the picturesque sea-front of the old town, with fishermen's houses below which pointed arches serve as boathouses. Other monumental remains of the ancient city walls are visible from the *Bastione di Marchiafava* (Marchiafava Bastion), situated on the cliff north of the town. The **Rocca ❹**, reached by a path leading up from Piazza Garibaldi, comprises remains of some *fortifications* which are probably Byzantine in date, and the ruins of the 13th-century *castle*.

CORLEONE [58 km]

This farming town is situated in a dip in the heart of fertile, well-irrigated land. To the east and south of the town, the yellowish-green calcareous sandstone has been eroded into shapes resembling bastions and towers. They include the "Castello Soprano" (Upper Castle), to the east, with a *Saracen tower* on the top, and the "Castello Sottano" (Lower Castle), a huge mass of rock which stands out on the right bank of the river to the south of the town. Corleone probably already existed in the Byzantine period, and gained economic and military importance during the period of Saracen occupation (Corleone was on the old route across the island from Palermo to Sciacca) and was conquered by the Normans in about 1080. Several times the town was the victim of landslides which were sometimes further aggravated by severe flooding, but the general decline in the economy and the resources of the island in the 17th century led to a slow process of social and economic degradation.

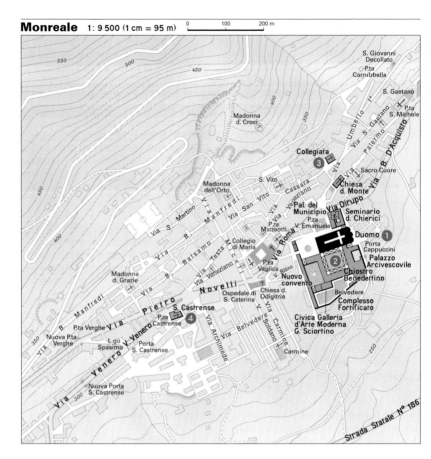

Monreale 1:9 500 (1 cm = 95 m)

The **Chiesa Madre** (Mother Church), dedicated to St Martin, was built in 1382, probably on the site of an existing church, and was subsequently altered (the dome dates from 1663). Its current appearance dates from the 18th century, when it was further extended and the dome was decorated with frescoes. The 18th-century *Chiesa dell'Addolorata* (Church of Our Lady of Sorrows) (1753), is built on a central plan, and the interior is decorated with stuccoes and frescoes dating from the same period. The church of **Santa Rosalia** (17th century) contains many works of art of diverse origin.

ISOLA DELLE FEMMINE [15 km]

This wind-battered little island, situated 600 m off the coast, has a square tower dating from the 16th century. The island was designated a Riserva Naturale (Wildlife Reserve) in 1997, with the aim of protecting the numerous species of birds on

migration which use the island as a stopping-place, and the many plant species which grow here. Its name, which means "Women's Island" - seems to be derived from the Arabic word "fim", or inlet - also applies to the seaside resort on the coast opposite the island.

MONREALE [8 km]

High on a spur dominating the Oreto Valley and the Conca d'Oro (the broad fertile fan-shaped plain behind Palermo), this small town is the main attraction outside Palermo. Having grown up since the 13th century around the Benedictine monastery on the site, the current appearance of the town is Baroque, but it clusters round one of the rarest jewels of Italy's artistic heritage: the **Duomo ❶**, an extraordinary architectural achievement by any standard, an outstanding blend of the Arabic, Byzantine and Romanesque styles. It was founded in 1174 by William II, the last of the great Norman kings, and was soon completed with the addition of the Abbey, the Royal Palace and the Archbishop's Palace, forming a single complex. The top of the facade, framed by two mighty towers, is decorated by intersecting blind arcading and is preceded by an 18th-century porch over a portal* decorated with carving and bands of mosaic. The bronze doors, by Bonanno Pisano (1186), depict Biblical scenes with inscriptions in the vernacular. On the left side of the cathedral is a 16th-century porch, underneath which is a bronze portal* with panels bearing reliefs (depicting the saints) by Barisanus of Trani (1179). The apse* is covered with intersecting arches and polychrome inlay work in limestone and lava. The interior is built on a basilica plan with a nave and two side-aisles separated by columns, most of them re-used columns from classical sites. The beams supporting the roof

were replaced after the fire of 1811, whereas the mosaic floor is original. The upper walls are decorated with **mosaics**** on a gold background (covering a total area of 6,340 m2) dating from the 12th and 13th centuries. They depict the cycle of the Old and New Testament, with inscriptions in Latin and Greek. Those in the nave depict the stories of Genesis* and in the central apse, below the figure of Christ Pantocrator, are the figures of the Virgin Enthroned, angels, apostles and saints. Above the two thrones - one for the king, the other for the bishop - at the sides of the sanctuary are two panels. One depicts William II as he receives the crown from Christ; the other depicts William II in the act of offering the church to the Virgin Mary. The left-hand side of the sanctuary leads into the 17th-century Cappella del Crocifisso (Chapel of the Crucifix), built on a hexagonal plan (1687-92). From here there is access to

Monreale: the Cathedral and the Cloister

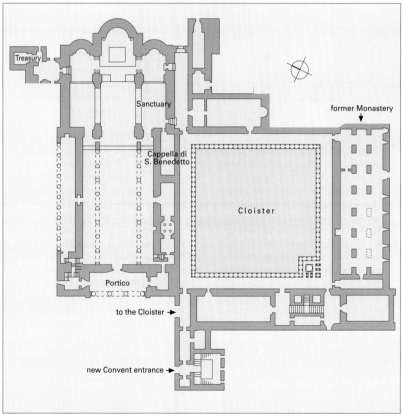

the *Treasury*, which contains Gothic reliquaries and sacred objects and vestments dating from the 13th to 17th centuries. Stairs lead up to the *terraces* above the Duomo, from where there is a splendid *view** over the Conca d'Oro. To the right of the facade of the Duomo is the entrance to the magnificent **cloister ❷**, dating from the reign of William II (12th century). It consists of a square surrounded by a portico of pointed arches supported by 228 small paired columns with exquisitely carved Romanesque capitals, all decorated with marble inlay and mosaics or reliefs with Arabic motifs. In the south corner of the cloister, a low wall* supporting three arches on each side encloses a small fountain with a central column in the form of a stylized plaited palm. On the north side stands the wall of the old church pierced by a portal and two-light windows decorated with

The splendid cloister of the Duomo at Monreale

limestone and lava. On the north side of the square in front of the church is the Baroque facade of the new convent (1747), now a school. An archway on the right leads through beyond the courtyard to the *Belvedere* (viewpoint), a public garden with a view over the Oreto valley and across to Palermo. At the far end of the Belvedere is the *Galleria Civica d'Arte Moderna Giuseppe Sciortino* where paintings, works on paper, sculpture, and pottery by contemporary artists are exhibited. In the highest part of the town is the **Collegiata ❸** (Collegiate Church), built in the 17th century, with a crucifix on 17th-century majolica tiles and 18th-

century stucco decoration. There is also some fine stucco decoration in the 16th-century church of **San Castrense ❹**.

PETRALIA SOTTANA [99 km]

The names of the two towns ("Soprana" means Upper; "Sottana" means Lower) refer to the division in the 15th century of the ancient town of Petra, which appears in records as far back as the 3rd century BC. The town acquired importance during the Arabic period and, later, under the Normans who, in the 11th century, began to build a fortress here. The dominion of aristocratic families over the two towns is testified by the grandiloquence of their civic buildings and their splendid churches. In the upper town, the Chiesa Madre (Mother Church) is an early church extended during the Baroque period, while the nearby 18th-century church of Santa Maria di Loreto stands on the site of the ancient fortress. At Petralia Sottana, churches of interest include the Chiesa Madre, with a late-Gothic portal and the Santissima Trinità, which has a remarkable marble altar-piece (1542) with 23 bas-reliefs depicting the Life of Christ.

SOLUNTO [2 km]

Together with Motya and Palermo, this was one of the three main Phoenician cities in Western Sicily. Having been founded by the Carthaginians in about the mid-4th century BC, in approximately 250 BC, it was conquered by the Romans. Hellenistic and Roman forms prevail among the ruins (the city was destroyed by the Saracens). The excavations, which began in the 19th century, have yet to uncover a large proportion of the settlement. Many of the finds from the site are in the Museo Archeologico di Palermo.

The town was built on a regular orthogonal plan. The main street and the streets parallel to it are perpendicular to the streets that cross them, thus forming residential "insulae"

Solunto

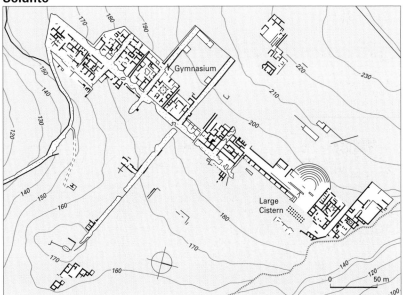

Gymnasium

Large Cistern

50 m

or blocks, built on terraces. The paving is particularly well preserved and is a typical feature of the site, the main street being paved partly in brick and partly in stone. The walls of the houses were plastered and often painted, with floors of "opus signinum" (a conglomerate of clay and mortar) or mosaic. There are many cisterns (one for each house) some of which had complex systems for collecting rainwater because of the lack of spring water on the steep hillside.

TERMINI IMERESE [36 km]

This seaside resort and health spa is situated on the Tyrrhenian coast of Sicily, east of the Bay of Palermo. The lower part of the town is a commercial area associated with the harbor. The upper part of the town, which is older and more typical, is built on terraces on a promontory. Its name points to the existence of hot springs ("terme"), which have been famous since antiquity and are still active today.
The civic and religious focus of the town is Piazza del Duomo. There are four small early 16th-century statues on the modern facade of the **Duomo ❶**, built in the late 15th century and rebuilt in 1614. Inside there are statues and reliefs dating from the 16th and 17th centuries and a crucifix painted on both sides

dating from the late 15th century. On the same square stands the 17th-century *Palazzo municipale* (Town Hall), and, beyond it, the *Belvedere Principe Umberto*, a viewpoint with beautiful views of the town and along the coast as far as Cefalù.
Via Mazzini ❷ is the main thoroughfare of the upper town. On it stand the Baroque church of *Santa Maria della Misericordia* (St Mary of Mercy) and the 17th-century *Chiesa del Monte* (Church of the Mount).
The **Museo Civico "Baldassare Romano" ❸** (Municipal Museum), created in 1873, occupies a former hospital and a late-medieval building. The *archeological section* contains exhibits from prehistoric times up to the late Imperial Roman period. The *historical and artistic section* includes works of figurative art from the Arabic-Norman period up to the 19th century. The visit ends at Villa Palmeri, a public park with the ruins of a Roman curia dating from the 2nd century AD, the remains of the *Roman Amphitheater* and the 15th-century church of *Santa Caterina d'Alessandria*, with 15th-century frescoes given a popular slant by adding inscriptions in the Sicilian dialect of the period.
East of the town lie the ruins of *Himera*, the ancient Greek colony, destroyed by

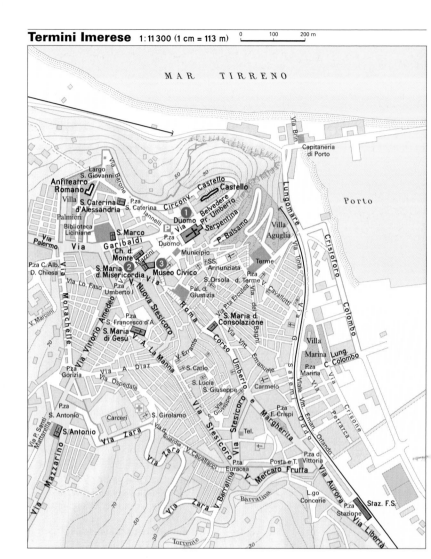

the Carthaginians in 409 BC. The archeological park includes the famous Doric temple (Temple of "Victory") and three small sanctuaries situated to the north of the ancient town.

USTICA [75 km]

Situated 52 km north of Capo Gallo (a cape a few km NW of Palermo), the island of Ustica is the top of a huge extinct submarine volcano.

Inhabited since prehistoric times, for centuries it was the target of Saracen incursions before it was fortified and settled by the Bourbons in the 18th century. For many years common prisoners and political deportees were banished to the island.

In recent years, imaginative initiatives to attract tourism have joined forces with the traditional activities of farming and fishing, but without altering the landscape of fertile plains where wheat, figs and prickly pears are grown.

The town of Ustica stands on a shelf of tuff between two bays, dominated by the hill of Capo Falconara. On the top of the hill stands a *Bourbon fortress*, which has wonderful views of the Sicilian coast. The town was laid out in 1763 according to a regular plan of perpendicular streets and rectangular blocks. South of the town, the Torre di Santa Maria is being converted into a museum of submarine archeology, with finds from ancient shipwrecks.

RAGUSA

Two important factors have influenced Ragusa: the earthquake in 1693 and the town's relations with the surrounding countryside. After the earthquake the town was rebuilt in two parts: Ragusa "supra", the new Baroque town built on the plateau by the landowning nobility; and Ragusa "iusu", or Ibla, the lower part of the town, also rebuilt in Baroque style after the terrible earthquake, but on the medieval town layout, with stairs and winding alleys. The town's relations with the local peasant farmers of the surrounding countryside were based from the 15th century onwards on "emphyteusis", or perpetual lease: this revolutionary economic arrangement meant that peasants were only required to pay their landlords rent, not a portion of the produce of the land as well. The fields of the small farms were enclosed by the dry-stone walls typical of the area. Over the centuries a strong local culture and sense of identity developed in the people of Ragusa; today it is seen as 'an island within the island'.

From ancient times to Arab and Norman medieval times, the city has always acted as a fortress. The ancient town of Hibla Heraia, at the time of the Greek colonies, had been fortified by the Siculi; the remains of the medieval fortifications may still be seen today.

San Giorgio ❶

The Duomo, designed in 1739 by Rosario Gagliardi, looks grandly down over a beautiful flight of steps, which lie at an angle to the square. It has an impressive Baroque facade, with a bell tower which is convex in the center, and a neo-Classical cupola built in 1820; the interior, with nave and two side aisles, is illuminated by stained-glass windows (1926). The church of **San Giuseppe** (St Joseph) stands in nearby Piazza Pola; it is attributed to Rosario Gagliardi or his school, and has a dynamic Baroque facade and an oval-shaped interior, decorated with stuccoes.

Giardino Ibleo ❷

This park in Ragusa Ibleo was created in the 19th century, near the church of *San Giorgio Vecchio* (St George the Old), which was damaged by the 1693 earthquake. It has a Gothic-Catalan doorway (second half of the 14th century) with a lunette in relief. Inside the park is the 14th-century church of *San Giacomo Apostolo* (St James the Apostle), which was rebuilt in the 18th century. At the south-east corner of the park, the

Chiesa dei Cappuccini Vecchi (Church of the Old Cappuchins) preserves at the high altar a large altar-piece by Pietro Novelli (Our Lady of the Assumption between Angels and Saints, 1635-36), and a Nativity (1520).

Museo Archeologico Ibleo ❸

The Ibleo Archeological Museum has material from excavations carried out in

Enchanting view of Ragusa Ibla

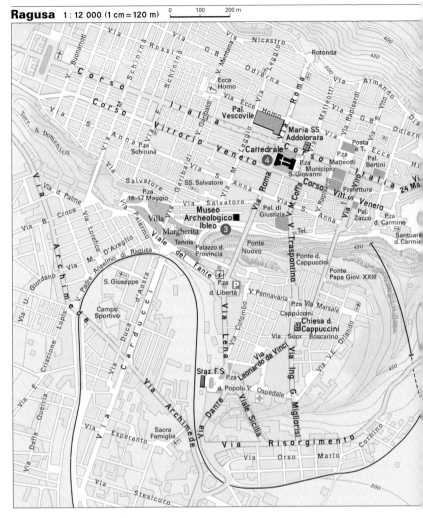

Ragusa 1 : 12 000 (1 cm = 120 m)

0   100   200 m

the area of Ragusa, and is divided into six sections: prehistoric sites, Camarina, Archaic Siculian towns, Hellenistic towns, late-Roman settlements, collections and purchases. The prehistoric section includes finds from Bronze Age villages and necropolises; there is interesting ceramic material from Archaic and Classical Siculian towns; particular emphasis is given to pottery production in the Hellenistic towns (a kiln has been reconstructed); and there are numerous objects from Roman and late Roman towns (mosaic floors, epigraphs, glass and bronze objects).

RAGUSA
IN OTHER COLORS...

- ITINERARIES: P 121
- FOOD: P 142, 147, 166
- SHOPPING: P 176
- EVENTS: P 188, 194
- PRACTICAL INFO: P 231

Cattedrale ❹

The cathedral was built between 1706 and 1760; it stands on a wide terrace on a loggia, overlooking the central Piazza San Giovanni. A cuspidate campanile makes the monumental facade asymmetrical. The interior is decorated with stuccoes. Below is *Palazzo Zacco*, a Baroque building with grotesque masks. On **Corso Italia**, the main street of Ragusa Superiore, *Palazzo Bertini*, built in the late 18th century, also has distinctive grotesque masks - the "three powerful ones" - on the window keystones.

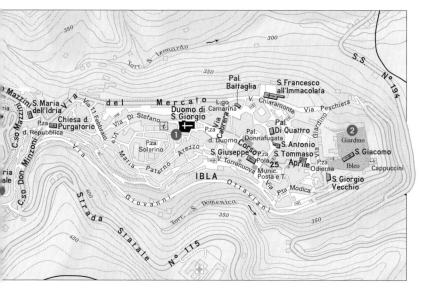

Le Scale ❺

These picturesque steps (over 300) lead down to the lower part of the town, from the church of Santa Maria delle Scale (St Mary of the Steps). Along the way, among stairs and buttresses, there are interesting examples of Baroque architecture, notably *Palazzo Nicastro* or *Palazzo della Cancelleria* (1760). From here, if you turn left into the alley named *Salita Commendatore*, you will find the church of *Santa Maria dell'Itria*, built in 1626 and rebuilt in 1739, as well as the *Palazzo dei Cosentini*, dating from the early 18th century, with its fine balconies. The *Chiesa del Purgatorio* (Church of Purgatory), with

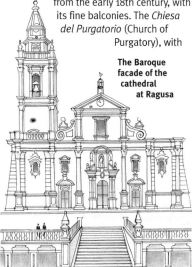

The Baroque facade of the cathedral at Ragusa

an ornate Baroque doorway, overlooks from the top of a flight of steps *Piazza della Repubblica*; this square is the point of juncture between the old town below and the 18th-century town above.

Santa Maria delle Scale ❻

The church was built in the 14th century and rebuilt in 1693. Parts of the earlier building may still be seen: outside, at the foot of the campanile, the remains of a doorway and a pulpit; inside, Gothic-Renaissance arches in the chapels on the right aisle. In the 3rd chapel in the right aisle, Transit of the Virgin, a polychrome terracotta of the Gagini school (1538). From the sacristy there is a wonderful view of Ragusa Ibla.

DAY TRIPS

CAVA D'ISPICA [9 km]

The calcareous plateau of the Monti Iblei (Hyblean Mountains) has many cuttings carved out by streams and rivers: they are locally known as "cave" (or quarries). The most noteworthy of these is the Cava d'Ispica, to the south east. It is interesting because it contains numerous signs of human habitation, from the Eneolithic age to the beginning of last century, and has thus much evidence related to pre-Classical and late-Ancient Sicily. Excavations carried out after 1904 have revealed: prehistoric rock villages and necropolises; Christian cemeteries; Byzantine rock churches in ruins; rock churches and villages some with surviving fragments of rock paintings; primitive cave dwellings on several levels; and late-Ancient and medieval rock settlements (the Castello), with cave houses used until recent times and then abandoned. For those who want to visit the Cava, custodians and guides may be contacted on site.

MODICA [14 km]

The town is situated on the southern slopes of the Monti Iblei (Hyblean Mountains). The upper part is on a wedge of plateau, while the lower part surrounds it in the unusual shape of a "Y". It has been described as a town growing from the rock: because of its caves that were inhabited until a few decades ago, its stairs and steps carved out of the rock, and its position. After the 1693 earthquake, it was rebuilt in Baroque style. One of the town's architectural

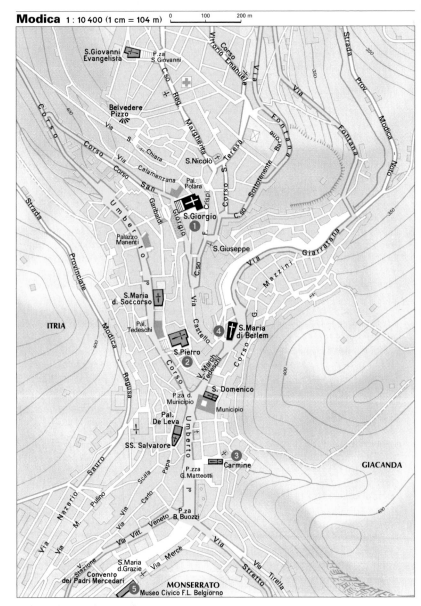

Modica 1 : 10 400 (1 cm = 104 m)

The church of San Giorgio in Modica, a dramatic combination of architectural design, creative vision and town-planning

treasures is the church of San Giorgio. The poet Salvatore Quasimodo, who won the Nobel Prize for literature, was born here. **San Giorgio ❶** (St George), in the upper part of the town, at the top of a picturesque flight of steps, is an 18th-century church with an unusual tower **facade** designed by Rosario Gagliardo. The *interior*, with nave and four side aisles, has many artworks from the 16th and 17th centuries. The transept pavement has a meridian (1895).

On Corso Umberto I, you will find the church of **San Pietro ❷** (St Peter). It was rebuilt after 1693 with an elaborate facade; in front there is a flight of stairs with statues of the Apostles. The same street has the 18th-century *Palazzo Tedeschi*, whose balconies have decorated 18th-century supports, and the 18th-century *Palazzo Manenti*, with a beautiful view over the high part of the town. There is another good lookout point at the *Belvedere Pizzo** near the church of San Giovanni Battista. Other important churches are the 17th-century **Chiesa del Carmine ❸**, and the church of **Santa Maria di Betlem ❹**, with the 15th- to 16th-century *Cappella del Sacramento** (Chapel of the Sacrament), a rare example of late Gothic-Renaissance architecture. South of the town is the **Museo Civico "F.L. Belgiorno" ❺**. The museum occupies the 18th century former monastery of the Padri Mercedari (Mercedari Fathers), and

houses archeological finds, fossils and early Christian art objects. The ethnographic section, the **Museo Ibleo delle Arti e Tradizioni popolari**, is very interesting. It has faithfully reconstructed traditional artisan workshops and an old country farmhouse.

SCICLI [24 km]

This small Baroque treasure of a town is reached through a series of roads arranged like the spokes of a wheels. Its prosperity over the centuries was the result of its position, which enabled it to control the navigable rivers and the coast. It was conquered by the Arabs in 864, and became a royal city under the Normans, after a fierce battle with the Arabs. The 1693 earthquake devastated the medieval town, which was rebuilt along Baroque lines.

The Mother Church, dedicated to **Sant'Ignazio** (St Ignatius), was previously the College of the Jesuits (1629), and preserves the Madonna delle Milizie (Madonna of the Militias), a work in papier mâché that depicts the Virgin on a white horse fighting the Arabs. From the square, you walk up to the 16th-century church of *San Bartolomeo*, located in the marvellous setting of the St Bartholomew quarry; it has an elegant facade and inside, a Neapolitan Crib Scene (1773-76) with 29 statues. The interior of the church of *Santa Maria la Nova*, decorated with stuccoes, houses a revered statue in cypress wood, the Madonna della Pietà, which is possibly Byzantine.

Scicli, the church of Santa Maria Nova

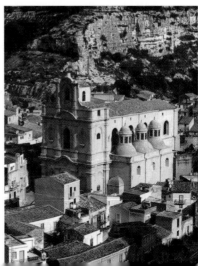

Situated in one of the Mediterranean's most beautiful bays, today Siracusa is a dynamic, modern town, with many visible signs of its grand and noble past. The haphazard growth of the new part of the town has not affected the little island of Ortigia (Ortygia), just off the coast, where the ancient Greek colony was founded, and neither has it spoiled the fascination of its classical monuments and the splendor of its Baroque facades. Visiting Siracusa is like taking a journey back in time. The ancient Greek city was as important as Athens and Rome in the Mediterranean, especially under the tyrant Gelon, in the 5th century BC. In medieval times, the arrival of the Arabs and Normans brought changes to the town's appearance and layout, and enriched it economically and culturally. The 1693 earthquake led to reconstruction on a vast scale, making Siracusa into an important capital of the Baroque style in Europe.

Siracusa not only has an extremely rich cultural past. It is set in breathtakingly beautiful natural surroundings: the peaceful bay of Porto Grande, with the Maddalena Peninsula, and in the background the magic of the Monti Iblei (Hyblean Mountains) and Etna.

Many famous contributors to culture and learning have been born in Siracusa: Epicarmus, the great Greek playwright; Theocritus, the bucolic poet; Archimedes, one of the greatest scientists of the ancient world; Ibn Hamdis, the Arab poet; and the modern Italian men of letters, Salvatore Quasimodo and Elio Vittorini.

An important cultural event in Siracusa is the performance of the classical Greek tragedies in the summer months.

Parco archeologico della Neàpoli ❶

The Neapolis Archeological Park was created in 1952-55, and contains most of Greek and Roman Siracusa's classical monuments. For security reasons, today tourists only have access to the Greek theater and part of the Latomia del Paradiso, one of the ancient stone quarries; the other monuments can be viewed from a distance. This doesn't detract in any way from the powerful fascination of this unique place, where the work of both man and of nature has such a strong impact. A wonderful view, taking in the Intagliatella and Santa Venera latomies, and the Grotticelli necropolis, can be seen from Via Romagnoli. **Viale Rizzo**, also with a wonderful view, runs north of the archeological area: once past the hair-pin bends and magnificent scenery of the Colle Temenite (Temenite Hill), you have a superb view of the town and harbor, the Greek Theater, three latomies (Paradiso, Intagliatella and Santa Venera), and on the right the Grotticelli necropolis.

The Greek theater cut out of the bedrock on Temenite Hill

Teatro greco ❷

The Greek Theater is one of the finest examples of Greek architecture of this type which has survived until our times. It was enlarged by Hieron II in the 3rd century BC. Mention was made of it as early as the 5th century BC when the tragedies of Eschylus and the comedies of Epicarmus were performed here. Public assemblies were also held here. It is completely carved out of the rock, and has a *cavea* (auditorium) measuring 138m in diameter, with seating capacity for as many as 15,000 spectators, divided into 9 sectors, with 61 rows of steps (of which 46 survive). About halfway up, the steps are separated by a wide ambulatory (*diazoma*), whose rock cornice is engraved with the names of the gods and of Hieron II's family members. At the foot of the steps, is the semicircular *orchestra* pit, which was modified in Roman times. In front stretches the vast area where the *scena* (stage) was; very little remains of it today. A large part of the limestone block structure was dismantled on the orders of Charles V, from 1526, to obtain material for building the fortifications around Ortigia. In the rock wall behind the theatre, there is a temple-grotto

Dionysius's Ear has extraordinary acoustic effects

dedicated to the muses and little niches for votive images (*pínakes*) associated with the cult of heroes. On the left is **Via dei Sepolcri** (Street of the Tombs), cut deep into the rock: along the sides are Byzantine votive niches and hypogea. From the terrace, to the west, the remains of a *Santuario di Apollo* (Sanctuary of Apollo) can be seen. Colle Temenite, the hill where the theatre is built, is named after the temple's sacred enclosure (*temenos*).

Latomia del Paradiso ❸

This is the largest and most famous of the Siracusa latomies: these are the very ancient stone quarries or pits at the southern edge of a rocky plateau, from where blocks of white-grey limestone were carved out for use in the construction of the town's building and walls. Excavation created vast pits in the

sheer rock walls, sometimes open, and sometimes under vaults supported by tall pillars. The heat of the sun and the intense humidity transformed these spaces into fertile gardens. The Latomia del Paradiso ranges in depth from 25 to 47 meters; the vault has partially collapsed. It's a very impressive sight, and is also interesting because of the famed Orecchio di Dionisio (Dionysius's Ear) and the Grotta dei Cordari (Rope-makers' Grotto).

Orecchio di Dionisio ❹

Dionysius's Ear is a man-made grotto, 65m long, from 5m to 11m wide, and 23m high, gradually narrowing at the top, almost like a pointed arch. The name derives from its resemblance to the shape of the human ear, and is said to have been first used by Caravaggio in 1608. According to legend, Dionysius converted the grotto into a prison, so that he could hear whatever prisoners were saying below, however softly they spoke. In fact, the Grotto is renowned for its amazing acoustics: the slightest sound is amplified, and can be easily heard at the entrance.

Grotta dei Cordari ❺

The Rope-makers' Grotto is next to Dionysius's Ear, and is named after the rope-makers who worked here for centuries, in the damp conditions that were perfect for their trade. The deep pit, with its vault supported by pillars, is a beautiful place with mosses and ferns growing everywhere, and interesting light effects. In some parts of the walls and the ceiling, sketches of plans for extracting the blocks of limestone can be clearly seen.

Anfiteatro romano ❻

The Roman amphitheater is reached through a garden whose entrance is opposite the church of San Nicolò dei Cordari (St Nicholas of the Rope-makers), with stone sarcophaguses from the necropolises of Siracusa and Megera Hyblaea. On the left of the amphitheater, numerous votive niches (*pìnakes*) used in the hero cult are carved in the rock. Built under the Roman empire (3rd- to 4th-century AD), it's just slightly smaller than the Roman Arena in Verona. The oval structure is mostly cut out of the rock, with the cavea divided into 4 sections, and separated by 2 corridors.

The doorways in the vaulted corridor beneath the high podium gave gladiators and animals access to the arena. Seat-owners' names can still be seen carved in the marble balustrade.

San Giovanni Evangelista ❼

The Church of St John the Evangelist was destroyed by the 1693 earthquake and never rebuilt. It had been built on the site of a 6th-century basilica, reconstructed in Norman times. In front of the church there are three surviving arches of a portico which was reassembled with 14th century materials. Behind stands another church, *San Giovanni Battista* (St John the Baptist), built in the 18th century. In a courtyard to the right are the remains of the ancient basilica, as well as the entrance to the **Cripta di San Marciano** (Crypt of St Marcianus), the first bishop of Siracusa. The Greek-cross crypt has three apses (6th century); the capitals of the four pilasters at the junction of the four arms of the cross bear the symbols of the Evangelists. On the walls, remains of frescoes ranging from medieval times to the 17th century can be seen. From here, you reach the **Catacomba di San Giovanni*** (Catacomb of St John), a 4th- to 5th-century underground necropolis, which was built by enlarging a Greek aqueduct carved out of the rock. It suffered considerable damage over the centuries as people searched for the remains of saints and treasure. Smaller tunnels lead off from the main central gallery, to circular chambers and crypts: there are thousands of loculi of various sizes along the walls and on the floor.

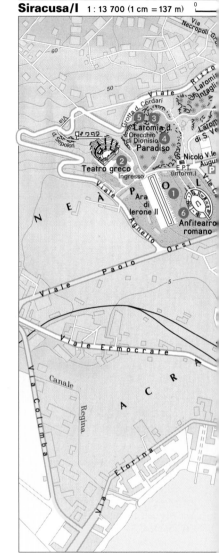

Siracusa/I 1 : 13 700 (1 cm = 137 m)

SIRACUSA
IN OTHER COLORS...

ITINERARIES: P 122
FOOD: P 147, 154, 156
SHOPPING: P 176, 178, 181
EVENTS: P 188
PRACTICAL INFO: P 236

Museo Archeologico Regionale "Paolo Orsi" ❽

The museum is dedicated to the archeologist Paolo Orsi, who worked in Sicily between 1888 and 1934. It's the most important Sicilian archeological museum, and one of Europe's largest, with an area of more than 9,000 square meters and over 18,000 exhibits. It portrays a picture of the civilizations which succeeded each other in Sicily, from prehistoric and

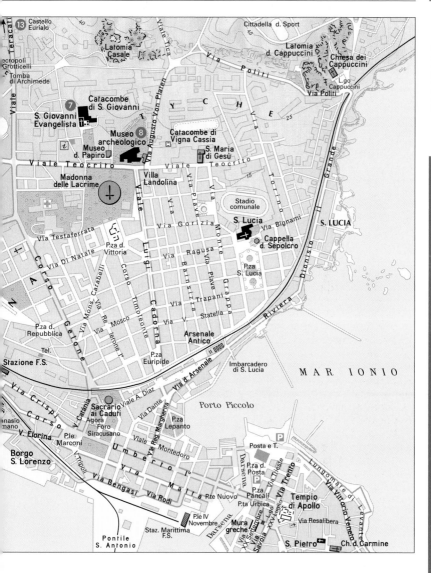

proto-historic times, to paleo-Christian times. The museum's new premises, made necessary by the growing size of its collections, were designed by Franco Minissi and opened in January 1988. The large triangular building has three sections arranged around a circular hall, where the entrance is. Section A is on prehistory and proto-history, from the Paleolithic Age to Greek colonization. Section B covers the Greek colonies in Sicily, especially Megara Hyblaea and Siracusa. Section C has finds from Eloro (Helorus) and Siracusa's sub-colonies (Akrai, Kasmenai and Kamarina), from

the local indigenous settlements of the interior, and from the Doric colonies of Gela and Agrigento. A basement floor (3000 square meters) houses storage space, laboratories and, an auditorium where films are shown.

Just before **Section A**, there is a *geological section*, with fossils, rock samples and displays illustrating the region's geology. The visitor is guided on a tour through the various stages of Sicily's earliest inhabitants. The oldest finds, from *Upper Paleolithic* and *Mesolithic* deposits (5th millennium BC), are almost always in stone, and largely

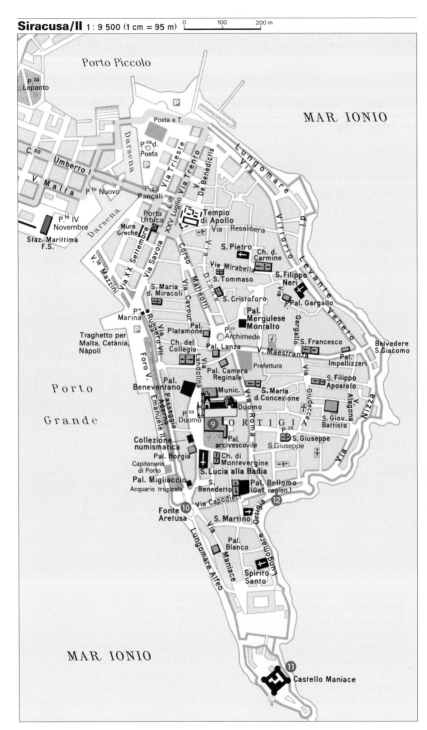

Siracusa/II 1 : 9 500 (1 cm = 95 m)

0   100   200 m

Porto Piccolo

MAR IONIO

p.za Lepanto

Darsena

Posta e T.

P.za d. Posta

C.so Umberto I

V. Malta

P.te Nuovo

P.za Pancali

Via Trieste

Via Trento

V. De Benedictis

Lungomare Via

P.le IV Novembre

Porta Urbica

Tempio di Apollo

Staz. Marittima F.S.

Mura Greche

XXV Luglio

Via Savoia

Via Resalibera

S. Pietro

Ch. d. Carmine

Via Mirabella

S. Filippo Neri

Vittorio Levante Veneto

Darsena

V. Mazzini

Via XX Settembre

Corso Matteotti

S. Maria d. Miracoli

S. Tommaso

S. Cristoforo

Pal. Gargallo

P.za Marina

Via Cavour

Pal. Platamone

Pal. Mergulese Montalto

Gargallo

S. Francesco

Belvedere S.Giacomo

Traghetto per Malta, Catània, Nàpoli

Foro V.

V. Ruggero VII

Ch. del Collegio

Pal. Lanza

P.za Archimede

Via Maestranza

Pal. Impellizzeri

Porto

Via Landolina

Pal. Camera Reginale

Prefettura

S. Filippo Apostolo

Grande

Pal. Beneventano

passeggio Adorno

Munic.

S. Maria d.Concezione

Via Giudecca

Pal. Alagona

Via Nizza

Foro Emanuele II

P.za Duomo

Duomo

S. Giov. Battista

Via Roma

ORTIGIA

9

Collezione numismatica

Pal. Borgia

Pal. arcivescovile

S.Giuseppe

S.Giuseppe

Capitaneria di Porto

Ch. di Montevergine

Pal. Migliaccio

Acquario tropicale

S. Lucia alla Badia

S. Benedetto

Pal. Bellomo (Gall. region.)

Via Capodieci

Fonte Aretusa

10

S. Martino

12

Ortigia

Lungomare Alfeo

Pal. Blanco

Via Maniace

Spirito Santo

MAR IONIO

11

Castello Maniace

microlithic. In the subsequent *Neolithic* layers (4th to 3rd millennium BC), finds include bone objects and pottery. The *Copper Age* (late 3rd and early 2nd

millennium BC) shows various influences on decorative styles in pottery. The *Bronze Age* (early 2nd millennium to 15th century BC) was the period when the so-called Castelluccio culture (named after a site near Noto) was established in eastern Sicily, with its typical painted pottery, flint tools, and early metal objects. Grave goods from necropolises explored by Paolo Orsi, local pottery and interesting imported pottery are also exhibited. The section ends with objects from the *Iron Age*, just before the foundation of the first Greek colonies.

Secion B covers the Ionic and Doric Greek colonies. Finds from *Megara Hyblaea* feature superb Archaic works of *sculpture** (a funerary stele of the physician Sambrotidas and a limestone statue of a mother nursing twins, both dating from the 6th century BC), Archaic and Classical architectural remains, grave goods, local pottery, and pottery imported from Greece. Standing at the entrance to the *Siracusa* section is the famous **Venere Anadiomene*** (Venus Anadiomenes, or Venus Arising from the Sea), also known as the Lanolina Venus because the statue was discovered by Lanolina in 1804. The section includes objects from the town's two oldest quarters (Ortigia and Acradina) and from the necropolises, ranging from the 8th century to the 4th century BC. There are some particularly interesting terracotta remains from the temples of Apollo and Athena. There is also, from the temple of Athena, part of a *marble cornice**, with gutter spouts shaped as lion heads (480 BC), as well as the extremely finely-crafted acroterial statue of **Winged Victory***, in an Archaic depiction of flight. This section ends with objects from sanctuaries outside the town: the most remarkable piece is the *limestone Archaic head** found near the source of the Ciane River.

Section C covers the sub-colonies and the indigenous towns of the interior. There are objects from *Eloro* (Helorus), which was an outpost of Siracusa as early as the end of the 8th century BC, as well as exhibits from the three Siracusa sub-colonies of *Akrai*, *Kasmenai*, and *Kamarina*. Finds from some Hellenized indigenous towns include particularly interesting objects from *Grammichele* and superb statues dating from the second half of the 6th century BC. There is also a series of very delicate *terracotta pìnakes** from

Francavilla di Sicilia related to the cult of Persephone (470-460 BC). A bronze statuette, known as the Mendolito Ephebus, found at the archeological site of *Mendolito*, also dates from around 460 BC. There are many exhibits from Gela and Agrigento, excavated by Paolo Orsi in the early 1900s.

Duomo ❾

The Duomo was built in the 7th century, on the remains of the ancient Doric temple of Athena (5th century BC). It was modified in Norman times and again in the 16th century, and then largely reconstructed in the 17th- to 18th-centuries. The Baroque facade (18th century), with a flight of steps and statues in front, has two rows of stately columns and statues by Marabutti. The central nave and side aisles of the basilica **interior** were created by closing

Siracusa: the Duomo

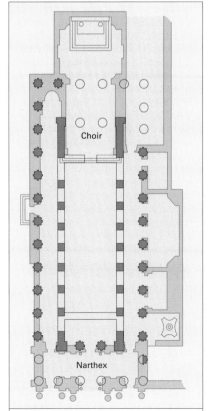

Choir

Narthex

▮ Greek temple
▯ Later building phases

Baroque buildings in Siracusa: the Duomo and the City Hall

off the spaces between the columns of the ancient temple, and converting the cella into the nave. Eight arches were built into each side of the cella walls. The *nave* has a fine wood ceiling (1518). Along the *right aisle* there are a number of chapels, including the outstanding *Cappella del Sacramento* (Chapel of the Sacrament). It was designed by Giovanni Vermexio in 1653, and has an elaborate interior, with scenes from the Old Testament in the vault. Right at the end is the *Cappella del Crocifisso* (Chapel of the Crucifix): on the left of the altar, a panel on a gold background depicting *St Zosimo** is attributed to Antonello da Messina. In the *presbytery*: the impressive Baroque altar (1659), two bronze candelabra (1513), 17th-century wood choir stalls and beautiful 16th-century singing galleries. The ten Doric columns of the original temple of Athena can be seen along the *left aisle*; a lovely statue of the *Madonna della Neve** (Madonna of the Snow) by Antonello Gagini (1512) can also be seen here.

Fonte Aretusa ⑩

The Fountain of Arethusa is an ancient spring, celebrated in ancient times by Pindar and Virgil. It is now in the form of a pool planted with papyrus, created in 1843. According to the myth, the nymph Arethusa, Artemis's hand maiden, flung herself into the waters of the Èlide to flee from the river god Alpheus, and then reappeared here in the form of a spring. From the nearby terrace, there is

a view over the bay of *Porto Grande* which has been Siracusa's port since ancient times. In the distance, the Monti Iblei and Etna.

Castello Maniace ⑪

This castle on the southernmost tip of the island of Ortigia is an interesting example of Swabian military architecture. It was built by Frederick II in 1239 and, despite considerable restyling over the centuries, retains its original 13th-century external structure: square with round towers at the corners. There is a noteworthy pointed-arch doorway* at the entrance, in polychrome marble. The *interior* was damaged in the 1693 earthquake and by the explosion of a gunpowder magazine in 1704. More recently it was used as a prison and a barracks; almost nothing remains of the original structure.

Galleria Regionale di Palazzo Bellomo ⑫

The Gallery has important collections of painting and sculpture from late-medieval times to today, and collections of applied art. It's in the former *Monastero di San Benedetto* (Monastery of St Benedict), and consists of two parts: the 14th-century *Palazzo Parisi* and the much larger 13th-century **Palazzo Bellomo**. The ground floor of this building has features typical of Swabian architecture; the floor above has been considerably altered and is clearly Catalan in style. You enter through a vestibule and porticoed courtyard, parts of which (arches and half-pilasters) are original to the 13th-century building. The portico pilasters are 15th-century, like the beautiful flight of stairs outside leading to the floor above, decorated with Catalan motifs. Adjoining the monastery is the church of *San Benedetto* (St Benedict), with a 17th-century facade and, inside, a magnificent 16th-century Baroque ceiling. The gallery divides into various sections. The *sculpture section* displays

5th- to 9th-century paleo-Christian and Byzantine sculptures and 12th- to 14th-century medieval sculptures. Renaissance works include the *Madonna of the Bullfinch**, a marble statue by Domenico Gagini, and the tomb of Giovanni Sabastida, in the manner of Francesco Laurana. The courtyard holds a collection of coats-of-arms from various times, taken from public buildings and churches in Siracusa. Part of the *Pinacoteca* on the first floor is housed in 15th-century rooms. Some of the most important works are the famous **Annunciation**** by Antonello da Messina (1474) and the **Burial of St Lucy**** by Caravaggio (1609). This was Caravaggio's first Sicilian work and comes from the Siracusa Church of St Lucy. The collection also includes 15th- to 18th-century Italo-Byzantine and Slavo-Byzantine panels, as well as 14th- to 15th-century Catalan, Sicilian and Venetian paintings. There is an excellent *applied art section*: silver ware, furniture, fabrics and goldsmithery; ceramics, terracottas from the Bongiovanni-Vaccaro workshop, and 18th- to 20th-century crib figurines.

Castello Eurìalo ⑬

The Castle of Euryalus is about 8km from the center of Siracusa: it's the best place to admire the town's Greek remains from, and also provides one of the most beautiful and spectacular views in Sicily.

Euryalus was built at the beginning of the 4th century BC by Dionysius the Elder, and successfully protected Siracusa until the city fell to the Romans. Various modifications were made as it adapted to changes in the art of war. Its strategic position, as well as its internal and external design, which was innovatory for the time, make it an exceptional example of military architecture. However, the ruins cover a vast area (one and a half hectares) and you really need a map to find your way around.

The castle was originally formed of a single block in the form of a ship's prow. Today it consists of two parts: a rectangle to the west and a trapezoid to the east. The front of the east side has various defensive features: a *blockhouse*, once connected to the castle by a massive 15-meter drawbridge whose pillars can still, just,

Castello Eurialo

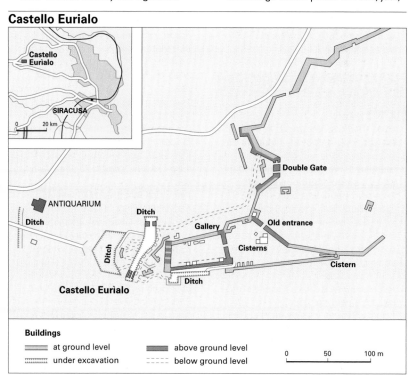

Castello Eurìalo

Buildings
- ▬▬ at ground level
- ⌇⌇⌇ under excavation
- ▬▬ above ground level
- ╌╌╌ below ground level

0   50   100 m

Megara Hyblaea

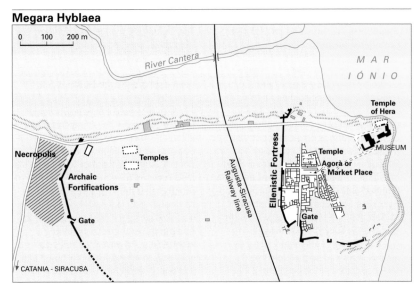

be seen; and *five towers* where the catapult platforms were situated. The defence system provided by the various *moats* is interesting. Their function was to slow enemy attacks and provide a variety of escape routes for the soldiers. The longest north-east side of the eastern trapezoid-shaped part of the Castle is joined to the walls built by Dionysius. Inside, there are three *cisterns*, for the castle's water supply, as well as ingenious defence and concealment systems.

DAY TRIPS

ELORO [7 km]

Eloro (Helorus) lies on a low hill near the sea just north of the mouth of the Tellaro river. The settlement was founded at the end of the 8th century BC by a group of Corinthian colonizers. Excavation work was begun in the late 19th century, and revealed quite an extensive part of the town, inside the *fortification walls** with double curtain, dating from the 6th century BC, with some 4th-century BC rebuilding. The south-west area is the most excavated. Houses here date from the end of the 8th century to the middle of the 4th century BC, and it was here that the *Santuario di Demetra* (Sanctuary of Demeter) was discovered. The **Villa Romana del Tellaro*** (Tellaro Roman Villa) was discovered on a farm just

past the river. The building hasn't yet been completely excavated. It was built in late imperial Roman times (4th century AD) and is especially interesting for its colored **floor mosaics****. They are being kept in Siracusa until excavation on the villa has finished, when they will returned there for conservation work. The mosaics depict hunting scenes, and a scene of the ransom of Hector, portrayed in a very original and untraditional way.

ROVINE DI **MEGARA HYBLAEA** [14 km]

The area contains the ruins of the ancient town of Megara Hyblaea: it has been saved from the intense industrial and urban development that has taken place around here, and has survived as a green and peaceful oasis.

Paolo Orsi first excavated here at the end of 1800; more recent work has made it possible to fit together the pieces of this Greek colony's past. It was founded in 728 BC by Greeks from Megara, razed to the ground in 483 BC by Gelon, tyrant of Gela, and again destroyed in 213 BC, during the 2nd Carthaginian War. Excavation of the town and the nearby necropolises has brought to light some priceless treasures of Greek sculpture, which today are displayed in the Siracusa Archeological Museum.

NOTO [32 km]

Noto was built after the earthquake of January 1693, and was designated 'Baroque Capital' by the Council of Europe. Its wonderful buildings and elaborate facades in honey-colored sandstone make it a real "garden of stone", as it was once described by a famous art critic. A number of excellent architects were involved in the rebuilding

The broad facade of the Duomo with a bell-tower on each side

of the town, on a slope, a couple of kilometers south-east of the old town. Some overgrown ruins of the old town can still be seen amongst the vegetation.

The town has a strictly regular layout around **Corso Vittorio Emanuele** ❶. At the beginning of the street is the impressive *Porta Reale* (Royal Gate), and then there follow a series of Baroque buildings and three beautiful squares. On the first of them: the steps and the church of **San Francesco all'Immacolata** (St Francis to the Immaculate Virgin); the *Monastero del Santissimo Salvatore* (Monastery of the Holy Savior), and its tower with tiered arches; and the oval church of **Santa Chiara** (St Clare). These last two buildings house the **Museo Civico Archeologico** ❷ (Municipal Archeological Musuem), which has interesting sections on archeology and Norman art.

Piazza del Municipio ❸, the town's

central point, is a Baroque square, with elegant 18th-century architecture.

Palazzo Ducezio stands on its own on the south side of the square, and is enclosed on three sides by a columned loggia. Today it's the town hall. Opposite, three striking flights of stairs lead up to the **Cattedrale** (Cathedral) which was completed around 1776. It has a two-tier facade, flanked by two bell towers. It is not possible to visit the interior (nave, two side aisles and transept) because the cupola and nave roof collapsed in 1996. They are currently undergoing complex restoration work.

There's a 19th-century garden, and the Baroque fountain of Hercules, in

The majestic Piazza del Municipio and the Duomo

Piazza XVI Maggio ❹. Looking onto the square is the convex façade of the church of **San Domenico*** (St Dominic) built in 1703-27, to a design by Rosario Gagliardi, and one of the best examples of Sicilian 18th-century Baroque architecture. The interior is interesting with its central plan and five cupolas. Next door, the former *Convento dei Domenicani* (Dominican Monastery) has a large ashlar doorway (1727). On the opposite side of the square is the 19th-century *Teatro Comunale*, or Municipal Theater, (*B-C2*) with allegorical statues and bas-reliefs decorated with music motifs. Not far away is the *Chiesa del Carmine* (*B1*), built in the second half of the 18th-century, with its concave three-tier facade.

From **Via Nicolaci** ❺, which has been closed to traffic at the top and is very pretty, and the Chiesa di Montevergine with its concave facade, you reach the upper part of the town. The **Chiesa del Santissimo Crocifisso** ❻ (Church of the Holy Cross) is here, with its

unfinished facade. Inside, at the right transept altar, a *Madonna and Child**, known as the Madonna of the Snows, an important work by Francesco Laurana (1471).

PALAZZOLO ACREIDE [41 km]

The town stands on the hill where ancient *Akrai* was situated, which the Greeks of Siracusa founded in 664 BC and which the Arabs later destroyed. The center is largely 18th-century, but had medieval origins: the Normans built a castle here.

On the central square of **Piazza Umberto I** ❶: elegant *Palazzo Zocco*, with its balcony supports adorned with figures, and the *Chiesa dell'Annunziata* (Church of the Annunciation). The church was rebuilt in the 18th century, and has a Baroque doorway with spiral columns, and marble inlay work inside. The large church of **San Sebastiano** ❷ (St Sebastian) in *Piazza del Popolo* has a sumptuous Baroque facade, and a long flight of steps in front.

The **Area Archeologica** ❸, on the hill

south-west of the modern town, contains the ruins of ancient *Akrai*, one of the main Greek settlements in the interior of Sicily, which survived to early Christian times.

Remaining monuments include the 3rd-century BC **Teatro Greco ❹** (Greek Theater), which is not that large but very well-proportioned, a small *bouleutèrion* where the town council met, and the *agorà*, or town square.

Detail of the Baroque facade of the Church of the Annunciation

Behind the theater are the **Intagliata ❺** and **Intagliatella** latomies; these Greek stone quarries were later used as rock dwellings and hypogea in Byzantine times. Some of them have traces of bas-reliefs.

East of the hill are other latomies: the **Templi Ferali ❻** (Temples of Doom) have walls lined with votive tablets (pinakes) dedicated to the cult of the dead. The **Santoni ❼**, further along, are 12 large sculptures hewn out of the rock, dating from the 3rd century BC,

and connected to the worship of Cybele. They are among the most important known figurative works related to this goddess, the Roman Magna Mater, depicted standing or sitting, with lions and sometimes with other figures.

NECROPOLI DI PANTALICA [30 km]

This rock necropolis, a warren of 5000 tombs spread over 80 hectares, is the largest in Sicily. It belonged to the ancient town of *Hybla* which was the capital of a small 'state' in the Anapo valley, between the 13th and 8th centuries BC. Today it's part of a **Nature Reserve** and the visit here winds around 5 burial areas with cave-tombs for multiple burials, dating from the 12th to the 8th century BC. Near the Cavetta, there are some remains of the *Anaktoron* (12th- to 11th-century BC), the palace of the prince of *Hybla*.

Palazzolo Acreide 1 : 15 000 (1 cm = 150 m) 0   100   200 m

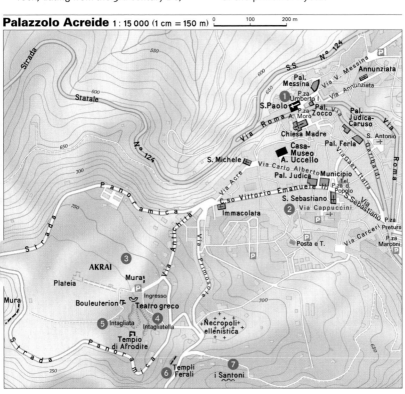

TRANPANI

Situated on a curved promontory on the west coast of Sicily, Trapani was an important port and a thriving industrial center until quite recently. The fish-processing industry and shipbuilding yards, the salt-pans and business enterprise have thrived here over the centuries, but now it is mainly a services center and the point of departure for tourists heading for the Egadi Islands. However, this part of the island's historical ups and downs over a long period of time have left important testimonials and some real artistic gems, both in the provincial capital and inland.

Originally, the Greek colony of Drepanon (meaning "sickle") was founded on a small archipelago of islands. Over the centuries it has been many things: an Arab town, full of winding narrow streets and courtyards, a craft center during the Norman period, specializing in the working of coral, and a modern fortified peninsula under Spanish rule in the 16th century.

The cathedral dedicated to St Lawrence

Corso Vittorio Emanuele ❶

The main thoroughfare of the historic center is lined by small, elegant 18th-century palazzi. At its eastern end

stands the graceful three-tiered facade of *Palazzo Senatorio*, built in the Baroque style between 1699 and 1701. Next to it is the 12th-century *Torre dell'Orologio* (Clock Tower), one of the five depicted in the town's crest. Further along, on the right, is the *Chiesa del Collegio* (Collegiate Church), begun in 1636, with the Baroque former *Collegio dei Gesuiti* (Jesuit College) on one side.

Cattedrale ❷

Erected in 1635, the cathedral facade, dating from 1740 and designed by Giovan Biagio Amico, is preceded by a portico. Inside, the 4th altar on the right contains an anonymous 17th-century Crucifixion by a Flemish artist of the Van Dyck school. The street opposite the

Trapani   1: 18 500 (1 cm = 185 m)

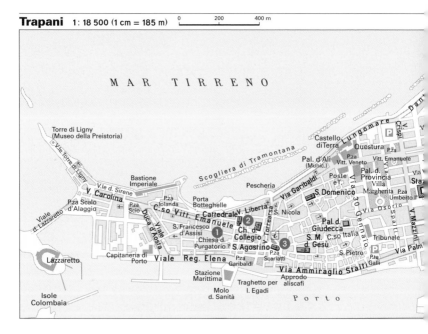

cathedral leads to the 17th-century *Chiesa del Purgatorio* (Church of Purgatory), where the *Misteri* (Mysteries), twenty 18th-century wooden statues traditionally paraded round the town on Good Friday, are kept.

S. Agostino ❸

The church dedicated to St Augustine stands in a small square graced by the *Fontana di Saturno* (Fountain of Saturn), of 1342. Of the original 14th-century building, which was damaged by bombing in 1943, there remains the simple facade with intersecting arches and a sloping roof, a Gothic portal and a *rose-window**. Close by, the former church of San Giacomo Maggiore (St James the Greater) is now the *Biblioteca Fardelliana* (Fardelliana Library), which contains priceless incunabola, manuscripts and illuminated codices from the 14th and 15th centuries.

Santuario dell'Annunziata ❹

This sanctuary dedicated to the Virgin Annunciate is one of Trapani's most interesting monuments, erected between 1315 and 1332 but

Santuario dell'Annunziata

subsequently altered. The facade dates from the original building, with a huge rose-window and a Gothic portal of Norman influence (early 15th century). Next to it stand the imposing 17th-century Baroque bell tower and the 16th-century Cappella dei Marinai (Sailors' Chapel). The **interior** was transformed in 1760 into a single vast nave. On the right of the nave is the *Cappella dei Pescatori** (Fishermen's Chapel), dating from 1486, with a fine Gothic arch and and an octagonal dome, frescoed in the 16th century. On the left of the presbytery is the entrance to the interesting *Cappella dei Marinai** (Sailors' Chapel), which is mainly Renaissance in form but still has Gothic and even Arab-Norman features. Behind the main altar is the 16th-century *Cappella della Madonna* (Chapel of the Madonna), the true sanctuary, decorated with reliefs. Above the altar is the much revered marble statue of the *Madonna and Child**, known as the *Madonna di Trapani*, a work by Nino Pisano or his pupils (14th century), at the foot of which is a silver model of the town.

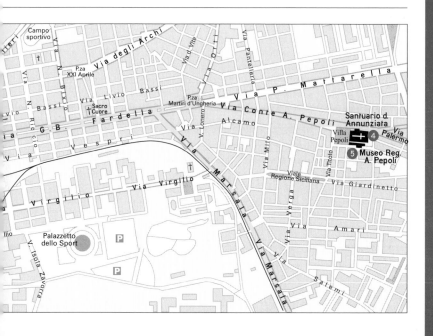

View of Trapani and the Egadi Islands

Museo Regionale "Conte Agostino Pepoli" ❺

Housed in the premises of a former convent dedicated to the Virgin Annunciate, this museum contains collections of archeological artifacts, sculpture, paintings and sections devoted to the decorative arts, which illustrate the artistic and cultural heritage of Trapani and its surroundings. In the section devoted to *sculpture* there are funerary inscriptions dating from the Arab period, Byzantine friezes, sarcophagi and statues. The *Pinacoteca* contains paintings from the 13th to 18th centuries, in particular some 15th-century polyptychs by Trapani's unknown Master of the Polyptych (*Madonna and Child and saints**); a Pietà* by Roberto di Oderisio (c. 1380); *St Francis receiving the Stigmata**, a large canvas attributed to Titian (1522); and other works by Ludovico Carracci, Giuseppe Ribera, Mattia Preti and Salvator Rosa. The *decorative arts section* is particularly interesting, with artifacts made by Trapani craftsmen in the 17th to 19th centuries: *gold- and silverware**, ceramics, fabrics and cribs* made of wood, alabaster, ivory and semi-precious stones. The traditional Trapani skill of working **coral** is well documented, with pieces created in the workshops of the coral-workers of Trapani in the 17th and 18th centuries. These include a crib, a *copper chalice** with cameos and coral inlay, and a *Crucifix** made from a single piece of coral.

DAY TRIPS

ALCAMO [52 km]

The name and origins of the town, built on a hill on the slopes of Monte Bonifato, about 11 km inland from the Bay of Castellammare, are Arabic: Manzil al-Qamah, was a stopping-place on the trading route between Palermo and the south-west coast of the island. The oldest part of the town, with perpendicular streets and regular blocks of houses, dates from the 14th century. The fact that several religious orders decide to move to the town (during the 15th to 17th centuries) encouraged the growth of the Baroque town, which was organized into districts beyond the medieval walls to the west, towards the modern Piazza Ciullo. Unfortunately, in recent times, haphazard urban development has marked the gradual decline of this historic town.

Corso VI Aprile, built on the line of the old "Imperial road" and historically the town's main street thoroughfare, cuts straight through the town center with the main religious buildings on either side, built in the Baroque style. At the beginning of the corso is the 17th-century church of **San Francesco d'Assisi** (St Francis of Assisi), which has two remarkable statues by Antonello Gagini (1520). Not far beyond it is **San Tommaso**, with a fine Gothic portal surmounted by a one-light window and crowned with small arches. A brief diversion to the right leads to the church of **San Salvatore** (St Savior), annexed to the Benedictine monastery of *Badia Grande* (Great Abbey), which dates from the 14th century.

The **Chiesa Madre** (Mother Church) was founded in the 14th century and rebuilt in 1669. The bell tower with two-light windows and the marble portal belong to the original church. The interior, with a nave and two side-aisles, contains works by Antonello Gagini. Not far away is the *Museo d'Arte Sacra* (Museum of Sacred Art), with some 17th-century paintings and vestments dating from the 16th century. Beyond **Piazza Ciullo**, the focus of life in the town, is the **Castle**. It overlooks the vast *Piazza della Repubblica*, which has been laid out as a park. The castle, which is rectangular and has round towers at

Landscape near Alcamo

the corners, dates from the 14th century. It has been converted to house the *Museo agricolo pastorale e artigianale* (Museum of Farming and Craftsmanship).

CALATAFIMI-SEGESTA [35 km]
Founded, according to the legend, by soldiers fleeing from Troy, the town's name (from "Kalat al-Phini") is of clear Arabic origin. The town acquired importance in the 14th century, when the Aragonese built a castle and fortified the town by building defensive walls. On May 15, 1860, a historic battle took place near Calatafimi during which Garibaldi's troops defeated the Bourbons. Just outside the town is a monument commemorating the followers of Garibaldi who died in battle: the **"Pianto romano"**. Churches worth visiting in the town include the Neoclassical **Chiesa del SS. Crocifisso**

(Church of the Holy Crucifix), the **Chiesa Madre** (Mother Church), with a splendid marble Renaissance triptych, and the ruins of **Castello Eufemio**.

CAMPOBELLO DI MAZARA [66 km]
The area surrounding these ancient quarries ("cava" means quarry), just outside the town of Campobello di Mazara, has an unusual atmosphere. This is where the enormous masses of tufa used for building the temples was quarried. The huge drums of columns that lie around the site, together with capitals and other architectural features, are overgrown with vegetation. The site was probably abandoned in 409 BC, when the quarries were attacked by Hannibal's Carthaginian troops.

CASTELLAMMARE DEL GOLFO [36 km]
The town began as a trading post for Segesta and Èrice. In late-medieval times, under the Arabs, it became a stronghold that was made impregnable by the building of a small fortress on a promontory jutting into the sea. It was the Arabs who succeeded in making the town into an important commercial center by setting up tuna fisheries here. The town developed further when a new town was built behind the castle, in 1560. Urban expansion took place between 1600 and 1800, based on a grid plan, with a later phase of streets and blocks stretching back as far as the slopes of the mountain behind.

The **Norman castle** stands on a small promontory beside the harbor, between two sandy beaches. It is now the *Museo delle attività marinare* (Museum of Marine Activities) and contains tuna-fishing gear, models of boats, photographs of tuna-fishing expeditions and a few marine archeological finds. In the square in front of the museum stands the little *Chiesa del Rosario* (Church of the Rosary) with a 16th-century portal. Behind is the *Chiesa Madre* (Mother Church), rebuilt several times between the 16th and 18th centuries.

ERICE [14 km]

A famous sanctuary dedicated to the Mediterranean goddess of fertility and protector of sailors - Astarte to the Phoenicians, Aphrodite to the Greeks, Venus Erycina to the Romans - stood here in the ancient city of Eryx, on the top of an isolated mountain called Monte San Giuliano, near the north-west tip of the island. The modern town, surrounded by ancient walls, is reserved and quiet, and has a charming medieval layout. The narrow, winding streets, paved with cobbles and stone paving slabs, provide occasional glimpses of peaceful courtyards full of flowers. The streets are lined with houses built of stone, now dark with the patina of time. It is a favorite haunt of intellectuals, who come here for its subtle charm, magnificent views and special atmosphere.

Entering the town by Porta Trapani, one of the three gates in the defensive **walls** ❶, still well-preserved with their square towers, you come to the **Chiesa Matrice*** ❷ (Mother Church), dating from 1314. Under the pronaos in front of the church, which dates from 1426, is a Gothic portal. Opposite stands the bell tower, decorated with two-light windows. It was built in 1312, possibly as a lookout tower. Continuing up Corso Vittorio Emanuele, a short diversion to the right leads to the church of **San Martino** ❸, founded by Count Roger the Norman, but rebuilt at the end of the 17th century. Back on the corso, the church of **San Salvatore** ❹, once attached to a monastery, has traces of 14th-century windows and a portal dating from the 15th century. At the end of the street is *Piazza Umberto I*, redesigned in the 19th century. Here, the *Town Hall* also houses the **Museo Civico "Antonio Cordici"** ❺ (Municipal Museum), with archeological finds from the necropolis, a coin collection and paintings and sculptures from the 15th to 18th centuries. Not far away stands the church of **San Pietro** (St Peter), built in the 14th century together with the convent of the Clarisse. The former convent now now houses the *Ettore Majorana Center for Culture and Science*, which attracts scholars from all over the world.

In the highest part of the town stands the church of **San Giovanni Battista** ❻ (St John the Baptist), dating from the

Erice 1:10 400 (1 cm = 104 m)   0   75   150 m

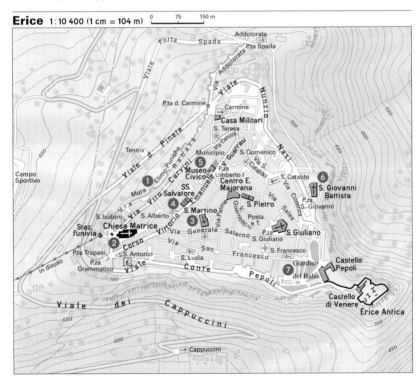

Erice, the Castle of Venus

promontory of Lilybaeum (now Capo Boeo), in the far west of the island, and thus became a naval base of key importance in Roman times. The town is famed for the robust wines which bear its name, which were first exported in the late 18th century by the English merchant, John Woodhouse. The town also has the distinction of having witnessed a particular moment of Italian history. It was here that, on May 11, 1860 Garibaldi and his Thousand disembarked, to begin the historic expedition which would eventually lead to the Unification of Italy.

The historic center, which is well-preserved, consists of a square surrounded by 16th-century walls and old districts with elegant Baroque buildings.

Via XI Maggio ❶, which follows the line of the old Carthaginian "càssaro", is the town's main thoroughfare, and ends at the 18th-century *Porta Nuova* (New Gate), built into the 16th-century walls. Nearby is the public garden of *Villa Cavallotti*.

The focus of the city is **Piazza della Repubblica ❷**: *Palazzo Senatorio*, finished in the 18th century with an arched facade and a square clock-tower, and the Baroque **Duomo** dedicated to St Thomas of Canterbury, begun in 1628 on the site of an earlier Norman foundation. Inside are sculptures by the Gagini and their pupils (16th century).

The **Museo degli Arazzi ❸** (Tapestry Museum) is housed in some rooms near the apse of the Duomo. It has some extremely fine 16th-century *tapestries**, given by Philip II of Spain to the Archbishop of Messina, and by him to Marsala's Mother Church.

12th century, set in a splendid position on the edge of a precipice, and the **Giardino del Balio ❼**, a lovely 19th century English-style garden laid out on a shelf of the citadel of the ancient city. On an isolated rock protruding from the citadel stands the **Castle of Venus**, built in the 12th and 13th centuries. It contains the ruins of the *Temple of Venus Erycina*, a sacred well and other buildings. From here there are *wonderful views** across the salt-pans of Trapani and out to the Egadi Islands.

GIBELLINA [49 km]

The town was completely rebuilt after the earthquake of 1968 which struck the Bèlice Valley.

A colossal metal star spanning the road, created in 1980 by Pietro Consagra, marks the entrance to the town, while the streets of Gibellina, laid out on a regular grid plan, are dotted with other sculptures by contemporaries artists.

MARSALA [31 km]

The name is Arabic and derives from: *Marsa Alì* or *Marsa Allah* (the port of Ali or God). some traces of the old Arab town can still be seen in the modern urban layout. However, originally, the town was Phoenician. It was situated on the

Marsala, windmills in the Lo Stagnone Nature Reserve

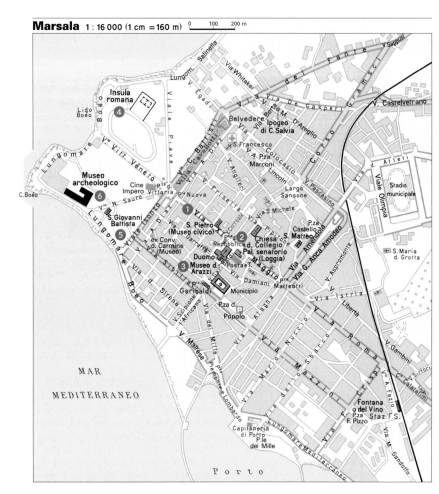

Marsala 1 : 16 000 (1 cm = 160 m)

In the area towards Capo Boeo is the **Insula romana** ❹, where excavations have brought to light a villa dating from the 3rd century AD and two smaller houses of a later date. You can also see the ruins of the Roman baths and a paleo-Christian necropolis.

Nearby is the 16th-century church of **San Giovanni Battista** ❺ (St John the Baptist), built above the *Antro della Sibilla Lilibea* (grotto of the so-called Lilybaean Sybil) where, according to the legend, the sybil lived and was buried, with the remains of a 3rd-century Roman mosaic and traces of early frescoes. Not far away is the *Baglio Anselmi*, once a typical winery and now housing the **Museo Archeologico** ❻.

The museum contains prehistoric artifacts from the local area and mosaic floors from the *Roman site*. The most interesting exhibit is the wreck of a **Punic ship*** dating from the 3rd century BC. This is the only example in the world of a *liburna*, a fast warship about 35 m long, which would have had a crew of 68 oarsmen. In the same room are exhibits and equipment associated with the ship.

MAZARA DEL VALLO [53 km]

The Phoenicians set foot on this site on the west coast of the island between the 6th and 5th centuries BC.
The Arabs, having disembarked at nearby Capo Granìtola, began their conquest of the island from here and made

TRAPANI
IN OTHER COLORS...

■ ITINERARIES: P 118
■ FOOD: P 147, 154, 167
■ SHOPPING: P 176, 178, 181
■ EVENTS: P 188, 195
■ WELLNESS: P 199
■ PRACTICAL INFO: P 241

Piazza della Repubblica at Mazara: the Baroque square *par excellence*

sarcophagi depicting the Amazonomachia (or battle with the Amazons) and Meleager Hunting the Calydonian Boar. In the apse is a majestic sculpture of the *Transfiguration** by Antonello and Antonino Gagini (1537) and, below, a fine marble Renaissance altar.

Between the cathedral and the sea-front is the **Jolanda Public Garden ❸**. This was where Count Roger built his castle in 1072, but little remains to be seen today.

The **Diocesan Museum ❹**, housed in the Seminario dei Chierici, contains important liturgical furnishings from the churches of Mazara and the diocese, while the **Museo Civico ❺** (Municipal Museum) is housed in the former *Jesuit College* (1675-86), an elegant Baroque building. The museum contains archeological finds (including the splendid statue of the **Dancing**

this town the capital of the Val di Mazara, one of the three Arab divisions of Sicily and the derivation of its modern name. The historic center lies in the rectangular area on the left bank of the River Màzaro. It has narrow, winding streets, cul-de-sacs and courtyards dating from Islamic period. Around it are the new quarters which sprang up in the early 20th century. The population earns a living mainly from wine-production and fishing. In fact, today, Mazara del Vallo is one of Italy's largest and best-equipped fishing ports. The center of the town is **Piazza della Repubblica ❶**, a Baroque square designed and built between the 17th and 18th centuries. It is graced by the statue of San Vito, the town's patron saint, and the most important public buildings.

The **Cathedral ❷**, founded in 1093 by Count Roger, conqueror of Sicily, and rebuilt in 1690-94 has a splendid *interior*, with a nave and two side-aisles separated by monolithic columns. In the right-hand aisle, a marble portal by Bartolomeo Berrettaro (1525) leads into the chapter-house, the hall of which contains two Roman

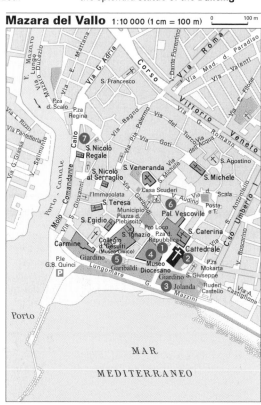

Mazara del Vallo 1:10 000 (1 cm = 100 m)

satyr*, dated to the 3rd or 2nd century BC and discovered on March 4, 1998 in the sea between Pantelleria and Africa), fine medieval sculptures, 18th-century paintings, and sculptures and drawings by the Mazara-born artist, Pietro Consagra. The palazzo is also the seat of the Historical archive of the Municipal Library.

Behind the Palazzo Vescovile (Bishop's Palace) is the **Città Vecchia** ❻ (Old Town) with its strongly Arabic flavor, typified by cul-de-sacs, archways, closed courtyards and various very old religious buildings.

Not far from the *harbor and shipping canal*, one of the most important fishing towns in the Mediterranean, overlooking the mouth of the River Màzaro stands the church of **San Nicolò Regale** ❼, (St Nicholas Royal), a small Norman building dating from 1124. Built on a square plan, it has a triple apse and is crenellated with merlons. The exterior is decorated with blind arcading and one-light windows.

The ruins of the Punic city on the island of Motya in Lo Stagnone lagoon

MOZIA [21 km]

The ancient city of Motya was founded in the late 8th century BC by the Phoenicians on the island of San Pantaleo in the beautiful shallow lagoon called "Lo Stagnone". The island was protected from enemy attacks and provided a safe haven for their ships. Because of its fortunate position on trading routes to Africa, Spain, Sardinia and central Italy, it soon became one of the most prosperous Punic colonies in the Mediterranean. It was destroyed in

397 BC by Dionysius, tyrant of Siracusa, during the wars between the Greeks and the Phoenicians.

Today, the ruins, discovered in the early 20th century by the Englishman Joseph Whitaker, can be reached by boat from a jetty on the nearby coast. The recommended itinerary incorporates the *House of the Mosaics*, a Greek house built after 397 BC on Phoenician foundations, the floor of which is decorated with mosaics, the remains of the *walls* and the *gates*, the *cothon*, or artificial basin connected by a channel to the sea, dug by the Phoenicians for repairing damaged ships, the *tophet*, a sacred area dedicated to the Phoenician god Baal Hammon, whose sacred rites are thought to have involved the sacrifice of animals and children, the so-called *area K*, a sector of the old industrial quarter where pottery was produced and the *necropolis* with numerous funerary pillars and votive stones.

The 19th-century Villa Whitaker has been converted into a **Museum**, containing about 10,000 finds from the excavations conducted by the British archaeologist and others discovered during more recent excavations. Perhaps the most beautiful find is the **Young man in a Tunic***, a magnificent Greek marble statue from the 5th century BC.

PANTELLERIA [150 km]

Situated in the middle of the Canale di Sicilia, the island of Pantelleria has a wild beauty, a jagged coastline with bays and little headlands, inlets and caves, dominated by precipitous rocks: ideal for fishing or underwater-photography enthusiasts. It was the Arabs, who dominated the island for 400 years (its name derives from "Bent el-Rhia", meaning "daughter of the wind"), who transformed its landscape by cultivating every tiny piece of land (and introducing the zibibbo grape). You can still detect traces of the Arab occupation in the place-names, the dialect, and features of the houses and gardens. The town of Pantelleria is clustered around the *Barbacane Castle*, built of black lava, which possibly dates back to the Byzantine period (c. 535) and was later extended by the Normans (in 1123).

Pantelleria, the Lago di Venere Nature Reserve

pools used for fish-farming. The 17th-century **Chiesa Madre** (Mother Church) stands on the town's main street. There are numerous **lookout towers** dotted along the coast, built with the aim of spotting enemy ships.

On the hills south of the town are remains of some *fortifications*, which probably defended the citadel of the Punic settlement of *Cossyra*.

SAN VITO LO CAPO [39 km]

A well-known seaside resort on a headland jutting out into the Tyrrhenian Sea. This sandy stretch of wild and beautiful coastline lapped by crystal-clear water is now the *Riserva Naturale Lo Zingaro* (Lo Zingaro Wildlife Reserve). During the Roman period, the town was an important fishing center. At the **Tonnara del Secco** (a tuna fishery), which was active until the 20th century, you can still see the remains of ancient

SCOPELLO [10 km]

This small farming town grew up around an 18th-century "baglio" (Marsala warehouse) built on the site of a group of houses dating from the Arab period. Famous for its interesting "tonnara" (tuna fishery), which dates back to the 13th century, the town is popular with tourists not only because of its crystal clear water but because of the picturesque rocks offshore which add charm to this section of the coastline.

SEGESTA [6 km]

One of the most beautiful and best-preserved examples of Doric architecture, the temple dominates the ancient city of Segesta (ancient Egesta), situated on the green slopes of Monte Barbaro. The city founded by the Elymians, a people consisting of the Sicani, a local tribe, and immigrants from Greece, was the adversary of Selinus (Selinunte) and was one of the first cities on the island to side with the Romans in the First Punic War. It was destroyed by the Vandals and then by the Saracens, and a violent earthquake during the Byzantine period reduced the monuments of the ancient city to rubble.

Segesta 1 : 23 500 (1 cm = 235 m)

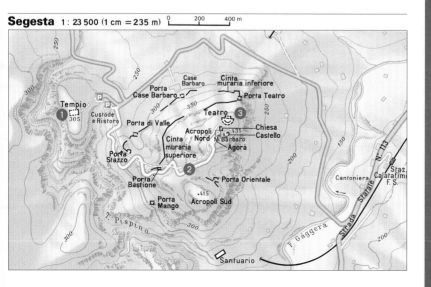

The **Temple ❶**, built in the 5th century BC, is peripteral and hexastyle, on a stepped stylobate, with 36 unfluted columns which still support the two pediments and the whole of the entablature. The lack of a cella has given rise to several interpretations. According to some, the building of the temple was interrupted by the conflict which broke out with Selinus in 416 BC. Others regard it as an open structure built to ennoble a cult area where indigenous rites were performed. What little remains of the **ancient city ❷** includes an imposing square tower, another tower, the ruins of the ancient fortifications, a fortified gate and the remains of a later set of defensive walls. North of the settlement stands the **Theater ❸**, which has been dated to the mid-3rd century BC. Facing north, possibly with the aim of allowing the audience to enjoy the spectacular view* across the hills to the sea in the distance, it is semi-circular (diameter 63 m), with rows of seating cut out of the bedrock, and divided into seven wedge-shaped sections. Excavations under the stage (of which little now remains) have uncovered the ruins of buildings of an earlier date.

SELINUNTE [14 km]

When he came here in the 12th century, the Arab chronicler al-Idrisi called this site *Rahl' al'Asnam*,

a *village of columns*. One of the most important archeological sites in the Mediterranean, ancient Selinus, founded in 650 BC by Greek settlers from Megara Hyblaea, is situated on low hills overlooking the south coast of Sicily, on the left bank of the River Modione. These are the ruins of the most powerful Greek city on the island. The site was first excavated in the early 19th century by Fagan, who was British Consul General in Palermo at the time.

Today, as they did 2,600 years ago, the huge Doric temples dominate the sea from the heights of the acropolis, or citadel, now part of a huge archeological park with an area of 2,700 hectares. Our visit includes the eastern temples, the acropolis, the ancient city and the sanctuary of Malaphoros.

Eastern Temples. Once possibly enclosed within a single immense wall, the eastern temples are a testimonial of the city's wealth and importance in the 6th century BC. The colossal *Temple G*, one of the largest temples to be built in antiquity (110.36 x 50.10 m), was possibly dedicated to Zeus. Begun in approximately 550 BC, it was still under construction when the city was destroyed at the hand of the Carthaginians. *Temple F* is the smallest and least well-preserved of the three temples on this part of the site. **Temple E****, reconstructed in the mid 1950s,

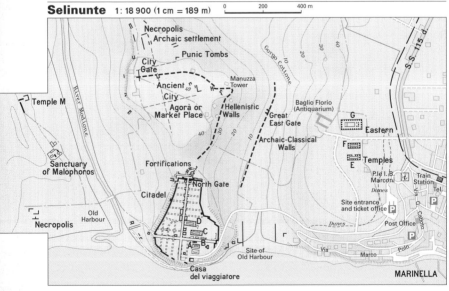

Selinunte   1: 18 900 (1 cm = 189 m)   0   200   400 m

Aerial view of the Archeological Park at Selinunte

towers majestically over the landscape of Selinunte. Possibly dedicated to Hera, the temple was built in the pure Doric style, is peripteral and hexastyle and dates from the early 5th century BC. Four metopes from this temple are displayed in the archeological museum in Palermo.

Acropolis. The citadel was built on a terrace of irregular shape sloping down slightly towards the sea, and was widened to the north-east with buildings that are supported and enclosed by a massive stepped defensive wall. Divided into districts by two perpendicular main streets, regularly intersected by smaller streets, the acropolis contains the ruins of various public buildings or buildings associated with cult worship,

Selinunte, Temple E

and five temples, with their main facade facing east, as was the custom. The largest and oldest temple is **Temple C** (6th century BC), from which three of the famous metopes in the Palermo archeological museum derive. The temples are surrounded by the ruins of *Punic houses* dating from the 4th to 3rd centuries BC. To the north, lie the impressive **fortifications***, consisting of a long gallery several storeys high, of which only the lower storey remains.

Ancient City. Destroyed in 409 BC, the city lay on the hill to the north of the citadel. Today you can still see the remains of a road, the agorà and parts of the residential area.

Sanctuary of Malophoros. A sacred area enclosed by walls on a hill on the other side of the River Modione, the ancient *Selínon*, from the citadel. At the mouth of the river, it is thought that there was a once a port, lying slightly west of the citadel. On the "sacred way" within the rectangular enclosure you can see the ruins of a large sacrificial altar and a temple, dedicated to Malophoros (literally, "bringer of pomegranites"), a divinity who can be identified with the Greek goddess, Demeter. It is thought that the temple was used during funeral processions which stopped here before continuing to the *necropolis*.

The salt-pans of Trapani and Marsala

The traditional salt-pans of this area are separated from the sea by the *traversa*, a causeway made from blocks of tufa from the island of Favignana. A sluice-gate (*purteddu*) regulates the flow of sea-water into the *fridda*, the largest and deepest tank in the complex. Here, the water deposits the heaviest sediments, and is then pumped by windmills (of the Dutch or American type) into the *vasi*, tanks at a slightly higher level. One of them, known as the *vasu cultivu*, also collects the liquid from the previous salification process, which acts as a sort of "yeast". The untreated sea-water (*acqua crura*) is then conveyed into the intermediate tanks (called *ruffiana* and *ruffianedda*) and subsequently, into a series of hot tanks (*càuri*), ending in the *sintina*. From here, the acqua fatta (that is, with a high level of salinity) flows into the *caseddi*, where the crystallization of the sodium chloride takes place. After the harvest (from June to September), the salt is deposited on the banks (*ariuni*) of the salt-pans in long piles (*munzidduni*), and is then covered with terracotta tiles (*ciaramiri*) to protect it from the elements.

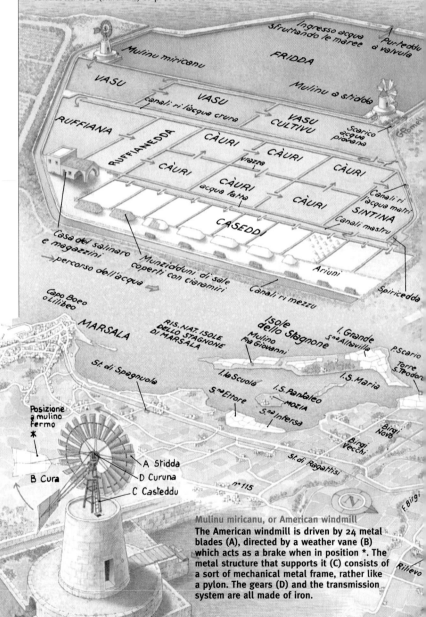

Mulinu miricanu, or American windmill
The American windmill is driven by 24 metal blades (A), directed by a weather vane (B) which acts as a brake when in position *. The metal structure that supports it (C) consists of a sort of mechanical metal frame, rather like a pylon. The gears (D) and the transmission system are all made of iron.

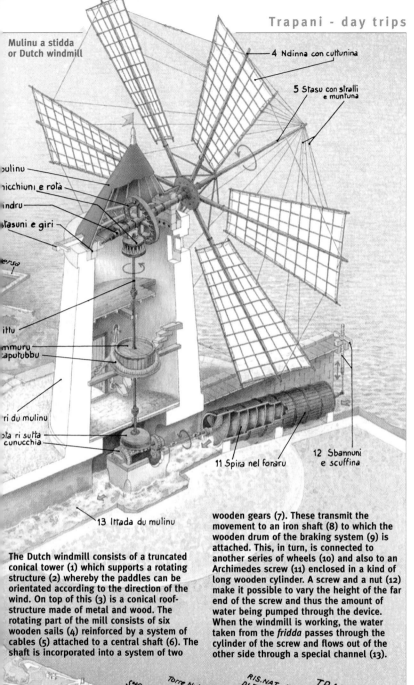

Mulinu a stidda
or Dutch windmill

4 Ndinna con cuttunina

5 Stasu con strali
e muntuna

ulinu

nicchiuni e rota

indru

stasuni e giri

ersa

ittu

mmuru
caputubbu

ri du mulinu

ota ri sutta
cunucchia

11 Spira nel foraru

12 Sbannuni
e scuffina

13 Irrada du mulinu

The Dutch windmill consists of a truncated conical tower (1) which supports a rotating structure (2) whereby the paddles can be orientated according to the direction of the wind. On top of this (3) is a conical roof-structure made of metal and wood. The rotating part of the mill consists of six wooden sails (4) reinforced by a system of cables (5) attached to a central shaft (6). The shaft is incorporated into a system of two wooden gears (7). These transmit the movement to an iron shaft (8) to which the wooden drum of the braking system (9) is attached. This, in turn, is connected to another series of wheels (10) and also to an Archimedes screw (11) enclosed in a kind of long wooden cylinder. A screw and a nut (12) make it possible to vary the height of the far end of the screw and thus the amount of water being pumped through the device. When the windmill is working, the water taken from the *fridda* passes through the cylinder of the screw and flows out of the other side through a special channel (13).

S.na Grande

Torre Nubia

RIS. NAT. SALINE
DI TRAPANI E PACECO

TRAPANI

MUSEO DEL SALE

Marausa

S.na Chiusa

S.na Alfano

Nubia

cograndе

A 29 dir.

Palma

S.na Vecchia

S.na Paceco

S.na Reda

Pietretagliate

S.na Galia

S.na Bella

Guarnato
n° 115

Fontanasalsa

S.na Maria Stella

Paceco

EOLIE

The distance between the seven islands of the archipelago and the mainland is negligible, yet, here, it is as if time moves at a different pace. Declared a UNESCO World Heritage Site, the islands are named after Eolus, the ancient god of the winds, who made them his home. They are all of volcanic origin, but differ from one another in the colors which make up the landscape. Vulcano (named after the ancient Roman god of fire) is yellowish-green, because of the sulfurous incrustations on the summit and black because of

Ris. nat.
Isola di Filicudi
e scogli Canna-
-Montenassari   **I. Filicudi**
Fossa delle Felci
Ris. nat. Isola   GROTTA DEL   773   Filicudi Porto
di Alicudi   BUE MARINO
Pecorini   *C. Graziano*
I. Alicudi
675
▲ Filo d. Arpa
Alicudi Porto

I. SALINA

Isole   Eolie

(Messina)

Ris. nat.
Isola di Filicudi
GROTTA DEL   *e scogli Canna-*
BUE MARINO   *-Montenassari*
Fossa delle Felci   **I. Filicudi**
773   Filicudi Porto
Pecorini   *C. Graziano*

I. Salina
P. di Perciato   Malfa   Capo F
Pollara   ▲860   SANT. MAD.
Ris. nat. Montagna   Leni   D. TERZIT
d. Felci e monte dei Porri   ▲962
Rinella   M. Fossa   S. Ma
d. Felci   Salina
P. Grottazza   Lin

Canale

I. ALICUDI

I. Lipa

Terme d
San Calògero

I. Eolie
I. Ègadi   Palermo
Trapani   Messina
Enna   Catania
Caltanissetta
Agrigento   Siracusa
Ragusa
I. di Pantellerìa

M A R

its beaches of black volcanic sand. Lìpari is a dazzling contrast of shining black obsidian and white pumice. Strómboli is black during the day and glows an incandescent red at night, on account of its continuous eruptions. Salina is bright green, its now extinct craters being covered with dense woodland. Filicudi, like Alicudi, is dark green, because of the beautiful caper plants which burst out of the basalt rock all over the island. Panarèa is a golden color, dotted with the bright green of the vines and the white of the whitewash of the "dammusi", the name given to the houses flat, terrace-roofs large typical of these islands. The water around the islands is crystal-clear and cobalt blue, revealing a rocky sea-bed. The islands have not been inhabited continuously, and their soil, much of which is still virgin, has thrown up a few fragments from early settlements dating from the 5th millenium BC without yielding any further finds from the historic period.

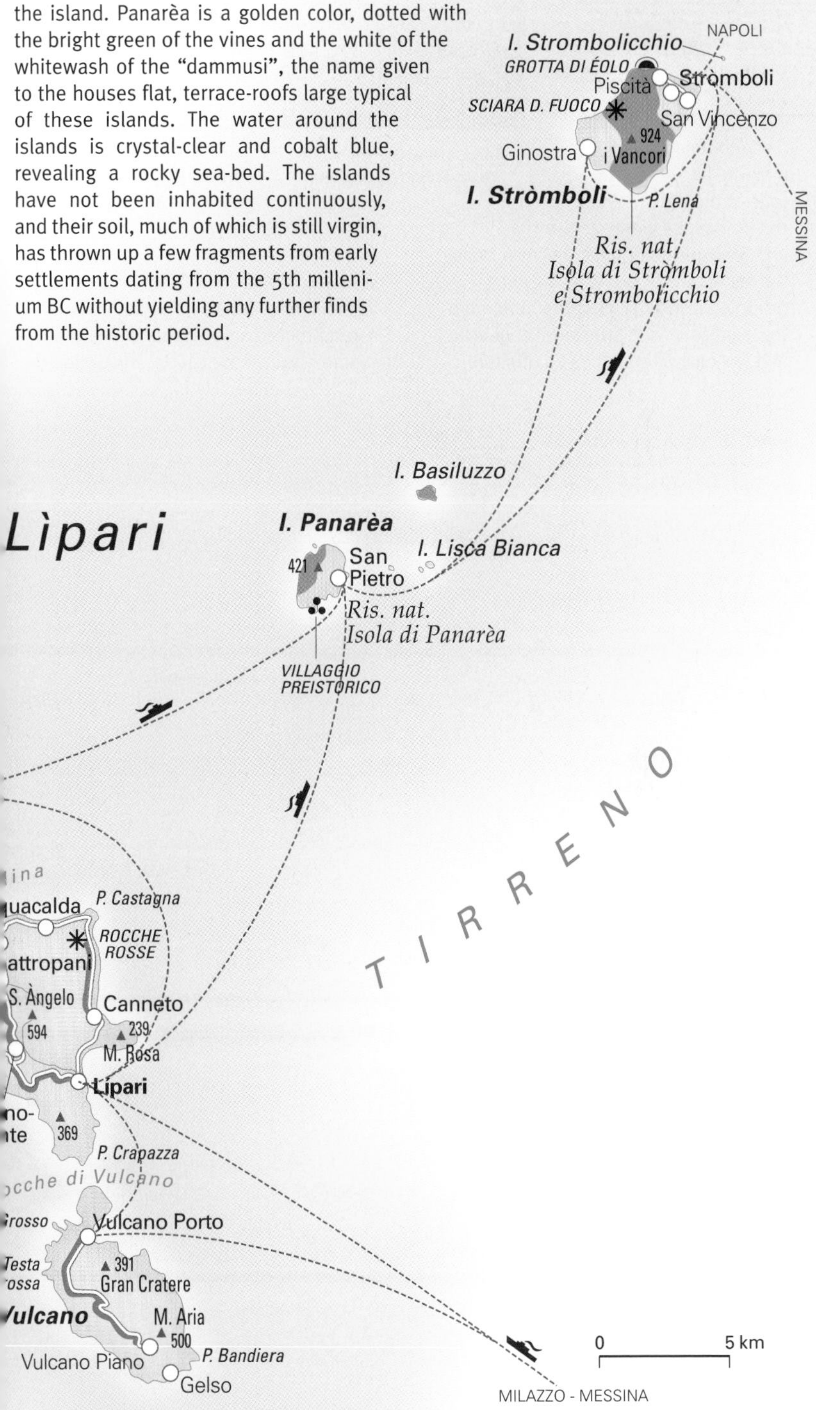

NAPOLI

I. Strombolicchio
GROTTA DI ÉOLO · **Stromboli**
Piscità
SCIARA D. FUOCO
San Vincènzo
Ginostra · ▲ 924
i Vancori
I. Strómboli · P. Lena

MESSINA

*Ris. nat.
Isola di Strómboli
e Strombolicchio*

I. Basiluzzo

Lìpari

I. Panarèa
421 · San Pietro · *I. Lisca Bianca*
*Ris. nat.
Isola di Panarèa*
VILLAGGIO PREISTORICO

T I R R E N O

ina
uacalda · P. Castagna
ROCCHE ROSSE
attropani
S. Àngelo · Canneto
594 · 239
M. Rosa
no-
te · 369
Lìpari
P. Crapazza
cche di Vulcano
rosso · Vulcano Porto
Testa ossa · ▲ 391
Gran Cratere
Vulcano
M. Aria
▲ 500
Vulcano Piano · P. Bandiera
Gelso

0   5 km

MILAZZO - MESSINA

Lipari

Lipari, one of the many fine views at Sottomonastero

It is the largest and mostly highly populated of the seven islands. A tarred road runs right around the coast, while a network of cart-tracks makes it possible to explore inland. In fact, it is possible to drive right round the island, passing through tiny villages, making detours to the tops of the hills to enjoy the marvelous views across the archipelago (don't miss the view from the viewpoint of Quattrocchi), and dropping down to the shore to admire the pumice caves, little creeks, beaches and the characteristic rocks offshore known as the faraglioni scattered along the coast. The most important town is *Lìpari*, the millenary history of which focuses on its Castello (castle). Having become prosperous in the Middle Ages, thanks to the exploitation of sulfur, alum and pumice mines and the export of these minerals to Sicily, in 1544, Lìpari was destroyed in a raid led by the Turkish corsair Khair ad-Din, better known to posterity as Barbarossa. Within a few years, the Spanish had reconstructed an effective defensive system around the castle, which now

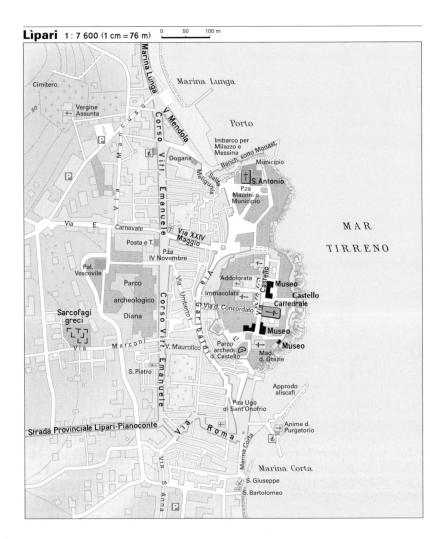

Lìpari 1 : 7 600 (1 cm = 76 m)

houses a small archeological park. The cathedral of San Bartolomeo, built on the site of the ancient acropolis, is of Norman origin.

Vulcano

Vulcano has never been permanently inhabited, but has always attracted people for various reasons. They came for the therapeutic properties of its mud and hot water springs, to exploit its alum and sulfur deposits and to graze their sheep, and, according to some, to bury the dead. Today, the interesting volcanic activity (fumaroles, jets of steam rising out of the ground) make it possible to enjoy hot-water and mud baths all the year round.

Strómboli

The island of Strómboli is the only volcano in the archipelago which is permanently active. Many people come to the island to watch its spectacular eruptions (there is also an interesting Centro Vulcanologico (Volcano Center) to visit). From the sea, at night, visitors can enjoy the unforgettable spectacle provided by the "sciara del fuoco" (or red-hot lava flow), on the north-west side of the island, where a stream of incandescent lava flows down to meet the sea.

Panarea

Panarea is the smallest island in the Eolian archipelago. For the last few decades, it has been bombarded by merciless development to build tourist facilities. The best way to enjoy the magical charm of the island is to approach it by sea
Above the delightful bay known as Cala Junco, you can visit the remains of a prehistoric village dating from the Middle Bronze Age.

Panarea, the cobalt-blue water of Cala Junco

Filicudi and Alicudi

They are the two islands least visited by mass tourism. Filicudi consists of a group of craters covered by typical Mediterranean maquis vegetation. Do not miss the chance of going on a nature walk accompanied by a guide who is an expert on the island's plant and animal species.
Half of the island of Alicudi is completely uninhabited. Here, the only means of transport available - apart from your feet - is a donkey.

Stromboli seen from Strombolicchio

EGADI

The coastlines of these islands of calcareous rock and sandstone consist of many caves and just a few enchanting beaches. The inland plateaus are dominated by fields of wheat, vineyards and meadows. Today, its popularity as a tourist destination is on the increase. The designation of the archipelago as a marine and land nature reserve is an attempt to slow down development and safeguard this precious environment.

Favignana

It is the largest island, the nearest to mainland Sicily, less wild and more highly populated than the other islands of the archipelago. There are numerous buildings of historical and architectural importance on the island, including the *Villino Florio*, the villa belonging to the Florio family of Marsala fame, built in 1876 in the Art Deco Style. There is also a *tonnara* or tuna fishery, one of the largest industrial complexes in Europe at the end of the 19th century and, today, a marvelous example of industrial archeology. Favignana also distinguishes itself for its interesting archeological sites and for its many tufa quarries, tufa being an ideal building material. But the island's main resource has always been the sea. Tourists come here to enjoy Favignana's splendid beaches, its bays, its rocks. Tuna fish use the island as a huge buoy, since it lies on the route they use when returning to the coast to reproduce. As a result, many of them are caught in the nets laid by the tuna fisheries.

Levanzo

Levanzo has an enchanting coastline and clear blue water. Many archeological remains have been discovered in the sea around the island (Punic and Roman ships and Spanish galleons). But Levanzo is worth visiting just for the **Grotta del Genovese**, a cave famous for its prehistoric wall paintings and incised drawings, dated to between 9,000 and 10,000 BC. They depict *human figures* in the act of performing a ritual dance and a *series of animals*, including a *deer* and are of particular artistic value because of the successful way that movement has been expressed.

Marettimo

The island situated furthest from Sicily, is a natural paradise. From the wild, steep sides of Monte Falcone, there is a direct drop down to the sea. There are no hotels here, but the islanders who live in the little town between the two small harbors are happy to put tourists up in their houses. Every day fishermen set out in little boats to perform the ancient rite of fishing, pitting their strength and skill against the might of the sea.

Favignana, the splendid stretch of coastline at Calamoni

PELAGIE

The Scattered among the southernmost of Italy's territorial waters (they are closer to Africa than to Sicily), the islands of Lampedusa, Linosa and Lampione form the little Pelagian archipelago (from the Greek word "pelagos", meaning "high-sea"). The islands differ in their geological make-up: Lampedusa and Lampione are calcareous, whereas Linosa is of volcanic origin. Although they are too small and exposed to have

been used as military bases, the fact that they have always been so isolated has preserved them from negative environmental transformations. As a result, today, the diversity of the marine and land species which live there constitute a major attraction for naturalists. The sea around the island of **Linosa**, which is of volcanic origin, is a paradise for scuba divers. Accommodation can be found in the village of the same name with its picturesque, brightly-colored houses.

Linosa, with its brightly-painted houses

Lampedusa

Lampedusa, once famous for its sponges, resembles a rocky platform tipped at an angle. Its steep cliffs overlook water that is crystal-clear and teeming with fish, while its coastline is full of caves and rocks interspersed with little sandy bays.

It has only been permanently inhabited since 1843, when the Bourbon King Ferdinand II established a penal colony here. Until 1940, it was used as a detention center. The population of the island is concentrated in the small town of *Lampedusa*, in the south of the island. In 1995 the **Riserva Naturale Isola di Lampedusa** was created to preserve the Mediterranean maquis and the habitats of certain species of plants and animals on the verge of extinction. The charming **Spiaggia dei Conigli** (Rabbit Beach) is one of the few remaining places where the loggerhead turtle (Caretta caretta) lays its eggs. Linosa is really the cone of a volcano which has been inactive for almost 2000 years. The sea around the island is deep and full of fish, a true paradise for

scuba divers. Accommodation can be found in the village of Linosa, in one of its colorful houses.

High cliffs on Lampedusa

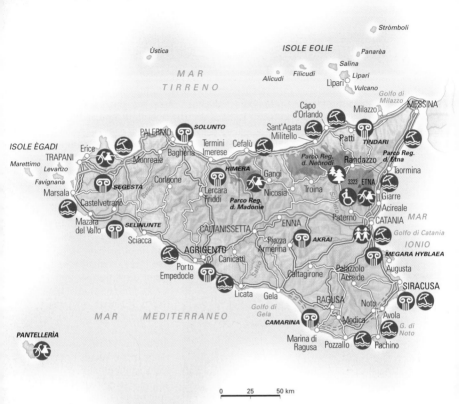

From obscure baroque towns to the major archeological sites of ancient temple ruins, the perfect itinerary to suit your interest is at your fingertips. Explore heavenly beaches, majestic mountains and Europe's number one hot spot—Mount Etna. No matter the season Sicily provides ample opportunity to experience it's natural beauty in a variety of methods. Hike the trails around Mt. Etna or follow the ancient temple roads by bike.

HISTORICAL ITINERARIES

PARKS

CHILDREN

BEACHES

BIKING ROUTES

Itineraries & special interest

Explore the beaches on horseback and discover the craggy coast and hidden coves that remain unchanged since the first explorers stepped ashore. Well-marked roads lead to endless adventures thorough the heart of Sicily and past miles of citrus, almond, and olive groves.

Highlights

- An extraordinary journey discovering the island's major archeological sites
- The Park which protects Mount Etna, Europe's highest volcano
- Discovering Sicily's finest beaches along its almost 1,500 km of coastline
- Four interesting suggestions for entertaining your kids

Inside

AMONG THE VESTIGES OF THE PAST

Perhaps the most interesting and pleasurable way to discover the development of Sicily's artistic heritage is to follow an itinerary based on visits to the island's archeological sites. This, after all, was why Sicily was one of the main stops on the Grand Tour during the 18th and 19th centuries, of which Goethe's "Italian Journey" is the most famous and most romantic celebration. But, although what most fascinated the German poet about Sicily were the traces of its Greek past (so much so that he wrote that, rather than describing Sicily as Magna Grecia (Greater Greece), that is, a mere colony of Greece, it should be described as one of the most authentic parts of the Greek motherland), we should not forget the important testimonials left here by other cultures and civilizations.

Sites dating from the **Paleolithic** include the rock engravings at Addàura near Palermo and at the Grotta del Genovese on the island of Lèvanzo. The **Neolithic** is represented by the remains of the villages at Stentinello and Megara Hyblaea. Another aspect of the Neolithic period is the evolution of pottery on the

Eolian Islands, providing evidence of the first contact with the Aegean area and Mycenae, and the dissemination of obsidian. Finds from the period are exhibited at that little jewel which is the Lìpari Archeological Museum. During the Bronze Age (1800-900 BC), there was an intensification of economic trade and cultural links between Sicily and the Greek and Mycenaean world. Sites associated with this period include the villages on Panarèa, Salina, and Lìpari, and at Thapsos, whereas later colonization by the Sicani and other Italic peoples finds testimonials in the rock-cut necropolis at Pantàlica, and in the excavations conducted at Sabucina and Morgantina.

Top: Selinunte, tourists visiting Temple E. Bottom: another view of the Acropolis at Selinunte, with Temple C in the background. Right: Morgantina, the *cavea* of the Greek theater and (below) a kiln

But the true turning-point in the island's history is the mid-7th century BC, when the **Greek colonization** of the island began. The first Greek "poleis" (cities) were founded at Zancle, Naxos, Catania, Leontinoi, Megara Hyblaea, Siracusa and Gela, which, in turn, led to expansion along the coast or inland, resulting in the foundation of new towns or fortified cities (Himera, Selinunte, Camarina, Agrigento, Akrai and Casmene). During the 7th century BC, the **Punic presence** was also consolidated in Western Sicily, with the founding of settlements at Motya, Palermo and Sòlunto. In the century that followed, the Greek cities of Sicily reached a level of opulence and power that can be seen in the development of the architecture of the time. This is documented particularly by the building of sanctuaries and **temples**, for example the first large stone temples at Siracusa and Selinunte. For Sicily, the 5th century BC was a Golden Age which saw the culmination of its political and cultural splendor, leading to urban expansion and architectural development in the cities. Everywhere, new temples were built (Himera, Siracusa, Selinunte, Agrigento). Increasingly, they reflected the architectural canons of classical Greece, which were also adopted - albeit with occasional variations - in the non-Greek

settlements on the island (Segesta). Thus Sicily became one of the great centers of the Mediterranean, following the historical and artistic transformations of this cultural area. After the Carthaginian offensive and the destruction which resulted therefrom, in the 4th century BC, we see the resurrection of the most important cities and the foundation of new ones: Gela (whose splendid stone and brick walls on Capo Soprano are still intact), Camarina, Agrigento, Halaesa and Sòlunto. The 3rd century BC marks the transition, in terms of town-planning and art, to Hellenistic forms: cities such as Tyndaris, Tauromenion (Taormina), Sòlunto, Akrai (Palazzolo Acrèide), Morgantina and Iaitas reflect the new canons of urban planning in the imaginative and scenic layout of their monuments and squares, as shown in the agorà at Morgantina. **Stone theaters** suddenly underwent an important phase of development (Siracusa, Segesta, Palazzolo Acrèide, Sòlunto, Morgantina, Tyndaris, Catania, Iaitas, Eraclea Minoa and Taormina).

Among the vestiges of the past

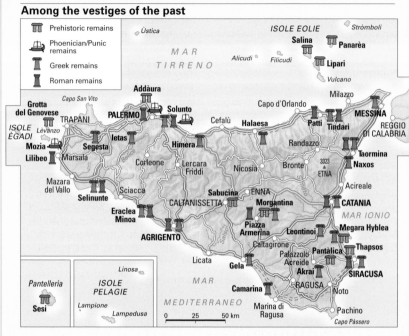

In 212 BC, Sicily became a **Roman province**. Some of the cities in western Sicily seem to have undergone a certain amount of development, particularly Sòlunto, Lilybaeum (Marsala) and probably Palermo. In the 1st century AD, the construction of sumptuous residential villas testifies to the development of the latifundium (large estate) system (the most notable example being the Roman villa of at San Biagio). Finally, in the Imperial period, in addition to the restoration of Greek monuments (the theater of Taormina being the prime example), we see the development of important architectural projects at Tyndaris, Agrigento, the mouth of the Tellaro and at Patti. The economy based on the latifundium system, which also characterized the late Imperial period, gave rise, in terms of architecture and art, to splendid Imperial or senatorial villas, like the one justly celebrated on account of its magnificent mosaics, at Piazza Armerina.
It is therefore clear that an archeological itinerary in Sicily offers great variety and potential to visitors. And although we certainly cannot

ignore the great monumental complexes such as Siracusa, the Valley of the Temples at Agrigento, Selinunte, Sòlunto and Piazza Armerina, nor the fabulous collections of the archeological museums of Agrigento, Palermo (with the extraordinary metopes from Selinunte), Siracusa and Catania (to mention only the most important), it is right that we should also consider the marvelous surprises concealed in less well-known sites, often located in superb natural settings. This is certainly the case of the Phoenician settlement on Motya, a tiny island in the Lo Stagnone lagoon off Marsala; Eraclea Minoa, with the remains of its tufa theater built next to a glorious beach; Morgantina, set in the green heart of Sicily, which, despite the fact that it has no great monuments, enables us to understand what a Greek city was really like; and Segesta, where a gravel track leads up from a perfectly preserved Doric temple, to an equally well-preserved theater where, for some years now, performances have been staged at dawn, as the sun rises above the Golfo di Castellammare.

ETNALAND

BELPASSO (CATANIA)

FACILITIES: BARS, SELF-SERVICE CAFETERIAS, PICNIC AREAS, NURSERY, PLAYGROUND. VISITORS ARE NOT ALLOWED TO BRING PETS OR GLASS CONTAINERS INTO THE PARK.

HOW TO GET THERE

BY CAR: A19 PALERMO-CATANIA MOTORWAY, EXIT AT GERBINI; SS 121 CATANIA-PATERNÒ EXIT AT VALCORRENTE-BELPASSO.

BY TRAIN: CATANIA TRAIN STATION.

INFO: ETNALAND, LOCALITÀ VALCORRENTE, 95032 BELPASSO (CATANIA), TEL. 0957913333.

E-MAIL: INFO@PARCOZOO.IT, WEB: WWW.PARCOZOO.IT

OPENING TIMES

ZOO PARK: 22 MARCH - 30 SEPTEMBER AND SUNDAYS IN OCTOBER

WATER PARK: 21 JUNE - 14 SEPTEMBER. THE ZOO PARK IS CLOSED ON WEDNESDAYS EXCEPT ON PUBLIC HOLIDAYS.

ENTRANCE CHARGES

LOW SEASON: (21 JUNE-18 JULY AND 1 SEPTEMBER-14 SEPTEMBER) FULL TICKET € 17.50, REDUCED TICKET (HEIGHT LESS THAN 1.40 M) € 9

HIGH SEASON: ADULTS € 19, REDUCED TICKET € 10; ZOO PARK ONLY (WHEN THE WATER PARK IS CLOSED) FULL TICKET € 8.50, REDUCED TICKET € 5.50

Park, which experts have judged to be exceptional in terms of the number and the diversity of the attractions it offers. The zoo park covers an area of more than 32,000 m² and includes a zoo where more than 600 animals from all five continents live in an area with bridges, waterfalls and huge bird-cages. There is also an area that can only be visited in a open 2-person cabin on a Rope Safari, which completes the pentagonal route in about half-an-hour. This unusual means of transport enables children (and adults) to see the animals from above without disturbing them. Species include the rare oryx, with their long, sword-like horns, lion, elephant, tiger, lynx, panther, llama, maned sheep and mouflon. Etnaland also has a Prehistoric Park, sub-divided into four areas - the Paleozoic, Mesozoic, Cenozoic and Neozoic - with about 20 life-size reproductions of animals that are now extinct, such as the Brontosaurus, the Tyrannosaurus Rex and the mammoth, all displayed as part of a botanical itinerary which you can visit on the "Time Train". The park is situated at the foot of Mount Etna in dramatic landscape, around a large lake (20,000 m²) populated with aquatic species. The new area of the Acqua Park has an approximate area of 80,000 m² and includes two huge water-slides with rubber dinghies that can accommodate up to five people and automatic uphill ramps to take you back to the top. There is a Twin Twister with 4 tracks, a Rio Anaconda which is like a bob track on water, the Wild River tunnel with laser- and sound-effects, Niagara Falls which are negotiated in two-seater rubber dinghies, Slow River, Blue Lagoon, one of the largest swimming-pools with waves in Europe, waterfalls, bubble water, geysers and hydro-beds. Then

When Etnaland was first opened in 1985, it was a zoo park. In 2001, it was transformed into a huge theme park, with the inauguration of the new Acqua

there are special attractions for younger visitors such as the lagoon with the Water Castle, Mini Foam, the Mini Dodgems and the Dolphin Slide.

CIRCUMETNEA RAILWAY

(Catania)

HOW TO GET THERE

By car: A19 Motorway, exit at Catania.

By train: Catania train station.

INFO: Ferrovia Circumetnea, Stazione Catania Borgo, 95100 Catania, tel. 095541250/095541251, e-mail: info@circumetnea.it, web: www.circumetnea.it

TRAIN SCHEDULE Runs all year, consult the timetable for the train times. Tickets: Catania-Randazzo € 3.85

CASTAGNO DEI CENTO CAVALLI

Sant'Alfio (Province of Catania)

HOW TO GET THERE

By car: from the Messina-Catania motorway, exit at Giarre, follow the SP 5 for approximately 7 km and follow signs for Sant'Alfio.

By train: get off the train at Giarre Riposto. There is a bus to Sant'Alfio every two hours.

INFO: Castagno dei Cento Cavalli, 95010 Sant'Alfio (Catania), tel. 095968772 (Local Information Office),

It's the only narrow-gauge railway line in Sicily. It was opened in the late 19th century and was altered several times when lava flows from Mount Etna invaded the track. The route starts at the terminus in Catania. During the first section in the city, it's like being on a tram, and the train often has to stop to allow traffic to cross. The railway line proper begins after Catania Borgo and continues with the marvelous landscapes of the volcano in the background. The highest point of the journey is at Rocca Calanna (976 m above sea-level), after which the train begins its descent to the sea, with more splendid views along the Ionian coast. To return to Catania you can either catch a normal Trenitalia (the Italian national railway company) train at Giarre (a stop on the Messina-Catania line); or you can continue to the terminus at Riposto. The train's maximum speed is 60 km per hour. Many of the stations, once used by farmers to reach their farms from the towns where they lived, are now starting-points for nature walks. From Passo Zingaro, for example, a mule-path leads up across old lava fields to Monte Minardo.

WEB: www.comune.sant-alfio.ct.it

OPENING TIMES: all year.

Sant'Alfio is a small farming town on the eastern slopes of Mount Etna. Not far from the center of the town, on the Linguaglossa road, is one of Italy's most famous monumental trees, the millenary Castagno dei Cento Cavalli (Hundred Horse Chestnut). The name of this ancient tree derives from a legend according to which Queen Joan of Aragon and her entourage of one hundred knights sheltered beneath its branches having been surprised by a storm during a royal outing to Mount Etna. The chestnut tree, which is thought to be one of the oldest living creatures in Europe, has had its share of bad luck. For example, in 1923, the main trunk was burnt by the inhabitants of Giarre who did not want their village to be separated from the town, and it has often been damaged by people trying to pick chestnuts. Today, it is protected by a fence and by the local council's plan for safeguarding the natural environment.

PARCO MONTE SERRA

VIAGRANDE (PROVINCE OF CATANIA)

FACILITIES: BAR-RESTAURANT AREA, PICNIC AREA WITH BARBECUE FACILITIES, NATURE WALKS.

HOW TO GET THERE

BY CAR: FROM THE A18 CATANIA-MESSINA MOTORWAY, EXIT AT ACIREALE, FOLLOWING SIGNS FOR VIAGRANDE. THE PARK IS ON THE ROAD BETWEEN VIAGRANDE AND TRECASTAGNI. FROM CATANIA, TAKE THE PROVINCIAL HIGHWAY IN THE DIRECTION OF ZAFFERANA.

INFO: PARCO MONTE SERRA, 95029 VIAGRANDE (CATANIA), TEL. 3472686906, WEB: WWW.PARCOMONTESERRA.IT

OPENING TIMES: OPEN ALL YEAR. ON SUNDAYS AND PUBLIC HOLIDAYS OPEN FROM 10-18.

Parco Monte Serra is a suburban park which takes its name from the mountain on which it is situated. It covers about 30 hectares of land from the lower slopes up to its peak. Ideal for walking and for children, the park contains the only Butterfly House in southern Italy. A natural habitat for butterflies has been recreated inside a huge cage, where they are free to fly about and breed. The Butterfly House has some of the most beautiful butterflies in the world, and some strange species such as leaf butterflies and owl butterflies, which use artful disguises to fool predators. There are three paths leading through the park, which you can explore on foot or on the back of a donkey. There is also a small, fast, comfortable train which enables visitors to visit the various parts of the park easily. When you reach the top, you can walk all round the volcanic cone admiring the splendid views of Mount Etna, Taormina and even Calabria. To reach the top, there is also a flight of 350 steps carefully built in lava. For children there's also a playground and a large green area for picnicking.

e spurge (*Euphorbia dendroides*) one of the most common species of plant found on Monte Serra.

113

PARCO NATURALE REGIONALE DELL'ETNA

Province of Catania.

AREA

58,095 hectares. Active volcano, extensive tree vegetation, extensive areas at high altitude with pioneer vegetation.

HEADQUARTERS

Ente Parco dell'Etna, via Etnea 107/a, 95030 Nicolosi (Catania), tel. 095821111, fax 095914738, e-mail: ufficiostampa@parcoetna.it

VISITORS' CENTERS

Environmental Education Center at Fornazzo di Milo, tel. 03382993077.

WEB

www.parcoetna.it

The park incorporates one of Europe's few active volcanoes, in a spectacular setting in terms of colors, landscapes and human activity. It also protects everything that lives or exists on the volcano, including its volcanic activity: the low walls built of lava, the old farm-houses, the woods of birch and Austrian pine, beech and flowering ash, the striking Etna broom, the plants

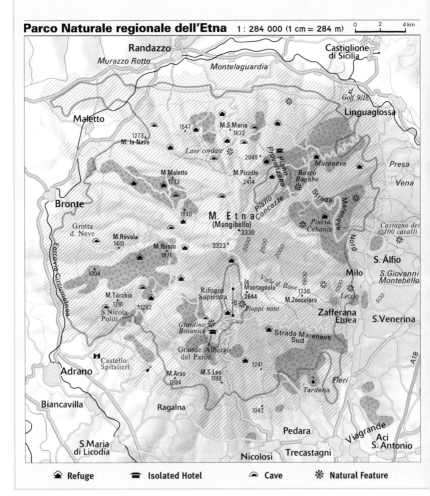

Parco Naturale regionale dell'Etna   1 : 284 000 (1 cm = 284 m)   0   2   4 km

Randazzo
Murazzo Rotto
Montelaguardia
Castiglione di Sicilia
Golf 9/18
Linguaglossa
Maletto
1547
M.S.Maria 1832
Lave cordate
2049
Piano Provenzana
Mareneve
Presa
Vena
M.Maletto 1773
M.Pizzillo 2414
Bosco Ragabo
Strada
Bronte
1840
M. Etna
(Mongibello)
3330
Piano Concazze
Pineta Cubania
Mareneve Nord
Castagno dei 100 cavalli
Grotta d. Neve
M.Rúvola 1410
M.Rosso 1876
3323
3000
2500
2000
S. Álfio
1304
Valle del Bove
1600
Milo
S.Giovanni Montebello
M.Túrchio 1291
1282
Rifugio Sapienza
la Montagnola 2644
1739
M.Zoccolaro
Leccio
1000
600
S.Nicola Politi
Pioppi nani
Zafferana Etnea
S.Venerina
Giardino Botanico
Strada Mareneve Sud
Grande Albergo del Parco
Castello Spitalieri
1241
Adrano
M.Arso 1084
M.S.Leo 1198
Fleri
Tardaria
A18
Biancavilla
Ragalna
1042
Pedara
Viagrande
Aci S.Antonio
S.Maria di Licodia
Nicolosi
Trecastagni
Ferrovia Circumetnea

Refuge   Isolated Hotel   Cave   Natural Feature

and animals living in extreme conditions. Just observing the lava shapes, veritable sculptures of Nature, provides scholars with an endless task. One of the wonders of the volcano is Valle del Bove (Bove Valley), an enormous basin situated on the eastern slope of the volcano with walls as high as 1,000 m, which, according to some theories, is the result of the collapse of the original crater complex.

Although the diversity of wildlife species has diminished in recent times, the fact that humans find much of the environment inhospitable allows many species of birds to survive. Diurnal raptors such as the sparrow-hawk, the peregrine falcon and the golden eagle; nocturnal raptors such as the barn owl and the long-eared owl; grey herons, duck and other water birds inhabit Lago Gurrida, the only stretch of water in the mountainous area around Etna. Areas of dense woodland are home to many species of woodland species, such as various species of tit and the common cuckoo. Finally, mushrooms, rare flowers, reptiles, little-known insects and small mammals all add their charm to this strange environment, admired for more than two centuries by travelers on the Grand Tour, possibly the best-known being Goethe and the Englishman, Patrick Brydone.

Ascending the volcano

The **Strada dell'Etna** is the simplest way to ascend the volcano. Leaving Catania by the Via Etnea, follow directions for **Gravina di Catania** and **Nicolosi**, seat of the *Etna Vulcanological Museum*, the

base of the Parco dell'Etna. Nearby is the **Astrophysical Observatory of the Università of Catania** and the *Nuova Gussonea Botanical Garden*, then continue on foot or with an off-road vehicle to the *Torre del Filosofo*.

Gurrida Path

Of all the walks in the park, the Sentiero Gurrida deserves a special mention. The fact that there are no architectural barriers means that everyone can enjoy the experience.

Suitable for visitors in wheelchairs or on foot, the path winds along for 1.5 km beside Lake Gurrida. A wooden walk-way follows the edge of the lake (dry in summer) and then continues to the bank of the artificial pool where, two specially-built observation huts (with wheelchair access) enable visitors to birdwatch or enjoy photography. The path starts and finishes at the wine-cellar of an old farm, where visitors can taste and purchase local products.

Etna, birchwoods in autumn. Top and left: pictures of the volcano in action.

DISCOVERING SICILY'S FINEST BEACHES

Sicily is the largest island in the Mediterranean and has almost 1,500 kilometers of coast-line. The territory of Sicily includes the Island of Ustica, the archipelagoes of the Eolian Islands, the Egadi Islands and the Pelagian Islands (with the islands of Lampedusa and Linosa) and the Island of Pantelleria. In the north and east, the Sicilian coast is high and indented, where the rocks run down to the sea, resulting in a series of promontories inter-laced with bays and small flood-plains which make the coast flatter and more sandy. In the west of the island, this uniformity can also be seen in some of the less indented bays. The following is a list of the best beaches for tourists to visit, starting at Messina and traveling in an anti-clockwise direction.

Beach of the Santuario

(Province of Messina) The beach is at Capo Milazzo, north of Messina, near the sanctuary of the same name. The beach is an isolated area of rocks overlooking the deep blue water. You can get there by car or by bus from Milazzo. When you get there, you walk down the hill to the sanctuary, which is full of old votive offerings. Beyond it, a path leads down to the sea.

Marinello Beach

(Province of Messina) This beach is located in the municipality of Patti and deserves special mention because of its vast sandy shore which stretches east for approximately 2 km. It is situated below the imposing headland that was once the site of ancient Tyndaris, with a series of rock-pools of ever-changing shape, in a beautiful and unspoiled natural environment. Because of their environmental importance, the beach and the rock pools of Marinello have been designated a "Riserva Naturale Orientata" (Special Nature Reserve). A few hundred meters west of here is the delightful, unspoiled beach of Valle Tindari, situated between the headlands of Mongiove (Monte Giove) and Tindari.

Capo Calavà Beach

(Province of Messina) Coming from Messina on the SS 113, you come first to Capo Schino and then to Capo Calavà, the bay of which is entirely occupied by a magnificent beach stretching from one headland to the next. Capo Calavà is 137 m high. On the seaward side, the cliff walls are almost vertical, dropping down to the level of the sea, where there are many caves with gravel or sandy floors. The beach is well preserved because, until now, it has benefited from the supply of sand coming from the erosion of Gioiosa Marea beach just west of it. To reach the beach, you can catch a train (either from Palermo or Messina) and alight at the station of Gioiosa Marea. Coming by car, leave the highway at the Brolo turn-off, then follow the SS 113 for about 8 km in the direction of Messina. You can park on the road and walk down the steep paths leading to the beach. The most beautiful stretch of the beach is still in its natural state. It extends beyond the cape towards Messina and is covered with pebbles.

Testa di Monaco Beach

(Province of Messina) If you continue along this section of the coast, you will come to the long sandy beach which

stretches from Brolo towards Testa di Monaco, which you can reach by following the SS 113 west. Before you reach Capo d'Orlando, there are many paths leading down through the citrus groves to the beach, which is several kilometers long. The easiest path down to the sea runs parallel with the left-hand side of the River Naso. Leave the car on the road and walk down to the beach on foot.

San Gregorio Beach

(Province of Messina) Today, the beach of San Gregorio is the most varied section of all the coast around Capo d'Orlando, full of small ravines and inlets. Before you get to Capo d'Orlando, on the eastern slopes of the headland, you will see a tiny salt-water lake formed by the accumulation of sand. The beach was formed in the 1960s behind a jetty built for a harbor project that was never completed. To reach the beach from Messina, follow the A 20, leave the highway at Brolo and continue west along the coast, or take the SS 113. The beach is well sign-posted.

Pollina Beach

(Province of Messina) The whole coast

from Patti Marina to Cefalù is spectacular. State highway 113, which follows the coastline slightly higher up, runs along very close to this beach, where long sandy stretches alternate with pebbles. Various lanes and good paths lead down onto the beach.
At Pollina, park in the large car park on the right before the town of Finale di Pollina. A path leads down to the beach from the left-hand side of the car park, past some imaginative graffiti.

Lido di Cefalù

(Province of Palermo) Although often crowded, the Lido di Cefalù deserves a mention because of its beautiful beach and enchanting views. To the east lies the old harbor of Cefalù, dominated by the castle and the Norman cathedral. You can see the older part of the town higher up, towards the crag. To the west is Santa Lucia, where there is a cave, but, sadly, the water there has been polluted for some time. The beach at Cefalù is very long and is famous for its lovely fine white sand. There is only one official bathing establishment on the beach, the rest being free for the public to use. When you get to Cefalù, leave the car in a car park.

Cala Gallo

(Province of Palermo) The bay lies north-west of Palermo, on a rocky, north-facing part of the coast. Behind it is the splendid reserve of Monte Gallo, its lush Mediterranean vegetation and garrigue dotted with giant fennel, euphorbia, almond and carob trees providing a green lung for the area. This is one of the few sections of coast near Palermo which still has clean water. Although the coast is owned by the State, the area behind it is all privately owned. Access to the sea is therefore forbidden (although a sentence issued by the Supreme Court of Appeal in March 2001 forbids this practice) unless you are prepared to pay a fee to go through a gate. Once you reach the rocks, the greenish-blue water is crystal-clear. The landscape, which was recently designated as a Marine Nature Reserve, consists of at least 3 km of wild coastline.

Sferracavallo Beach

(Province of Palermo) This is an old fishing village, built on the sea where there is still a beautiful beach with sand and rocks. Unfortunately, today, the area has been spoiled by modern building and the sea water is no longer clean, due to effluent. All of which has ruined a marine environment which was once regarded as one of the most beautiful in western Sicily. To reach it from Palermo, take the ring-road as far as Tommaso Natale. From here simply follow signs for Sferracavallo.

Capaci Beach

(Province of Palermo) Also called "Tien An Men Beach", this beach is low-key compared to the most beautiful beaches on the island. Yet it has something to offer since it still has a stretch of fine white sand that is open to the public, albeit surrounded by bathing establishments which have altered the original natural environment of blue water, sand and reed-beds. The only surviving stretch of public beach was dedicated to the square in Beijing where, at that time, people were endeavoring to recover even more important areas of public liberty. To reach Tien An Men beach from Palermo (about 20 km away), take the A 29 in the direction of Trapani and leave the highway at the turning to Capaci. In fact, the highway follows the line of the coast here and, once you have turned off it, just follow the signs to the town of Capaci to find access-points leading down to the sea.

Lo Zingaro Nature Reserve

(Province of Trapani) Follow the highway in the direction of Trapani to reach the beaches of Lo Zingaro, leaving the highway at the Castellammare del Golfo exit. From here, follow signs to the "Riserva Naturale dello Zingaro". The park has finally recovered after the disastrous fire of 1996, which almost destroyed it. When you reach the park, leave the vehicle in the large car park and ask at the information center (where people are eager to help) for a map showing the footpaths of the area. Dogs or other pets must be left in the cages provided at the gate. In fact, the wild animals living in the reserve must not come into contact with their domestic counterparts. Special picnic areas with barbecue facilities are provided near the footpaths within the park. To reach the delightful little bays dotted around the reserve, take one of the steep paths (all of medium difficulty) leading down to the sea.

Beaches of San Vito lo Capo

(Province of Trapani) It is not easy to access these beaches, but they are worth visiting. They are close to Castellammare del Golfo as the crow flies, but the road to reach them is full of bends and, therefore, is not only uncomfortable for the passengers but takes some time. From Castellammare del Golfo, take the SS 187 in the

Mediterranean vegetation and the sea off the Lo Zingaro Nature Reserve

The splendid colors of the beach at San Vito lo Capo

reached on foot or with an off-road vehicle. The splendid long beach at Capo Feto is preserved by a protected area edged with Mediterranean maquis and marshy land. To get there, follow the sandy track which starts at the end of the tarmac road of Tonnarella, to the west of Mazara del Vallo.

Cala dei Turchi

(Province of Trapani) This beach of rocks and sand is tucked away in the Cala dei Turchi ("Turks' Bay"), a tufa inlet with many smooth rocks, where Arab pirates are supposed to have disembarked when raiding this part of Sicily. To reach it, follow the coast-road between Mazara del Vallo and Torretta di Capo Granitola and stop just before the lookout tower.

River Belice Special Nature Reserve

(Province of Trapani) This reserve lies approximately 12 km from Castelvetrano. In the 1970s, numerous attempts were made to divide the land into lots. Now it is a protected area. In 1984, the administration of the reserve was transferred from the Sicily Regional Council to the Trapani Provincial Council. The final section of the River Belice is an important stopover for birds on migration and the many species which come here to breed, thanks to the wetland and its lush vegetation. Along the coast, the sand dunes provide the ideal habitat for a few typical species of flowers and wild animals. The reserve, which is approximately 4 km long and is bisected by a disused railway line, is situated between Marina di Selinunte and the headland of Porto Palo. It covers an area of 214 hectares. The western end of the beach has splendid dunes which gradually give way to a limestone ridge with Mediterranean maquis to the east. The sea is almost always calm, the water is shallow and has a sandy bottom, making it ideal for children. To get there by car, take the Palermo-Mazara del Vallo highway (A 29) and turn off at Castelvetrano. Now follow signs for Selinunte, until you come to the turn-off for the old road to Agrigento. A little further on, on the left, two ancient tufa columns mark the

direction of Erice, and, after a few kilometers, turn north (right) and keep following signs for San Vito. Several more kilometers of wiggly roads eventually lead to your destination. It is truly worth the journey. The long beach, situated in the town, has beautifully clean water. Instead of sand, there is a carpet of tiny shells. Don't be put off by the areas of beach taken over by the hotels, which are some of the finest in the area. In fact, there are still long stretches of open beach which can also be reached from the beach of Lo Zingaro by a path through the Nature Reserve (time taken about 2 hours on foot).

Punta Tramontana Beach

(Province of Trapani) The beach lies at the northern end of the Stagnone di Marsala, a shallow lagoon sheltering a coastline of great environmental importance. You can access the sandy beach from the SS 115, between Marsala and Trapani, turning off at Birgi. Follow the tarmac road next to the Birgi Cantina Sociale (winery) to the end, then turn off along a road that runs round the edge of the salt-pans to the beach, situated on the tip of the headland.

Capo Feto

(Province of Trapani) This wild beach near Mazara del Vallo can only be

The River Belice estuary, now a nature reserve

beginning of a lane suitable for cars that leads almost to the mouth of the river. You can reach the beach by crossing the disused railway track.

Capo San Marco

(Province of Agrigento) The cape lies 7 km west of Sciacca. The predominant color here is yellow, due to the unusual hue emanating from the hills around the bay, the same color that illuminates the valley of Agrigento, afflicted by the results of illegal building speculation. In fact, the temples and the other architectural remains of the ancient city were built using stone from these very hills. To reach the sea, leave the car on the main road at Baia Renella and continue on foot along a path lined with palms and euphorbias. You can thus access the small inlets where the yellow calcarenite gives way to fairly rough sand. From the beach you can see Capo Bianco to the east and Capo Granitola to the west. From the shoreline, the sea-floor shelves steeply. This is a sort of natural paradise for sub-aqcua divers who come in search of rocks with luxuriant marine vegetation teeming with fish. Beyond the promontory is Sciacca beach, with all kinds of facilities, highly recommended to families with children, and surfers.

Borgo Bonsignore - Mouth of the River Platani

(Province of Agrigento) An enchanting sandy beach, almost 4 km long, bordered by a low coastline consisting of the alluvial deposits from the River Platani. The beach has broad stretches of golden sand edged with lines of dunes. This is a place where nature and

history blend. In fact, not only is the mouth of the river of great environmental importance, but it is also of great historical value. The area is now a nature reserve. On the headland above the left bank of the River Platani is the archeological site of the ancient city of Eraclea Minoa, founded by Greek colonists in the 6th century BC . To reach the beach, take the SS 115 and follow signs for Borgo Bonsignore.

Eraclea Minoa (Capo Bianco)

(Province of Agrigento) A wonderful sandy beach more than 5 km long, with several lines of dunes, overhung by cliffs, set on "trubi" (a typical local white sedimentary rock) and on shelves of chalk containing large crystals. The combination of the broad expanse of golden beach, with a thick wood behind the dunes, protected by the splendid white cliffs of "trubi" and gray chalk, makes the beach quite unique. From the SS 115, follow the signs for Eraclea Minoa and Capo Bianco.

Beaches of Torre Salsa

(Province of Agrigento) This is an area of great environmental importance and is now protected, having been designated as a nature reserve. Here, various ecosystems overlap and arable and animal farming are still practiced using traditional methods. The beaches are sandy and approximately 4 km long. Some are narrow and fringed with splendid white cliffs set on "trubi" (calcareous marl), others are broad and edged with lines of dunes covered with the typical natural vegetation of coastal environments. There are marvelous contrasts of color here: the dazzling white of the "trubi", the deep blue of the sea, interrupted here and there by the black of the fields of posidonia (sea-grass), the golden yellow of the beaches and the green of the vegetation. At sunset, the white cliffs are tinged with red and, at low tide, unusual light effects are created when the tops of the "trubi" emerge at the bottom of the cliffs. The name of the area derives from the ruins of an old lookout tower dating from about 1500.

Gelonardo

(Province of Agrigento) This is a beautiful long beach with fine sand situated east of the town of Siculiana Marina. Behind the areas of golden sand are cliffs formed of alternating white chalk and gray marl formations. Since the rock contains large chalk crystals, they flash constantly (Sicilian miners used to call this kind of chalk "specchiolino", meaning little mirror) creating interesting light effects. There is nothing more pleasant than walking along this beach next to the cliff under a blue sky watching the light being reflected off the water.

Pergole - Torre di Monterosso

(Province of Agrigento) This section of coast lies between Siculiana Marina and Realmonte. It consists of small sandy bays sheltering below cliffs, separated from each other by little headlands shaped by the sea and the wind. Here you can see the same yellow sandstone that was used to build the famous Doric temples of Agrigento. If you can, walk here at sunset, when the sandstone is tinged with wonderful nuances of gold.

Scala dei Turchi

(Province of Agrigento) This is a real gem of the coast around Agrigento. It is easy to recognize, since it consist of a white promontory which has been carved by the sea and the wind into a stair-like shape, hence its name (the "Turks' Stair"). The beaches lying to the east and west of the promontory are delightful, with their golden sand and white cliffs behind. For a truly thrilling experience, try to go there on a night with a full moon.

Punta Bianca - Monte Grande

(Province of Agrigento) This is the promontory marking the east end of the bay of Agrigento and, like Scala dei Turchi, is formed of white calcareous rock. The coast is dotted with small inlets with beaches of sand or pebbles, separated by little headlands. Along the slopes of Monte Grande, near the coast, there is evidence of sulfur mining, an activity which goes back many centuries, and for which Sicily was once famous. There is a particularly charming bay next to Castello di Palma in the area known as Capreria. There are plans to make this area into a nature reserve because of its natural beauty and the species of flora and fauna present in this habitat.

Castellazzo di Palma

(Province of Agrigento) This is an especially wild section of coastline halfway between Agrigento and Licata. The high coast features peaks of calcareous rock and chalk and, in some places, it is possible to get down to beautiful little bays with pebble beaches. You can reach this section of the coast by taking the SS 115 and following signs for Marina di Palma.

Punta Braccetto

(Province of Ragusa) Following the coast south-east from Scoglitti, you come to Punta Braccetto, a few kilometers away from Marina di Ragusa. Here there are two quiet little beaches, one on the left-hand side and the other on the right-hand side of the point. The last section of the access road is a dirt track. If, on the other hand

ITINERARIES

121

you head west from Scoglitti in the direction of Gela, you come to an area where the land directly behind the beaches has been taken over by greenhouses, however, there are still some points of access to beautiful, isolated stretches of beach.

Irminio Estuary Nature Reserve

(Province of Ragusa) The section of the coast between Marina di Ragusa and Punta Corvo, ending with the protected area near Sampieri, is the part which has been most altered by human intervention. It includes the beaches (and the little towns of the same name) of Donnalucata, Cava D'Aliga, Bruca and Arizza. These are worth avoiding unless you are able to visit them in the months of June

or September. About 4 km west of Donnalucata is the village of Plaia Grande, where there is a beautiful beach, but it is now dominated by a car park and various facilities. Just beyond it, on the same stretch of sand, you come to the "Macchia Foresta del fiume Irminio" Nature Reserve, which preserves intact an area of habitat of Mediterranean maquis and the sand-dune structure hundreds of years old. The only problem is that, on the reserve, swimming is forbidden.

Costa di Carro

(Province of Ragusa) Before you reach Sampieri, there is a stretch of unspoiled coastline including the little beach known as "Costa di Carro". The loggerhead turtle (Caretta caretta) still regards this habitat, with its typical dune vegetation, as ideal for laying its eggs. There is no car park in this area and, in order to reach the sea, you must leave the car by the road and follow the footpath leading down to the beach. Beyond the beach is a narrow coastal strip about 4 km long with typical Mediterranean vegetation,

including agave and the dwarf palm. The whole area is restricted but there is free public access. We recommend you avoid the central part of the beach (about 2 km from Costa di Carro), where the sewer from the town of Sampieri enters the sea.

Sampieri Beach

(Province of Ragusa) The territory of Scicli, which includes about 20 km of coastline, does not have many long stretches of unspoiled beaches owing to the high density of greenhouse cultivation in the area. Often the view is dominated by the plastic used to cover crops or the shiny roofs of the glasshouses. Few areas still have a natural habitat, although the beaches are still all accessible to the public. The little town of Marina di Modica is preceded by the lovely Sampieri Beach which, protected by a small area of forest, still has part of its original dune-structure and typical vegetation. At one end of the beach is the burnt ruin of a factory, an interesting piece of industrial archeology. A new holiday camp has altered the habitat around a small marsh next to the beach. It is situated next to the small town of the same name where there are car parks and tourist facilities.

Maganuco Beach

(Province of Ragusa) This area is targeted by large numbers of tourists and finding a stretch of isolated beach is virtually impossible. However, the high dunes of the beach at Maganuco are splendid to see, formed by a wind which often blows the sand up onto the road. It's 800 m long and 100 m wide and is only 2 km from the road between Sampieri and Pozzallo.

Santa Maria di Focallo Beach

(Province of Ragusa) The beaches in the Province of Ragusa are longer than those in the Province of Siracusa (Siracusa). However, the sea is rougher (we are now in the channel called the Stretto di Sicilia) and the sand is much rougher, so much so that the fisherman can drive across it with their vehicles. Some stretches of the long beach at Santa Maria di Focallo (7 km) are quite interesting, with their dunes and rich Mediterranean maquis vegetation. To get there, stop at one of the access-points on the coast road between km 6 and km 8, right opposite Isola dei Porri ("Leek Island").

Spiaggia delle Formiche ("Ant Beach") - Amber Coast

(Province of Siracusa) The beach links three little bays, dotted with headlands and caves. Although the best way to approach it is by boat, you can also get there by car. Follow the road that goes from Pachino or Porto Palo to Maucini. At Maucini, continue along the dirt road towards the Costa dell'Ambra. The total distance is approximately 7.5 km. The bays have a sandy bottom and there are some interesting caves to explore.

Isola delle Correnti Beach

(Province of Siracusa) We are at the southernmost tip of Sicily, even further south than Tunis or Algiers. It's also one of the most windy places on the island and a great attraction to surfers, who come here to enjoy the sea currents and

the winds caused by the meeting of the Canale di Sicilia and the Ionian Sea. The "isola" (island) is actually a promontory, connected to the mainland by a narrow neck of land which is usually submerged. The beaches lying to the east and west of the promontory are fringed with lines of dunes. You can get there from Pachino and Porto Palo by following signs for Isola delle Correnti.

Marzamemi Beach

(Province of Siracusa) The name comes from the Arabic Marsa el Hamem, meaning "harbor of doves", because it lies on a migration route used by birds flying between North Africa and Sicily. The splendid beach to the north of the town of Marzamemi ends with the promontory of Punta Bove Marino, a habitat of the monk seal until the 1950s. The town is worth stopping at, too. It's a small fishing town with a tuna fishery and a little market where you can buy all the delicious specialties made at the local tuna processing plant, ranging from "bottarga" (a strong paste made with tuna roe) to "lattume" (tuna sperm).

Vendicari Beach

(Province of Siracusa) Perhaps one of Sicily's most beautiful beaches, on a nature reserve dominated by a Swabian tower and the ruins of a tuna fishery. It lies on the road between Pachino and Noto, in a section of the coast which has been successfully preserved, thanks to moves to protect a wetland which hosts large populations of flamingoes. This spotless beach is on a par with those in the Caribbean. The thick Mediterranean maquis vegetation also provides shelter from the heat.

Cala Mosche ("Fly Bay")

(Province of Siracusa) If you ask people for directions for Cala Mosche, you are unlikely to find anyone who can help you. In fact, as far as the locals are concerned, this little bay between Vendicari and Noto is called "Funni Musca". To get there, you follow the provincial highway from Pachino towards Noto and, after 6 km, take the dirt road which crosses an old railway line. After about 1.5 km you come to the gate of the

Forestry Commission, who look after the Riserva Naturale di Vendicari. From here, continue for another kilometer on the dirt road and along a path through dwarf palms. When you reach the beach, it is a strip of sand at least 200m long hugged between two rocky promontories dotted with caves and inlets. Behind the dunes is a wetland used by birds on migration. No boats - not even canoes - are allowed to land here.

Do 'Iancu Beach

(Province of Siracusa) About 1 km north of Cala Mosche is the beach known as "Do 'Iancu", which is very isolated and, for this reason, was once much frequented by nudists. You can get there on foot by following a path starting at the mouth of the River Tellaro. Start at Lido di Noto and follow signs for Eloro (Helorus), a Greek city founded in the 6th century BC. Leave the car near the archeological site, cross the river and continue on foot for about 2.5 km along the only track. You'll find the beach at the end of the path: approximately 600 m of dunes and Mediterranean maquis.

Gallina Beach

(Province of Siracusa) This beach is also part of a nature reserve which protects the mouth of the River Cassibile. Until the 1980s, the river had a reputation for containing pure drinking water from the source to its mouth. This land used to belong to the Marquis of Cassibile, who prevented it from being broken up into lots for the purposes of speculation. The beach, about 500 m long, is unique because of the vast pine-forest which protects the lines of sand-dunes. At each end of the beach is a rocky promontory with steep cliffs, natural rock arches and caves.

Fontane Bianche Beach

(Province of Siracusa) 15 km south of Siracusa, near the town of Cassibile, is a beach with 3 km of beautiful white sand reminiscent of beaches in the Caribbean. The water is crystal-clear and part of the beach is open to the public and part taken over by bathing establishments. However, the concentration of discos, hotels and camp-sites along the road detracts from

its charm. Although there is no danger of getting away from it all here, it's worth stopping just to admire what was once a lovely beauty-spot.

Punta Asparano

(Province of Siracusa) Despite the relentless expansion of tourist facilities in the area, this small section (about 1 km) of headlands and bays, with little beaches tucked between ravines, crystal-clear water and vast fields of posidonia (sea-grass) which almost reach the shore, has survived. On the headlands are the last patches of Mediterranean maquis and dwarf palms. To get there, set off on the provincial highway from Siracusa in the direction of Fontane Bianche, and turn off at Ognina, where there is a little fishing harbor unusually situated in a fjord.

Maddalena Peninsula

(Province of Siracusa) To reach the Maddalena Peninsula, drive south from Siracusa for a short distance on la SS 115 and turn off at the junction towards Faro Carrozzieri (lighthouse). When you reach the office of the Guardia di Finanza (Financial Police), turn towards Punta Mole. Here, you must leave the car and proceed on foot for about 3 km along the only footpath, along the top of a cliff. Finally you reach the inlet, with steep cliffs dropping down to the sea and dominated by a cave (Grotta del Pellegrino) which is about 300 m deep. There are plans to make the area of sea off the peninsula into a marine nature reserve.

Agnone Beach

(Province of Siracusa) This beach is situated in the territory of Augusta, about 40 km north of Siracusa. Part of the beach is open to the public, while the rest is occupied by bathing establishments. To get there, follow the SS 114 east-coast road and turn off at the sign for Lentini-Agnone Bagni. When you get there, you will see a long stretch of rough, dark sand about 8 km long, fringed with eucalyptus trees. The water is clean, but the coast, once dotted with citrus groves, has been transformed by illegal building speculation, except in the few areas which have been re-planted with trees.

River Simeto Estuary

(Province of Catania) The mouth of the River Simeto, a few kilometers south of Catania, has a beach of white sand which extends into the nature reserve bearing its name. It can be reached by following the state highway from Augusta towards Catania. You will see the signs for the "Oasi di Simeto" before reaching Catania. You must leave the car and follow a footpath which follows the riverbank. To the north and south of the Simeto estuary there are long, sandy beaches which belong to the "Oasi del Simeto" Nature Reserve. Swimming is forbidden in many sections of the beach,

Bathing establishments at La Plàia

because of serious pollution (the sewer of Catania enters the sea here!) and for other reasons associated with environmental protection. The coast is interesting from an environmental point of view because of its wetlands, vital to many species of birds for breeding and on passage, and because of its stretches of well-preserved dunes. However, unfortunately, the area is a target of extensive illegal building speculation, against which the measures taken by the local council have hitherto proved to be ineffective. The entrance to the nature reserve is on the SS 114, north of the bridge over the River Simeto.

La Plàia

(Province of Catania) To reach this beach on the outskirts of Catania, take the SS 114 north and follow signs to the sea (Il

Mare). La Playa is the traditional city beach, recently the subject of controversial development plans for new hotels and sporting facilities. The beach is almost entirely occupied by bathing establishments, but there are also three areas of public beach administered by the city council. The land on the opposite side of the coast road from the sea is in serious danger of being transformed by building contractors. Land which was formerly cultivated and is in the process of spontaneous re-naturalization, is now threatened by plans to develop the area with new holiday camps and sporting facilities, involving a total of more than 200 hectares.

Costa della Timpa (Timpa Ridge) and Mulino Beach at Santa Maria La Scala

(Province of Catania) The rocky Timpa Ridge is part of a nature reserve and covered with dense Mediterranean maquis vegetation and citrus groves. The ridge, which can be reached by some quite difficult paths, is rocky and swimming is not always easy. In the town of Santa Maria La Scala, in the municipality of Acireale, there is a small sandy beach at the end of the coast road which leads to an old mill, now converted into a restaurant. There is a natural spring on the beach, the River Aci, dear to classical mythology. Sadly, the spring is now polluted by the local sewer and the water is no longer suitable for drinking.

Praiola Beach and the Chiancone area

(Province of Catania) The coastal area of "Chiancone", in the municipality of Giarre, is a vast area used for citrus cultivation, traversed by rivers with vegetation on their banks. There is only one road leading to Praiola Beach, where the coast has sadly been ruined by recent building. The beach of volcanic sand is edged by a very scenic tufa ridge.

San Marco Beach at Calatabiano, and the beaches at Fiumefreddo and Mascali

(Province of Catania) The area of the coast south of the mouth of the River Alcantara has a broad beach several kilometers long with sand and pebbles. The land behind it has been replanted with eucalyptus and acacias.

Development along the coast is still fairly limited (there is a small holiday camp at San Marco, and a paper factory at Fiumefreddo) and citrus groves and fields of crops run down to the edge of the beach. This part of the coast is important from an environmental point of view because it has many springs and water courses with extremely cold water, providing the ideal habitat for acquatic plants of particular importance.

TONNARE: AN ANCIENT TRADITION

The word *tonnara* (tuna fishery, pl. *tonnare*) refers to the complex of rectangular nets through which the tuna fish are guided once they have been captured, but also applies to the buildings on the coast where the tuna is processed and stored. During the 16th century, in the area around Trapani, there used to be eight tuna fisheries. Today, only two are still functioning, at the island of Favignana and at Bonagìa, just north of Trapani, where, between May and June, the ritual killing of the tuna known as the *mattanza* still takes place.

Not much remains of the old tuna fisheries: a few distinctive protection towers and the buildings and warehouses where the tuna is processed and stored and the equipment used for catching the tuna is kept. Some of these buildings have been converted into state-of-the-art "Maritime museums", whereas others have been turned into tourist accommodation. The finest tuna fisheries in Sicily were located on the stretch of coast between Castellammare del Golfo and just beyond Mazara del Vallo. Just beyond Castellammare is the perfectly preserved tuna fishery of Scopello, protected by two lookout towers. If we proceed further along the coast of the Lo Zingaro Nature Reserve, we come to the Tonnarella dell'Uzzo, which operated until the end of the 19th century. The nets of the Seco or Sevo tuna fishery were lowered offshore from the tip of the Lo Zingaro reserve. You can still see the remains of the considerable land complex associated with it: a factory where the tuna was processed, the owner's house, the garden, a chapel and the Sciere Tower. Towards San Vito Lo Capo you can see the Torrazzo Tower, which is still in good condition. In the bay of Còfano, where tuna fishing has been practiced since the 15th century, only one tower is still standing. Bonagìa was the land-base of one of the tonnare with a reputation for bringing in the largest catch.

The extensive buildings have now been converted into a hotel and other tourist facilities. However, the original structure has been preserved, even its tower which dates from 1626. Immediately beyond Bonagìa lay the tuna fishery of San Cusumano. The buildings are now an industrial complex for processing tuna. Nearby is the tuna fishery of San Giuliano, of which the old factories and one small tower are still standing. Heading out towards the Ègadi Islands, we come to the tuna fishery of Formica, which once caught huge quantities of tuna, the land-complex of which has been converted for other uses. Between Trapani and Mazara del Vallo there are numerous tonnare which have been abandoned: Nubia, Boeo, and Santa Maria la Nuova or Canonizzo, the small tuna fishery of Mazara and, beyond Granitola Point, the tonnara of Tre Fontane.

The tuna fishery at Scopello with the picturesque rocks known as the *faraglioni*

PARCO DELL'ETNA

M. Spagnolo 1547
Caserma
Grotta delle Palombe
Linguaglossa, Taormina
Rifugio di M. S. Maria
Grotta dei Lamponi
Caserma Pitarrone
Rifugio Brunek
M. Maletto 1773
Grotta del Gelo
Rif. M. Maletto
Grotta delle Vanette
M. Scavo 1785
Rifugio M. Scavo
Monte Etna (Mongibello)
Rifugio Cifelli
Poggio La Caccia 1904
Cratere Centrale 3323
Rifugio di M. Palestra
M. Palestra 2020
Rifugio d. Galvarina
Valle del Bove
Milo
Rifugio Forestale
Rifugio Sapienza
Zafferana Etnea
Giardino Botanico
Gr. Albergo del Parco
Catania
Catania

chilometri 0 2 4

Key to symbols

- Point of departure and arrival
- Stop en route
- *i* Tourist Information Office
- Train station
- Castle
- Tower
- Church
- Refuge
- Viewpoint
- Spring
- Ancient monuments, ruins
- Cave
- Beach

ROUTE 40KM: RIFUGIO BRUNEK - PASSO DEI DAMMUSI - RIFUGIO DI MONTE SANTA MARIA - RUINED BARRACKS - RIFUGIO DI MONTE SCAVO - PASSO MONTE PALESTRA - GALVARINA PLATEAU - RIFUGIO SAPIENZA. ON DIRT ROADS ON THE SOUTH SLOPE WITH CONSIDERABLE SECTIONS OF UPHILL AND DOWNHILL.

THE STARTING-POINT OF THE ROUTE CAN BE REACHED BY LEAVING THE A18 MESSINA-CATANIA MOTORWAY AT THE FIUMEFREDDO JUNCTION, TAKING THE SP 92 TO LINGUAGLOSSA, THEN TURNING LEFT UP THE MARENEVE ROAD.

FROM RIFUGIO SAPIENZA YOU CAN RETURN TO THE RIFUGIO BRUNEK ON TARMAC, PASSING THE TOWNS OF ZAFFERANA ETNEA AND MILO (42 KM).

DIFFICULTY: FOR SOME SECTIONS YOU MUST BE FAMILIAR WITH USING A MTB; THE ROUTE IS FAIRLY DEMANDING AND REQUIRES A HIGH LEVEL OF FITNESS.

BIKE SERVICE AND INFORMATION

LE DUE RUOTE, F. SALVATORE, VIA N. MARTOGLIO 93/M, SANTA VENERINA.

SALVATRICE CARCATIZZO, VIA ROMA 265 A/B, BELPASSO, TEL. 0957912802, 0957912577.

TOURIST INFORMATION

TOURIST INFORMATION OFFICE, CATANIA, VIA CIMAROSA 10, TEL. 0957306211; LINGUAGLOSSA, PIAZZA

ANNUNZIATA 7, TEL. 095643094; NICOLOSI, VIA GARIBALDI 63, TEL. 095911505.

PARCO DELL'ETNA OFFICE, VIA ETNEA 107, NICOLOSI, TEL. 095821111.

WEB

WWW.PARCOETNA.IT

OTHER USEFUL CONTACTS

ETNA FREE BIKE MTB CLUB, VIA LANZEROTTI 33, CATANIA, TEL. 3473554381, 368663031.

MUSEO VULCANOLOGICO, VIA BATTISTI 30, NICOLOSI, TEL. 095914722.

SOCCORSO ALPINO (MOUNTAIN RESCUE), TEL. 095914142.

Exploring the slopes of the volcano

The Parco dell'Etna was created in 1987 on Europe's largest volcano, Mount Etna, situated north-west of Catania.

For some years now, the volcano, which is more than 3,300 meters high, has been extremely active.

Take the Altomontana track from Rifugio Brunek, as far as the Pitarrone barracks, and keep left here. Pass an iron barrier, and continue to climb along a section where woods of beech and birch

127

alternate with older and more recent lava flows.

At the junction after 6km, turn left uphill (towards the Grotta del Gelo and Monte Spagnolo), then along a level section which goes through a pine-wood and across a bare slope of lava. A long straight section leads to some ripple-effect lava formations. Just beyond them, a sign points to the track leading off towards the Grotta dei Lamponi (Raspberry Cave).

The Altomontana track continues to the right towards the Passo dei Dammusi (1,710 m, after 8 km, wooden refuge), then re-enters the wood, also passing the Rifugio di Monte Santa Maria. The road descends to 1,450 m and, after 13 km, on a hairpin bend to the right, take the mule-track sign-posted (Riserva Integrale - Zona A), maintaining altitude and passing through a recent lava flow. Having re-joined the Altomontana track, you pass through a beech-wood and the ruins of the small barracks of Monte Spagnolo. Then the road heads south along the volcano's vast western slope. After 17 km, go through a wooden gate and continue through the oak forest, heading straight towards Monte Maletto, which lies on your left, as does the refuge of the same name.

Having emerged from the pine-forest onto a vast lava field at the bottom of the smooth, black slope of Bronte, continue towards Rifugio Monte Scavo which, like the others, has no warden running it but is open. Passing round to the right of the hill called La Caccia, you pass Rifugio Monte Palestra and climb up to the pass of the same name (1,985 m), the highest point on this route. From here, as you descend past clearings and spectacular larches to the Rifugio della Galvarina, you then cross the Galvarina plateau. Continue down through the splendid and highly-perfumed larch-wood, and, after 33 km, re-join the tarmac. Keep right until you come to the large green forestry gate across the road. Beyond the gate, turn left, and continue uphill until you reach the junction with the SP 92 from Nicolosi which goes up to the Rifugio Sapienza, where you can either stop or continue on tarmac along the eastern side of the volcano to Rifugio Brunek.

THE ISLAND OF PANTELLERIA

ROUTE 34 KM: PANTELLERIA - SESI NECROPOLISES - GROTTA DI SATERIA (CAVE) - SCAURI - REKHALE - TRACINO - KHAMMA - CALA CINQUE DENTI - CAMPOBELLO - PANTELLERIA. ALONG ROADS SUITABLE FOR A MTB OR A RACING BIKE WITH GOOD GEARS.

DIFFICULTY: A ROUTE WITH FREQUENT ALTERNATING UPHILL AND DOWNHILL SECTIONS. THE DOWNHILL SECTION ON THE PAVED ROAD AFTER THE SERRAGLIO ALLA GHIRLANDA PASS IS QUITE DEMANDING.

BIKE + FERRY/PLANE

BY SEA: (FERRIES AND HYDROFOILS TO PANTELLERIA LEAVE FROM TRAPANI) SIREMAR, TEL. 199123199 OR 0923911120; USTICA LINES TEL. 0923873813

BY AIR: PANTELLERIA AIRPORT, TEL. 0923911172.

BIKE SERVICE AND INFORMATION: POLICARDO, VIA MESSINA 31, PANTELLERIA, TEL. 0923912844, 0923911741. BIKE HIRE (ALSO CAR- AND MOTORCYCLE-HIRE).

USEFUL CONTACTS AND TOURIST INFORMATION

PRO LOCO, PIAZZA CAVOUR, PANTELLERIA, TEL. 0923911838, WWW.PANTELLERIA.IT/PROLOCO

AGENZIA GIRA L'ISOLA, VICOLO MESSINA 21, PANTELLERIA, TEL. AND FAX 0923913254, WWW.PANTELLERIATRAVEL.CO/AGENZIAGIRALISOLA

In the Mediterranean, land of "dammusi" and hot springs

Set in the cobalt-blue heart of the Mediterranean, life in Pantelleria is

Isola di Pantelleria

Pantelleria
Campobello
Cala Cinque Denti
Punta Spadillo
Kattibugal/Denti
Lago di Venere
Lave del Khaggiar
Necropoli neolitica dei Sesi
San Vito
Bugeber
Bonsulton
Cufira
Contrada Tihirriki
Khamma
Mueggen
Tracino
Sibà
Montagna Grande ▲ 830
Sateria
Monte Gibele ▲ 700
Tanche
Piano di Ghirlanda
Scauri
le Favare
Rekhale
Passo del Serraglio

0   1,5   3
chilometri
Balata d. Turchi

the left marks the road to the "Favare" (geysers) and Monte Gibele. Continue to pedal downhill on the other side of the pass along the road which, after a while, becomes paved and more demanding. Approx. 1 km beyond the pass you come to an obvious bend near a "dammuso" (typical island house) built close to the rock behind on the right. On one side, areas of terracing ("tanche") are surrounded by a small holm-oak wood. Leaving the bike, walk down through the terraces to the Byzantine rock-cut tombs (on the right).

sometimes hard but holds great potential for the tourist. Like its wines, its landscapes are not only spectacular but exhilarating.

The "dammusi" are the typical island houses. Leaving the harbor of Pantelleria, take the road that runs west along the sea-front (Via Borgo Italia) until you come to a crossroads. Go straight across it along a flat road which soon emerges from the town, following the coast. After approx. 2 km, the road climbs gradually and passes the neolithic necropolis called the "Sesi". On the left, a sign marks the road leading to the nearest necropolis of Sese Grande (a large stone neolithic multiple burial chamber). Continue along the the coast-road with uphill and downhill sections and, after approx. 5 km, at the bottom of a short downhill slope, on the right you will see steps leading down to the Grotta (cave) di Sateria, where you can swim in the water from the hot springs. Continue along the coast to (after 3 km) via a steep uphill section. Here the route leaves the coast-road. Past the center of the town there is a double junction. Turn left and then right following signs for Rekhale along a long, straight road with a slight uphill gradient. When you reach Rekhale, instead of going into the town, continue up the tarmac road to the col of Passo del Serraglio where a sign on

Once back in the saddle, continue along the road which loses height and then levels out as it crosses the Ghirlanda Plain, the most fertile part of the island. A short uphill section leads to the little village of Tracino. In Piazza Perugia, opposite the new church, turn right down a road that drops down towards the sea and, after approx. 100 m, take the first road on the left which crosses the village passing some old houses and then continues uphill to Khamma. Continue straight along this road for approx. 3 km, losing height very gradually, until you re-join the coast-road. Turn left and cycle through the magnificent lava landscape of Kaggiar and pass Cala Cinque Denti ("Five Teeth Bay"). From here, continue along the coast of the Kattibugal plain.

The road climbs again, with two hairpin bends, passing the sign on the left marking the road leading to the Lago di Venere (Lake of Venus), after which it begins to descend towards Campobello. After cycling downhill for 500 m, leave the coast-road and take a small road on the left (forbidden to heavy traffic) which continues in the same direction with a less steep gradient. Keep straight on, ignoring the signs to left and right. Finally you join a tarmac road where it curves to the left and, at the next junction, to the right, leading down into the center of Pantelleria.

PARCO DELLE MADONIE

Case di Mastro Peppino
Isnello
Pzo. Colla ▲ 1676
Monte Cervi 1600
1794 ▲
M. dei Cervi
M. Fanusi 1472
Portella Colla 1420
▲ Czo. di Castellazzo 1440
Casa Crisanti
Vallone San Nicola
C.T rapani
C.Bettini
Palermo, Cefalù
F. Fichera
R ovola
Donna Lavia
Rio Secco
Polizzi Generosa
Caltanissetta, Enna
chilometri
0 1 2

Start at Polizzi Generosa on the SP 119 (head for Piano Battaglia) which climbs slowly for the first 6 km, then more steeply for another 6 km, until it reaches the pass of Portella Colla (1,420 m). Here, leave the tarmac road and turn left onto a dirt track (No. 11), following signs for Rifugio di Monte Cervi and Case di Mastro Peppino. After 1.5 km, path No. 11 diverges from the road. Continue along the dirt track which climbs more slowly now until it re-joins the path again further ahead. Pedal uphill for 0.7 km, then downhill for 0.8 km then start to climb through a beautiful beech-wood to the pass of Rifugio Monte Cervi (1,600 m). Pedal along a good road with several uphill and downhill sections and, after 1.9 km, there is a beautiful view to the right over Isnello. On a fine day you can even see the archipelago of the Eolian Islands. Pedal on for 1.5 km down this stony but good track with wonderful views until you reach Case di Mastro Peppino. From here, keep left following a track that contours round half-way up the side of the mountain to the spectacular cleft in the rock where the dirt road begins to follow the ridge of Monte Fanusi (1,472 m). This is one of the most spectacular parts of the route. Having reached the end of the ridge, the track begins to lose height with a series of tight bends till it reaches Casa Crisanti (approx. 5 km), where you will see a typical Madonie shepherd's hut. Here, keep left (with the house still on your right) in the general direction of the mountain. After 4.2 km, go through the farmyard of the Ficile family (who make cheese). Shortly after the farm, keeping to the main road, you pass a group of rustic houses. Continue downhill until the road re-joins the tarmac and turn left towards Polizzi Generosa (9 km). The road climbs steadily but there are no steep sections.

ROUTE 40 KM (21 KM ON TARMAC + 19 KM ON DIRT ROAD): POLIZZI GENEROSA - PORTELLA COLLA - RIFUGIO MONTE CERVI - CASE DI MASTRO PEPPINO - CASA CRISANTI - POLIZZI GENEROSA. A MIXED ROUTE WHICH REQUIRES A MTB WITH GOOD SHOCK-ABSORBERS.

DIFFICULTY: FOR THIS ROUTE BIKERS NEED TO BE VERY FIT, SINCE THERE IS A HEIGHT GAIN OF 1,200 M. THE DESCENT TOWARDS CASA CRISANTI IS QUITE DEMANDING ON ACCOUNT OF THE STONY ROAD SURFACE.

BIKE SERVICE AND INFORMATION: BICI & MOTO SHOP, LARGO ZINGARI 10/11, POLIZZI GENEROSA, TEL. 3805034532, 3284020453. BIKE ACCESSORIES, GEARS, CLOTHING.

TOURIST INFORMATION

PARCO DELLE MADONIE, CORSO PAOLO AGLIATA 16, PETRALIA SOTTANA: TEL 0921684011, FAX 0921680478, WWW.PARCODELLEMADONIE.IT

CLUB ALPINO ITALIANO (OR CAI, THE ITALIAN ALPINE CLUB), POLIZZI GENEROSA LOCAL BRANCH, TEL. 0921688521, FAX 0921649314.

From Polizzi Generosa towards Monte Fanusi

Very fit bikers will enjoy the challenge of the roads and paths of this unspoiled area in the heart of the mountains of the Madonie National Park.

BETWEEN PALERMO AND TRAPANI

Capo S. Vito

0   2   4
chilometri

Golfo di
Castellammare

Riserva
Naturale
dello
Zingaro

Scopello

Visicari

Balata
di Baida

Castellammare
del Golfo

SS187

Buseto
Palizzolo

Terme di
Segesta

Palermo

Bruca

Segesta

ROUTE 70 KM: SCOPELLO - BAIA DI GIUDALOCA - TERME DI SEGESTA - BRUCA - BUSETO - BALATA DI BAIDA - VISICARI - SCOPELLO. ALL ON TARMAC ROADS.

DIFFICULTY: THE ROUTE REQUIRES BIKERS TO HAVE A BASIC LEVEL OF FITNESS. A ROAD BIKE OR GOOD TOURING BIKE IS RECOMMENDED.

BIKE + TRAIN: THE ROUTE CROSSES THE CASTELLAMMARE DEL GOLFO-TRAPANI RAILWAY LINE AT THE STATIONS OF SEGESTA AND BRUCA.

BIKE SERVICE AND INFORMATION: CICLOMANIA PIZZITOLA, CORSO G. MEDICI 41/A, ALCAMO, TEL. AND FAX 092426392.

TOURIST INFORMATION AND ORGANIZED BIKE TOURS

SICICLANDO, VIA M.T. CICERONE 19, BAGHERIA, TEL. AND FAX 091906086, WWW.SICICLANDO.COM. SPECIALIST TOUR OPERATOR WHICH ORGANIZES BIKING HOLIDAYS AND ITINERARIES IN SICILY ACCORDING TO VARIOUS FORMULAS, WITH VEHICLE SUPPORT, WITH A GUIDE, OR FOR INDEPENDENT TRAVELERS WITH A CUSTOMIZED ROUTE-BOOK.

TOURIST INFORMATION OFFICE, PIAZZETTA SATURNO, TRAPANI, TEL. 092329000, FAX 092324004.

From Scopello to the Temple of Segesta

The west of Sicily is particularly enchanting. Travelling by bike is the ideal way to discover its spectacular coastline and its hilly inland landscapes, its old towns and villages with their rich monumental heritage. Welcome to the part of Sicily which faces the sunset, is not far from the salt-pans (on the coast between Trapani and Marsala) and has a spectacular viewpoint in Erice, built high on a hill.

The route starts at Scopello, an old village built on the sea and a popular seaside resort, famed also for its tuna fishery, which operated until quite recently. It ends at Segesta, the city of the Elimians, a people who sided with the Romans during the Punic Wars and the arch-rivals of Selinus (Selinunte).

Leave Scopello, following signs for the Riserva Naturale dello Zingaro. After approx. 700 m of descent turn right. After 1 km, on the left, you will see the old tuna fishery of Scopello, against the background of the splendid "faraglioni" (the curiously-shaped rocks lying offshore), and some ceramics shops. After 900 m, turn left onto a long, straight road ending in a series of sharp bends leading to the white sandy beach of the Baia di Giudaloca. The route continues across the little bridge you can see to the left and then climbs to the right towards Castellammare del Golfo. When you reach the SS 187, turn left towards Palermo. Take extreme care when crossing the road. At the second traffic light, turn right and continue to Terme di Segesta. From here, merely follow the signs for Segesta. At the top of the hill, the road curves left and passes under the bridges of the railway and the highway. Keep following the signs for Segesta. You now come to the train station, a cafè and the archeological site. To get back to Scopello, return to the station, cross under the railway and continue for 2.7 km to the junction where you turn right towards Buseto Palizzolo, passing through the village of Bruca. Here the road follows the edge of the Riserva Naturale del Bosco di Scorace and then continues towards the center of Buseto passing close to Lago Rubino (Ruby Lake). From here, continue towards the SS 187 in the direction of Palermo. Leave the state highway at the junction of Balata di Baida and, once you reach the town, follow signs for the 14th-century castle. The final part of the route passes through Visicari and eventually arrives back at Scopello, completing the circular route.

ITINERARIES

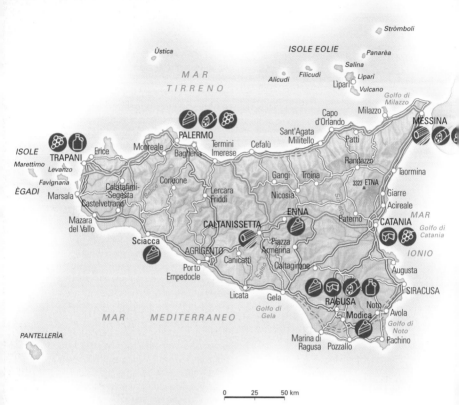

The soul of Sicily is best experienced through its exceptional food and wine. The distinct palette of the island reflects its multi-layered culinary history and is nothing less than transcendent. The Sicilian method takes the staples of Italian cuisine—Pasta, Ham, Salami, Cheese, Olive oil, Wine, Liqueurs, Sweets— and bring them to a new level of epicurean expression. The originality of the dishes and unexpected tastes of traditional specialties such

Food

as Caponata, Arancine, Pasta con sarde, and the superlative desserts—Cannoli, Cassata and Frutta di Martorana (almond pastries shaped to resemble real fruit)— create a sensational variety of complex flavors and imaginative combinations found nowhere else in the world.

Highlights

- Today, Sicilian *pecorino* (cheese made from ewe's milk), the first cheese to be produced on the island, is still made using traditional techniques and equipment
- Dressed meats, sausages and salami are often very spicy and flavored with garlic, origano and wild fennel
- The best of the Sicilian art of pastry-making: cassata, *cannoli* and ice-creams
- Thanks to the soil-type and a warm climate with gentle breezes, Sicily produces excellent high-quality wines

Sicily is an island with many souls and many regions. Since the island underwent foreign rule for many centuries, the influence of the different cultures is still clearly visible in the Sicilian cuisine: on the one hand seafood (mainly tuna and swordfish), on the other hand the typical products from inland Sicily with the unexpected tastes from the mountainous areas.

A land of contrast

The result of a wild and sometimes cruel nature, the landscape has been tamed by the creative presence of man, and defeated by the fury of time. This island in marked by great climatic change: cold and snowy in the central hilly areas, mild and sunny along the coast. This multi-shaped environment has developed a deep-rooted fishing tradition where tuna and swordfish (the former fished in the open sea, the latter in the Straits of Messina) are the main source of living. Excellent grapes are also grown here, and improvements have led to a number of new wines with the Doc label. Cattle breeding (sheep breeding, mainly) and cheese making are typical of the mountain areas. The area around the Etna volcano, a land of noble grapes and Doc wines, is the land of almonds and pistachios, pine seeds and hazelnuts, which enrich the Sicilian cuisine along with mushrooms and citrus-fruit honey. The bare and limestone area of the Siracusa province is given over to olive trees, carob and fig trees, while Modicana cattle and Comisane sheep are bred around Ragusa, with its intensive agriculture. Blessed by the sun, olive and fruit trees abound along river valleys and planes.

Picturesque stalls at a street market

the New World. The influence of foreign traditions on Sicily and its cooking is also evident by the way flavors are mixed: vinegar and sugar sauce came from the Arabs, as did the mixing of pasta with raisins and pine seeds, or the use of cakes with almonds or honey. From the Spanish, the generous use of ingredients and a unique love for colorful sweets. The typical rural dishes of Ragusa and Siracusa come from Greece, while the generous use of onions is French. Pastry making goes back to three main sources: cake making in monasteries, where cakes were prepared for religious festivities; the Arab tradition of almonds, with the addition of a few other ingredients in sugar cakes and the use of sherbet; creams and fillings by Swiss Masters.

Hybrid cooking

The heir to so many traditions, the culinary art in Sicily is a hybrid cuisine. Although most traditional dishes have the same origin, Sicilian chefs have elaborated on and adapted recipes to make them unique. As a result, couscous is cooked with fish (the economy being mainly based on fishing), dried cod and stockfish (brought in under Norman rule) are now cooked to a special recipe. "Caponata" is made with local eggplant instead of Catalan chicken.

The Mediterranean character of Sicilian cooking changed with the introduction of rice, sugar, exotic spices as well as tomatoes, red peppers and potatoes from

Popular cooking and top chefs

Over the years, Master Chefs (the renowned 'monsù') and enologists (including the inventor of "Marsala" wine) have come from abroad to take charge of the "haute cuisine" for the Sicilian elite, thus introducing new recipes, which has put restaurants in Sicily at the forefront of experimental cooking. At the bottom of such experimental tradition is the rediscovery of old, traditional recipes that Master Chefs enhance. More and more restaurants now serve dishes prepared to old recipes. Nonetheless, the true symbol of popular cooking in Sicily is all those small shops that open right onto the streets, and where you can go in at any time of the day, buy something and eat it while strolling along: the 'polipari' (men selling octopus) on the seashore in Palermo, the 'panellari', fried-food shops, the 'focaccerie' (selling a flat salty bread called focaccia) in Messina, and all those shops selling 'scacciate' in Catania, 'scaccie' in both Ragusa and Siracusa, not to mention those kiosks in any square in Catania selling drinks and soda.

PASTA

While speaking about the production of *tryia* (a sort of forefather of spaghetti) in his book *The Delight of Him Who Wishes to Traverse the Regions of the World*, 1154, which he dedicated to his patron Roger II of Sicily, the Arab geographer Al-Idrisi mentioned Trabia, which is not very far from Palermo. This is the first written account of the production of dry pasta, which spread from Sicily throughout Italy. One of the most delightful of cuisines (one only has to remember the colorful cakes and desserts), Sicilian food triumphs in pasta dishes that range from the opulent timbale to more common but just as refined dishes: at the beginning, a variety of pasta sizes and shapes developed to enhance their being eaten with the wide variety of sauces, from fish to cheese to vegetables. One outstanding Sicilian tradition are the "anelli" (spaghetti hoops), born to be finished by putting them in the oven, eaten with eggplant and cheese. Even the *maccaruni* are fairly common throughout the island: this is a short pasta made from durum wheat and water. A needle or a piece of cane is then used to make the hollow in the dough. Then there is (above all) the extremely fine Angel's hair pasta which is referred to with its more poetic name *scuma* (mousse), to underline the lightness of this pasta.

Agnolotti siciliani

A square or retangular ravioli. The filling has ricotta cheese, Sicilian sausage, sage and cinnamon.

Anelli

Also called *anelletti* (little spaghetti rings) this is indeed little pasta hoops made of durum wheat. Produced at an industrial level, this pasta is used to prepare timbale and baked pasta dishes. Various sauces can be used including the traditional Bolognese sauce with the addition of small pieces of cheese (usually a hard, smooth or strong pear shaped cheese from the South of Italy called caciocavallo) or an eggplant sauce again with pieces of cheese.

August: Macaroni Festival p. 168

Cannaruzzuni

This is a durum wheat pasta very similar to today's rigatoni pasta. *Cannaruzzuni* is actually the augmentative word for *cannarozzu*, which was once used to describe the largest size of the Sicilian macaroni.

Capiddu d'ancilu

(*scuma*)The Sicilian word for Angel-hair pasta or Venus-hair pasta, this very small diameter spaghetti is served in a broth or with a tomato or Bolognese sauce, in any case a light sauce. In Sicily this sort of spaghetti (fried with honey then poured over it) is also used in a delicate dessert called "scuma cc'u meli" (mousse with honey).

Catanesella

Catanesella is a large short macaroni from the area around Catania. It is also used to make timbale.

Cùscusu

Just as the name implies, *cùscusu* (namely couscous) has Arabic origins. It corresponds to cous cous and indeed both words come from the Arabic *kuskus* and is one of the earliest forms of pasta known to man. The semolina flour is put into a container called a "mafaradda" and salted water is poured in a little at a time and the ingredients are hand mixed using a rotary action until tiny balls are formed. The mixture is then steam cooked in a special pan called a *cuscusera* which has three parts: a container with high sides that is filled with water or broth; a second container, with tiny holes, to hold the semolina, and then the lid. When the semolina is half cooked the pan is removed from the stove and the semolina is sprinkled with cold water and then left to stand for about 15 minutes until the semolina grains start to swell. The pan is then put back onto the flame for another 20 minutes to finish cooking. At this point it is ready to be mixed with the required sauce. Particularly popular around Trapani where it is the main ingredient for a fish soup dish, couscous can also be served with a lamb or pork stew, vegetables, broad beans and wild fennel.

Ditalini

"Ditalini" (little fingers) is a short smooth or rough macaroni used throughout Sicily in traditional local dishes such as pasta with ricotta cheese (pasta simply mixed with fresh ricotta cheese and a few spoonfuls of the hot water the pasta was cooked in), or the *pasta chi vruocculi 'rriminati* (pasta with broccoli); the latter recipe varys from area to area (in Palermo they add raisins and pine seeds; in Siracusa they add "caciocavallo" and "pecorino" cheese).

Filatu

This is a sort of "vermicello" pasta and is part of the family of hand made pastas. The name comes from the action of hand drawing the dough, which is made of durum wheat, egg and saffron.

Lasagne cacate

This is egg lasagna pasta, a wide pasta with ruffled edges. It is usually used with a very rich and dense Bolognese sauce with meat, ricotta cheese and other cheeses. This pasta is typically found around Palermo, particularly in Termini merese. Tradition has it that the recipe for this lasagna was invented during the Aragonese (Spain) dominion. The name ironically refers to the fact that once only the nobility ate this pasta (the term "cacato" is still used today to refer to people who are a little snobish).

Maccaruna

The word *maccaruna* (macaroni) referes to the various types of pasta traditionally prepared in Sicily using a long thin needle-like tool called a "ferretto". The dough is prepared from durum wheat, lukewarm water, salt, egg (though some recipes do not include egg), and then rolled out into thin rolls as thick as bread sticks, 20 cm long. The macaroni is then made from these long rolls of pasta by pressing *spiti* (skewers or long needles), or a thin rod similar to a piece of cane, into the pasta. The macaroni (*maccaruna cu purtusu*, or macaroni with a hole) are then removed and left to dry in the open air. The housewife's skill lies in being able to make more than one macaroni at a time. The most widespread recipe throughout Sicily, and typical around the carnival period, is *maccaruna ca sasizza* (macaroni with sausage). The lasagna is made with a beef, sausage and pecorino cheese sause. One variant to this recipe is called *maccarruna di sdirrimarti* and is eaten for lunch on Shrove Tuesday in the county of Modica; once, this meal went on until the bell towers struck midnight, thereby announcing the start of lent. In the area around Trapani, macaroni is called *busiati*: the dough does not have egg in it and the pasta is typically eaten with Trapani pesto which is made of tomatoes, almonds, garlic, breadcrumbs and basil.

Maccu di granu

Once widespread throughout Sicily, this pasta is similar to couscous. This dish is made from wheat that is initially roughly ground between two stones, then boiled in salted water and mixed with olive oil, salt and peper, or with wild fennel. Though it is a much sought after dish these days, during the war, when it was difficult to carry corn on mules, it was quite a common dish and was eaten in place of bread and pasta.

Sciabò

This lasagna has ruffled edges (festooned) and is also known as "reginella". This sort of pasta is typical of central Sicily, particularly around Enna, and gets its name from a French word meaning *ruche* used for trimming ladies garments and the edges of men's shirts. The recipe for the sauce features a mixture of flavours that remind one of the great traditions of aristocratic food. Indeed, we are dealing with a Bolognese sauce with minced meat, onion and tomato with sugar, cinnamon and chocolate.

Taccuna di mulinu

Homemade lasagna made from durum wheat, salt and water. The main feature of this sort of lasagna pasta, which is mainly found in the Siracusa area, in Noto, is that the pasta is rather think. Having made the pasta it is cut into long strips which are left to dry for at least two hours before cooking. This very thick sort of tagliatelle is then usually prepared with a tomato sauce with the addition of fried eggplant and an abundant sprinkling of salted ricotta cheese.

Tagghiarina

A Sicilian dialect term meaning very thin tagliatelle, even though the initial pasta sheet is rather thick. The tagliatelle is served with a variety of sauces, though one of the most typical ways is with a broad bean sauce.

AGRIGENTO

CAMMARATA
Pastificio Gesù Nazareno

Via Venezia 171, tel. 0922901127
In the town of Agrigentino at the foot of the mountain Monte Cammarata, with its hundreds of years of history and clearly reminiscent medieval layout, this shop makes homemade fresh pasta from durum wheat flour from Sicilian mills . Among the various sorts of pasta one should notice the macaroni, tagliatelle, tortellini, ravioli filled with spinach and ricotta cheese, or with meat, tagliatelle colored with chilly pepper and spinach.

A typical first course: *pasta alla Norma*

CALTANISSETTA

Pasta Fresca Campisi Catena Giovanna

Via don Giovanni Minzoni 203/205
tel. 0934555012-3479664074
Delicatessen and fresh pasta shop rolled into one. The durum wheat semolina and fresh eggs are the main ingredients in making homemade cavatelli, bucatini, tagliatelle, pappardelle, fettuccini, spaghetti alla chitarra, gramigna, tortellini, ravioli and pansotti. Some sorts of pasta are even colored, such as the tagliatelle and the cavatelli, using tomato and spinach. As for the delicatessen, there are local products like Sicilian pesto, but also Bolognese sauce, Genoese pesto, walnut sauce, spinach and meat rolls.

ACQUAVIVA PLATANI
Pastificio Gierre

Capodici, tel. 0934953407
The pasta made by this homemade pasta maker is excellent. The firm is located in Acquaviva Platani and has a wonderful view over the Valle del Planani and the mountain Mounte Cammarata. You will be able to buy the traditional national pasta made of Sicilian durum wheat that does not cook quickly. It can be used with a variety of sauces as it will absorb the tastes and smells of the sauces.

CATANIA

FIUMEFREDDO DI SICILIA
Food Service Primula

Via Umberto 20, tel. 095642222
This homemade fresh pasta maker sells directly to the retail trade and the small supermarkets. All the pasta is hand made except for the filled pasta (tortellini, ravioli) for which they use special machines. They use durum wheat flour (with 20% soft wheat), buckwheat flour, a flour mixture of 5 cereals, chickpea flour, chestnut flour, and pumpkin. They will also make organic pasta and gluten-free pasta to order. Out of the various sorts of pasta the highest demand is for macaroni, hand made every morning, conchiglione (large shells), the "spring roll", ravioli filled with vegetables, tomato and mozzarella cheese, ham and mozzarella cheese, eggplant and basil; and yet more, tortellini, agnolotto, round tortelli and tortelli with pistachio nuts. Every Sunday they make pre-cooked pasta that only has to be warmed up: gnocchi from Sorrento, macaroni timbale and a mixed lasagna-pasta dish.

Pastificio Barbagallo

Via Regina Margherita 56
tel. 095641059, www.barbagallo1911.it
This old pasta maker is located at the foot of mount Etna. The pasta is made using the traditional methods for making dry pasta. They have specialised in making organic pasta; the grain is bought straight from the Sicilian farms and ground on the premises. The firm then makes the pasta and dries it at low temperature. They use wholemeal flour, cereal flour, as well as barley, spelt and buckwheat flour. The firm produces to order and makes all the

FOOD

traditional sorts of pasta. They also make organic flour and lemon, mandarin and bergamot essential oils.

MISTERBIANCO
La Sfoglia d'Oro
Via Nobel 4, tel. 095474707
This fresh homemade pasta maker produces for the small supermarkets and retail trade. The local flours and fresh eggs are kneaded both by hand and by machine, depending on the sort of pasta to be made. They make both traditional and standard sorts of pasta, including filled pasta. The range includes caserecci, potato gnocchi, tortelli, pansotti, ravioli with ricotta cheese and spinach, or with eggplant, gnocchetti sardi (Sardinian gnocchi), conchiglioni (large shell-shaped pasta), tagliatelle.

Pasta with broad beans

MESSINA

Specialità Emiliane
Via Dei Mille 204, tel. 0902932503
As the name implies this pasta maker has specialized in the preparation of the most common sorts of fresh pasta typical of the Reggio Emilia region of Italy. All the pasta is traditionally hand made using durum wheat, both with and without egg. They make the most traditional pasta: tortellini, tortelloni, ravioli, agnolotti (a sort of ravioli) with various sorts of filling, from the classic ricotta cheese with spinach filling to mushrooms, artichokes, or fish. Look out for the Crêpe, both filled and plain, sweet or savory, the potato gnocchi and the macaroni, hand made using a needle, a typical specialty in Southern Italy. This pasta shop also sells a range of regional products: stuffed eggplant, Parmesan cheese, a sardine dish called "sarde allinguate" small calamari and stuffed artichokes.

ACQUEDOLCI
Sapori di Grano
Via Giuseppe Ricca 12, tel. 0941726130
This small homemade pasta maker sells its own fresh pasta over the counter. They use Sicilian durum wheat flour and soft wheat flour . Macaroni, fusili, conchiglie, tagliatelle, spaghetti alla chitarra and Sicilian anelli are all made using a bronze die. There is also pasta colored with tomato, spinach and hot red peppers.

They also make filled pasta: ravioli, tortellini, raviolini, agnolotti; the fillings include meat, ricotta cheese and spinach, cooked ham, raw ham. The delicatessen sells an excellent sauce made with onions, carrot, celery and meat.

BARCELLONA POZZO DI GOTTO
Fantasia di Sapori
Via Kennedy 344, tel. 0909763729
This homemade fresh pasta maker buys its durum wheat semolina from a Sicilian mill. Even the other ingredients (vegetables, eggs) are all fresh and prime quality goods. The shop produces various sorts of classic pasta, though not necessarily tied to the local area: macaroni, lasagne, tagliatelle, bucatini, pappardelle, as well as various other filled pastas such as velette (a triangular ravioli) with ricotta cheese and spinach, or pumpkin, eggplant, salmon, sward fish, dentex, radicchio. They even make some pasta that has been colored using tomato, spinach and also sepia.

CONTESSE
Industrie Alimentari Triolo
4 km along the SS 114
tel. 090621848
This firm makes both dry and fresh pasta on an industrial scale. The fresh pasta is sold locally and the dry pasta is sold to the wholesale market. The Sicilian durum wheat flours are used in all the production processes. The firm also produces various sorts of stuffed pasta.

PACE DEL MELA
Pastificio Puglisi
Giammoro, tel. 0909384395
www.puglisipasta.com
This firm is over a hundred years old. It melds a respect for traditional pasta

production with advanced mechanisation. The pasta production is based on the use of Sicilian durum wheat semolina. Some sorts of pasta are even shaped through bronze dies. The pasta is dried at an average temperature. They makes all the most common sorts of pasta, though greater attention is placed on the sorts of pasta that have set their mark in Sicilian gastronomic history, such as spaccarelle, home made macaroni, pici. They even sell organic pasta and wholemeal pasta.

PALERMO

CORLEONE
Pastificio Corleone Tipica
Via S. Lucia 3, tel. 0918463612
www.corleonetipica.com
This shop has been open since 1840. Though it made a change to its production in 1999 it has kept the original artisan production technology. Located in the historic centre of the town, this pasta maker produces pasta that is dried at low temperature, in wood cells where the temperature never goes above 40ºC. Durum wheat semolina from the Corleone area and water, these are the ingredients used in the 32 different sorts of pasta, from the "lunghe" pasta (a long pasta that can even reach one meter in length) to spaghetti, to the more typical shapes: margherita corleonese, anelli siciliani (shaped with bronze dies), maglie siciliane, maglie di ziti, tiny "pastina" of all shapes. The shop also sells cheese, olive oil, preserves, cakes, "rasoli" (don't miss the ones made with prickly pear).

TERRASINI
Il Mastro Pastaio
Via Benedetto Saputo 66
tel. 0918681173
This small homemade pasta maker and delicatessen makes fresh durum wheat pasta and sells it to the retail trade. The flour is ground in a local mill though the dough is made using machines. They make the most traditional Sicilian pasta such as macaroni, caserecce, bucatini (original sort of macaroni) as well as tagliatelle and many other sorts of filled pasta: tortelloni, tortelli, raviolini. They will make just about any filling to order.

RAGUSA

MODICA
Molino e Pastificio della Contea
Via Fontana 246, tel. 0932943680
This homemade pasta maker makes dry pasta right from the flour grinding stage. The local durum wheat flour and semolina are actually ground on the premises using their rotary grinder. The pasta is then made using a Teflon die and then dried at low temperature. They make the various sorts of regional and national pasta, such as spaghetti, ditali, macaroni, penne, the very small pastina for broth, all packaged in 1kg packets.

POZZALLO
Delizie Modicane
Via Giuseppe Mazzini 49
tel. 0932797200
This homemade fresh pasta maker does almost all the production by machine, except for the macaroni, which is made to order. The shop uses Sicilian durum wheat flour and durum wheat semolina. The pasta ranges from tagliatelle to cavatelli, to caserecce, rigatoni and bucatini. The ravioli have various sorts of filling: ricotta cheese, eggplant or fish. They also sell tortellini with a meat filling.

TRAPANI

MAZARA DEL VALLO
Pastificio Poiatti
Via Circonvallazione 90
tel. 0941726130, www.poiatti.it
This firm is at the forefront of the industrial production of durum wheat semolina pasta.
The firm uses a selection of Sicilian durum wheat semolina, sourced both domestically and from abroad, which is ground in technologically advanced mills. This firm is a leading firm in the area and produces 250 tons of pasta a day in a range of over one hundred sorts of pasta, both regional and national (capellini, spaghettini, spaghetti, spaghettoni, rustichelli, bacati, bacatini, maccheroncelli, linguine), all sold in Italy and abroad.

FOOD

HAMS AND SALAMI

Sicily is basically a rural land, but high-quality pork meat products are also produced in those areas where breeding is not deeply rooted. This is the result of the careful choice of meat and masterly processing. Sausages still dominate popular tastes (and production), and spicy sausages are often added to many dishes, with their strong flavors of wild fennel, garlic, oregano and red peppers, of course!

Among the other local products, the Nebrodi Mountain area is renowned worldwide for its excellent dressed pork meats, its bacon and ham.

Budello origanato

Nicosia in the province of Enna is home to this specialty. It is made using the meat of rather small free-range animals. Eaten both raw and cooked, it has a characteristic ribbon-like shape and is brown. It can sometimes be a whole metre in length.

Pancetta arrotolata dei monti Nebrodi

This cold rolled underbelly of pork meat is eaten raw. It is made in restricted quantities using the underbelly of free-range pigs that are bred all around the area of the Nebrodi mountains. Once the meat has been cleaned it is salted and put into special covered wood containers for fifteen days, completely covered in a brine mixture of salt, pepper, red chilly pepper, wild fennel, garlic, oregano and vinegar. After the fifteen days the pieces of pork underbelly are rolled very tightly and then seasoned.

Prosciutto dei monti Nebrodi

This famous raw ham (Prosciutto crudo) is made in restricted amounts. They use the whole legs of a breed of free-range black pig that are initially only fed on a kind of acorn and berries from the Nebrodi mountains. During the last 30 days, before they are sent to the butchery, they are fed on cereal and broad beans. The legs are left to lie for some days. Then they are trimmed and salted, which takes a few days. After some 20-40 days the hams are sent to the seasoning room for a number of months, having first been covered in garlic, wild fennel and oregano.

Salame di Chiaramonte Gulfi

This pure pork salami is made in restricted amounts in Chiaramonte Gulfi in the province of Ragusa. They use the meat from free-range pigs. To make the salami, they use the lean cut-offs of pork from the prime pieces of pork with a high fat content that are being prepared for other sorts of preparations. The pork is roughly minced and then mixed with fat and mixed until they have obtained a consistent mixture. Then they add salt, pepper corns, fennel seeds and red pepper. The mixture thus obtained is then wrapped into the sausage covering and tied to form the long salamis. They are then hung in the kitchen for a few days and then left to season for a month in special cool rooms.

Salame di San Marco

Also know as Fellata, this salami is from the area around the Nebrodi mountains. Once the pork has been trimmed it is hand cut using a knife into a large rough mince. This meat is then mixed with salt, black pepper and red pepper, put into fine pig's gut and tied to make the salamis which, after a short maturing time, are left to season for 2-3 months.

Salame di Sant'Angelo

One of the most well known Sicilian salamis in the region, the history dates back to the 16th century. It is made using pieces of top quality lean meat (thigh, loin, rib and underbelly) that are initially cut into strips then into cubes using the tip of a knife. The mince is then put into special wood containers called "madia" (for kneading purposes) and hand mixed with salt and pepper corns.

Salame di San Marco, originally from the area of the Nebrodi Mountains

Salsiccia di Chiaramonte Gulfi

This pure pork meat sausage gets its name from the town it comes from. The pork is taken from the cut-offs of prime pieces of pork used for other products, and fat. The ingredients are minced and then mixed with salt, black pepper, red pepper and fennel seeds. The mixture is then put into gut and tied to look like a sausage. It is eaten fresh.

Salsiccia di Nicosia

Another salami that is made in restricted quantities in Nicosia and, more generally, throughout the province of Enna, using the cut-offs of prime and second quality pieces of locally bred pigs. The meat is mixed with a high amount of fat and the mixture thus obtained is mixed with salt, ground black pepper, fennel and perhaps red pepper. This mixture is then put into pork gut and fashioned to look like a sausage.

Supprissato di Nicosia

This sort of salami is prepared throughout the province of Enna. It is made of cut-offs of prime pieces of pork and about half the amount again of fat. Once the supprissato has been left to lie for a few days in warm rooms it is then left to season for about a month in a cool room and then it is moved to special containers, covered in ash and left to flavor for more than three months.

Beaches of Torre Salsa pag. 120

Suzu

This is a jelly mold of second choice mixed meats. It is made between November and May almost throughout the whole region even though the most delicious sort comes from the area around Catania and Ragusa. It is made by boiling calf and pig's trotters, pig's skin and beef with bay leaves, red chilly pepper and lemon juice. The bones are then removed and the mixture pressed and left to cool. It is really nice eaten fresh. In any case it does not keep.

U suppesato

This seasoned meat comes from the area around Monti Nebrodi and is made using prime quality meat, usually haunch of beef or fillet steak. When the meat has been cured and covered with red and black pepper, garlic and oregano it is tied

under pressure between two sticks and left for a few days in a warm well ventilated room. The U suppesato is then moved to the seasoning area in the loft for three months, and then to the cellars for the same length of time.

AGRIGENTO

Antichi Sapori Prodotti tipici di Cacciatore Maria
Via C. Battisti 20, tel. 0922554585
This is Sicily and much more. The salamis on show have been chosen personally by the owner from all over Italy, and the sight before your eyes is quite something. Apart from the traditional salamis, there are many specialties to temp your taste buds.

CAMPOBELLO DI LICATA
Enoteca La dispensa di Ulisse
Via Edison 233, tel. 0922870335
This shop has a good selection of typical Sicilian products: cold meats, cheeses, ready-made sauces, sweet and savory jams, olive oil, wine, liqueurs and cakes and pastries. Among the various products, lovers of salami certainly must not miss the "capocollo", the various sorts of sausage and the very tasty salami from Sant'Angelo.

CALTANISSETTA

MUSSOMELI
Salumeria Enoteca Delizie di Diliberto Bruno
Via Madonna di Fatima 4
tel. 0934951621
This shop has a good stock of regional specialties from all over Italy, including a number of local homemade products.

CATANIA

Salumeria Macelleria Vasta di Anna Vasta
Via Martino Cilestri 27, tel. 3280766690
This shop is famous for the vast range of Sicilian salamis, cheeses and wines as well as the careful choice of products from the rest of Italy. They also have a range of genuine foods, ready to be put into the oven, including a very tasty

sausage with a sauce, a house specialty. There is also a wide choice of products for people with nutritional disorders, including a number of salamis.

MESSINA

MIRTO
Macelleria Salumeria La Paesanella di Agostino Ninone Sebastiano
Via S. Rocco 40, tel. 0941919403
You must try the "fellata", a typical local salami, as well as the sausage, the capocollo, pig underbelly, pig's cheek, lard and the ham.

SAN SALVATORE DI FITALIA
La Vedetta dei Nebrodi di Carmelo Armeli
Bufana Alta, tel. 0941421977
This wood and stone building is covered in farm-yard tools. There is a breathtaking view from the refreshment area, where clients can choose from many typical homemade products or products chosen from the local producers. Among the products on sale we must mention the black pig salami, the meat, porcini mushrooms, hazelnuts, jams and marmalades, Sicilian durum wheat, quality grapes and rosolio.

SANT'ANGELO DI BROLO
Salumificio Sapori di Sant'Angelo
Via sant'Elia 17, tel. 0941533016-3472467970-34734927199
This salami maker uses the original old traditional methods to make its salamis. It is now the last firm to make salamis using selected meats from the finest of locally bred pigs. The whole homemade method adheres to both the traditional methods as well as to modern health regulations. The salami are made using selected fresh local pork that is cut into cubes, put into pig's gut and then simply covered in salt and black pepper. Then it is naturally seasoned in large well ventilated rooms.

PALERMO

Enoteca Mi manda Picone
Via Marconi 36, tel. 091331300
The Picone wine shop is a prime stop off for anyone wanting to try and buy both excellent wines as well as quality salamis and cheeses. One part of the

shop has been set aside just for tasting: there are tables where all sorts of titbits are served, including the locally-made salamis and cheeses.

CAMPOREALE
Salumificio Amato
Via Roma 30, tel. 092436076
The Amato shop has been open since 1920 and has made a name for itself as a seller of a line of personalised products that are made, packaged and sold as genuine and traditional products. Do not miss the two house specialties: the pasqualora, a take on a salami with spices and wild fennel, and the Sicilian mandolino, a Sicilian raw ham that has been treated with local herbs.

Rolled bacon, typical of the Nebrodi Mountains

RAGUSA

Punto Formaggi e Salumi di Dicunta Sebastiana
Corso Italia 32, tel. 0932621694
This shop sells traditional food, a place where, amidst an array of colors, tastes and smells, one can find just about everything, from the extremely fresh provola, made by a master cheese maker, to the highly sought after delicatessen foods for the more refined taste buds, and the local Caravello salamis.

MODICA
Salumi Artigianali Napolitano
Via Modica Sorda 89, tel. 0932751531
www.salumiartigianali.it
Years and years of trials and experience, together with a good deal of enthusiasm and love of the art of salami making, have allowed Vincenzo Napolitano and his entire family to reach the quality they have managed to reach. The family sells its own versions of traditional Modica salamis.

CHEESE

A land of culture and natural beauty, Sicily was once a region of immense estates, and grain was its main agricultural resource. Thanks to its sunny, hot climate, Sicily was the granary of the Roman Empire, first, and an Arab garden, later. Today, Sicily is getting a reputation for its wines. Sheep and cattle breeding date back to ancient traditions, though they have always been a minor activity due to poor pasturelands. Legend has it that Polyphemus was offered Pecorino cheese and wine. Pecorino cheese may have different names: "Tuma", "canestraio", "Piacentinu" (which is flavored with wild saffron) but they all have one thing in common: the same, unmistakable taste. What about ricotta cheese, then? Shepherds used to sell ricotta cheese from house to house till a few years ago. Fresh, baked or dried, ricotta is delivered every morning in little straw baskets and is often the main ingredient either for a tasty first course or for pastries (cannoli, just to mention one). Cow's milk, instead, is the main ingredient for Caciocavallo cheese from Ragusa, which flavors a pasta dish called 'ncasciata.

Caciocavallo palermitano

A cheese with a long history, no aristocratic home or monastery ever went without it. It is made throughout the province of Palermo, with Godrano and Cinisi being the main areas, and can even be found in some towns in the province of Trapani. This is a cow's milk cheese made into rectangular shapes. It is a firm cheese and shows stripping when it is quite ripe.

Caciotta degli Elimi

This is a typical cheese from Calatafimi and Vita in the province of Trapani. This is firm sheep's milk cheese made using a special fermenting process that makes it different from other sorts of pecorini cheese. The name comes from the old Elimi, legendary descendents of Enea who were principally located in Segesta.

Canestrato

Referred to as Tumazzaor or Cacio in the old trade parchments, this cheese is common around the region. It is a semi-cooked hard cheese made from full cow's milk mixed with sheep's milk. It is made in round molds and has a crust with the imprint of the basked in it. It also comes under the names of Tuma (when it is fresh and unsalted), Primosale (8-10 days old), Secondosale (2-4 months old), Stagionato (over four months old).

Canestrato cheeses maturing

Cofanetto

Caciocavallo cofanaro. This is a typical cheese from the area around Monte Cofano, in the province of Trapani, though especially found in Custonaci, San Vito Lo Capo, Castellammare del Golfo and Calatafimi. It is made from a mixture of milk from the Cinisara breed of cow (70-80%) and milk from the Valle del Belice breed of sheep (20-30%). It is a rectangular shape and is left to ripen for between 20 days and one year.

Ericino

The name of this cheese comes from the town of Erice in the province of Trapani, which was famous in ancient times for their belief in the god Venus. Among the various gifts offered to this god there was a cheese that reportedly increased a person's virility. In keeping with this tradition today, this firm cheese is made from the milk of a breed of sheep called the Valle del Belice (80%) and the milk of a breed of cow called the Cinisara (20%). The full cheese weighs some 2-7 kilograms and the production area includes Erice, Val d'Erice, Custonaci, San Vito lo Capo, Castellammare del Golfo, Calatafimi and other places around.

Formaggio di capra siciliana

Sicilian goat cheese also known as Caciu di capra. This round goat's milk cheese is found throughout

FOOD

143

the region. It is a hard cheese. One important piece of writing comes from Pliny the Elder who recounts the trade with Rome of a 'caprino from Agrigento, which is improved with smoke.

Formaggio di Santo Stefano Quisquina

Sicilian flowers, Cow's milk Tumazzu. This is a typical cheese from the central area of the Sicani hills on the border between the provinces of Agrigento and Palermo, particularly from Santo Stefano Quisquina, Castronovo di Sicilia, Prizzi, Palazzo Adriano and Cammarata. It is a raw or soft full cow's milk cheese made in round molds and weighs some 2 kilograms and has a thin slightly moldy crust.

Maiorchino

This cheese typically comes from Messina, particularly from Novara di Sicilia where they hold a race during carnival and roll the 10-12 kilogram cheeses along the streets. Made from full sheep's milk, sometimes with the addition of goat's milk, it is a firm cheese with a delicate taste (the fully ripe cheese has a stronger taste).

Sicilian *pecorino* cheese

Pecorino siciliano Dop

This is probably the oldest cheese on the island; indeed, it was mentioned by Homer in the Odyssey as well as by Pliny, who was enthusiastic about the production in Agrigento. This cheese represents the best sort of sheep's cheese on the island and is still made using traditional methods and tools, like the *fascedde* which is made of rush and surrounds the cheese rounds. The base product is uncooked full milk taken from pasture sheep. Once the cheese rounds are made they are left to mature for 4-8 months. At the end of this time the cheese looks compact, it has a very strong smell, a

DOP: Protected Origin Denomination

characteristic sharp taste. It can be eaten at various stages of the seasoning process and thus has different names: when it is fresh and not salted it is called Tuma; when it has been salted it is called Primusali; when it is well seasoned, no more than two years old, it is called Canistratu or Tumazzu. It may even have pepper corns inserted into it.

Piacentinu

This is a traditional cheese from around Enna and is made from full sheep's milk with a little saffron, an idea, so they say, that was introduced by the Norman king Roger. It is a hard, firm, yellowish cheese with a slightly aromatic taste. Though there is uncertainty where the name comes from some believe it is from the town of Piacenza and the Longobards. Others say it comes from the word *piangentinu* as it tends to sweat. Finally others believe it comes from the word 'piacente': sharp taste.

Picurino

This red Pecorino cheese is found throughout the region. It is the most common sheep's milk cheese and is made in round molds. Sometimes it is covered in black pepper or red chilly pepper. It is a firm cheese that comes in various names: Tuma, when fresh and unsalted; Primosale between 8-10 days after salting; Secondosale, 2-4 months; Semistagionato and Stagionato (semi-ripe and ripe), over 4 months.

Provola dei Nebrodi

This cheese comes from a wide area around Messina, though mainly from Floresta. One special feature is that there is a knob of butter in the middle to refine the cheese, or a greenish lemon which will give the cheese a lemony taste as the cheese ripens.

Provola delle Madonie

This pear-shaped cheese comes from the area east of Palermo, especially Collesano, Petralia and Castelbuono.

Provola ragusana

This cheese comes in small pear shaped pieces (0.5 - 1 kg). Apart from this it is the same as the traditional local caciocavallo, which is better know as

Ragusano Dop. The best sort is made from the milk of the pasturing cows from the Ibleo hills.

Provola siciliana

This name brings together all the unmistakable kinds of provola in Sicily. The main features are: a pear shape with a tiny head shaped by the bow at the top, a slightly amber-colored thin smooth skin. The cheese itself is pale and firm and the taste sweet and delicate.

Ragusano Dop

The typical production area of this cheese includes the province of Ragusa as well as Noto, Palazzolo, Acreide and Rosolini in the province of Siracusa. Historically know as Caciocavallo ragusano or Cacio ibleo, this is one of the oldest traditional Sicilian cheeses and was traded outside the Kingdom of Sicily as far back as the 14th century. It is a firm cheese made from untreated cow's milk and takes the shape of a parallelepiped. Two cheeses are tied together and are left to ripen hanging astride a bar, traditionally inside caves, for between three months and one year. The cheese is firm, quite pale, and has a delicate taste when it is young and a strong intense taste when it is ripe. The smell changes as ripening progresses. There is even a smoked version. The cheese obtained from a local breed of cow called the Modicana is particularly sought after, especially when the high "Ibleo" pastures are in full bloom. Usually eaten as a table cheese, it can be sliced, coated in breadcrumbs or fried. The fully ripe Ragusano can be grated and is used as an ingredient or a condiment in many Sicilian dishes.

Ricotta di pecora, di capra, di vacca o mista

Sheep's, goat's, cow's and mixed milk ricotta cheese

In the work *Le venti giornate dell'agricoltura e dei piaceri in villa* (4th century A.D.) this cheese was described in detail and the caprino was considered the best. Today's production in the region includes fresh, salted or oven-baked ricotta.

Ricotta iblea

The term Iblea refers to the Ibleo hill pasture land and is closely tied to the production of Ragussa caciocavallo and

provola. It is a creamy, ivory white cheese shaped like a short cone taken from the molds. It smells like whey and tastes sweet.

Ricotta infornata

Produced throughout Sicily this cheese is obtained from cow's, sheep's or goat's milk whey. After 1 - 2 days it is transferred into clay basins with a butter layer or ground black pepper and then baked in the oven until a thin brown-red skin is formed. The end product is creamy, ivory white and has an aromatic taste.

Tumazzu di vacca

Cow's milk tumazzu

A product from Canestrato, and specifically from Nicosia (En), this firm cheese has differing colors from white to yellow. Depending on the time of year the taste varies from acidy to sharp. The cheeses weigh between 5-15 kg and are sometimes covered in black pepper or red chilly pepper.

Vastedda della Valle del Belice

From the provinces of Trapani, Agrigento and Palermo this sheep's milk cheese is typically made and eaten in summer. It has a flat, oval shape (*vastedda*) and is white. It tastes slightly acid and fresh.

Vastedda palermitana

The history and production of this cheese goes hand in hand with the sort of Caciocavallo made around Palermo. It is known for its oval shape, not too thick and not too thin, the weight of about 1 kg, and the freshness of the cheese itself.

AGRIGENTO

SANTO STEFANO QUISQUINA
La Casa del Formaggio
Via Maranzano 11, tel. 0922982035
Direct and retail seller of cheese and salamis they also sell tuma, primo sale, pecorino siciliano and pecorini aromatizzati.

SCIACCA
Antiche Tradizioni
Viale della Vittoria 41, tel. 0925905025
For many years now Enzo and his wife have been delighting the taste buds of the most exacting of clients. They sell an

enormous range of delicacies: cheeses and cold meats, both local and not, as well as many other special delicatessen goodies with special sauces like the sauce used in making pasta with sardines, cherry tomatoes in oil.

Salumeria del Buon Sapore

Via Cappuccini 20, tel. 092526562
This is one of the key shops for the local inhabitants and tourists alike. You will find local cheeses and cold meats as well as a highly enticing delicatessen.

CATANIA

Salumeria Dagnino Carlo

Via Etnea 179, tel. 095312169
This shop sells both cheese and cold meat specialities. Among the range of products, try the Sant'Angelo salami, the pickles, olive pate, capers and red chilly pepper.

Vineria Picasso

Piazza Ogninella 4, tel. 3478632282
This wine bar has its own kitchen and will let you try the local cheeses. Make sure you try the pecorini siciliani, especially the traditional one, though the new ones with Nero d'Avola or with Zibibbo should not be missed.

ENNA

Salumi Formaggi Di Dio

Via Mercato S. Antonio 34, tel. 093525758
This shop sells all the Sicilian cheeses including a very good piacentinu ennese that has been left to ripen for 12 months.

AIDONE

Az. Agrozootecnica Biologica Casalgismondo

13 km along the SP 103, tel. 093587900
Right in the heart of Sicily, and not far from the Morgantina and Piazza Armerina architectural sites, this farm breeds some 1,000 Comisana sheep and, in the cheese making process, only uses its own lamb's whey. You can visit the farm and taste the products on arrangement only.

ASSORO

Caseificio San Giorgio

Pietramaggiore, tel. 0935669438
www.caseificiosangiorgio.com
The cheeses are made from uncooked milk, which is absolutely necessary for the milk to obtain the classical taste and smell. This cheese maker can be visited by appointment only.

MESSINA

BARCELLONA POZZO DI GOTTO
Caseificio Cosimo Grasso

Via Spine Sante 12, tel. 0909710398
This cheese maker has been going since 1987 and can be visited on booking. They produce mozzarella cheese, scorze, provole, burrini, milk and cream.

TAORMINA
La Torinese

Corso Umberto I F2459, tel. 094223321
Since 1936 generations of women have taken over from each other to sell from this well supplied counter. They also sell organically made pasta made from the wheat grown on land that has been confiscated from the mafia.

PALERMO

Cambria

Via Liguria 49, tel. 091517791
This shop has about one hundred different local and national cheeses ranging from pecorino siciliano to ragusano, primo sale and formaggio delle Madonie, pecorino sardo from Sardinia. They also sell cold meats, olive oil and pickles as well as fresh and dried pasta.

Gastronomia Mangia

Via Principe di Belmonte 116 tel. 091587651
This shop has a wide variety of quality products both Sicilian and national as well as a selection of foreign items. The owner also owns a restaurant called "Gigi Mangia" that serves food all based on the food from his shop.

Pizzo & Pizzo

Via 12 gennaio 1Q, tel. 0916014544
This is a food boutique. The Pizzo couple themselves go to great trouble to find the best Italian cheeses for their clients.

CAPACI
Industria Alimentare Puccio

Via Mons. Siino 52
tel. 0918671322-8696068
Both direct and wholesale trade.

Santa Rosalia celebration pag. 193

The interior of a Sicilian cheese-production plant

CASTRONOVO DI SICILIA
Az. Agr. Rotolo Francesco
*Marcatobianco, Via Roma, 47
tel. 0918214964*
The Anfosc brand ensures the quality of the products on this farm. You may visit the farm by appointment.

PARTINICO
Fattoria Manostalla - Villa Chiarelli
*Contrada Manostalla, tel. 0918787033
www.villachiarelli.it*
15 km from the Zingaro natural reserve and surrounded by a wonderful natural environment, Villa Chiarelli is a great stop off with wonderful food. They have their own home grown cheese and meat dishes, homemade fresh pasta, vegetables and fruit from the garden and organically grown citrus fruit. Telephone if you want to shop or visit the farm.

RAGUSA

Casa del Formaggio S. Anna di Di Pasquale
Corso Italia 387, tel. 0932227485
This outlet produces and sells its own fresh and ripe cheeses such as Ragusano Dop and canestrato. They also sell certain British and Spanish cheeses.
Fratelli Baglieri
Via G. Puccini 7, tel. 0932826061
This firm is thirty years old and has just been renovated. They sell local cheeses such as ragusano Dop, the various sorts of provols and ricotta.
Gastronomia Dicunta
Corso Italia 32, tel. 0932621694
This shop sells the classical Dop products, such as fresh and ripe caciocavallo ragusano, from all the Sicilian regions. There is also a wide choice of ready-made sauces at the delicatessen.

ISPICA
Floridia Rosario
Scorsone, tel. 0932952370
This firm has been run by the same family for over 40 years. They sell all their own cheeses: caciocavallo ragusano Dop, provola, canestrato and ricotta.

SIRACUSA

Fratelli Burgio
Piazza C. Battisti 4, tel. 093160069
Among their own products there is a label called "Il gusto dei sapori smarriti dei F.lli Burgio" (lost tastes by the Burgio brothers). They sell Sicilian cheeses and cold meats, jams and marmalades and Sicilian pesto.

TRAPANI

Salumeria Renda
*Via G.B. Fardella 80, tel. 092322270
www.renda.it*
This rather small family-run shop sells Sicilian wines, cold meats and cheese such as fresh sheep's milk tuma, pecorino and the Sant'Angelo di Brolo salami.

CALATAFIMI-SEGESTA
Spatafora
Kaggera, tel. 0924951502
This firm has focused on the production of the various sorts of pecorino cheese with red chilly pepper, black pepper, and with rocket salad.

CASTELVETRANO
Caseificio Forte Benvenuta
Via Selinunte al km 75,00, tel. 3488021285
This cheese maker also makes cheese with red chilly pepper and black pepper, with olives, thyme, fresh and smoked cheeses as well as the typical 'mandarin' provola. Telephone before going there.

MARSALA
Gerardi Gastronomia
Piazza Mameli 14, tel. 0923952240
This shop has a wide range of both Sicilian, Italian and Swiss cheeses as well as butter, cold meats, pasta, meat and rice. The delicatessen is quite breathtaking with a number of specialties like the red tuna fish and couscous.

FOOD

OIL

Sicily has been a major olive-oil producing area for centuries. It now has an area of some 110,000 hectares of land dedicated to olive tree plantations, with an average of 100 to 150 trees per hectare. Sicily is now the most dynamic region, after Puglia and Calabria, producing a little more than 10% of total Italian output. The most widespread method of olive-oil extraction is by continuous cold pressing so as not to affect the olives in any way (68%); only in the province of Ragusa do they still use traditional olive pressing methods.

Rediscovery of an antique treasure

Olive-oil producers and the regional administrations are doing a great deal of agronomic research and experimentation to modernize olive tree production, they are fighting the use of pesticides and improving oil extraction methods. The various kinds of soil and the difference in climate from one area to another gives Sicily one of the widest varieties of olive tree throughout the Mediterranean, the "olive kingdom".
The most widespread olive trees are original of their area, plants like Moresca, Tonda iblea, Zaituna, Ogliarola messinese, Passalunara, Biancolilla, Giarraffa, Nocellara del Belice, Nocellara etnea, Santagatese, Minuta, Verdella, and none of them have particularly been influenced by any foreign variety.

The gnarled trunks of ancient olive-trees in the Province of Messina

Another vocation

This silver-lined olive garden has a number of distinct features, particularly productive areas: the area around Trapani, particularly around Erice, and the highland valleys extending as far as Castellammare del Golfo with old and new olive trees. New mechanized methods are now used to reduce production costs; Mazarese and the Belice valley, the center being Campobello di Mazzara, Castelvetrano and Partanna; the area around Agrigento, the rolling coast line as far as the mountains of Caltabellotta and Ribera and Calamonaci; the area around Ragusa with its south-western lie on the slopes of the Iblei mountains and its towns: Chiaramonte Gulfi, Comiso, Modica, Ispica; along the streams from the Nebrodi mountains, the most southerly point of Sicily, around Reitano and Mistretta; the silted coastline valleys to the north of the Madonie. There is excellent olive production around Siracusa, Catania (especially on the slopes of the enormous Etna volcano), Messina and Palermo; though a mixed production, it should not be frowned upon.

A guaranteed variety

So, high olive-oil output but, above all, quality oils; most of the olive oils produced are extra-virgin olive oils. Sicily has four European Union quality certificates, testifying to the quality and authenticity of the olive oil from the various parts of the island.
The Monti Iblei Dop olive oil (distinct green color) has a maximum acidity of 0.6% and is in the same league as the other extra-virgin olive oils from Calatino, Frigintini, Gulfi, Monte Lauro, Trigona-Pancali, Val d'Anapo, Val Tellaro and Valle d'Irmino. The quality is only very slightly different, the best being Tonda iblea, Moresca or Nocellara etnea from the province of Siracusa, Catania and Regusa. The Valli Trapanesi Dop label, which gathers together many areas including the province of Trapani, contains no less than 80% of the Cerasuola and Nocellara olives from Belice (maximum acidity 0.5%, green with golden-yellow highlights, clear olive smell with herb undertones, fruity with a slight tang and bitterness).

Monte Etna Dop and Val di Mazara Dop are recent oils. The former is from around Catania and Messina, particularly two areas. Monte Etna is a gold-green oil with at least 80% Brandofine olives. The Val di Mazara Dop is from the province of Palermo and Agrigento. 100% obtained from Biancolilla, Nocellara del Belice, Cerasuola, Ogliarola messinese olives, it is gold-yellow with green highlights and a fruity smell (sometimes a little almond) and taste with a sweet aftertaste. Two other extra-virgin olive oils are seeking the highly sought-after quality certification from the European Union. Valdemone, province of Messina, is obtained from the small Minuto olives. The oil is light, sweet, fragrant with a bay-leaf aftertaste, very low acidity. The Valle del Belice is from a few towns south of Trapani; it is 90% Nocellara del Belice olives, has almost no acidity, is green with gold-yellow highlights and is fruity with a slight tang.

MESSINA

CARONIA
Frantoio Ricciardi
Canneto, Via Nazionale 13, tel. 0921331322

PALERMO

CASTRONUOVO DI SICILIA
Colle San Vitale S.R.L.
Via Kassar 66, tel. 0918217862
www.collesanvitale.it
I.A.M.I. S.R.L.
Candelora 1.5 km along the SP 36 road.
tel. 0918217002, www.iamifood.com

RAGUSA

Azienda Olivicola F.lli L. e R. Gafà
Via Roma 140, tel. 0932682303

CHIARAMONTE GULFI
Andolina Rosario
Contrada Gerardo 100
tel. 0932926155
Azienda Agrobiologica Rosso
Via Cimarosa 75
tel. 0932621442
www.agrobiologica-rosso.it
Cutrera Giovanni
Contrada Piano dell'Acqua 71
tel. 0932926187, www.frantoicutrera.it
Gravina Silvana
Contrada Gerardo, tel. 0932922389
Guccione Maria
Contrada Ponte Biviere, via S. Vito 11
tel. 0932927479
Gulino Giovanni
Cicimia, corso Umberto 162
tel. 0932921249
Mediterranea di Lucio Paravizzini
Piazza Duomo 52
tel. 0932922342
www.mediterraneasrl.it/index.htm

In Ragusa:
Cheese Art pag. 168

TRAPANI

Azienda Agricola D'Alì
Via G.B. Fardella 24, tel. 092328890
www.tenutazangara.it

CAMPOBELLO DI MAZARA
Azienda Agricola Filpi
Viale Risorgimento 11, tel. 092447860

CASTELVETRANO
Azienda Agricola G. Becchina - Antica Tenuta Casina Pignatelli
Via Trinità, tel. 092489295
Azienda Agricola Lo Sciuto C. - Smeraldo Belice
Via Palestro 33, tel. 360295109
Azienda Agricola Agro Verde di Murania
Piazza Matteotti 70, tel. 092481067
Azienda Agricola Barbera Gaspare Oleum
Via Civiletti 3, tel. 092481858
Azienda Agricola Carbona di Benedetto Giuseppe
Contrada da Carbona, tel. 092462611
www.olioincoronati.it
Azienda Agricola Moliture Infranca
Piazza Dante 3, tel. 0924907222
Azienda Agricola Pantaleo
Contrada Terrenove 72-74, tel. 0923969482
Azienda Agricola Tenuta Rocchetta
Via Ugo Bassi 12
tel. 0924904364
Aziende Agricole Filippo e Cecilia Becchina
Contrada Seggio, tel. 092524982
Ditta Maurizio Genco
Via V. Emanuele 59, tel. 0924902388
Oleificio Girolamo Campagna
Via XX Settembre 33, tel. 092489213
Oleificio Peruzza srl
Via Maffei, tel. 0924905133
www.peruzzaolio.com

MARSALA
Baglio Caruso e Menini S.p.A.
Via Salemi 3, tel. 0923982356
www.capricciodisicilia.it

FOOD

WINE

Vineyards in Sicily were long bound to the production of strong wines that were used for blending. However, in the last few years the quality of Sicilian wines has steadily improved due to better vine growing techniques and new wine ageing methods.

Vine growing, as indeed Sicily itself, is divided into three major areas: western vineyards (Trapani and surroundings) with the famous wines produced in Marsala; north-eastern vineyards and the wines produced around the Etna volcano; southern vineyards and the wines from the area around Ragusa. This land is perfect for vine growing thanks to the composite nature of the soil and a warm and windy climate, which favor the best output with minimum intervention by man. The local vine growers highlight this aspect to underline the quality of their products.

Sicily, a land of resources

Being rich in natural resources and extremely sunny, it is no wonder Sicily, with its Roman and Arab inheritance, ranks first in Italy for yearly wine production (7 million hectoliters - more than 154 million gallons). Under the present circumstances, it is hard to believe that Sicily had been producing strong wines only for blending until a few years ago. As a matter of fact, until the 1950s most wines from Sicily were used to strengthen weak wines. Then a dramatic change occurred in a matter of a few decades. First, better growing techniques (with a more careful selection of vine stocks) and the introduction of a thermo-conditioned wine-making process led to the wine no longer being sold by the measure, but in bottles (thus quality instead of quantity). The second change, which is still on-going, is the attempt to boost the production of quality red wines. This is Sicilian vine growers' latest bet and their new endeavor is evidenced by big wine companies from northern Italy investing capital in Sicily.

Traditional wines, new wines

The vine-growing scenario in Sicily is dominated by traditional vines: Cataratto Bianco Comune, Cataratto Bianco Lucido and Trebbiano Toscano are worth mentioning among white wines, while Nero d'Avola (also called 'Calabrese'), Nerello Mascalese and Nerello Cappuccio stand out among red wines. Minor white wines include Grecanico Dorato, Grillo and Zibibbo; among other red wines we have Perricone and Frappato di Vittoria. As for vine-growing techniques, bush vines are still dominant (they produce grapes with a strong alcohol content), but the "spalier" suspension system (or guyot system) is also evidence of the endless quest for quality. The use of covering the vines is still widespread in vineyards where dessert grapes called 'Italia' are grown. Although most vine growers still love tradition, the situation is rapidly changing. Local vine stocks are being improved through cloning and are ever more often grown side by side with foreign vines (French vines).

Awaiting the great 'Doc Sicilia'

The change is particularly taking place in the fermenting cellars. On the one hand, local grapes are extensively used and highly appreciated both as single-grape wines - Nero d'Avola is appraised as one of the best red wines in the world: the grapes are excellent for dessert or, again, can be mixed with imported grapes which not only improve their quality, but make local grapes more suited to the changing tastes of consumers. On the other hand, growers tend to widen their output of non-Sicilian single-grape vines such as Chardonnay, Cabernet Sauvignon, Merlot and Sirah, which grow better in Sicily than anywhere else. Seventeen areas are now labeled as 'doc' (a quality label) - including Sciacca and Delia Nivolelli - but other areas - Doc Riesi, the Valley of Temples and Madonie - will be labeled soon. Sicily will soon obtain the 'Doc Sicilia' quality label, an international label designed as a sort of multi-product brand including all products from Sicily (today a similar brand is the "Indicazione Geografica Tipica" (Typical Geographic Area) label).

Bianco d'Alcamo

This is probably the most well know Sicilian white wine. It is mostly made from Cataratto grapes, a long-time mainstay of Sicilian wine making. The other grapes used are the traditional Inzolia, Grillo and Grecanico as well as the non-Sicilian grapes Chardonnay, Müller Thurgau and Sauvignon. This wine is dry with a strong scent, the various grapes used being quite evident. It has been registered as a "Classico", and has to be made from 80% Cataratto grapes and late harvest grapes, as well as the sort of grapes used for sparkling wines.

Cerasuolo di Vittoria

The name refers to the town in the centre of the Ragusa province, the very cultural heart of the area and quite likely the native town of the Frappato grapes it is made of. The mix of Frappato and Nero d'Avola makes this cherry-red wine a little dry, vigorously alcoholic with a warm and pleasant taste.

Doc Marsala

The oldest known documentation referring to Marsala dates back to 1773, when a ship left Trapani bound for England with barrels of wine that had a high alcohol strength so that they would stand the long voyage. This voyage marked the extraordinary history of a liqueur-like wine which, over the centuries, has gained popularity throughout the world. The situation has not changed that much these days. The Doc certification brings together many traditions. First and foremost, it sets out the production area as being the area around Trapani, except for the areas of Alcamo, Pantelleria and Favignana, considered border areas of Palermo and which has its own special wine production, and the islands that fall

within the administrative government of Palermo. Marsala is made from a wide variety of both white and red grape: the numerous varieties of Catarratto, Damaschino, Grillo, Inzolia; Nerello Mascalese, Nero d'Avola, Pignatello. They even add alcohol produced from grapes or wine brandy and, if need be, concentrated must. The end product comes in a number of varieties depending on the sugar content (dry, semidry, sweet), color (golden, amber, ruby red) and ageing, which goes from a minimum of one year to over ten years (Fine, Superiore, Superiore Riserva, Vergine and/or Soleras, Vergine and/or Soleras Stravecchio or Vergine and/or Soleras Riserva). Traditionally, Marsala is drunk with traditional Sicilian cakes and pastries - cannoli, cassata, Martorana marzipan fruit - and, a more modern twist, with herb cheeses. However, Marsala is still considered the wine for thought and contemplation par excellence.

Etna Rosso

The area around Etna volcano is well known for its local grapes, namely Nerello Mescalese which is about the only variety of grape used to make this dry red wine. It is a little towards a purple color and is full-bodied, warm and robust. It will certainly make a name for itself in coming years. There are other wines from the area between Catania and Messina made from similar grapes.

Malvasia delle Lipari, Moscato di Noto, Moscato di Pantelleria

Sicily can boast an outstanding show of sweet wines and dessert wines, sometimes even sparkling wines. Malvasia from the island of Lipari is made from a particular variety of grape that comes from the Aeolian

Vineyards and *dammusi* on the island of Pantelleria, kingdom of the *Zibibbo* grape

WINE CATEGORIES

Three labels define Italian wines according to quality. IGT (Typical Geographic Indication) guarantees vine cultivation according to certain regula-tions. DOC (Controlled Origin Denomination) indicates conformity to regulations on area of origin, and production and maturation procedures. The top label is DOCG (Guaranteed and Controlled Origin Denomination); there are around 20 DOCG wines in Italy.

Islands. This variety of grape gives a golden-yellow wine with a warm taste, sugary, with undertones of mature apricot and tamarind. The Moscato di Noto, from the area around Siracusa, is made from the unmistakable Moscato Bianco (white Moscato), heir to the sort of white grapes the ancient Romans used to indulge in called "uva appiana"; it was so sweet it used to attract bees. The particular taste of Moscato di Pantelleria, on the other hand, comes from the Zibibbo grape, originally from north Africa. This grape is also used to make a sort of strong sweet.

Marsala

This wine, which is made in Marsala, in the province of Trapani, really needs little introduction. It is probably better if we explain the importance and the sorts of these aperitif and after dinner wines, which are also drunk for the mere pleasure or in thought and contemplation. They have been divided into two categories: gold and amber, made from yellow-gold grapes, Cataratto, Inzolia; Damaschino, the typical Rubino, which is made from the red Perricone, Nero d'avola and Nerello Mascalese grapes. All these wines come as dry, semidry and sweet, and must meet the following requirements: Fine (17° alcohol strength, one year's ageing), Superiore (18° alcohol strength and four years' ageing), Vergine or Soleras (18° alcohol strength and five years' ageing), Vergine Stravecchio or Riserva (18° alcohol strength and ten years' ageing). Some special wines can be added, such as: Garibaldi Dolce (GD) - for Marsala Superiore; Italia Particolare (IP) - for Marsala Fine; London Particolar (LP) - for Marsala Superiore; Superiore Old Marsala (SOM) - for Marsala Superiore; Cremovo, Zabaione Vino Aromatizzato.

Nero d'Avola

Made from one of the most prized grapes on the island, this is an unblended cherry-red wine. It is quite dry and very strong, full-bodied and excellent for ageing. It is used as a blending wine for a number of Doc-certified wines such as Rosso, or wines with a specific grape variety, as well as some of the best non-Doc wines.

Zibibbo

The name Zibibbo is of Arabic origin and means "dry grapes". Indeed, one of the other names, Moscato d'Alessandria, underlines the probable Egyptian origin. It was the Romans who spread this sweet wine throughout the Mediterranean. A straw-yellow color, with gold highlights, it has an intense moscato aroma. It is sweet with a very high alcohol strength. These characteristics are enhanced by the way the raisins are obtained. Most of this sort of sweet wine comes from the island of Pantelleria.

AGRIGENTO

Le Botti di Antistene
Viale L. Sciascia 36, tel. 0934939007
www.lebottidiantistene.com

MENFI
Planeta
Contrada Dispensa, tel. 092580009
www.planeta.it
- ● *Cerasuolo di Vittoria - Doc*
- ● *La Segreta Rosso Sicilia - Igt*
- ● *Merlot Sicilia - Igt*
- ● *Santa Cecilia Sicilia Rosso - Igt*
- ● *Syrah Sicilia Rosso - Igt*
- ○ *Cometa Bianco Sicilia - Igt*
- ○ *La Segreta Bianco Sicilia - Igt*

SAMBUCA DI SICILIA
Di Prima
Via Guasto 27, tel. 0925941201
www.diprimavini.it
- ● *Villamaura Syrah Sicilia - Igt*
- ● *Pepita Rosso - Igt*
- ● *Gibelmoro Nero d'Avola - Igt*
- ○ *Sambuca di Sicilia Bianco Pepita - Doc*

CALTANISSETTA

BUTERA
Feudo Principi di Butera
Contrada Deliella, tel. 0934347726
www.feudobutera.it
- Calat Merlot Sicilia - Igt
- Deliella Nero d'Avola Sicilia - Igt
- San Rocco Cabernet Sauvignon
  Sicilia - Igt

CATANIA

CALTAGIRONE
Antica Tenuta del Nanfro
Contrada Nanfro S. Nicola Le Canne
tel. 093360525, www.nanfro.com
- Nero d'Avola in purezza Antica Tenuta
  del Nanfro - Igt
- ○ Nanfro Inzolia Sicilia - Igt
- ○ Tenuta Nanfro Sicilia Bianco - Igt

CASTIGLIONE DI SICILIA
Cottanera - Fratelli Cambria
Contrada Jannazzo, tel. 0942963601
- Barbazzale Sicilia Rosso - Igt
- Fatagione Sicilia Rosso - Igt
- Grammonte Rosso Sicilia - Igt
- L'Ardenza Rosso Sicilia - Igt
- Sole di Sesta Sicilia Rosso - Igt

LINGUAGLOSSA
Gambino Maria
Contrada Petto Dragone
tel. 348822130, www.agricolagambino.it
Tenuta Scilio di Valle Galfina
Contrada Arrigo 2 km
along the SP
Linguaglossa-Zafferana.
tel. 095647789

MILO
Barone di Villagrande
Via del Bosco 25
tel. 0957894339
www.villagrande.it

MESSINA

Colosi
Via Militare Ritiro 27, tel. 09053852
www.cantinecolosi.com
- L'Incontro Sicilia Rosso - Igt
- ○ Malvasia delle Lipari Naturale
  di Salina - Doc

- ◖ Malvasia delle Lipari Passito
  di Salina - Doc
- ◖ Moscato di Pantelleria - Doc
- ◖ Passito di Pantelleria - Doc

Palari
Santo Stefano Briga Contrada Barna
tel. 090630194
- Faro Palari - Doc
- Rosso del Soprano Sicilia - Igt

SANTA MARINA SALINA
Hauner Carlo
On the isle of Salina. Via Umberto I
S. Marina Salina, tel. 0909843141
www.hauner.it
- Antonello Salina Rosso - Igt
- Salina Rosso - Igt
- Carlo Hauner - Igt
- ○ Salina Bianco - Igt
- ◖ Malvasia delle Lipari Passita - Doc

PALERMO

Abraxas
Via Enrico Albanese 29, tel. 0916110051
- ○ Kuddia del Gallo Sicilia Bianco - Igt
- ◖ Passito di Pantelleria - Doc

CASTELBUONO
Abbazia Santa Anastasia
Contrada S. Anastasia, tel. 0921671959
www.abbaziasantanastasia.it
- Litra Rosso Sicilia - Igt
- Montenero Rosso Sicilia - Igt
- Passomaggio Rosso Sicilia - Igt
- Nero d'Avola Sicilia - Igt
- ○ Passomaggio Bianco Sicilia - Igt

> **WINE LEGEND**
> Wines are listed with
> symbols which indicate
> their type
> - red
> ○ white
> ◍ rosé
> ◖ sweet or dessert

MONREALE
Pollara
2 kim along the SP 4/bis
in Contrada Malvelli
tel. 0918462922
www.principedicorleone.it
- Il Rosso Principe di
  Corleone Sicilia - Igt
- Principe di Corleone
  Nero d'Avola Sicilia - Igt
- ○ Principe di Corleone Inzolia Sicilia - Igt

Spadafora
Contrada Virzì, tel. 091514952
www.spadafora.com
- Don Pietro Rosso Sicilia - Igt
- Schietto Cabernet Sauvignon Sicilia - Igt
- Schietto Chardonnay Sicilia - Igt
- Schietto Syrah Sicilia - Igt
- Sole dei Padri Sicilia Rosso - Igt

SCLAFANI BAGNI

Conte Tasca d'Almerita
Contrada Regaleali, tel. 0921544011
www.tascadalmerita.it
- ● *Contea di Sclafani Cabernet*
  Sauvignon - Doc
- ● *Nero d'Avola - Igt*
- ● *Rosso Doc Contea di Sclafani - doc*
- ○ *Contea di Sclafani Bianco Nozze*
  d'Oro - Doc
- ○ *Contea di Sclafani Chardonnay - Doc*

SIRACUSA

Pupillo
Contrada Targia 5, tel. 0931494029
www.solacium.it
- ◑ *Moscato di Siracusa Pollio - Doc*
- ◑ *Moscato di Siracusa Solacium - Doc*
- ◑ *Moscato di Siracusa Vigna di Mela - Doc*

NOTO

Coop. Interprovinciale Elorina
Contrada Belliscala
tel. 0931857068, www.elorina.com

In Siracusa: Euryalus Castle pag. 81

TRAPANI

Cantina Sociale di Trapani
Contrada Ospedaletto, tel. 0923539349
www.cantinasocialetrapani.com
- ● *Forti Terre di Sicilia Nero d'Avola Sicilia - Igt*
- ● *Forti Terre di Sicilia Rosso - Igt*
- ○ *Forti Terre di Sicilia Bianco Sicilia - Igt*

Fazio Wines
Fulgatore Via Cap. Rizzo 39
tel. 0923811700, www.faziowines.it
- ● *Pietrasacra Sicilia Rosso - Igt*
- ● *Torre dei Venti Sicilia Rosso - Igt*
- ○ *Torre dei Venti Inzolia Chardonnay*
  Sicilia - Igt
- ○ *Torre dei Venti Inzolia Sicilia - Igt*
- ◑ *Ky Moscato Passito Sicilia - Igt*

CALATAFIMI-SEGESTA

Vini Marzuko
Contrada Marzuko, tel. 0924951191
www.vinimarzuko.it

MARSALA

Baglio Hopps
Contrada Biesina 2, tel. 0923967020
www.infohopps.com
- ● *Incantari Sicilia Rosso - Igt*
- ● *Nero d'Avola Sicilia - Igt*
- ○ *Grillo Sicilia Bianco - Igt*

De Bartoli Marco - Vecchio Samperi
Contrada Fornara-Samperi 292
tel. 0923962093, www.marcodebartoli.com
- ○ *Grappoli del Grillo - doc*
- ○ *Pietra nera - Igt*

Fattoria Fratelli Lombardo
Via Vincenzo Florio 17, tel. 0923981003
www.lombardo.biz

Florio
Via Vincenzo Florio 1, tel. 0923781111
www.cantineflorio.com

Pellegrino
Via del Fante 37/39, tel. 0923719911
- ● *Gorgo Tondo Sicilia Rosso - Igt*
- ◑ *Marsala Superiore Riserva Dom*
  Pellegrino - Doc
- ◑ *Moscato Passito di Pantelleria Nes - Doc*

Rallo
Via Vincenzo Florio 2, tel. 0923721633
www.cantinerallo.it
- ● *Vesco Sicilia Rosso - Igt*
- ◑ *Marsala Vergine Soleras*
  Riserva 20 anni - Doc
- ◑ *Passito di Pantelleria*
  Mare d'Ambra - Doc

Tenuta di Donnafugata
Via Sebastiano Lipari 18
tel. 0923724200, www.donnafugata.it
- ● *Contessa Entellina Rosso Mille e Una*
  Notte - Doc
- ● *Contessa Entellina Rosso Tancredi - Doc*
- ○ *Contessa Entellina Bianco Vigna di*
  Gabri - Doc
- ○ *Contessa Entellina Chiarandà - Doc*
- ◑ *Moscato Passito di Pantelleria Ben*
  Ryé - Doc

PANTELLERIA

Cooperativa Nuova Agricoltura
Contrada Barone, tel. 0923915712

Enopolio di Pantelleria
Via Balate Contrada Arenella
tel. 0923912556, www.pantelleriadoc.it

Maccotta Cav. Fortunato
Contrada Kamma 165, tel. 0923915065
www.maccotta.com

Minardi Andrea
Contrada Karuscia 6, tel. 0923911160
www.viniminardi.it
- ◑ *Passito di Pantelleria Karuscia - Doc*

Murana Salvatore
Contrada Kamma 276, tel. 0923915231
www.salvatoremurana.com
- ◑ *Moscato di Pantelleria Mueggen - Doc*
- ◑ *Moscato Passito di Pantelleria*
  Khamma - Doc
- ◑ *Moscato Passito di Pantelleria*
  Martingana - Doc

LIQUEURS

Spices and flavors, which are so important in Sicilian cooking, are also generously used in local liqueur making. As a matter of fact, Sicily can boast a world renowned production of eau-de-vie (the renowned Grappa di Nero d'Avola or the scented Grappa made from the grapes used to make Malvasia wine are worth mentioning) but we must not forget Rosolio and other liqueurs in all their different flavors: mulberry, pistachio, hazelnut cream, coffee, cinnamon, lemon, prickly pear, vanilla, chocolate, orange, tangerine, fennel, bay leaves, almond-tree blossoms, rose, carob bean. All these liqueurs keep the delicate taste and smell of the fruits they are made with, and they are excellent digestive liqueurs which can be sipped either ice-cold after a substantial meal or as a dessert drink with traditional cakes.

Elisir di carruba
Carob elixir
This liqueur has a 24% alcohol content and a light pleasant taste. It is ideal after meals with desserts, cakes and cookies. From carob they also get decotto, Carrubone amaro and Karrubello, a digestive liqueur with carob syrup that is served chilled.

These highly-perfumed lemons are ideal for making *Limoncello*

Fuoco del Vulcano
A highly "hot" and strong liqueur, just like the Etna volcano. Made from an old recipe that has never been changed this liqueur blends a full flavor with a pleasant and refined fragrance. A wonderful digestive and very invigorating on cold winter days, it is delicate on ice-cream and cannot be substituted in the most refined of cocktails.

Grappa dell'Etna
This grappa is made by distilling the fermented marc of the top-quality grapes grown on the slopes of Etna volcano. The special vacuum distilling method and the aging in special oak barrels make this a highly prestigious grappa. It is usually sold in characteristic bottles covered in lava stone.

Limoncello di Sicilia
This is a sweet, thirst quenching liqueur with a distinct flavor. The fragrance reflects the smells of Sicilian citrus fruit. Served very cold, it is drunk at the end of meals as a digestive. It is really nice on ice-cream and on mixed fruit salads and also in preparing long drinks. The Limoncello cream is also a well know drink and has milk in it. Mandarinetto

and Arancello (respectively made from mandarins and oranges) also have very distinct flavors.

Liquore di cannella
Cinnamon liqueur
Highly aromatic, unique and unmistakable, the scent of this liqueur stirs memories of some bygone liqueurs called "rosolio". The liqueur is masterly prepared to strict homemaking techniques. Cinnamon has to steep for 120 days in pure alcohol, thereby releasing an intense fragrance, with undertones of spiciness. A slightly brown-amber color it is pleasantly dry. We suggest trying it at a temperature of around 10°C with chocolate and almond cakes.

Liquore di ficodindia
Prickly-pear liqueur
A very smooth liqueur for meditation, it is dark red. It has a light, sweet fragrance and is indeed sweet and creamy, very fruity. It is always served chilled in tiny glasses and goes exceedingly well with the small Sicilian cakes, with a creamy sugary pudding called "panna cotta" and

with mixed fruit salads. It can even be used in cocktails or just as a digestive liqueur. One particular combination is with sharp soft cheeses.

Rosolio di alloro

This liqueur is prepared using the original traditional methods. The bay leaves are picked from the local bay trees, that abound in Sicily owing to the wonderful Sicilian weather, and are left to steep in pure alcohol. Thanks to the traditional homemade methods used, this rosolio keeps its aromatic and digestive properties. It is served chilled and well shaken.

Sperlinga: Tortone Cake Festival pag. 169

Prickly pears used for making the *fichidindia* liqueur

AGRIGENTO

SCIACCA
Gioie di Bacco
Viale della Vittoria 35, tel. 0925902623
Grappa, wine and liqueurs
Nonsolovini
Via Cappuccini 69, tel. 092525052
Wine and typical liqueurs

CATANIA

SANTA VENERINA
Distilleria Fratelli Russo
Via Vittorio Emanuele 355
tel. 095953321, www.russo.it
Etna grappa, Limoncello, Mandarinetto, Fuoco del Vulcano, Rosolio
Liquori Cav. Rosario Giuffrida
Via Stabilimenti 257, tel. 095953494
www.liquorigiuffrida.com
Limoncello, Anice, Amaro

ENNA

Agricasale
Ciavarini, tel. 0935686034
Prickly-pear and wild herb liqueurs

GAGLIANO CASTELFERRATO
Fattoria Valle del Sole
Via Raffaello Sanzio 151, tel. 0935694052, www.ficodi.com
Prickly-pear liqueur

MESSINA

La Bouteille
Via Nino Bixio 141, tel. 090717326
Wine and typical liqueurs

BARCELLONA POZZO DI GOTTO
Liquori Messina
Via Carducci 96, tel. 0909795160
Limoncello, Arancello, Prickly-pear liqueur, Chocolate liqueur, Cinnamon liqueur, Rosolio and wine

PALERMO

Fratelli Tutone Anice Unico
Via Garibaldi 91, tel. 0916161908
Anice, Limoncello
I Peccatucci di Mamma Andrea
Via Principe di Scordia 67, tel. 091334835
Rosolio and sweets

SIRACUSA

Agrifanusa
Via Adorno 7/b, tel. 0931782146
Carruba decoction, Mandarinetto, Limoncello and Rosolio
Dieci e lode
Viale Zecchino 165 t. 0931442655
www.diecielode.it
Amaro Carrubone

TRAPANI

MARSALA
Morsi & Sorsi
Via A. Diaz 66, tel. 0923719481
www.morsiesorsi.it
Amaro and osolio, Arancello, Limoncello, dessert wines and typical products

CAKES

Positioned right in middle of the Mediterranean, Sicily has wonderfully preserved the customs of the different peoples that have conquered and ruled the island over the centuries, cleverly adapting them over the centuries. This is especially true of food (cakes and pastries in particular) where Arab and Spanish conquerors put their stamp, thanks to their cultural influence and to the introduction of new kinds of food. From the Eastern world came oranges, lemons, cedars, the peach-tree and the apricot tree, the pistachio tree, the carob tree, jasmine and the sesame, cane sugar and spices, all of which are fundamental ingredients in the most important cakes in Sicily. The Spanish galleons brought cocoa from the American continent, a product which Sicilian confectioners still use following the original Aztec recipe, combined with other unusual ingredients. In Sicily cultures never lie over each other. Rather, they complete each other. If the Arabs introduced cassata, the Spanish made it a baroque wonder. Likewise, the Arabs introduced marzipan, but the Spanish gave it all the colorful shapes of the Martorana marzipan fruits. The evolution of Sicilian culture (and food) reached its peak in the 19th century and was even mentioned in the novel "Il Gattopardo". This was the century of the great chefs who were inspired by the Paris cuisine, people who are conferred the title of "monsù", the Sicilian adaptation for the French "monsieur".

Agnello pasquale
Easter Lamb
Common in most Sicilian towns, though it can now even be found in Rome or Milan, this sugar lamb or marzipan lamb, with its citron marmalade filling, is one of the traditional Sicilian Easter cakes. Il looks like a white lamb, usually in a crouched position, holding a red banner with a white cross, the symbol of

Sweetmeats made with almond paste

the Risen Christ. You will more than certainly find it in Erice, in the province of Trapani, where it has a delicate outer covering of marzipan fruit.

Bevande dolci e dissetanti
Sweet and thirst-quenching drinks
Sicily boasts a wide range of thirst-quenching drinks for the hot summers. These drinks include: 'minnulata' or 'latti di mennula' and is based on the use of almond milk. Granatina, on the other hand, is made from the juice of pomegranate seeds. "Siminzata" is obtained from the seeds of the muskmelon, and lastly the very simple (and extremely cold) sugared milk called 'carapigna' and 'sciala cori'.

Biancomangiare
Traditional of the province of Ragusa, this dessert is made of diced almonds mixed with sugar, starch, lemon peel and powdered cinnamon mixed into a smooth cream. This cream is then put into special earthenware molds and left to thicken. The molds are then turned over onto lemon leaves placed on plates and the dessert is served like that.

Biscotti ennesi
Enna cookies
Flour, sugar, yeast, water and lard. These cookies need to stand a long time to rise (as long as 16 hours), in two separate steps. They are then baked in the oven at low temperature for about

40 minutes. They go very well with a southern Italian wine called "Cerasuolo di Vittoria".

Braccialette

Doughnuts: literally bracelets
Traditional of Nicosia in the province of Enna, these cakes are carnival doughnuts made of flour, water, egg, sugar and lard. They are fried in boiling oil and covered in sugar and cinnamon.

Buccellato

This is a typical cake from Aidone in the province of Enna, though it is also found in other areas from Palermo to the center of the Madonie Park. Originally, this cake was fig bread, but these days they use biscuit pastry with almonds, walnuts, sultanas, chocolate and boiled wine or honey. Cinnamon is added with orange peel and cloves, and the whole thing is then covered in icing sugar.

Cannoli

Cannoli are certainly among the most famous Sicilian pastries, indeed a byword of Sicily. Around Palermo, where they first appeared, you will find "cannolicchi" a smaller version as big as a finger. On the other hand in the "Piana degli Albanesi" they are the biggest you are likely to get in Sicily. From the traditional Sicilian cannolo grew the idea of a tiny one

stuffed with chocolate cream which, though, is not part of Sicilian tradition. This small cannolo has an outer oven baked spiral pastry crust, which must be light brown and crusty. When it has cooled down it is filled with ricotta cheese mixed with sugar, pistachio nuts, diced candied fruit and various flavorings.

Cassata siciliana

Experts do not agree on the origin of this name: some believe it comes from the Arabic word *qas'at* , a large deep bowl; others say it comes from the Latin word *caseus*, 'cheese'. Both schools are, however, compatible with the nature of this cake. It must have originally been a sort of chilled fresh cheese cake made from a dome shaped sponge. The cheese was later substituted with ricotta cheese sweetened with sugar. This cake was considered the Easter cake par excellence. The Cassata today has a sponge and marzipan base filled with fresh ricotta cheese mixed with cinnamon, vanilla, chocolate and pistachio nuts. The whole thing is then covered in icing of various colors and perfumes. It is then further decorated with candied fruit, marzipan, small almond pastries and other decorations. Among the numerous variations on the theme we cannot but mention the

Cherries decorate the summer *cannolo*, known locally as *ova murin*

cassata from Erice, which is filled with citron marmalade and covered in marzipan.

Cassatella di Agira

This is a specialty with the same name as the town it comes from. It is made from short pastry and looks like a crescent lace covered cake. It is filled with almonds, chickpea flour, sugar, cocoa, cinnamon and lemon peel and goes well with a glass of "Prosecco" sparkling wine.

Cedrata

Citron cake
This sweet is from Modica, in the province of Ragusa. Of Arab origins, as is orangeade, it has similar digestive properties to the citron drink. It is prepared using citron peel that has been washed in running water and then cooked in honey. It is as thick as nougat and eaten as small flaky pieces, especially after the large meals eaten at the most important festivities.

Colombina pasquale

Easter dove
This Easter cake is made from short pastry (soft flour, sugar, egg, butter, grated lemon peel) in the shape of a dove and is then covered in marzipan and lemon icing sugar.

Cubbaita

Of Arab origins, this sweet is also found in Calabria. It is a very soft nougat, made with almonds, honey and sesame seeds, and then cut into diamond shapes.

Cuccìa

Though of Arab origins this cake has taken on a Christian importance in Sicily. Traditionally it is prepared on December 13th , Saint Lucy's Day, based on the legend that on this day a ship berthed in the port of Palermo loaded with grain, thereby saving the city from terrible famine. The original recipe needs grain boiled in water for at least 10 hours. Then it is mixed with olive oil. The cake version adds a ricotta cheese cream mixed with sugar, chocolate flakes, pieces of candied pumpkin and pine seeds.

Dolci di riposto

"Long-life" cakes
This is the name of the small marzipan cakes that come in various shapes. They are filled with various sorts of jams and then covered in icing sugar. As the name implies these cakes can be kepy in the cupboard for a long time

Frutta di Martorana

Martorana marzipan fruit
These highly colored pastries shaped to look like fruit, vegetables and other things, bear a story that takes us way back in time and to far off places. Let's start with the raw material: almond pasta, or marzipan as it is better known as, a name that comes from certain kinds of vases from the Indian city of Martaban, a word that has passed through Arabic to mean "the mixture of sugar and spices" that was traditionally kept in those precious containers. Secondly, the tradition of celebrating All Saints Day and All Soul's Day at the beginning of November with auspicious cakes that reflected the abundance and colors of summer (Martorana fruit, packed into small baskets tied with ribbons were given to the good children; bad children received coal, though made of extremely sweet marzipan). Lastly, the courtesy title due to the aristocratic Eloisa Martorana, 1193, founder of the Palermo convent that made history, especially for the Benedictine nuns' ability in making pastries. As time passed by all religious events were bestowed with a special marzipan cake: little sheep for Christmas, small horses and donkeys for Saint Anthony, small pigs for Saint Sebastian, lambs for Easter. When the secret knowledge of how to make the cakes leaked from the convents into the hands of the confectioners, the Martorana fruit broke all boundaries with the calendar or indeed with imagination. The production from Erice, in the Trapani area, is worth mentioning as the fruit takes on the shape of flowers.

Genovesi

Genoese cake
These round cakes are the only cakes in Sicily to be eaten hot: straight out of the oven with a sprinkling of sugar.

FOOD

The shape of these little cakes reminds people of the traditional 'minni di virgini', an impertinent reference to the breasts of the novice in the convent of the same name in Palermo, or the 'minni di sant'Agata', a term used in Catania to honor the city patron saint, as depicted in the sacred iconography, with the symbols of her martyrdom lying on a tray.

Mostarda

The difference between this "mostarda" and the sort traditional of Northern Italy, which is a conserve of pickled candied fruit or vegetables in a thick mustardy syrup that is eaten with boiled meats or well seasoned cheeses, is that Sicilian "mostarda" is a special cake. It is made by cooking crushed grape must (or the juice of prickly pears) and flour. The mixture is then poured into small earthenware molds and left to dry in the sun. It is eaten year round as it has an extremely long life.

Mpanatigghi

Crescent shaped cakes typical of Modica, they were brought to Sicily by the Spanish during the Spanish domination. This is proved by both the etymology of the name (from *empanadas* or *empadillas*) and by the unusual match of meat with chocolate.

Nfasciatieddi

Baked cakes made of pastry filled with boiled wine, honey, sugar, toasted almonds, cinnamon and orange and lemon peel. On removing the cakes from the oven they are doused in boiled wine or honey and then covered in almond flakes.

Nougat

The abundance of honey and almonds in Sicily couldn't but have increased the output of nougat in Sicily. The range of types and qualities of nougat on the island is bewildering, many of them being made to local recipes. The basic recipe has almonds, sugar, honey and natural flavorings. Among the many kinds of nougat there is one that comes from the country and is very similar to the Calabrian ice-cream nougat. Around Ragusa, the white and the toasted sorts are renowned for the whole almonds.

Nucatoli

"S" shaped cookies from Modica in the province of Ragusa. These cookies are filled with dried figs, almonds, walnuts, quince jam and honey and are partially covered in white icing sugar.

Ova murina o Cannolo estivo

This cake dates back to the late 17th century at the monastery of the Badia Grande di Sciacca. The name might come from "Mori" (the Mores) who were extremely fond of spices and cocoa. The name might also come from the "moro" (brown) outer covering or even from the "murena" (moray eel), a dark colored fish on the outside and pale inside. Whatever the origin, this is a simply delicious dessert. Instead of using ricotta cheese (a winter ingredient) they use a vanilla milk cream with dark chocolate, cinnamon, candied pumpkin, toasted almonds and grated lemon peel. It is then covered in icing sugar with half a candied cherry on the top.

Pasta di mandorle o Pasta reale

Marzipan or almond paste
Almonds are one of the most important plants in Sicilian agriculture. The importance of almond paste, also known as "royal pastry" because it is considered the queen of all Sicilian cake shops, dates back to the Arab dominance of the island. The almonds are first boiled, peeled and then ground. Then they are mixed with sugar, egg white, honey, glucose syrup, a pinch of cinnamon and orange or lemon flavoring. The paste is then shaped into the various shapes which, having been covered in icing sugar, are then left to stand for 12 hours before going into the oven to make then golden (about 30 minutes). When diluted in water, almond paste terns into a thirst-quenching summer drink.

Pignolata di Messina

This is a typical Christmas cake found around the Messina area. It consists of balls of fried egg pastry half dipped into icing sugar (or honey in Palermo) and the other half into hot chocolate. The balls are then placed onto each other on a serving dish as a two-colored pile of balls, and the balls stick together.

Ravioli

These ravioli consist of a rather thin layer of pastry made with flour, sugar, lard, water and wine. The pastry is then cut into squares which are then filled (ricotta cheese, sugar, cinnamon, pieces of dark chocolate). The pastry squares are then closed to look like ravioli and fried in deep boiling oil. They are served with a sprinkling of icing sugar.

This *frutta di Martorana* made with almond paste incorporates all the colors of southern Italy

Sfoglio

This is the traditional cake in the Madonie area, especially in Castellana Sicula, Petralia Sottana and Polizzi Generosa. A short pastry cake filled with fresh cheese called "tuma", candied pumpkin, egg white, cocoa, sugar and lemon peel, it is cooked in the oven and eaten cold.

Sorbetti, granite, gelati

Sherbert, Granita, Ice-cream
From the Turkish word *serbet* meaning "a cool drink", this word was transformed into the Arabic word *sarab*, hence the word "sciroppo" (syrup). However, the most suggestive word is sorbetto (sherbert). The closest reference, however, is to the use of snow collected from the Etna volcano and kept in natural hollows or pits until well into the summer, ready for the preparation of what was the forerunner of ice-cream. Though it is quite likely this method dates to Roman or Greek times, it was the Arabs who turned ice-cream making into a real art and gave it the technology and tastes that have made ice-cream what it is today. From

Sherbert to granita, and from granita to ice-cream: the raw material changes, from water to milk, as does the consistency, from a semi-liquid substance to a creamy one. However, the outstanding feature of Sicilian ice-cream is the variety and the typical tastes, some of which just cannot be reproduced anywhere else. Sicilian ice-cream parlors fear no competition: the "spongata" are extremely mouth watering: They are a collection of various tastes mixed together with liqueurs. "Scumoni" is a covering of chocolate or pistachio with beaten egg and sugar in the center. As for granita, the range goes from lemon to coffee, which are two classic ones. But, there are specific Sicilian ones made from, say, almond milk, prickly pear and black mulberries. It is quite well known that Sicilians have breakfast at the local bar with a brioche and a glass of coffee and cream granita. Another of the many oddities is the watermelon ice-cream found in Palermo which smells of Jasmine, typically eaten on Saint Rosalie's Day.

Testa di turco

Turk's head
This is a sort of very large cream puff (more or less as big as a small head, hence the name) filled with pork meat, ricotta cheese, egg, cocoa and cinnamon. As this cake is not easy to make it is usually only made to order these days.

Vino cotto e mustazzoli

A cake made with prickly pears and boiled wine.

Zuccata

Candied pumpkin
This ingredient is traditional in Sicilian cake shops and fundamental in preparing the cassata. It is obtained from the long pumpkin (looks like a trumpet) but also from water melon peel. The pumpkin is pounded for about an hour in water and salt. Then it is washed in running water and left to dry for a number of hours. Lastly it is cooked, cut into pieces and mixed with

the same weight of sugar and a good amount of cinnamon. The candied pumpkin prepared by the nuns of the Badia del Cancelliere convent in Palermo was once very famous.

AGRIGENTO

NARO
Milazzo
Via Cappuccini 17, tel. 0922958489
This shop is very small but the bakery is quite large. They sell the most typical Sicilian cakes though we would suggest you try the sweet ricotta cheese ravioli.

SCIACCA
Bar Scandaglia
Piazza A. Scandaliato 5, tel. 092521665
Right on the main square, this bar has an evocative open-air terrace overlooking the port. A very smart bar, the cakes are very good, as are the savories like the stuffed pizzas, the small snack pizzas and the sfoglie. From the ice-cream bar you really must try the pistachio and the chocolate ice-creams.
Dolci Sapori
Via Cappuccini 33/C, tel. 092586986
Though this shop has not been open for very long it has quickly become one of the mandatory stops for people who are fond of homemade Sicilian cakes and sweets. The cakes include: cucchitelle, ricotta cheese cannoli, cassate, almond cakes, lemon mousse, fruit or almond semifreddi and many others.
Fratelli La Bella
Via A. De Gasperi 23, tel. 092521524
This is one of the best cake shops in the town. It is a classical shop, not particularly big, but full of many speciality cakes: iris, genovesi, cassatelle, small almond or pistachio cakes, pignolata, decorated cakes... The cassate and the cucchitelle ("cucchiteddi" in the Sicilian dialect) are particularly good. Then there are the traditional cakes with Arab origins made of durum wheat, sugar, almonds and candied pumpkin. The rotisserie is also very good.
Nuovo Fiore
Viale della Vittoria 24, tel. 092584218
The premises are simple but carefully planned, the cakes are freshly made every day: cakes, cookies and ice-cream

Ricotta cheese is used in Sicilian cuisine and pastry-making, especially to make *cassata*

made from wholesome ingredients. We suggest you try the ricotta cheese cakes and the "bucciddati", a typical Christmas cake made with dried figs, almonds and chocolate.

CALTANISSETTA

Bar Esperia
Via Malta 6, tel. 0934592234
Not far from the law courts, this bar has a vast selection of typical homemade cakes: almond cakes, almond or the Bronte pistachio croccanti, the classical cassata, cannoli and ricotta cheese ravioli.

CATANIA

Pasticceria Svizzera Caviezel
Corso Italia 123, tel. 0957222837
The name, which is so tightly tied to the town's cake traditions, appears once more in this very nice cake shop where the traditions of bygone recipes are continued for the pleasure of everyone with a sweet tooth. The assortment is extremely wide covering cakes of all sorts. You really must try the wonderful ice-creams and chilled cakes, melon ices and other seasonal specialities.

Savia
Via Etnea 302/304, tel. 095322335
www.savia.it
This is a historical cake shop on the main street. It is a traditional Sicilian shop selling the "sfoglie", the highly colored marzipan cakes, cookies, ice-cream, granita and, lastly, the chilled cakes called "semifreddi". The food is highly varied, especially at lunch time.

ACIREALE
Castorina
Piazza Duomo 20/21, tel. 095601546
www.pasticceriacastorina.com
This really nice cake shop has specialised in a wide range of almond cakes, cassata, ice-creams and granita since 1953.

BRONTE
Conti Gallenti
Corso Umberto 275, tel. 095691165
This cake shop has the bakery next to it. Pistachio nuts, the love of the Bronte, is celebrated in all possible versions: cassate, cannoli and ice-cream.

CALTAGIRONE
Scivoli
Viale Milazzo 121, tel. 093323108
The invincible 83-year-old owner still runs this warm, welcoming shop with its wood furnishing. Do not miss the cassatine siciliane, the cannoli, the ricotta cheese sfogliatelle nor the meat sfogliatelle which are still sweet and have almonds, bitter cocoa, cinnamon, vanilla and hazelnuts.

LINGUAGLOSSA
L'Alhambra
Via G.Marconi 62, tel. 095643156
Among the special cakes look for the hazelnut and honey "mustaccioli", the rice "zeppole" and the hazelnut marzipan.

RANDAZZO
Bar Arturo
Via Umberto 73, tel. 095921068
This bar is decorated in Liberty style. It is located inside the 15th century palazzo Rummolo. You will find the typical Sicilian cakes on the cake table, with the marzipan and pistachio cake in the forefront.

SANT'ALFIO
Vittorio Popotto
Piazza Duomo 12, tel. 095968153
This rather rustic shop in brick and lava stone has some excellent almond paste cakes, citrus-fruit-pastry cakes, cannoli, cassate and nougat. Do not miss the hazelnut and the walnut pastries.

ENNA

Biscottificio Savoia
Via Ospedale Umberto I 31
tel. 0935501371
This is a very small shop including the bakery and the outlet. Apart from the Enna sponge cake they make the buccellati and Saint Joseph's panuzzi.
Caffè del Centro
Piazza S. Cataldo 6/8, tel. 093522088
Right in the town center, with the bakery next to it, lies this bar and ice-cream parlor. The bar's speciality is the typical croccantino though you must not miss the giant cannolo.
Delizia Bar
Via Roma 446, tel. 0935500549
In the historic centre, in front of the cathedral, this shop has a bakery that is specialised in marzipan and cakes that look like monuments. There is also an ice-cream parlor and a rotiserie. Try the various sorts of rice croquettes called "arancini" (with meat or spinach, salmon or with eggplant).
Di Maggio
Enna Bassa, piazza Antonello da Messina 2/4, tel. 093529343
This is a large building on the road to Pergusa and to Piazza Armerina. Among the specialities: the "rametti di Napoli" (a sweet cookie with the ends covered in white chocolate and pure chocolate), the almond and fig buccellati, the cassatine di Agira with chocolate, almonds and chickpea flour and, lastly, nougat. Do try the almonds with rum.
Pasticceria Gelateria Campisi
Via Astronauti 27, tel. 0935504024
This shop makes artistic cakes, ice-cream cakes, fig and almond buccellati, nougat, pralineria and the traditional panuzzi.
Sant'Antonio
Viale IV Novembre 35, tel. 093537881
Though this is a bread shop you cannot leave Enna without trying their

FOOD

specialities: Enna cookies to be eaten with a nice glass of a special wine called Cerasuolo di Vittoria.

Tirrito
Via S. Leone 1, tel. 093525352
This cake shop makes the typical sponge cake used in Enna and, for 19th March, the artistic bread for Saint Joseph's Day.

PIAZZA ARMERINA
Antica Pasticceria Consoli
Via Sette Cantoni 32, tel. 0935680150
Again in the historic centre of the town, this cake shop, with the bakery next to it in view for all to see, is most welcoming. Apart from the marzipan cakes and normal nougat, try the torrone di campagna and the almond paste. At Easter the shop makes the traditional Easter dove cake and other cakes made with short pastry filled with marzipan.

Bar Pasticceria Europa
Via Roma 156
tel. 0935680235
www.pasticcerialberti.it
This bar is located at the entrance to the historic center and it sells, among the many traditional cakes, the traditional Easter dove cake and, above all, three cookies that have been registered and are dedicated to the people who have played an important role in the town's history and the famous town horse race called the "Palio dei Normanni": Ruggero (Roger) cookies, Normanno (Norman) cookies and Saraceno (Saracen) cookies.

Restivo
Via Mazzini 114, tel. 0935680048
This small cake shop specialises in almond paste cakes, nougat and marzipan.

Specialità Dolciumi Zingale
Via Gen. Muscarà 8, tel. 0935686111
There is a comfortable family feeling in this shop. They make excellent dry cakes and cookies; as your first taster we suggest the typical wine ones.

MESSINA

Bar Progresso
Viale S. Martino 33, tel. 090673734
This nice bar dates back to 1910. The furnishings are in marble and there is a gazebo outside. Apart from the semifreddi and granite they have coffee spongato; the recipe has been handed down for three generations.

De Stefano
Santo Stefano di Briga piazza S. Giovanni 1, tel. 090630275
This small bar on the town square has an enormous range of cakes on display. The ice-creams are really special; made like in the past using local products they come in many flavors: Avola almond, Bronte pistachio, Maletto strawberry. If this were not enough, they also have granite, anise cookies or the pignolate which is just as good. The service is exquisite.

MALFA
Cosi Duci
Via S. Lorenzo 9, tel. 0909844358
This cake shop is in an old house on the island of Salina and has a luring sign; it is ideal for people who are fond of the typical cakes: cannoli, nacatuli and vastedduzzi.

Villa Romana del Casale pag. 40

TAORMINA
Saint Honoré
Corso Umberto 208, tel. 094224877
While walking along the very long main street you cannot but help to notice this cake shop. It is not large, the assortment of cakes is highly concentrated. There are hundreds of specialties; the Martorana fruit are particularly good, as is the ice-cream in summer.

Turrisi
Castelmola via Pio IX 16 - on the corner with piazza Duomo, tel. 094228181
www.turrisibar.it
Spread over four stories, this historical cake shop is quite original in having apotropaic furnishings as well as other things hanging from the walls like almonds, Sicilian dolls, agricultural tools and many other things: a sort of multifunctional bazaar. The shop has many flavors of granite (the almond milk one is really special), ice-cream and, obviously, cassate. The sweet wine with almond, made using the traditionally recipe, is very famous (a dessert dish). It is one of the mandatory stops owing to the splendid view from the terrace and for the very charm of the town itself.

PALERMO

Accardi
Via G. Amoroso 1, tel. 091485797
Not far from the university area known as the "Cittadella Universitaria" this bar is a pleasant place where people meet and taste the savory and sweet goodies. It is also an internet point.

Cappello
Via Colonna Rotta 68, tel. 091489601
Not far from the cathedral, though a little hidden, this bar has to be hunted out as it really is worthwhile. This is probably the finest cake shop in the town with a vast assortment of cakes: both traditional and modern cakes and, as compared to other towns, a deep knowledge of chocolate desserts. Do not miss the pistachio "Sette Veli" and "Delizia" cakes.

Fratelli Magrì
Via I. Carini 42, tel. 091584788
This is a historical cake shop that is famous for its cassete, cannoli and the Martorana fruit. The "patate" (potatoes) are also well worth trying, a cake made with sponge cake filled with cream and then covered in marzipan.

Matranga
Via Cesareo 38, tel. 091306869
No one but women, and the result is clear for all to see. Apart from the premises, which are very nice, the service is immaculate. Coffee is served in small porcelain cups, and the same attention is paid in preparing the cakes; beautiful workmanship, but delicious at the same time. This is a powerful walk down traditional Sicilian cake making. Look out for the "lunette", shell-shaped sfogline filled with a milk cream, rice or pistachio nuts.

Mazzara
Via Gen. Magliocco 15, tel. 091321443
Very close to the Massimo theatre, this large cake shop is divided into areas: the cake area, the area for take-away pastry and, ever thronging, the

THE PISTACHIO NUTS OF BRONTE

Introduced to Sicily by the Arabs (in the 9th-11th centuries), the pistachio tree (Pistacia vera) has found an ideal habitat on the north-west slopes of Mount Etna, in the area around the small town of Bronte. Here, the extraordinary combination of the soil and the climate means that the pistachio nuts produced in Sicily are unique, and much in demand from top pastry-chefs all over the world. No other pistachio is such a bright green color – the locals call it "emerald green"– or has such a strong, rich, resinous perfume, as precious as it is rare.
The unevenness of the land makes them very difficult to harvest. The pistachio-nut harvest takes place in the fall. Usually, the husks of the pistachio nuts are removed by rubbing them together mechanically, after which the nuts are laid on tarpaulins on the ground and left to dry in the sun for three or four days. The pistachio nuts in their shells are then transferred to dark, dry rooms, where they are stored prior to being packed.
In the case of shelled pistachio nuts, the fruit is exposed briefly to high-pressure steam, then passed through rollers which remove the thin skin around the nuts. Finally, they are roasted. Local pastry-chefs produce mouthwateringly delicious specialities using pistachio nuts: do not miss the "fillette" (biscuits rather like large round sponge fingers); the soft little round or S-shaped pistachio cakes, and chocolate-flavored pralines; "olivette" (little balls made of chopped pistachio nuts and sugar), and "croccanti" (pistachio-nut brittle), "torrone" (nougat) in bars, or small, wrapped, bite-sized "torroncini".

caffetteria counter, a real triumph with enormous brioches and hot cakes, fried and baked focacce, dainty snack pizzas and small timbale.

Oscar
Via M. Mighiaccio 39, tel. 0916822381
www.oscarpasticceria.it
Out of the many places you could stop at to try Sicilian cakes, this shop is one of the most important in the area. The shop sells both traditional cakes as well as many others. The most widely known cake is the "Devil" cake.

Scimone
Via Imera 8, tel. 091584448
www.pasticceriascimone.it
For over half a century this shop has been offering cake lovers all the Sicilian specialities from cannoli to cassate, taralli to citron and croccantini. In summer the shop serves wonderful ice-cream. They have another shop in viale Regina Margherita 61, Mondello-Valdesi.

CASTELBUONO
Extra Bar Fiasconaro
Piazza Margherita 10, tel. 0921671231
www.fiasconaro.com
This is a bar-cum-cake shop with a room exhibiting the specialities, all home made: panettoni, citrus fruit or wild fruit mannetto, and the extremely difficult-to-find testa di turco (only made to ordered).

CEFALÙ
Pietro Serio
Piazza Duomo 18, tel. 0921921271
www.pietroserio.it
This is possibly the best cake shop in the town thanks to the assortment and the wonderful flavors on offer. The specialties include: cassata, almond cakes, orange cakes, pine seed cakes and Easter eggs.

USTICA
Bar Centrale
Piazza Umberto I 8, tel. 0918449534
Small, with tables outside in the square, this bar makes wonderful ice-cream and cassate, chocolate sweets, fruit cakes, cannoli and rice "sfinci".

RAGUSA

Di Pasquale
Corso Vittorio Veneto 104
tel. 0932624635

The town's historical cake shop, it is not that far from the cathedral. They have a good assortment of cakes inside of all sorts, though there is a good range of savory products and cookies. In the summer, ice-cream and granite. They also offer a delivery service as well as a catering service.

Dolce Barocco
Largo S. Domenico 18, tel. 0932246149
www.dolcebarocco.com
In the old area of Ragusa Ibla you will find the traditional tastes of Sicily. Try the carob and almond cookies, the Bronte pistachio cookies and simply do not miss the chocolate "Dolce Barocco".

MODICA
Antica Dolceria Bonajuto
Corso Umberto I 159, tel. 0932941225
It is to the famous master baker Franco Ruta that we owe the foundation of a small museum, a gem (not far from the cake shop). This shop is a real shop window, simply packed with flavors; bygone specialties like cedrata, almond cakes, the riposto cakes, as well as the more recent cakes with carob. Another of this shop's prime attractions is the cold-worked chocolate using the original techniques dating back to when, for the first time, chocolate came to Sicily from Spain. Do not go away without trying the chocolate with red pepper.

Antica Dolceria Gelateria Rizza
Corso Umberto I 268, tel. 0932752550
www.anticagelateriarizza.it
You simply cannot leave Modica without buying and tasting the famous chocolate or one of their numerous sorts of nougat.

Caffè dell'Arte
Corso Umberto I 114, tel. 0932943257
The house speciality is chocolate, in every way possible: hot, chocolate bars, little chocolates, pure or mixed with vanilla, with cinnamon, coffee, with carob and red pepper, with Sicilian citrus fruit or simply plain. And even more: the nucatoli, quaresimali, cardinali with almonds, candied fruit and chocolate, the impanatiglie with meat, chocolate, nutmeg and sugar.

Casalindolci
Corso Vittorio Emanuele 2/A
tel. 0932942064

In the historic centre of Modica Alta, this shop shows off its 'mpanatigghi, nucatoli, nougat, cubaita and other traditional cakes, including homemade chocolate cakes.

Spinello Dolci Pensieri
Via Tirella 11/G, tel. 0932751366
www.dolcipensieri.it
All round fantasy: marzipan "bomboniere", the traditional Christmas cake called "panettoni", hearts with cream and strawberries, nougat, cubaita and Modica chocolate.

SIRACUSA

Bonomo
Corso Gelone 48/50, tel. 093167845
Very close to the center, this is probably the best cake shop in the town. Though it is not particularly large it is packed full with cakes of all sorts. At the back the large bakery allows for and ensures quality products that can even be exported. The cassate are particularly good, even the oven-baked ones, as are the decorated cakes.

NOTO
Caffè Sicilia
Corso Vittorio Emanuele 125
tel. 0931835013
A real symbol of Sicilian confectionery works here: Corrado Assenza. It is thanks to him that many old recipes have been re-discovered, and especially the development of the products and the local traditions. He works hard at protecting the quality of the products that have made him famous the world over. He sells a wide variety of special cakes, all traditional Sicilian ones: In particular the cakes made with vegetables like pumpkin, zucchini and eggplant are overwhelming.

PALAZZOLO ACREIDE
Antica Pasticceria Corsino
Via Nazionale 2, tel. 0931875035
www.corsino.it
This cake shop has been in the hands of the Corsino family since 1889. It is a wide smart location and the right place to find wonderful traditional cakes made just like they were in the past: cassate, even

single slices, ricotta cheese cannoli with flakes of dark chocolate, almond cakes, nougat, croccanti, praline and jams.

TRAPANI

Colicchia
Via delle Arti 6, tel. 0923547612
A historical cake shop in the centre of the town. You can sit inside or outside and taste the wonderful cakes, in particular the cannoli and marzipan cakes, but also the ice-cream. The granite are not to be missed: we suggest the red mulberry and the more classical lemon ones.

ERICE
Bar Tulipano
Via Vittorio Emanuele 10
tel. 0923869672
This bar, with its wonderful windows, has classical furniture. They make the most traditional plain Sicilian cakes: cannoli, cassate and marzipan.

Grammatico Maria
Via Vittorio Emanuele 14
tel. 0923869390
This cake shop has a taste of medieval architecture. Skilfully constructed with an extremely high quality, this shop makes cannoli, genovesi, cassate ericine, marzipan and hazelnut and honey "mustaccioli". It has a secondary shop inside a deconsecrated church at via Gaurnotta 1, where there is a wonderful 14th century statute on show (tel. 0923869777).

FAVIGNANA
Due Colonne
Piazza Matrice 76, tel. 0923922291
This is a pleasant summer bar, and not to be missed by anyone wanting to try the real Sicilian granita, the house speciality. Apart from this, they have many fruit ice-creams. They only use local products.

MARSALA
Aloha
Via Mazzini 152, tel. 0923715460
This is a large shop with the bakery next to it. They make cassate and marzipan cakes, ice-cream, zuccotti and a Bavarian cake called "bavaresi". There is also a caffetteria and a snack bar.

FOOD

Food and wine festivals

JANUARY

January 6th
RICOTTA CHEESE FESTIVAL
Sant'Angelo Muxaro (AG)
Comune tel. 0922919506
Taste the sheep's milk ricotta cheese, muffoletti (traditional round rolls) and latri (home-made specialties made with cheese whey). Scenes of rural life and the shepherds visiting the Infant Jesus.

FEBRUARY

February and March
ORANGE FESTIVAL FROM ADRANO
Adrano (CT)
Comune tel. 0957606111
Orange festival with entertainment, fruit stalls and free tasting of fruits, marmalades and cakes.

During the Carnival Festival
CAVATIEDDI FESTIVAL
Palazzolo Acreide (SR)
Comune tel. 0933801431
While "cuturri" (the typical masks of Siracusa) are paraded on floats through the town, women cook cavatieddi, a typical pasta served with a pork sauce, sausage and trout-flavored toasted bread.

During the Carnival Festival
SAUSAGE FESTIVAL
Chiaramonte Gulfi (RG)
Comune tel. 0932711239
Chiaramonte celebrates Carnival with floats (also on Sunday and on Shrove Tuesday). Do not miss the sausage festival on Monday evening.

MARCH

March 19th
SALEMI LOAVES
Salemi (TP)
Tourist Board c/o Comune, tel. 0924991320
March 19th (Saint Joseph's Day), tables – called 'cene' – with flowers, bread and other food; drinks of all sorts. Children and the poor are fed as they wander the town dressed as members of the Holy Family. Stalls serve traditional food.

APRIL

April
ARTICHOKE AND BREAD FESTIVAL
Niscemi (CL)
Comune tel. 0933881631
Niscemi celebrates this local vegetable with traditional products. The fruit and vegetable market also has local glassware, wrought-iron and stone work. Meetings, entertainment and fun fairs; artichoke and local wine tasting.

April 25th
ARTICHOKE FESTIVAL
Cerda (PA)
Comune tel. 0918991003
A favorite event of lovers of Sicily and strong flavors. Yearly event with entertainment. Various artichoke dishes to taste with bread and wine.

April
EASTER LAMB FESTIVAL
Favara (AG)
Only in Favara is the traditional Easter lamb cake made with marzipan, pistachios and sprinkled with sugar. The festival is over two-hundred years old and Flavare is known as "the City of Easter Lamb"

MAY

May
LOQUAT FESTIVAL
Trabia (PA)
Comune tel. 0918146117
Try the local loquats. Folk-groups, flag wavers and street artists perform in the old city, while boys and girls wander around in traditional costumes. Baskets of loquats with the Nespola brand are on offer.

JUNE

June (every other year)
CHEESE ART
Ragusa
Milk and Cheese Union - tel. 0932660411
A two-yearly festival to celebrate the most delicious dairy products in the Mediterranean. Meetings, discussions, free food tasting, shows and concerts.

First week in June
STRAWBERRIES AND WILD FRUIT FESTIVAL
Maletto sull'Etna (CT)
Tourist Board in Catania tel. 0957306233
A traditional market for this most delicious cultivated and wild fruit from Maletto. All kinds of strawberries are on offer; renowned delicious local food. A huge cream cake (over 1,000 kg. or 2200 pounds) is cooked every year and decorated with wild strawberries.

June to October
THE TRAIN OF WONDERS
Province of Catania
Catania-Etna Railway - tel. 095541250 (web site: www.circumetnea.it)
19th century railway from Catania to the foot of Etna. After cooled streams of lava, citrus and prickly pear fields, in Randazzo a bus trip to local farms with genuine wines and traditional food.

JULY

First week in July
INYCON - MENFI AND ITS WINE
Menfi (AG)
Comune tel. 092570111
Named after the ancient town of Inycon, this yearly festival celebrates the fine Menfi wine. Entertainment, exhibitions, meetings and free tasting in old courtyards or in the city center.

AUGUST

August
MACARONI FESTIVAL
Librizzi (ME)
Comune tel. 094132281
Three-day feast with macaroni served hot in the streets on special dishes. Entertainment, fireworks, market stalls and exhibitions.

August
PROVOLA AND RICOTTA CHEESE FESTIVAL
Floresta (ME)
Comune tel. 0941602036
Held when shepherds move from the Catania plain to the Nebrodi mountains. Dairy products and the local provola cheese are sold in the streets.

Making couscous at San Vito Lo Capo.

August
CORN FESTIVAL
Antillo (ME)

Comune tel. 0942723031
August 14th. This festival
around Messina always
throngs with people. A big
market with local farm
products. Try the boiled and
grilled corn, homemade
bread, sausages and roast
suckling pig.

August
TORTONE CAKE FESTIVAL
Sperlinga (EN)

Comune tel. 0935643025
Old country life in caves or
poor houses depicted before
the majestic Sperlinga castle.
Try the "tortone", a
homemade cake made of a
risen dough mixed with olive
oil and sprinkled with sugar.

August
FISH FESTIVAL
Pozzallo (RG)

Local Tourist Board -
tel. 0932954441
This is the main summer event
in this wonderful seaside
town. Tons of cuttlefish, squid,
octopus and prawns are
cooked and served from
sunset to midnight with wine
and a tasty Russian salad. A
live orchestra and colorful
stalls add to the charm.

SEPTEMBER

September
"DA FRITTULA" FESTIVAL
Librizzi (ME)

Comune tel. 094132281, web
site: www.festadafrittula.it
"Frittule" is a simple dish
from the Nebrodi mountains;
the pigskin, pork fat and
other remains are boiled
together in a big copper pot.
Try the "frittule" with
crushed olives and red wine.

4th week in September
PISTACHIO FESTIVAL
Bronte (CT)

Comune tel. 0957747229
Local pistachio is free to
taste on the stalls. A "sweet"
weekend, discover the
secrets of the "green gold"
from the Etna area.

September
COUSCOUS FESTIVAL
San Vito Lo Capo (TP)

Comune tel. 0923974300,
web site: www.couscousfest.it
An international event,
renowned chefs from the
world over compete for "The
Best Couscous" award. Stands
with varieties of couscous,
demonstrations by food and
wine experts as couscous is
made, regional craftwork or
products from participating
countries. After sunset, the
"Couscous Live Music" venue.
Concerts and performances
underline the multi-cultural
nature of the event.

OCTOBER

October
PRICKLY PEAR FESTIVAL
Roccapalumba (PA)

Comune tel. 0918215207
A three-day event with music
and folk-groups. Taste the
fresh prickly pears, fig-
mostarda, fig-cakes and
a refreshing liquor called"
ficodì".

October
OCTOBER IN ZAFFERANA
Zafferana Etnea

Comune tel. 0957082825
Traditional food and
craftwork exhibitions on
Sundays, dancing and
traditional songs. Try the
local products: delicious
mushrooms from around
Etna, wine, honey, chestnuts
and mostarda.

October
HONEY FESTIVAL
Sortino (SR)

APT (Local Tourist Board)
in Siracusa - tel. 0931481200
Tradition beekeeping and a
leading honey producer (lime
tree, eucalyptus, and citrus-
honey). Typical cakes and
all sorts of honey on offer.
Culture events, music
and folk shows.

NOVEMBER

November 1st
VASTEDDA FESTIVAL
Capaci (PA)

APT (Local Tourist Board)
in Palermo - tel. 091586122
A local bread with extra-
virgin olive oil, anchovies
and strong caciocavallo
cheese from Palermo,
this is a simple dish dating
back to ancient times.
It was once sold
on November 2nd to people
on their way to visit dead
relatives in far-off places,
and thus no time to prepare
the evening meal.

October and November
MUSHROOM FESTIVAL
Pedara (CT)

Comune tel. 0957028111
Mushroom festival with
traditional products from
the Etna Park area.
Visit the old buildings in
Pedara and taste the various
mushroom dishes.

DECEMBER

December 13th
CUCCIA FESTIVAL
Paceco (TP)

Comune tel. 0923401111
The "Providence ship",
symbol of Saint Lucy's Day,
is driven through the streets
while people on the ship
dish out cuccìa, a local soup
with chickpeas and cereals,
eaten in homage to St. Lucy.

December
PATACÒ FESTIVAL
Licodia Eubea (CT)

Biblioteca tel. 0933801431
(town library)
"Patacò" is a chickling flour
polenta eaten soft or fried.
Entertainment, and street
stalls sell the dish.

FOOD

The major Arts and Crafts products traditionally made in Sicily include fine ceramics, fabric, marble, wrought iron, and terra cotta folk pottery. Place mats, tablecloths, napkins, and clothing decorated with fine embroidery can be found in shops and outdoor markets all over Sicily.

CERAMICS

WROUGHT IRON

MARBLE AND ALABASTER

PUPPET

GOLDSMITHERY

FABRICS AND EMBROIDERY

GLASS

Shopping

The ubiquitous markets are a great place for bargain shopping as well as a focal point of everyday life in each town. Sicilian marionettes and painted cart reproductions make great gifts for children of all ages, and the Trinacria, the heraldic symbol of Sicily which represents the island's three points is a must have souvenir.

Highlights

- Ceramics production includes vases, wine-jugs, lampshades and typical lamps with human or animal forms
- In eastern Sicily, many craftsmen work the lava that has taken millennia to form
- The most famous coral carvers are concentrated in Sciacca and the area around Trapani
- In Catania and Palermo highly prestigious puppets are still made according to the traditional 19th-century models

Inside

ARTS AND CRAFTS

The history of Sicily is a long interwoven list of events, civilizations and cultures that have molded both the landscape and the nature of the people. The influence of many foreign peoples: Phoenicians, Greeks, Romans, Arabs, Normans and Spanish conquerors (broken by long periods of total neglect), has produced stunning effects on both art and architecture; this is reflected in the popular craftwork. Sicilian carts, for instance, are so richly and beautifully decorated that they were - and still are - considered an example of artistic craftwork. As a matter of fact, the one feature that unites all the different areas of Sicilian craftsmanship is the craftsmen's ability to transmit part of their rich cultural heritage to any object they make, from the humblest to the richest items.

Ceramics

Ceramics were first made in Sicily 5,000 to 6,000 years B.C., but it was the Greeks who, in the 8th century, perfected pottery-making techniques and founded the best schools for potters and decorators in the Mediterranean area.

Events later led to neglected until the 18th century, when three major centers in Sicily for pottery decoration were founded: Santo Stefano di Camastra, Caltagirone and Sciacca.

The kilns in Santo Stefano di Camastra were re-lit by shepherds, and potters slowly specialized in majolica tiles and decorated pottery, with a vast production of flower pots, dishes, jugs, vases and bricks with the traditional multi-colored designs.

Potters in Caltagirone made a wide range of different objects such as vases, jars and lamps. But their most original objects were lamps with human shapes, either decorated with yellow/green leaves or in a plain turquoise against a white background. Nowadays, 150 workshops still produce majolica-objects, earthenware and statues using traditional methods.

Pottery-making started in Sciacca between 1400 and 1500 A.D, when barons and bishops needed decorated tiles to embellish palaces and churches (the Cathedral in Monreale is a good example). It reached its peak in the 16th century thanks to Giuseppe Bonachia, a renowned master potter. There are now some thirty workshops still making decorated pottery and the dominant colors are straw-yellow, orange, turquoise, blue and copper-flake green.

Coral

The production of coral-decorated objects evolved along with fishing, which supplied a wide range of coral: Catania and Messina were renowned for white coral; Palermo was the main source for black coral while Sciacca and Trapani had a good supply of red and pink coral. The most ancient technique is "retroincastro" where black pitch and wax is used to fix coral onto a gold plated copper plate, previously shaped and perforated. This was the most common technique for holy-water stoups, monstrances, plates, sculptures and jewels. In 1720 the "sewing" method was introduced, which consisting in coral being fastened using metal threads. There are still a few coral engravers in Sciacca and the area around Trapani, and they often fashion coral with traditional jewel-making techniques.

The delicate art of coral-working

Fabrics and Embroidery

The embroidered cloak that emperors of the Holy Roman Empire used to wear for their crowning ceremony was woven and embroidered in Palermo in 1134 (Royal Works), evidence of the ancient origins of Embroidery in Sicily. Messina was also renowned in the 18th century for its damask cloth. After a glorious period, weaving and embroidery slowly started

The decoration makes these ceramics even more valuable

to die out and it was only carried out by women as a hobby in their homes. Luckily, this decline did not put a stop to a highly original technique called "sfilato siciliano", which is still used today. The technique consists in removing threads from a piece of cloth, right where it must be embroidered; the cloth is then embroidered in a net-like pattern. Nowadays, "sfilato siciliano" is only practiced by skilled embroiders, mainly in eastern Sicily. On the other end of the island - in Erice (province of Trapani) - a different and less refined technique called "frazzata" is still used to make carpets. This technique consists in weaving colorful end-cuts of cloth and cotton yarns together on a hand loom.

Marble and lava-stone sculpturing

The fashion for marble sculptures, an art that flourished between the 17th and 18th centuries, is slowly disappearing due to high costs in marble-working, but a few family-run workshops still exist between Palermo and Trapani.

The use of lava stone is widespread in eastern Sicily, though, where most sculptors and stone-cutters living at the foot of Etna skillfully cut and work lava stone to produce a wide range of objects, including souvenirs, artistic objects and building materials (balustrades, pillars, seats and fountains).

This elephant, which has become the symbol of Catania, is made of lava

Sicilian string puppets

"Pupi siciliani" (traditional Sicilian string puppets) appeared around 1850, when marionettes, which were very popular in Rome and Naples, first reached Catania and, later, Palermo. The introduction of Pupi had very important effects on the typical puppet plays drawn from legends of the Carolingian periods. "Pupi siciliani" differ from any other marionette in the world because their right hand is moved by an iron rod (instead of a thread) and their armor is carefully manufactured right down to the finest detail. A few workshops in Catania and Palermo still make Pupi, mostly souvenirs for tourists, but collector's pieces are also produced, faithfully reproducing the original 19th century marionettes.

Among the most traditional marionettes you will see the classical Italian carabinieri wearing a hat with feathers and a big moustache; there are also comedy and tragedy masks from Greek and Roman tradition.

Wrought iron

The making of wrought iron objects is one of the most distinctive features in Sicilian architecture; the imposing windows of the buildings in Taormina and the richly decorated balconies adorning baroque palaces are only an example. Today, craftsmen still work iron using traditional

techniques (no soldering-irons, nor mass production dies are allowed) to make beds, candlesticks, lamps, flower-stands, lanterns and grating based on baroque and Arabic models.
The covers of some of the Italian Touring Club's most important publications are given in this section.

Making puppets is an art which involves carpenters, engravers, dress-makers... and blacksmiths, who make the armor

AGRIGENTO

SCIACCA
✳ **CERAMICS**
Ceramiche Cascio
Corso V. Emanuele 115, tel. 092582829
Art ceramics
Navarra Emiliano
Corso V. Emanuele 38, tel. 092522438
Art ceramics
Perconte Ceramiche Artistiche
Contrada Stanca Padrone, tel. 0925994005
Art ceramics

Typical floral decoration with hints of green and yellow

✳ **GOLDSMITHERY**
Dulcimascolo Sabrina Orafa
Via F.lli Argento 19/B, tel. 092584618
Coral

CALTANISSETTA

✳ **CERAMICS**
Arte e Creta
Via Xiboli 314, tel. 0934566987
Art ceramics

CATANIA

✳ **GLASS**
L'Inglesina di Paolo Dainotti
Via dei Sanguinelli 78, tel. 095571781

Art glass doors and windows
Orazio Privitera
Stradale Giovanni Agnelli 8
tel. 095291638

ACIREALE
✳ **FABRICS AND EMBROIDERY**
Appunti di Ricamo
Piazza Indirizzo 24, tel. 0957650090
Embroidery
✳ **METALS**
Leonardo Barbagallo
Via Nazionale 283, tel. 095809597
Wrought iron working
✳ **WOOD**
Lanzafame Maria Sculture Artigiane Siciliane
Via Vittorio Emanuele 97, tel. 095606805
Wooden objects
Salvatore Scarabelli
Via Vittorio Emanuele 100
tel. 095604254
Frames

BIANCAVILLA
✳ **STONE AND MARBLE**
Efesto
Via Scirfi 24, tel. 095981226
Lava stone working

CALTAGIRONE
✳ **CERAMICS**
Ceramiche Giraffa
tel. 093354217
Art ceramics
Dell'Aquila
Via Reburdone 7, tel. 093334076
Art ceramics
Maria Morales
Via Stazione Isolamento 82
tel. 093358398
Gifts and fancy goods

Riccardo Varsallona
Via Colombo 33, tel. 093326167
Romano Maurizio
Via Porto del Vento 10, tel. 093352121
Gifts and fancy goods

PATERNÒ
✳ **STONE AND MARBLE**
Lavica
Gianferrante, tel. 095621721
Lava stone working

SANTA MARIA DI LICODIA
✳ **CERAMICS**
Bottega d'Arte Athena
Via Po 5, tel. 095629392
Art ceramics

ENNA

CENTURIPE
✳ **CERAMICS**
Keramos Ceramiche Artistiche
Contrada Marmora 1, tel. 0935919126
Art ceramics

MESSINA

✳ **CERAMICS**
Ruggeri Ceramiche
Via Fabrizi Nicola 90, tel. 090675682
Art ceramics

GIARDINI NAXOS
✳ **METALS**
Patanè Gaetano
Via Regina Margherita III, tel. 094251149
Wrought iron working

LIPARI
✳ **CERAMICS**

Puppet Theater pag. 186

Stefano Panza
Marina Corta via Roma 1
tel. 0909812021
Art ceramics

SANTO STEFANO DI CAMASTRA
✳ **CERAMICS**
Ceramiche Fratantoni
SS 113, 94
tel. 0921331833
Art ceramics
Sebastiano Insana
Via Vittoria 1, tel. 0921337223
Art ceramics

PALERMO

✳ **CERAMICS**
Ceramica De Simone
Via Lanza di Scalea 960
tel. 0916711005
Art ceramics
Nino Parrucca
Via S.Lorenzo 291/R, tel. 0916790949
Gifts and fancy goods

Weaving, once a purely domestic activity, has become one of the island's most important craft industries

SHOPPING

The characteristic Sicilian carts are decorated with bright colors

✳ **GIFTS AND FANCY GOODS**
Sicily's Folk
Via Vittorio Emanuele 450, tel. 0916512787
Crib
✳ **GLASS**
Vetreria Silvio Greco
Viale Regione Siciliana 2621, tel. 091225701
Art glass doors and windows
✳ **GOLDSMITHERY**
Antonino Amato
Piazza G. Meli 5, tel. 091580287
Silver

RAGUSA

✳ **FABRICS AND EMBROIDERY**
L'Angolo del Ricamo
Via Napoleone Colajanni 9
tel. 0932245982
Embroidery
✳ **STONE AND MARBLE**
Sgarlata
Zona Industriale III, tel. 0932667475
Lava stone working

SIRACUSA

✳ **GLASS**
Tiffany's Studio and Art Work
di Giuseppe Santoro
Via Maestranza 76, tel. 0931463649
Art glass doors and windows
✳ **PAPER AND PRINTING**
Galleria Bellomo
Via Capodieci 15, tel. 093161340
Paper
✳ **WOOD**
La Bottega del Puparo
*Near the "Teatro dei Pupi" (puppet
theater) via della Giudecca 17
tel. 0931465540*
Sicilian string puppets

PALAZZOLO ACREIDE
✳ **CERAMICS**
Bottega dell'Arte
Corso V. Emanuele 26, tel. 0931883626
Art ceramics

TRAPANI

✳ **CERAMICS**
Ceramiche Perrone
Corso Vittorio Emanuele 106
tel. 092329609
Art ceramics
✳ **GOLDSMITHERY**
Coralli e Preziosi
Via Roasi 11, tel. 0923546171
Coral
✳ **CERAMICS**
Ceramica De Simone
Via Borgo Italia, tel. 0923913028
Art ceramics

ERICE
✳ **CERAMICS**
Antonino Catalano
Via G.F. Guarnotta 20, tel. 0923869126
Art ceramics
Ceramica Ericina
Fontanarossa, tel. 0923869040
Ceramiche Pipitone
Casa Santa via Marconi 193
tel. 0923552468
Art ceramics
✳ **FABRICS AND EMBROIDERY**
Ericina Tappeti e Ceramiche
Via Guarnotta 15, tel. 0923869126
Carpets
Pina Parisi by Vario Francesca
Via Pepoli 55, tel. 0923869049
Carpets

MARSALA
✳ **CERAMICS**
Ceramiche Marsa-Allah
Corso Calatafimi 36
tel. 0923718299
Art ceramics

The *carretto da parata* used at special festivals embodies the history, art and colors of the island

MARKETS

Sicily is rich in craftwork tradition and has been a crossroads for different cultures for thousands of years. Take a walk in the street markets, among their colorful stalls; this is the real heart and soul of the island. Colors, smells, voices all contribute to make a picturesque scene with Sicilians proudly exhibiting their local wares, the fruits of a deeply-rooted tradition and the skilful use of the raw materials the island has to offer.

AGRIGENTO

Antique market
Fourth Sunday of the month
Held in the town center this is a tiny antique and fancy goods market.
For further information: tel. 0922401566.

SAMBUCA DI SICILIA
Sambuca fair
21st September
The town hall in Corso Umberto. A one day exhibition of various kinds of craftwork goods: paintings, iron and stone sculptures and embroisdery work.

CATANIA

Antique market
Every Sunday
The biggest Sicilian antique market, it runs from early morning to 13 in piazza Carlo Alberto.
For further information: tel. 0957306222.

Flea market
Sundays
From 8 to 14 in Piazza Carlo Alberto: an art market-cum-mall antique market; excellent for collectors of coins, tokens and paper money.

Natale alle Ciminiere
At Christmas time
A yearly appointment that focuses on craftwork and typical local products.

Omnia antiquaria
February
This is a yearly antique fair and is held in Castello Ursino in piazza Federico di Svevia.

Pescheria
Every morning
The historical fish market spreads out around Piazza Pardo (near the Cathedral). The bloody tables at this market were supposed to have inspired the paintings of Francis Bacon.

ACIREALE
Fiera dello Jonio
First 11 days of September
This yearly craftwork market is held in the Palazzetto dello Sport in corso Italia.
For further information: tel. 095895267.

CALTAGIRONE
'A Truvatura
Every third weekend from mid October to mid June
This antique market in the town centre also has modern artwork.
The exhibitions, museums and shops stay open until late in the evening.
Traditional Sicilian string puppet show, concerts and folk dancing.
For further information: tel. 0933351073.

Kalat Expo
September
The town hall exibits local craftwork and food. Open meetings on particular topics, music and folklore.
For further information: tel. 09334181541809.

Rassegna Internazionale del Fischietto in Terracotta
Lasts two months starting from the Easter weekend
Since 1988 the bars and cafès in Palazzo Libertini di S. Marco have celebrated the yearly "Rassegna Internazionale del Fischietto in Terracotta", dedicated to this typical local craftwork product which, once, was sold just before Easter.
For further information: tel. 0933351073.

RANDAZZO
Market
Every sunday morning
Local craftwork market with local textiles, wood and iron goods from the Etna area.

MESSINA

Antique market
Every Sunday morning
Antique goods are put on display every sunday morning in Gazzi.

GIARDINI NAXOS
Mediterranean builders exhibition
October
Held in Palanaxos, this is the foremost regional exhibition for the building trade. Special attention is paid to basalt

lava and the way it is used both by craftsmen and by industry.
For further information: tel. 0957463355.

Nasso Antica Antique Fair
Every three months
This antique exhibition-cum-market in the Palanaxos trade-fair complex in via Apollo Archegeta.
For further information: tel. 094250050.

MILAZZO

Market
First Sunday of the month
A market for collectors' items, creftwork and bric-a-brack.

PALERMO

Ballarò
Every morning (except Sunday) until 14
The Ballarò market is held in the area around Piazza del Carmine, and the Capo. The first, more picturesque section is round Piazza Beati Paoli.

Flea market
Every weekday
Located in via Papireto in the city center near the cathedral and the Palatina chappel, this market runs all day.
You will find old furniture, period objects, precious jewellery and collectors' items.

Palermo in Soffitta
Saturdays and second Sunday of the month
In piazza Unità d'Italia, this antique market also has furniture and fancy goods.

Vuccirìa
Every morning (except Sunday) until 14
The Vuccirìa market is certainly Palermo's most famous, always bustling with colour and noise. Set back from the waterfront in Via Cassari-Argenteria and the surrounding area (stretching as far as Piazza San Domenico).

CORLEONE

Corpus Christi fair
From the Thursday of Corpus Christi until the following Sunday
Dry flower arrangements, cakes and local craftwork in "piazza Falcone e Borsellino".

RAGUSA

MODICA
Antique market
Last Sunday of the month
Held in piazza Principe di Napoli, this is a small antique market.

SCICLI

Antique market
Third Sunday of the month
This antique and craftwork market is held in via Francesco Mormina Penna and is locally known as "salotto di Scicli", a baroque street that is now under Unesco protection.

SIRACUSA

Fiera del Sud
December
Market-cum-exhibition, where you can buy all kind of traditional local and foreign things on sale.
For further information: tel. 0931464255.

CARLENTINI
Fiera di San Giuseppe
Easter Monday
Wood and wrought iron craftwork goods hold center stage in this market in piazza Diaz.

NOTO
Craftwork market
Third Sunday of the month
The exhibition in the square is completely dedicated to craftwork.

TRAPANI

Market
Every Thursday
Not far from Pala Ilio, near the port, this is a classical craftwork and clothes market.
For further information: tel. 092329000.

MARSALA
Antique exhibition
Last weekened of the month (from April to September)
Antiques as well as furniture and costume jewellery. In piazza della Vittoria.

MAZARA DEL VALLO
Fiera del Ponente
July
A yearly craftwork exhibition-cum-market, but there are also other things to see.

PANTELLERIA
Craftwork exhibition
August
This market-cum-exhibition focuses on local craftwork. The local stone masons' work on lava stone is particularly interesting.
For further information: tel. 092329000.

FASHION

Fashion is going through a period of growth and fame in Sicily. Doubtless, the amazing growth in this sector is mainly due to the inventiveness and hard work of young designers whose talent is ever appreciated by the market and by fashion magazines, too.

The young islanders who developed their talent in the Academies of Palermo, Catania and Rome are now the symbol of "made in Sicily" fashion. Most of these young people, who worked for other designers and later opened their own fashion houses, can now boast fashion shows in Sicily, Rome, Milan or even abroad, not to talk about co-operations with other fashion houses.

Talented designers from Sicily, like Domenico Dolce from Dolce&Gabbana, all share a strong tie with their land and its traditions, which include a rich background in ancient tailoring techniques; they have learnt to master and adapt clothes to the latest trends.

Sicilian style mirrors the island's history with a mixture of Baroque and Arab influence, aristocratic affectation, jewel making traditions and Mediterranean style. Warm and bright colors prevail, and they recall the sun, the sky and the sea of Sicily with its wild nature and its volcano. White is the dominant color for wedding dresses and Sicily can boast an ancient tradition in this sector. Many fashion houses are specialized in wedding dresses and offer a wide range of models: from classical dresses to rather daring ones.

The "made in Sicily" fashion stands out for the quality of its fabrics, the greatest care for details, and its original style.

The most famous fashion houses and fashion designers are locate in Palermo and Catania. If you love fashionable clothes, you must walk along via Libertà, via Principe di Belmonte and via Ruggero Settimo in Palermo, or along Corso Italia and via XX Settembre in Catania.

Models by the most famous Italian designers are often concentrated in multi-brand stores, some of which have an originally distinctive style. Do not miss a visit to the minor towns in tourist areas along the coast: you may find very good clothes by famous and non-famous designers at bargain prices.

AGRIGENTO

Pollini
Via Atenea 195, tel. 092220170
www.pollini.com
The elegance of Pollini stands out for the greatest care to detail and the handmade goods: footwear, handbags and leather items for both men and for women.

CATANIA

Alba Eloisa d'Alessandro
Via XX Settembre 19, tel. 095431705
www.albaeloisa.com
Very elegant wedding dresses, for all tastes, right in the center of Catania.

Emporio Armani
Corso Italia 68/70, tel. 095448516
www.giorgioarmani.com
This showroom selling garments designed by one of the top Italian designers is located in the most elegant shopping street in Catania.

Fortini Rossetti
Corso Italia 133, tel. 095382746
Opened as a furrier's shop in 1966, Fortini Rossetti later became a first-rate and exclusive boutique and a leather goods shop. Ready-to-wear

clothes can be found in Corso Italia 133, while furs and accessories are sold in a liberty-style apartment in Corso Italia 141.

Giampiero Nicita
Via XX Settembre 9/A, tel. 0957169600
The extravagant designer from Catania creates fashion wear for the most elegant and non-conventional woman.

Giovanni Cannistrà
Viale XX Settembre 56, tel. 095505067
www.giovannicannistra.it
This liberty-style atelier, adorned with muses, nimph statues, purple-red walls and richly decorated ceilings, is located in the most elegant street in Catania. An ideal location for high fashion wear, wedding dresses, men's wear and accessories by a very talented designer from Sicily.

Helmé
Largo Vespri 13, tel. 095552243
Women's wear and accessories, from top fashion clothes to casual wear. This department store is famous for its wedding dresses, bathing costumes, lingerie, accessories and household goods.

Malo
Corso Italia 262, tel. 095371292
www.malo.it
This has been a leading name for cashmere garments since 1972. A refined and colorful environment, there is great care to detail. Leather is wonderfully matched with cashmere,

much use of ribbons. Excellent soft-leather goods.

Marella Ferrera
Via XX Settembre 25/27
tel. 095446751, www.marellaferrera.com
Genuine creations fashioned on Sicilian traditions: simple lines combined with original materials like fired clay, rock crystal, copper wire, cork, lava stone. Top fashion collections and ready-to-wear clothes.

Nancy Licciardello
Viale Medaglie d'Oro 82, tel. 095365438
www.nancylicciardello.com
The young designer from Catania started her career with Ferrera. Today she creates top fashion clothes and wedding dresses.

Papini Store
Corso Italia 48, tel. 095536492
www.papinistore.com
Opened in 1972 as a top men's tailors, Papini Store now sells fashion wear by both renowned Italian designers (Missoni, Fay, Gucci, Dolce & Gabbana, Valentino, Cavalli and others) and by young Sicilian ones. Modern and trendy fashion wear for women and a sushi bar at Corso Italia 78.

Parco Naturale Reg. dell'Etna p. 114

MESSINA

Emporio Armani
Via dei Mille 67/69, tel. 090770563
www.giorgioarmani.com
Men's and women's wear by Armani in a single store.

Malia Club
Via Centonze 33, tel. 0906783406
www.maliaclub.it
Women's wear for all ages, hand-made articles. Top quality tailoring and refined elegance.

Petite Fleur
Via Croce Rossa 49/51, tel. 0902937111
www.petitefleur.it
Wedding hats and hats for special occasions since the 1960s. It is worth a visit for those who love different colors and shapes.

Pollini
Viale San Martino, tel. 0920934522
www.pollini.com
The small, unmistakable letter "p" enhances handbags and leather goods. Men's and women's footwear by Pollini are also worth mentioning.

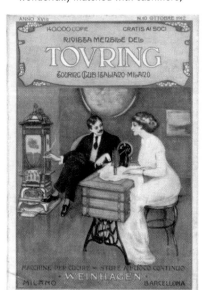

men's and women's wear, with accessories.

Giglio
Piazza Crispi 3, tel. 0916257727
Clothes designed by the best Italian designers for both men and women. Trendy articles are sold only by Giglio In (via Libertà).

Pollini
Via Libertà 20/F, tel. 091582372
www.pollini.com
Footwear, belts, handbags and ladies head scarves. Footwear, belts, and leather goods for men, with the unmistakable Pollini elegance.

RAGUSA

MODICA
Alfano Moda
Corso Umberto I, tel. 0932942747
www.alfano-moda.it
Men's and women's wear, accessories by the most renowned Italian and foreign designers.

Ottavia Failla
Via Blendini 5, tel. 0932941835
www.ottaviafailla.it
Matching cloth handbags and scarves by famous designers, enriched with braiding, buckles and original buttons. Unique and exclusive articles.

SIRACUSA

Emporio Armani
Corso Matteotti 31/33, tel. 093168439
www.giorgioarmani.com
The elegance and glamour of Armani's creations, one of the most renowned symbols of Made in Italy.

TRAPANI

Stefania Mode
Via delle Arti 21/25, tel. 092328398
www.stefaniamode.it
Three stores with the latest trends by the most famous Italian designers (Armani, Cavalli, Fendi, Moschino, Prada, just to mention a few), top fashion, ready-to-wear clothes, casual and sportswear (via delle Arti 15). Young people's wear and accessories are sold in via Torrearsa 95.

TAORMINA
Marella Ferrera
Corso Umberto I 23, tel. 094221112
www.marellaferrera.com
The creations by this very creative designer from Catania are a mix of new and traditional lines.

Parisi
Corso Umberto I 1, tel. 094223151
www.parisitaormina.com
This has been the focal fashion shop in Taormina since 1920: men's and women's wear by famous designers, classic and casual wear, accessories. Four big stores in the same street. Another renowned store is Ermenegildo Zegna (Corso Umberto 79), selling made-to-measure clothes.

PALERMO

Atelier Roberta Lojacono
Via Turati 17, tel. 091588862
www.robertalojacono.it
A wide choice of top fashion wear in a very elegant atmosphere resulting from a mix of refined materials and innovative lines. Wedding dresses, elegant dresses and women's wear for all ages complete the choice.

Daniela Cocco
Viale Regione Siciliana 6645,
tel. 0916888323, www.danielacocco.it
Top fashion showroom specialized in wedding dresses and elegant clothes.

Emporio Armani
Piazza Mordini 11/12/13, tel. 0916257727
www.giorgioarmani.com
The unmistakable class by Armani :

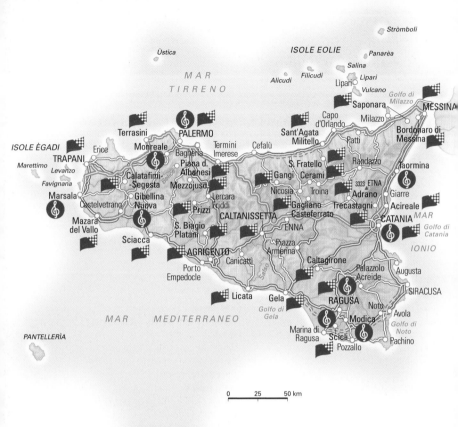

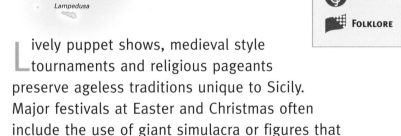

MUSIC

FOLKLORE

Lively puppet shows, medieval style tournaments and religious pageants preserve ageless traditions unique to Sicily. Major festivals at Easter and Christmas often include the use of giant simulacra or figures that are drawn along with ropes or pulleys.
In summer, the island comes alive with music. Sicily is a crossroads of culture and peoples, and provides a rich range of modern music, including jazz, rock, Arab and African-American pop music, as well as local music traditions.

Events

In addition to the many concerts promoted by music associations and institutes, there are ample opportunities to enjoy opera and ballet. Food and Wine Festivals occur all year long.

Highlights

- Palermo, the *Opera dei Pupi* and the *Festa di Santa Rosalia*
- Agrigento, *Il mandorlo in fiore*
- Numerous carnival and Easter celebrations held all over the island
- Gibellina, *Orestiadi*
- Catania, *Etnafest*
- *Taormina Arte*
- Modica, *Note di Notte*

MUSIC

Music has been performed in Sicily for thousands of years, in places which are fundamental to the history of western Europe. The magnificent, ancient theatres built in stone and dating back 2500 years, such as the Teatro Antico in Syracuse or in Taormina, have perfect acoustics. In summer, they are still used for concerts and performances.

Opera houses are important centers of musical life in Sicily today: Teatro Massimo and the Politeama Garibaldi in Palermo, Teatro Sangiorgi and Teatro Massimo Bellini in Catania (opened in 1890), the Vittorio Emanuele in Messina, and Teatro Comunale Vittorio Emanuele in Noto.

Concerts in Sicily also sometimes take place in beautiful religious buildings, such as the Duomo in Monreale, the medieval churches of Erice, and the Baroque churches of Val di Noto. Sicilians are also adept at making the best possible use of unconventional, contemporary locations, which are no less fascinating and appealing for this reason. Some old disused industrial areas and factories have been converted for cultural purposes: the Cantieri Culturali in the Zisa area in Palermo is used for many different types of events, and was once a furniture factory; the Auditorium Zò and the Centro Culturale le Ciminiere in Catania are in an area once occupied by sulfur-processing plants.

The island's natural scenery is also used for concerts. For example, Gibellina (severely damaged by the disastrous 1968 earthquake), with its "cretto" by Alberto Burri, has become the setting for contemporary works performed every year in the Orestiade, a festival of prose, music and poetry, named after the Orestea by Eschylus.

Sicily is a crossroads of culture and peoples, and provides a rich range of modern music, including jazz, rock, Arab and African-American pop music, as well as local music traditions. There are many concerts, promoted by music associations and institutes, and many opportunities to enjoy opera and ballet.

AGRIGENTO

Agrigento Musica Festival
Late August
Tourists visiting here in the summer will find that the Festival provides them with another reason to stay; the musicians participating are always of the highest caliber. The Festival aims to promote the historic and local features of interest of Agrigento and its Province.

Blues & Wine Soul Festival
July
Excellent music and fine wines to enjoy in July in Agrigento, Palermo, Catania and Syracuse. Top international blues and soul musicians take part in the festival. For further information: tel. 092220627, www.bluesandwine.com

Teatro Luigi Pirandello
Piazza Pirandello 1, tel. 092223199, www.teatropirandello.it

CALTANISSETTA

Concorso Internazionale di Danza Michele Abbate
September
A competition consisting of classical, modern and choreography sections, which enjoys the patronage of Italy's Council of Ministers and of the Senate. The panel of judges includes some big names in the dance world. For further information: www.concorsomicheleabbate.com

Concorso Internazionale Musica da Camera
Early December
A competition which began nineteen years ago, and attracts a large public, both to the auditions as well as the final performance, providing a great opportunity of exchange for all involved. For further information: www.musicamera.caltanissetta.it

Teatro Bauffremont
Via Matteotti 10, tel. 0934547030, www.teatrobauffremont.it

Teatro Regina Margherita
Corso Vittorio Emanuele 1, tel. 0934547599-0934547034

CATANIA

Art&Jazz Caffè
All year round
An interesting place, where the pleasures of the table combine with the energy of jazz.

For further information: tel. 0957477446, www.brassgroup.com

Catania Jazz
October-April
The two associations, The Brass Group and Catania Jazz, work together to produce a concert series with some of the world's best jazz musicians.
For further information:
tel. 0957465174, www.cataniajazz.it

Centro Culturale Le Ciminiere
Viale Africa 2, tel. 0957349911, www.provincia.ct.it

Etnafest
October-June
The festival concentrates on quality events and a range of art forms, including poetry, painting, and sculpture. The music section aims to cover a wide range of modern music, including jazz, swing, rock, and Arab and French popular music.
For further information: tel. 0957225340 -0957306222, www.apt.catania.it

Fondazione Teatro Massimo Vincenzo Bellini
Piazza Vincenzo Bellini, tel. 0957306111, www.teatromassimobellini.it

I Concerti dell'Anfiteatro
March-June
Places of historical interest in Catania provide the locations for an enjoyable cycle of classical concerts, towards the end of spring.
For further information: tel. 3396246788

Mappe
September
An international event, which stimulates thinking and ideas on the contemporary city, through events, seminars, workshops and performances.
For further information: tel. 095533871, www.mappefestival.it

Scenario Pubblico
All year round
A contemporary dance festival, organized by Compagnia Zappalà Danza, which hosts and co-produces events, shows and performances all through the year.
For further information:
tel. 0952503147, ww.scenariopubblico.com

SoFar Festival
December
An electronic music festival (the only one of its kind in Sicily), which also looks at research, experimentalization, and ethnic-based music
For further information: tel. 0957463122, www.sofarfestival.it

Teatro di via Tezzano
Via Tezzano 40, tel. 0957273686

THE ITALIAN GENIUS OF "PURE SONG"

Vincenzo Bellini, a unique figure in the history of opera and one of the most original characters in the whole history of music, was born in Catania in 1801 to a family of musicians. He showed a precocious sensitivity to music, completed his studies in Naples and soon established a reputation as a composer. Before long, he had won the approval of Italy's leading opera-houses: San Carlo in Naples, La Scala in Milan, the Fenice in Venice, but also of audiences in Vienna, London and Paris. In the French capital, he moved in the main aristocratic, cultural and artistic circles. These were already frequented by composers such as Rossini, Chopin and Liszt, and writers such as Alexandre Dumas and Victor Hugo. Bellini became a great friend of Rossini, and drew attention to himself for his unusual musical style, both because of the content of his music, through which he endeavored to "involve the heart", and for his expressive skills, in particular, the overpowering agility of his melodic expansion. Bellini is recognized as the greatest romantic composer of opera. Some of his most famous works include *Il Pirata* (The Pirate) (1827), *La Sonnambula* (The Sleep-walker) (1831), *Norma* (1831) and *I Puritani* (The Puritans) (1835).
Bellini died a lonely young man at Puteaux, a suburb

of Paris, in 1835. In 1876, his remains were finally returned to his native city and have lain in the cathedral of Catania ever since.
Many places in Catania are dedicated to his name: the solemn monument in Piazza Stesicoro, the theater and the city's largest public park.

Teatro Nuovo
Via Re Martino 195/197, tel. 095494028-095491871

Teatro Piccolo di Catania
Via F. Ciccaglione 29, tel. 095447603

Teatro Sangiorgi
Via Antonino di Sangiuliano 233, tel. 095316860-0952502963

Zò - Centro Culture Contemporanee
Piazzale Asia 6, tel. 095533871, www.zoculture.it

MESSINA

Jazz Time Messina
November-April
The festival, now in its fourth year, brings some big names of the jazz world to Messina and Catania.
For further information: tel. 0957465174, www.brassgroup.com

Teatro Vittorio Emanuele
Via Pozzoleone, tel. 0905722111-09045935, www.teatrodimessina.it

TAORMINA

Taormina Arte
June-August
Taormina Arte provides a great series of summer concerts and events, with famous pop and rock musicians.
For further information: tel. 094221142-094223348, www.taormina-arte.com

Teatro Greco Antico di Taormina
Via Teatro Greco 40, tel. 094223220

PUPPET THEATER

The Puppet Theater is one of Sicily's greatest traditional art forms; the cultural importance of this art form was recognized by Unesco in 2001, when it was included on the World Heritage list.
The "puppets" are not controlled by strings, but by iron rods; this means they can make certain very precise gestures, such as kneeling down or beating their breasts. There are two branches of puppet tradition: the Palermo tradition and the Catania tradition. Each has different techniques, both in making the puppets and in the performances. The former tradition has smaller, lighter, more flexible puppets; the latter are larger and heavier, as well as less flexible, and more elaborately decorated. Puppet theater has very ancient origins. Some sources document the skill of Syracusans in making and operating puppets, at the time of the ancient Greeks and Romans. The Puppet Theater, as we know it today, dates from the 16th century; the stories performed are inspired by Italian and French epic poems of chivalry. Subsequently, themes became simpler, and the puppets began to represent familiar subjects, related to everyday life, which are known and loved by Sicilians. The performances used to take place outside in town squares; in the 19th century they began to be performed in theaters, and the puppets became increasingly complex and detailed, requiring skilled workmanship by considerable numbers of carpenters, tailors, painters and sculptors. Today many companies work to keep the puppet tradition alive: the Cuticchio family run the Teatro dei Pupo Santa Rosalia in Palermo, where, every evening, spectators can enjoy the magic of the world of puppets, fighters, actors, knights and heroes.
The Compagnia di Mimmo Cuticchio also organizes the "Dream Machine": a wonderful festival for children and adults where the streets are filled with decorations and street performers, from afternoon to midnight in the second half of July. Another place which is very involved with puppet theater is the Catania Teatro Stabile.

Where to see Puppet Theater:

Catania
Teatro Stabile
Centro Culturale "Le Ciminiere", viale Africa 2, tel. 0957349911 www.provincia.ct.it

Palermo
Teatro dei Pupi Santa Rosalia - Associazione Figli d'Arte Cuticchio
Via Bara all'Olivella 45 tel. 091323400 www.figlidartecuticchio.it

PALERMO

Associazione siciliana per la musica-The Brass Group
June-July
In the superb setting of the Chiesa di Santa Maria dello Spasimo, The Brass Group presents a cycle of high-level summer concerts, with guest artists including top African-American musicians. For further information:
tel. 0916166480, www.thebrassgroup.it

Balarm Rock Festival
July-August
This is an interesting festival for up-and-coming rock groups performing new music, and is organized by the Associazione Culturale Balarm together with the Palermo Municipality.
For further information:
www.balarmrockfestival.com

Cantieri Culturali della Zisa
Via Paolo Gili 4, tel. 0916524942

Kals'art musica
December-January
This festival for female singers takes place in the splendid churches and oratories of the Kalsa area of Palermo, which provide unusual and charming locations for concerts.
For further information: www.kalsart.it

La musica attraversa/o i suoni
November-December
The fourth festival includes nine concerts, covering a range of genres, organized by the Associazione Culturale Curva Minore. Traditional performances from Turkey, Greece, the Balkans, and Sicily. Original compositions and improvization.
For further information: tel. 3476035179, www.curvaminore.virtuale.org

New Thing: immagini del suono
November-May
Festival organized by the Associazione Musiche and the Centro Polivalente Agricantus, with a cycle of concerts presenting new trends, such as nu-jazz, electronic music, and acoustic music.
For further information: tel. 091309636

Stagione Concertistica Associazione per la Musica Antica Antonio Il Verso
March-December
The Palermo "Associazione per la Musica Antica Antonio Il Verso" promotes a variety of activities related to Renaissance and Baroque music, especially by Italian composers, and is particularly attentive to Sicilian and southern Italian music.
For further information:
tel. 0916168373, www.antonioilverso.it

Stagione Orchestra Sinfonica Siciliana
All year round
A repertory mostly of classical symphonic music, but also some contemporary Italian music, for this orchestra which was founded over forty years ago and plays all over Italy. For further information: tel. 091588801, www.fondazioneorchestrasinfonicasiciliana.it

Teatro Biondo - Stabile di Palermo
Via Roma 258, tel. 0917434300-0917434341, www.teatrobiondo.it

Teatro di Verdura
Villa Castelnuovo, viale del Fante 60/b, tel. 800655858-800907080, www.teatromassimo.it

Teatro Massimo
Piazza G. Verdi, tel. 0916053111-800655858, www.teatromassimo.it

Teatro Politeama Garibaldi
Piazza Ruggiero Settimo 12, tel. 091588001, www.fondazioneorchestra sinfonicasiciliana.it

BAGHERIA
Stagione Concertistica
November-May
A series of events organized by the Associazione Unda Maris, together with the "Vincenzo Bellini" Conservatory of Palermo. A range of concerts and a variety of genres: classical, orchestral, gospel, chamber music and jazz.
For further information:
tel. 0916891808, www.undamaris.it

MONREALE
Festival Organistico San Martino delle Scale
July-August
This international festival of church music is held in the 6th-century Abbazia dei Benedettini (Benedictine Abbey). The Duomo has a superb organ with ten thousand pipes and six keyboards, an inspiration for the festival, held here every November.
For further information: tel. 091418104, www.abbaziadisanmartino.it

Settimane della musica
November
A week of church music in the superb setting of the Duomo in Monreale, and other churches with lots of atmosphere. For further information: tel. 0916398011, www.aziendaturismopalermo.it

RAGUSA

Teatro Tenda
Via Mario Spadola 1, tel. 0932683018

MODICA
Note di Notte
July-August
The Festival involves three
Unesco towns: Ragusa, Modica and
Scicli. Visitors can enjoy the music,
as well as this little-known area.
It's organized by The Entertainer, an
association which also organizes other
interesting events during the year.
For further information: tel. 3201945850

Teatro Comunale Garibaldi
*C/o Ufficio Cultura del Comune,
corso Umberto I, tel. 0932759111,
www.teatrogaribaldi.com*

SIRACUSA

Auditorium San Pietro al Carmine (ASAM)
*Via S. Pietro al Carmine, tel. 093168042-
093167249, www.asam.it*
Teatro Greco Antico di Siracusa
*Corso Matteotti 29, tel. 093167415,
www.indafondazione.org*

NOTO
Noto Musica Festival
Late July-August
Now in its twenty-ninth year, the Festival
attracts well-known performers, such as
Salvatore Accardo, Uto Ughi, and Ennio
Morricone. For further information:
www.notomusicafestival.com/index2.htm

Teatro Comunale Vittorio Emanuele
*Piazza XVI Maggio, tel. 0931896655-
800279505, www.comune.noto.sr.it*

TRAPANI

**Ente Luglio Musicale Trapanese-Teatro
Giuseppe di Stefano**
*Viale Regina Margherita 1, tel. 092321454,
www.lugliomusicaletrapanese.com*
Teatro Auditorium Provinciale dell'Università
*Lungomare Dante Alighieri,
tel. 0923560229-0923533888*

CALATAFIMI-SEGESTA
Ciclo di spettacoli classici
June-August

Segesta's ancient Greek theater has
much to offer in the summer time:
drama, music, opera and ballet. For real
enthusiasts, there are also drama, poetry
and literature events at dawn.
For further information: tel. 0924956246,
www.calatafimisegesta.com/
inner/eventi.html

Traditional
cheese p. 147

ERICE
Rassegna del premio "Zampogna d'oro"
First fortnight in December
International festival of traditional music
with musicians playing folk instruments;
organized by the Azienda Autonoma
Soggiorno di Erice. For further information:
tel. 0923869388, www.apt.trapani.it

GIBELLINA
Gibellina d'Inverno
December-April
Drama festival which includes plays,
operettas and ballets.
For further information: tel. 092467428
Gibellina Jazz Festival
July
A cycle of jazz concerts in a great
location, the Arco (Arch) by Nanda Vigo
For further information: tel. 092467428
Orestiadi
Late June-September
A event combining various performing
arts, where music plays an important part,
held at an old Sicilian country estate.
For further information: tel. 092467844,
www.fondazione.orestiadi.it

MARSALA
**Concorso pianistico internazionale "Città
di Marsala"**
December
The "Associazione Amici del Pianoforte"
(Friends of the Piano Association)
started this competition for young
talents twenty years ago. Contestants
come from all over the world, and are
judged by a panel of experts.
For further information: tel. 3280074939,
www.amicidelpianoforte.com
Marsala Doc Jazz Festival
Late July
Now a permanent summer event, the week-
long Festival features international artists and
attracts jazz enthusiasts from all over Italy.
For further information: tel. 0923993224
Teatro Comunale Eliodoro Sollima
*Via Teatro 1, tel. 0923953355-
0923993230*

FOLKLORE

Sicily has been occupied by various different peoples and cultures and this has had an effect on the region's folk traditions. Giant simulacra or figures appear at many festivals: they may be either fixed and drawn along with ropes or pulleys, or mobile, like the "santoni" (saints), whose internal supporting structures allow someone hidden inside to operate them and make them move. The fact that these figures are widespread in Catalonia and also in Flanders suggests that they originated in Sicily under the Normans. Sicily's large, spectacular processions seem to be Spanish in origin; during these processions, the trade associations parade for the community with their emblems and very recognizable hierarchies. Plays and shows performed during festivals have their origins in the religious performances of the Middle Ages and the 17th- and 18th-century religious plays: processional floats or carts ("vare"), and sculpture groups have substituted the real actors used in religious drama in the past. In celebrations of St Joseph, food is distributed at banquets and altars to mark the end of Lent, or to strengthen family and neighbourhood ties. In the "laurel festivals", usually in agricultural areas, branches and foliage are collected, decorated, and carried in the procession, in ways that testify to the strength and skill of the faithful. The various celebrations often follow "viaggi", or short trips from home to church; for the month before the festival, the faithful make these "journeys" every day, for votive or devotional reasons.

AGRIGENTO

Sagra del mandorlo in fiore
February
The almond blossom festival is a very popular spring festival in Agrigento. It was first started in the early thirties, to celebrate the beautiful white blossom which flowers in February here and in the surrounding area. The festival celebrates the coming of spring, as well as local folk traditions with puppeteers, singers, poets, and actors. In Akragas, the Fiaccolata dell'Amicizia (Torchlight Friendship Procession) is very popular, with international folk groups winding through the streets of the old town. The International Folk Festival is the central event; different peoples from all over the world come together to dance and sing, in the name of peace and brotherhood. For further information: tel. 092220500, www.mandorloinfiore.net

San Calogero
July
St Calogerus, a performer of miracles, is celebrated on a number of days in July; the most important is the day when the saint is carried in procession, by men in white shirts with the saint's crest; the privilege of wearing this shirt is hereditary. During the procession, the faithful throw pieces of bread or "muffuletti" at the procession from houses along the street. Some babies are undressed and placed near the statue to receive part of the saint's miracle-working powers. The following Sunday there is a parade with richly-caparisoned horses and mules. For further information: tel. 092220446

ARAGONA
Incontro dei giganti
Easter Sunday
Easter Sunday celebrations here feature paper mache simulacra, or holy statues, of St Peter and St Paul, which can move (each conceals a man inside). St Paul announces the resurrection to the Virgin, who lets her black mantle fall. For further information: tel. 092237170

LICATA
Sant'Angelo
May 3rd-6th
Sant'Angelo is celebrated three times: in January, in May and in August. The most important celebration is in May. The saint's relics are carried by runners in the procession held on May 5th; next in the procession are four large church candles (donated by the trade associations), also carried along at a run, and perched on four high towers surrounding the silver reliquary urn. In the past, there was a tradition of leading gaily-decorated donkeys into the church, with donations of money. There was also a sea procession, with the saint's statue in a boat. A boat race is held on the last day of the celebrations. For further information: tel. 0922868229

SAN BIAGIO PLATANI
Gli archi
Holy Week
Wooden structures are assembled by the Signurara (members of the Confraternity of the Holy Sacrament) during Holy Week. These structures, called Archi (Arches), are built to resemble parts of buildings, church facades, and so on, and are adorned with plants and loaves of bread.
For further information: tel. 0922910753

SCIACCA
Carnevale
Holy Week
Sciacca, a town near Agrigento, has one of Italy's best carnivals: every year thousands of visitors come here from all over the country to enjoy themselves. First mentioned in the 16th century, the Sciacca carnival is a festive occasion, with original masks and a strongly satirical streak. The undisputed protagonist is Peppe Nappa, a local carnival character, who dances and sings through the streets of the old town and invites people to enjoy themselves and forget the problems of everyday life. During the celebrations, he also distributes generous quantities of sausages, wine and sweets to visitors, thus expressing the local tradition of warm hospitality. There are also allegorical floats, made by groups who put enormous effort into making the festival a success. Over the following week there are also dance shows and music concerts. Carnival comes to an end on the night of Mardi Gras, when Peppe Nappa is burnt on a bonfire.
For further information: tel. 092522744-092584121, www.aziendaturismosciacca.it

Celebrazioni pasquali
From the Wednesday before Easter, to Easter Sunday
The main Easter celebrations intensify in the three central days of Holy Week. On Wednesday, there are two processions: the Corteo della Reale Maestranza and the Varricedde procession. The latter consists of small sculpture groups, belonging to various trade associations. The following day, the Mysteries procession takes place: sixteen groups of large figures make up the procession, representing scenes from the passion of Christ. When the Mysteries gather in Piazza del Duomo at the end of the procession, the "spartenza" takes place: suddenly all the groups of figures are quickly removed from the square, and returned to the trade association which they belong to.
For further information: tel. 093424001, www.aapit.cl.it

Sant'Agata
February 3rd-5th
Starting in January, St Agatha's Veil is displayed on Sundays for veneration in various churches in Catania; this important relic was used over the centuries to protect Catania against Mt Etna's eruptions. The festival of St Agatha features traditional processions with "cannalore", solid structures in wood painted

During the Festival of Sant'Agata the precious reliquary is processed around the city

with stories from the Bible and scenes of the martyrdom of St Agatha. In the past, the festival used to be attended by "ntuppateddi", women entirely swathed in black robes leaving only their eyes uncovered; on special occasions like this, they were allowed to move around the city unaccompanied. Sometimes the voluminous clothing disguised men.
For further information:
tel. 0957306211, www.apt.catania.it

ACIREALE
San Sebastiano
January 20th
St Sebastian's statue is carried in procession on a heavy silver "fercolo" or supporting structure, placed on a cart, which is pushed along at a fairly brisk pace by the members of various confraternities; meanwhile, "manilleri" (or "handlers") belonging to the fishermen's confraternity use special handholds to skilfully rotate the fercolo. St Sebastian is

also celebrated in Melilli, in the province of Syracuse, on May 1st. "Nuri", the faithful, who once went barefoot and almost naked, take part in the procession; today they dress in white with red sashes around their waists. St Sebastian is also celebrated in Palazzolo Acreide, on August 10th; in Syracuse; and in Totorici, in the province of Messina, where people in the procession carry laurel branches.

For further information: tel. 095891999

ADRANO
Diavolata
From the Thursday before Easter, to Easter Sunday

Easter celebrations in Adrano are like real theatrical performances. On the Thursday before Easter, the procession of Christ at the Column takes place; the simulacrum, or sacred image, advances very slowly, as the bearers take two steps back for every three steps forward. On the morning of Good Friday, there's a procession with the statue of Our Lady of Sorrows, and in the evening with the statue of the dead Christ. The most important event is the Diavolata, a play performed on Easter Day. It tells the story of the battle between the Devils and Death on one side, and the Archangel Michael on the other, who must save Humanity (a character played by a little girl). After the final victory of Good over Evil, another performance follows, known as the Angelicata.

For further information: tel. 0957698849

CALTAGIRONE
San Giacomo
July 24th-25th

The Luminaria is set up to celebrate the feast day of Caltagirone's patron saint, St James, and sometimes also for other festivals. It developed from 18th-century displays of illumination, and was first created in this form in 1860. Around four thousand "coppi" (paper cylinders each with an oil lamp inside) are placed on the 142 steps in front of the church of Santa Maria del Monte; when lit, they create a picture in three colors (white, red and green).

For further information: tel. 093353809

TRECASTAGNI
Santissimi Alfio, Filadelfo e Cirino
May 1st-17th

The three saints, Alphius, Philadelphus and Cyrinus, brothers of Turkish origin, are worshipped in a number of towns in Sicily (such as Lentini). At Trecastagni, festivities celebrate the three holy men over a number of days. On the night of May 9th, the procession of the "Nuri" (naked ones) is held, with the important reliquary of the heart of St Alphius. The Nuri wear white trousers and a red sash across the shoulder.

For further information: tel. 0957806502

ENNA

CERAMI
San Sebastiano
August 27th-28th

In the month leading up to the festival of St Sebastian, the faithful make "journeys" (short trips from home to church). The festival itself consists of two main events. On August 27th, there is a procession with the heavy "bbanneri", enormous banners made of large laurel branches tied together and opened out fan-style, which the faithful carry for votive purposes over certain distances. On August 28th, another procession takes place, with the "vara" containing the saint's statue.

For further information: tel. 0935931109

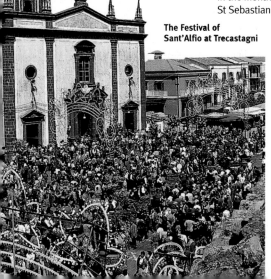

The Festival of Sant'Alfio at Trecastagni

GAGLIANO CASTELFERRATO
San Cataldo
August 29th-31st

Before the festival, a pilgrimage is held on August 22nd, from the town to the woods of Baronia, where people collect foliage and large branches of holly and laurel. At the procession on August 29th, the saint's relic is followed by the faithful, who walk along carrying small branches; next come riders on horseback in single file, bearing the "rods", or long branches of holly stripped of leaves, decorated with paper and fabric, with a cross or a bunch of laurel leaves at the top. Over the following days, other processions take place with the saint's relic or statue.
For further information: tel. 0935694130

MESSINA

Madonna della Lettera
August 14th-15th

The festival of the Madonna of the Letter includes two events, one on June 3rd and another on August 15th, at the same time as the Feast of the Assumption. On August 14th, the giants Mata and Grifone, also known as Cam and Rea, parade through the city streets. The giants – a Moor who has come from afar, and a local woman – represent the city's mythical ancestors, as in other processions of giant figures (in Sicily and Calabria, in Catalonia, and in Flanders). On August 15th, the "Vara" is carried in procession. This pyramid structure portrays the death and assumption of the Virgin, along with numerous other characters, some played by live people and some not. The overall visual spectacle is heightened by the mechanical clock, at the top of the Duomo, with its various symbolic figures representing time, striking the hour regularly.
For further information: tel. 090674236

ALCARA LI FUSI
Festa de' muzzuni
June 24th

The festival takes place around the summer solstice; it was probably once an ancient agricultural feast day, which was Christianized and associated with St John. The women of the town set up small rug-covered altars in the streets, where they display pitchers, known as muzzini', filled

with young wheat shoots grown in the dark, and decorated with the family jewelry and woven ears of wheat.
For further information: tel. 0941793010

BORDONARO
Festa del pagghiaru
Epiphany

The "pagghiaru" is assembled in the town's main square, in the days preceding the festival. It's a structure made from a large chestnut pole around nine meters high, a ring made of iron and wood known as the

The *Festa dei Giudei* (Festival of the Jews) is the oldest festival of popular sacred plays

"crucera", and a cone-shaped covering of interwoven branches and flowers. Fruit, bread, hams and salamis hang from a cross at the top. In the afternoon, a competition is held. The young men of the town climb up the "pagghiaru" to the cross and the prizes hanging there. Then the whole structure is destroyed and its various parts thrown on the crowd. Later there's an open-air performance. Two men, one disguised as a horse and the other as a savage, have a mock fight, with firecrackers.
For further information: tel. 0906411047

NASO
San Cono
September 1st

The St Conus procession generally takes place without any church authorities being present; the bearers run with the simulacrum, although they stop at various houses many times along the way. In August preparations for the festival are made by setting up arches covered in foliage. Some of the faithful go to collect earth from the grotto where the saint is believed to have died, to obtain protection from illness. Others, before the procession, tie olive branches to the "fercolo" (the structure which the simulacrum is carried on), or ears of wheat, to mix with sowing seed, for a good harvest.

For further information: tel. 0941961060

Every year, the traditional Festival of Santa Rosalia involves a huge number of devoted followers and tourists

SAN FRATELLO

I giudei

Holy Week

The usual Easter ceremonies (the Washing of the Feet and processions) are performed here. In addition, from Wednesday to Good Friday, a performance takes place which resembles the holy plays of the past where key religious events, such as the birth of Christ, or the resurrection, include negative characters who try to obstruct what is happening. During the Good Friday procession, groups of Judeans, move swiftly amongst the public, blowing trumpets and acting as "disturbers" of the ceremony's holiness. They are dressed in red, military-style costumes, and wear helmets. They never speak, and their faces are covered, so they

cannot be identified. Many of the costumes have been handed down for generations from father to son.

For further information: tel. 0941794030

SAPONARA

Carnevale

Mardi Gras

The Carnival parade in Saponara winds its way through the streets of the town; masked figures include the Prince, the Princess, the Scribe and Dignitaries. The Bear leads the procession, dressed in goat skins, with four dangling cowbells; he's accompanied by two Hunters and three Tamers, to restrain him with ropes and chains. Often the Bear breaks away from the procession to lunge at girls and women, but is always kept under control by the Tamers; sometimes he becomes gentlemanly, and invites a girl to dance. The role of the Bear has always been played by members of the same family.

For further information: tel. 090333747

PALERMO

Santa Rosalia

July 9th-15th and September 3rd-4th

Santa Rosalia, the patron saint of Palermo, who lived as a hermit on Monte Pellegrino (Mt Pilgrim), is celebrated on two occasions. The Festino lasts from July 9th to July 15th, in the city. The pilgrimage to Monte Pellegrino, where the sanctuary is, takes place on September 3rd and 4th. The Festino features a procession with the triumphal cart, an enormous structure shaped like a ship, where singers and players are seated; there are also horse races (although some years these are cancelled); and sometimes it is possible to hear the blind street singers singing the "Songs of the Blind" about the life of the saint. For the pilgrimage on September 3rd and 4th, the faithful walk up to the sanctuary on Monte Pellegrino. Some stay the night in temporary shelters. There are celebrations, a banquet and dancing, and then the return to the city.

For further information: tel. 091346075, www.comune.palermo.it

GANGI

Celebrazioni pasquali

Palm Sunday

The Grandi Palme procession, with large

decorated palms, takes place on Palm Sunday; the town's ten confraternities take it in turns to organize the procession from year to year. Confraternity members go to Cefalù to collect palms; they are decorated with flowers, dates and objects made from woven palm leaves, and are then carried in the procession.
For further information: tel. 0921644076

Festa dei Burgisi
1st week in August
The festival of the Burgisi (or the Bourgeois) expresses the strong religious sense of a people who have close connections with the land and its produce, and who celebrate the miracle of the cycles of the seasons and the fruits of the harvest, by giving thanks to God. All the earth's produce is central to the festival, especially bread: six enormous loaves are carried in the procession by young people dressed in costume.
For further information: tel. 0921644076

MEZZOJUSO
Carnevale
Last Sunday of Carnival
On Carnival Sunday, "Mastro di Campo" is performed. It was probably inspired by a historical event involving Bernardo Cabrera, Count of Modica, who fell in love with Bianca di Navarra. The play takes place in the open air and tells the story of Mastro di Campo's successful assault on the castle; he won over the Queen and imprisoned the King. With his red mask and enormous nose, Mastro di Campo is a stock character in traditional carnivals in the Palermo area.
For further information: tel. 0918203237

PIANA DEGLI ALBANESI
Epifania e Pasqua degli albanesi
6th January, Holy Week
The Albanian community, which settled here and in other parts of Sicily from the 15th century, maintains its identity and traditions by celebrating Epiphany and Easter, according to Greek Orthodox rite. On January 6th, a ceremony takes place at the Fonte dei Tre Cannoli, where the cross is immersed in the fountain, symbolizing the baptism of Christ in the River Jordan. In Holy Week, there are the usual ceremonies (the Last Supper, the Washing of the Feet, the Procession, Baptism by immersion). After the service on Easter Sunday, red-painted eggs are distributed. Many women taking part in

the celebrations dress in ethnic Albanian costumes: some of these are very old and have been passed down from mother to daughter over the centuries.
For further information: tel. 0918571787

PRIZZI
Abballu di li diavuli
Easter Sunday
On Easter Sunday afternoon there is a procession with the figures of the Virgin and of the Risen Christ. While the procession advances, at least five groups of masked players move around the statues and among the public; each group is composed of four Devils (in red, with grotesque masks and goat skins) and Death, dressed in yellow and holding a wooden crossbow. The Devils scare the public, and Death shoots off symbolic arrows, but they collapse to the ground whenever the two statues of the Resurrection come together.
For further information: tel. 0918344360

TERRASINI
Festa de li schetti
Easter Sunday
The festival centers around a competition to test the strength and skill of the town's young unmarried men, known as "schetti" in local dialect. On the day before Easter Sunday, the contestants go out to the surrounding countryside and each cut down a previously-selected orange tree. All the trees are decorated with colorful ribbons and various objects, and on Easter Sunday are blessed in front of the church. The competition consists in holding the tree in the palm of one hand for the longest possible time. A mutton feast follows.
For further information: tel. 0918686194

RAGUSA

San Giorgio e San Giovanni
Last Sunday in May, August 29th
Ragusa has two patron saints: St George Knight for Ragusa Ibla, and St John for Ragusa Superiore. The simulacrum of St George, on horseback, is carried in procession together with the Holy Casket, holding various relics of saints; the statue is not very heavy, and the bearers dance, and spin the simulacrum, sometimes even throwing it up into the air and then catching it. In Ragusa Superiore, the

The statues carried during the *Processione dei Misteri* were made in the 17th and 18th centuries

statue of St John and the Holy Casket with relics are paraded in a large procession; people carry lighted candles or torches.
For further information: tel. 0932663094

ACATE
San Vincenzo
Third Sunday after Easter
The festival of St Vincent first took place in 1722, and has its origins in a terrible deed carried out by Anna, wife of Prince Vincenzo Paternò Castello. She took revenge on a rival in love, a young girl, by having her kidnapped and locked away in the castle. The girl had been totally coated in honey, was attacked by bees, and died. As punishment for this crime, the Prince and Princess were made to bring St Vincent's "holy body" from Rome to Acate. The saint's festival is celebrated with church services, a horse race with jockeys, and a religious procession.
For further information: tel. 0932989189

SCICLI
Madonna delle Milizie
Last Sunday in May
The Virgin of the Militias is portrayed as a warrior maid on horseback, her sword unsheathed. The cult developed from a historical event: a Saracen raid into Norman territory, which failed because of the Virgin's intervention. In the past, the people used to perform a play about the event, telling the story of the battle between the inhabitants of Scicli and the Normans on one side, and the Saracens on the other. Then for a while the tradition was abandoned; since 1988 the play has been performed by an amateur theatre group.
For further information: tel. 0932932782

TRAPANI

Processione dei Misteri
Good Friday and Easter Saturday
The procession of the Mysteries consists of twenty sculpture groups, depicting scenes from the passion of Christ. Each sculpture group, representing a different trade association, is carried by sixteen men, today from the church's congregation, but once upon a time workers from the port of Trapani. The procession takes place on Good Friday, and then on Easter Saturday, the statues are returned to the church of Holy Purgatory; the bearers move and sway them around to the sound of music.
For further information: tel. 092329000

CALATAFIMI-SEGESTA
Santissimo Crocifisso
May 1st to 3rd, once every five years
The festival of the Holy Crucifix includes various processions. The children's procession takes place on May 1st, with each child holding a precious object used in religious services and ceremonies. In the afternoon, there's a procession with allegorical floats, showing stories from the Bible, with scenery and real people. The main procession is on May 2nd. The various trade associations all participate, with their banners and symbols: the Workers, Burghers, Farmers, Horse-handlers, Millers, Greengrocers, Shepherds, St Joseph's Burgers, Butchers and Trawl Fishermen. The festival ends with another procession where a silver simulacrum of the Crucifix and an image of the Madonna del Giubbino (Madonna of the Jacket) are paraded.
For further information: tel. 0924951988

MAZARA DEL VALLO
San Vito
Last 2 Sundays in August
There are various processions on the feast day of St Vitus (protector from bites of rabid dogs). The annunciation procession, with characters in 17th-century dress; the procession of the "quadri viventi" (living pictures), with characters mounted on allegorical floats depicting the virtues, Christian symbols, and scenes from the life and martyrdom of the saint; and the procession with the silver simulacrum on a cart drawn by fishermen.
For further information: tel. 0923941727

EVENTS

Sicily's bubbling sulfur springs have become an important destination for health and fitness aficionados. The therapeutic properties of the hot springs and mud rich in minerals are ideal for treating a variety of ailments and maladies.

The benefits of Sicily's many wellness centers are enhanced by the mild climate and abundant natural beauty of the island.

Sicily's blend of endless beaches, rolling orchards, lush forests and stunning mountain landscapes, create the perfect environment for renewing the

mind, body and spirit.
Modern spas facilitate deep
relaxation and rejuvenation in
one of the most magical places
on the planet.
Experience the healing mineral
waters and indulge in some
of the same timeless spa
treatments that the ancients
used to relax after a long day
of conquering.

Wellness

Highlights

- Acireale: the Greeks were the first
  to build systems for exploiting the
  sulfurous waters which surface here
  at a temperature of 22°C/72°F

- Montevago: the waters here are rich
  in sulfur, calcium and magnesium
  and are recommended in the
  treatment of the respiratory and
  motory systems

- Island of Vulcano: the fumaroles near
  the coast heat the sea-water, making
  it a perfect temperature for
  swimming all the year round

An itinerary devoted to wellness and health in Sicily must first incorporate the ancient therapeutic properties of its thermal springs, found in modern "remise en forme" centers but also in the hammams and spas of its cities.

Amongst its many treasures, Sicily has an extremely rich heritage of hot springs, which were known about in the times of Magna Grecia ("Greater Greece" as the Ancient Greeks called Sicily), but also makes the island an important destination for fitness and spa tourism today. In fact, the Sicily lies on the fault line of great volcanic fissures between the African and Eurasian tectonic plates and is largely composed of igneous rocks. Springs of mainly sulfurous mineral water are to be found in almost all of the provinces of Sicily. They are used mainly for balneo-therapy and mud therapy and are ideal for treating arthrosis, the after-effects of fractures, gout, bronchitis, acne, psoriasis and leukorrhea.

An added attraction is the natural beauty of the island. The spa towns and other structures

dedicated to wellness are situated in the finest parts of the Sicilian landscape, where there are plenty of opportunities to enjoy cultural excursions to famous tourist sights or swim off its splendid coastline. The benefits of coming to Sicily for wellness treatments are compounded by the climate, which is always mild, with a high number of hours of sunlight and very little rain, even in winter. The region also offers the option of staying at wellness centers where there are many therapies and esthetic treatments available. The addresses and the description of the offering can be found in the Practical Info Section under "Health Centers".

ACIREALE

Azienda Autonoma Terme di Acireale

via delle Terme 47, tel. 0957686111
www.terme.acireale.gte.it
Open all year round

Acireale is built on a lava plateau above a vertical drop down to the sea on the stretch of coastline known as the Riviera dei Ciclopi (Cyclops Riviera, named after the one-eyed giants of ancient legend). Since antiquity, this place has been renowned for its mild climate and thermal springs. In this vast area dominated by expanses of citrus plantations situated between Mount Etna and the Ionian Sea, the Ancient Greeks built their first settlement, which they called *Xiphonie*, in order to exploit the sulfur-bearing water from the volcano. Later, the Romans built a bath complex on the same site at Santa Venera al Pozzo, the remains of which are still there today.

The water which gushes from the spring bearing sulfurous salt bromine iodic water at a temperature of 22°C/72°F

is effective for the treatment of circulatory diseases, skin complaints, and motory and respiratory problems. The bath houses date from 1873, and new facilities were opened at Santa Caterina in 1987. The facilities offer the following: inhalations, angiology and pneumology, mud therapy and balneo-therapy, physiokinesitherapy and dermocosmetics. The treatments available include: aerosols, therapeutic baths, nasal douches, mud therapy, humage, hydro-massage, hot and cold inhalations, insufflations, nebulizations, nasal irrigations, psammotherapy and lung ventilation, as well as kinesitherapy, breathing exercises, massage, esthetic medicine, rehabilitation, and physical therapy. In the summer, in the huge garden of the spa, where there is no shortage of swimming-pools and children's playgrounds, concerts of classical music and jazz alternate with theatre and dance performances.

ALÌ TERME

Terme Granata-Cassibile
via Crispi 1/13, tel. 0942715029
Open June-November

Terme Marino
via Roma 21, tel. 0942715031
Open June-November
People began to exploit the therapeutic properties of the springs and the natural mud of the area - which were famous even in Roman times - in the 16th century, when large pools were dug in the rock, of which one example remains at the Terme Granata-Cassibile. But Alì Terme didn't become famous until the following century, thanks partly to the fact that Renè Descartes, the French 17th-century philosopher, who visited the spa during his journey to Italy between 1623 and 1625, mentioned it in his journals.
The hot springs supply two separate spa buildings: the *Terme Granata-Cassibile*, down by the sea, and the *Terme Marino*, higher up, built in 1848 after the discovery of the *Nuova sorgente* (New Spring). The sulfurous salt bromine iodic water from the springs surfaces at a temperature of 47°C/116°F from the first spa and 40°C/104°F from the second. This water is beneficial for skin ailments, motory and respiratory problems, and the therapies offered here are as follows: aerosols, therapeutics baths, nasal douches, therapeutic showers, mud therapy, humage, hydro-massage, humid-hot inhalations, insufflations and nebulizations.
Both establishments offer therapies, beauty treatments, massages and accommodation. An open-air swimming-pool is in the process of being built at the Terme Marino.

The Terme Granata-Cassabile faces the Ionian Sea

CALATAFIMI - SEGESTA

Terme Gorga
Gorga, tel. 092423842
www.termegorga.com
Open all year round

The center of the town, which is in the Province of Trapani, is clustered around a rock bearing the remains of a medieval castle. The spa, on the other hand, is out in the country, only a few miles away from the archeological site of Segesta, on the east bank of the River Caldo. The spring water, which gushes from *Fonte Gorga* (Gorga Spring), accumulates in a natural depression between clay agglomerates at a constant temperature of 52°C/126°F. From here, a pipeline conveys it to the bath-house in an old mill that was converted in the 1960s. The alkaline and sulfurous water is beneficial in the treatment of skin complaints and problems associated with the motory and respiratory systems. The other therapies offered by the Calatafimi spa include therapeutic baths, nasal douches, aerosols, mud therapy, humage, humid-hot inhalations, insufflations and nebulizations.
The offering of the spa complex is completed by two open-air hot-water swimming pools, hydro-kinesitherapy and massage.

Terme Segestane

Ponte Bagni, tel. 0924530057
Open June to mid-November
Castellammare del Golfo is situated near the Riserva Naturale Regionale dello Zingaro (Lo Zingaro Nature Reserve), in one of the most spectacular parts of the Tyrrhenian coast, near Scopello. The hot springs are located at Ponte Bagni, on the River Caldo. According to one legend, a nymph created a spring here to revive Hercules, while another account tells how the companions of Aeneas benefited from its waters after their flight from Troy.

The spa complex itself dates from 1958. It was extended in 1990 and has two swimming-pools and a natural sauna known as the Grotta Regina ("Queen's Cave"), with a vault dating from Roman times.

In addition to the cave, the hot springs are at *Bagno delle Fimmine* and *Fonte Nuova*. Here, the sulfurous earthy salt sulphate alkaline water surfaces at a temperature of 44°C/106°F.

The Terme Segestane at Castellammare del Golfo

The water of Castellammare del Golfo is beneficial in the treatment of skin ailments, and of motory and respiratory problems. The treatments available include aerosols, therapeutic baths, mud therapy, steam caves, hydro-massage, humid-hot inhalations, nasal irrigations, a swimming-pool fed with hot spring water and massage.

MONTEVAGO

Terme Acqua Pia

Acque Calde, tel. 092539026
www.termeacquapia.it
Open all year round
This town in the hinterland of the Province of Agrigento was completely destroyed by the earthquake of 1968. Today it is a spa resort thanks to the hot spring known as *Acqua Pia*, situated about 7 km away from the town. In the luxuriant park near the spring, a large pool collects the water which gushes out of the many small veins in the calcareous rock.

The spa complex, opened in 1976, has been extended and modernized and is now a whole village, ideal not only for treatments but also for relaxing and leisure activities.

The water from this spring, which surfaces at a temperature of 39°C/102°F, is recommended in the treatment of the motory and respiratory systems thanks to its high levels of sulfur, calcium and magnesium. The treatments available at the spa include aerosols, therapeutic baths, mud therapy, steam caves, hydro-massage, humid-hot inhalations, and a swimming-pool fed with hot spring water. Other treatments available include sessions on kinesitherapy, health education, fitness, breathing exercises, de-stress programs, massage and personal consultancy.

The Terme Acqua Pia at Montevago

SCIACCA

Azienda Autonoma delle Terme

viale delle Terme, tel. 0925961111
Open all year (except January)
Surrounded by 16th-century walls, Sciacca is a delightful little town, situated on a flat shelf on the south coast of Sicily, between Agrigento and Mazara del Vallo. Popular as a seaside resort, it is also one of the island's oldest spa towns. Its origins date back to Roman times, when it was called Thermae Selinuntinae (Springs of Selinus) and it was thought that the steam caves had been created by Daedalus. Today the vapor grottoes are known as the *Stufe di San*

promontory with a vertical drop down to the sea. Sciacca is famous as a center for pediatric inhalatory ailments, physiokinesitherapy and hydro-kinesitherapy, both of which encourage motory rehabilitation. The spring water at Sciacca is also beneficial in the treatment of disfunctions of the circulatory, motory and respiratory systems and the following treatments are available: aerosols, baths, nasal douches, mud therapy, steam caves, humage, hydro-massage, humid-hot inhalations, insufflations, nasal irrigation, nebulizations, politzer crenotherapy

The swimming-pools known as the 'Molinelli' (whirlpools): the largest public hot-spring complex in Sciacca

Calogero, after the name of a hermit monk who used to cure people in them. The caves, dug out of the living rock, create a hot, damp environment (with a temperature of 38°C/100°F-33°C/91°F and 95% humidity) and are used as sweating rooms in the treatment of chronic joint pain, rheumatism, arthrosis and myalgia. The 19th century spa was built in the Bagni Valley, inland from the coast, whereas the new complex is housed in an Art Deco building perched on a

and lung ventilation.
The sulfurous salt bromine iodic water at Sciacca gushes out of the springs called *Cammordino R1* and *R3*. The following therapies are also offered by the spa: kinesitherapy, breathing exercises, hydro-kinesitherapy, massage and rehabilitation, whereas, if you want to relax, there are the swimming-pools at the Molinelli ("whirlpools"), a large complex fed by the hot springs, with marvelous views.

TERME VIGLIATORE

Fonte di Venere
viale delle Terme 85, tel. 0909781078
Open May-October

The Fonte di Venere spa complex, at Terme Vigliatore

Set in a panoramic position on the Bay of Patti, the town of Terme Vigliatore in the Province of Messina is an important spa and seaside resort, surrounded by an area dominated by vineyards, citrus groves and olive groves.
The area was famous even in Roman times, as confirmed by some of the archeological remains found nearby. These include a mid-1st-century AD Roman villa which had a small bath complex with floors supported by a hypocaust and terracotta pipes to circulate hot air and steam around the building.
However, the reputation of Terme Vigliatore as a spa town began in 1841, when the first spa complex was built. The *Fonte di Venere* (Fount of Venus) gushes out of terrain composed of sandstone and sand and, thanks to its chemical and physical properties, the water can also be taken by mouth to treat pathologies of the digestive tract, such as hyper-acidic gastritis, and to disintoxicate the liver. The temperature of the water, which is of the sulfurous bicarbonate alkaline type, is 33°C/91°F. It is also useful in the treatment of malfunctions of the circulatory system, the liver and the bile ducts, gynecological problems, and respiratory and motory problems. The following treatments are available: aerosols, therapeutic baths, hydropinic treatments (drinking the spring water), mud therapy, humage, hydro-massage, humid-hot inhalations, insufflations, vaginal irrigation, nebulizations and politzer crenotherapy. Sessions of kinesitherapy, hydro-kinesitherapy, massage, rehabilitation and physical therapy are also available.

TERMINI IMERESE

G.H. delle Terme
piazza delle Terme 2, tel. 0918113557
Open all year round
Situated in the Province of Palermo, Termini Imerese lies on the Tyrrhenian coast between Zafferano and Cefalù, 36 km from Palermo. Its Roman name was Thermae Himerensis, belying its ancient origins: its hot springs ("Terme") with salt bromine iodic spring water were famous in antiquity and Himera was the name of the Greek colony destroyed in 409 BC by the Carthaginians.
The hot springs, known as *Grand Hotel delle Terme 2* and *Grand Hotel delle Terme 3*, are located below the Grand Hotel and have created natural caves which are used for steam-cave therapy, in addition to the departments specializing in inhalations, mud therapy and balneo-therapy.
The spring water at Termini Imerese is of the salt bromine iodic type, with a constant temperature of 43°C/109°F. This water is beneficial in the treatment of disorders of the circulatory, motory, respiratory and gynecological systems, and also for skin diseases. Guests of the spa also have access to a swimming-pool fed with hot spring water, a beauty farm and a gym.

VULCANO

The volcanic activity for which the island is famous did not encourage the establishment of settlements in antiquity. However, the ancients did come here occasionally to benefit from the therapeutic properties of the hot water and the mud heated by the numerous fumaroles, which were less powerful than the ones in the bowl of the crater.

Today, the island of Vulcano still has a few hot springs of sulfurous water, tiny mud volcanoes and fumaroles to the north near Porto di Levante.

The sea off the coast near the fumaroles is noticeably warmer.

Not far from the coast is the Sorgente Termale (hot water spring).

The spa of the island of Vulcano consists of a natural open-air well surrounded by hills from which jets of steam emerge. They are used for insufflations and various beauty treatments. The mud here is composed of clay laden with micronized sulfur, heated to a temperature ranging from 40°C/104°F to 80°C/176°F by the gases present in the underground springs.

The sulfurous salt bromine iodic water is beneficial in the treatment of rheumatism, arthritis, nervous disorders and skin complaints.

Dense fumes of sulfur dioxide emanating from the potent fumaroles

WATER, MYTH AND LEGEND

The noble and melancholy myth of Acis and Galatea, celebrated by the poets Callimachus, Hermesianax, Theocritus, Virgil and, to an even greater extent, by Ovid in his Metamorphoses, tells the story of a sixteen-year-old shepherd boy called Acis, who used to graze his flocks on the slopes of Mount Etna, and the beautiful fair-skinned sea-nymph, Galatea, daughter of Nereus and Doris. In vain the terrible cyclops (one-eyed giant) Polyphemus tried to win Galatea's heart. The nymph remained deaf to the giant's continuous amorous entreaties. However, she responded willingly to the charms of Acis, until she fell in love with him and they made tender love by the sea, under a full moon. Polyphemus was overcome with jealousy, and, as soon as the nymph had dived back beneath the waves, hurled a boulder of lava at poor Acis, killing him instantly. The fair-skinned nereiad wept over the broken body of her lover, and the gods, moved to compassion, decided to acknowledge her devotion and console her by restoring life to the now inert body of the boy. They transformed him into a fresh-water spring whose waters would eventually re-join Galatea, now changed into sea foam. The origin of the myth which associates the figure of Acis with local place names may be the real presence of the River Akis, of which very little remains today, its course having diverted by a lava flow so that it now flows underground.

Acireale: sculpture of Acis and Galatea

WELLNESS

GETTING TO SICILY

By plane

PALERMO – Falcone e Borsellino International airport
Freephone: 800541880
Lost luggage information: 0917020574, www.gesap.it
To and from the airport: Trinacria Express subway from Palermo Central Station, departures every hour from 5 to 23; buses Prestia and Comandè connect the terminal with Palermo Central Station; departures every 30 minutes from 5 to 24 (for information tel. 091586351).

CATANIA –Fontanarossa International airport
Freephone: 800605656
Ticket office: 0957239320
www.aeroporto.catania.it
To and from the airport: Alibus shuttle service from Catania Central station, every 20 minutes from 5 to 24; inter-city coach services S.A.I.S. and Scionti.

TRAPANI –Vincenzo Florio National airport
For information, reservations, tickets tel. 0923842502, www.airgest.com
To and from the airport: A.S.T. bus/shuttle service from Trapani Coach station, departures from 5 to 23 connecting with AirOne flights

PANTELLERIA Airport
For information, reservations, tickets tel. 0923912213

By boat

FS, links Reggio Calabria-Messina:
FERRY (car and train transport); leaves every 20 minutes; length of crossing 30 minutes
HYDROFOIL (passengers only); afternoon departures; length of crossing 20 minutes
For information tel. 892021
TIRRENIA NAVIGAZIONE, operates the following routes:
Cagliari-Palermo
Napoli-Palermo
Cagliari-Trapani
For information and reservations tel. 199123199, www.tirrenia.it
GRANDI NAVI VELOCI, operates the following routes:
Genova-Palermo
Livorno-Palermo
Civitavecchia-Palermo
For information and reservations: tel. 0102094591 (Genova), tel. 0289012281 (Milano); www.gnv.it
S.N.A.V., runs between Naples and Palermo. For information: tel. 0814285555 (Napoli), tel. 0916317900 (Palermo); www.snav.it
GRIMALDI FERRIES, runs between Salerno and Palermo. For information: tel. 081496444, www.grimaldi-ferries.com
MERIDIANO LINES, runs between Reggio Calabria and Messina. Leaves every hour; length of crossing 45 minutes. Information and tickets: tel. 0965810414 (Reggio Calabria), tel. 0906413234 (Messina)
TOURIST FERRY BOAT/TOURIST SHIPPING, runs between Villa San Giovanni and Messina. Leaves every 20 minutes; length of crossing 20 minutes. Information and tickets: tel. 0965751413 (Villa San Giovanni), tel. 0903718510 (Messina)

By train

For timetables and fares:
TRENITALIA, tel. 892021, every day, from 7 to 21, only from Italy, www.trenitalia.com; telephonic ticket office 199166177, every day from 7 to 21.

By car

Motorway information center: tel. 0643632121 (road and traffic conditions, toll information 24 hours a day, freephone 800269269, www.autostrade.it
Radio information: Isoradio, FM 103,3 and Viaradio FM 102,5
For information on non-payment of tolls: tel. 0554210452.
To get to Sicily by car you must take the A3 Napoli-Reggio Calabria to Villa San Giovanni or Reggio Calabria, where ferries leave for Messina.

By coach

Links with other Italian regions: Etna Trasporti: long distance links between Sicily and Abruzzo, Emilia Romagna, Marche, Tuscany, Puglia, Umbria, Veneto. For information tel. 0957461333.
Segesta Internazionale: links Sicily with Germany, Belgium, France, Luxembourg. For information tel. 091342525

TRANSPORT WITHIN SICILY

Train

Travelling by rail is a comfortable and economical way of moving about the region. Every provincial capital is on the rail network. Here are some ideas for saving money: :
Carta Verde: reserved for young people up to the age of 26 and valid for a year. It allows you travel with a discount of 10% on 1st and 2nd class trains (including regional transport) and 25% on international routes. It may be purchased in all ticket offices and Trenitalia travel agencies.
Carta Argento: Reserved for people aged over 60, valid for one year. It grants price concessions with a discount of 40% in 1st class and 30% in 2nd class. It can be purchased in all ticket offices and Trenitalia travel agencies.

Coach

Ideal for reaching places which are not on the rail network. Some of the companies which operate in Sicily are:
AZIENDA SICILIANA TRASPORTI, runs between numerous towns in Sicily (Catania, Gela, Palermo, Ragusa, Siracusa); for information freephone 840000323, www.aziendasicilianatrasporti.it
SAIS AUTOLINEE, runs between numerous towns in Sicily (Catania, Enna, Messina, Palermo): for information freephone 800920900
INTERBUS, covers almost the whole of Sicily with frequent connections: www.interbus.it; for information tel. 199166188

Boat

All major companies link Sicily with the principal tourist islands: frequency and timetables vary depending on the season.
SI.RE.MAR. operates the following routes:
Palermo-Ustica
Milazzo-Isole Eolie
Trapani-Isole Egadi
Trapani-Pantelleria
Mazara del Vallo-Pantelleria
Porto Empedocle-Linosa-Lampedusa
For information:
tel. 199123199, www.siremar.it
N.G.I. runs between Milazzo and Isole Eolie; freephone 800250000
USTICA LINES operates the

CLIMATE

The climate of the island is typically Mediterranean with hot and dry summers and mild and rainy winters. Winter has the most rainfall, with mild temperatures along the coast and harsher temperatures inland; on the other hand, summer is the dry season par excellence, with almost no rainfall and particularly high temperatures. The typical wind of the island is the sirocco, which gathers a considerable volume of sand from desert regions and transports it northwards.

REGIONAL CUSTOMS

In Sicily some traditional customs still permeate the life of the islanders. One of these is the afternoon siesta, above all in summer when everything comes to a standstill after lunch. Stores are shut from approximately 13 to 16 and close for the night at around 20.

The streets and squares are the nub of social life: in small towns you will often come across people, especially elderly folk, sitting out on the doorstep of their houses chattering and doing the chores. While, in the evenings, the ritual of the evening stroll is a regular occurrence: from 18 to dinner time, the streets ring with the voices and footsteps of the parading crowd.

Sicilians have lunch at about 13.30 and dinner no earlier than 20.30. Restaurants too usually observe these times.

TOURIST INFORMATION

Web-site of Regione Sicilia: www.regione.sicilia.it
Islands of Sicily: www.isole-sicilia.it

following routes:
Milazzo-Isole Eolie
Cefalù- Isole Eolie
Palermo- Isole Eolie
Trapani-Isole Egadi
Trapani-Ustica
Trapani-Pantelleria
Porto Empedocle-Isole Pelagie
For information:
tel. 0923873813,
www.usticalines.it
In summer it also operates a hydrofoil service between Trapani-Favignana-Ustica-Napoli

Car hire

You will find all the major car hire companies in Sicily with an efficient network of agencies

AVIS
Booking center 199100133
www.avisautonoleggio.it
"Falcone e Borsellino" airport – Palermo, tel. 091591684

"Fontanarossa" airport – Catania, tel. 095340500
"Vincenzo Florio" airport – Trapani, tel. 0923842290

HERTZ
Booking center 199112211
www.hertz.it
"Falcone e Borsellino" airport – Palermo, tel. 091213112
"Fontanarossa" airport – Catania, tel. 095341595
"Vincenzo Florio" airport – Trapani, 0923842665

EUROPCAR
Booking center 800014410
www.europcar.it
"Falcone e Borsellino" airport – Palermo, tel. 091591688
"Fontanarossa" airport – Catania, tel. 095348125
"Vincenzo Florio" airport – Trapani, 092322874

EMERGENCY NUMBERS
112 Military Police (Carabinieri)
113 State Police (Polizia)
115 Fire Department
116 Road Assistance
118 Medical Emergencies

ACI CASTELLO

How to get there

BY CAR: exit Catania Est, A18 motorway Messina-Catania

BY TRAIN: FS Railway Station stations in Catania and Acireale; bus connections

Hotels

President Park Hotel ★★★
Via Litteri 88, tel.0957116111
www.presidentparkhotel.com
96 rooms. Restaurant, parking, air conditioned, swimming pool, gym
Credit Cards: American Express, Diner's Club, Mastercard, Visa
On a hill-top with a splendid view of the bay. A modern structure with a park and roof garden. Pleasant ambience with immaculately kept rooms. Congress center and restaurant serving Sicilian and classic cuisine.

Restaurants

Oleandro ¶¶ &
Cannizzaro, via A. Musco 8/10, tel.095491522
www.baiaverde.it
Cuisine: Sicilian and classic
Credit Cards: American Express, Diner's Club, Mastercard, Visa
Elegant ambience with large windows overlooking the sea and a terrace for al fresco dining; excellent fish.

ACI TREZZA

How to get there

BY CAR: exit Catania Est, A18 motorway Messina-Catania

BY TRAIN: FS Railway Station stations in Catania and Acireale; bus connections

Hotels

Acitrezza Ciclopi ★★★
Via Provinciale 3, tel.095276839
39 rooms. Restaurant, parking, air conditioned, swimming pool, tennis
Credit Cards: American Express, Diner's Club, Mastercard, Visa
Comfortable, quiet complex 50 meters from the beach. Conference rooms and a restaurant for hotel guests only.

Eden Riviera ★★★ & ★
Via Litteri 57, tel.095277760
www.hoteledenriviera.it
31 rooms. Restaurant, parking, air conditioned, swimming pool

Credit Cards: American Express, Diner's Club, Mastercard, Visa
Surrounded by countryside, built in the fifties with a swimming pool. Restaurant with Sicilian cuisine and a beautiful terrace with a sea view.

Restaurants

I Malavoglia ¶
Lungomare dei Ciclopi 167, tel.0957116556
Closed Tuesday
Cuisine: Sicilian
Credit Cards: American Express, Diner's Club, Mastercard, Visa
Sicilian family run trattoria, with rustic style rooms and al fresco dining in the small square in the summer. Local, traditional cuisine, serving dishes such as fish soup and pasta with sea urchins. Booking is advisable.

ACIREALE

🛈 **Azienda Autonoma di Cura Soggiorno e Turismo**
Via Oreste Scionti 15, tel. 095891999-892129, www.acirealeturismo.it

How to get there

BY CAR: exit Acireale, A18 motorway Messina-Catania

BY TRAIN: FS Railway Station via S. Girolamo

Hotels

Aloha d'Oro ★★★
Acireale, via De Gasperi 10, tel.0957687001
www.hotel-aloha.it
113 rooms. Restaurant, parking, tennis
Credit Cards: American Express, Diner's Club, Mastercard, Visa
Complex made up of a central body and two small annexes in a large park. Rooms with hand painted floors. Beauty center, restaurant and pizzeria in the summer.

Rural Lodgings

Il Limoneto ★
Scillischenti, via D'Amico 41, tel. 095886568
www.illimoneto.it
Open April-October
Restaurant
Ancient private house, with terrace and gorgeous pergola facing the sea and Etna; free fruit.

Bed & Breakfast

Aci e Galatea
Via S. Carlo 22, tel.095604088
www.aciegalatea.com

A cosy, renovated, elegantly furnished 19th century house in the old city center. Breakfast is served on the beautiful terrace with a view.

Restaurants

Molino ¶¶
Santa Maria La Scala, via Molino 104-110, tel.0957648116
Closed Wednesday
Cuisine: Sicilian
Credit Cards: American Express, Mastercard, Visa
Rustic ambience with spacious terrace, where one may dine pleasantly overlooking the sea; cuisine inspired by whatever ingredients are available from the market (especially fresh fish from the nearby sea),served with local wines.

Health Centers

Aloha d'Oro ★★★ ⚕
Via A. De Gasperi 10, tel. 0957687001
www.hotel-aloha.com
Open January - October
In one of the most picturesque spots in Sicily, opposite Etna, the hotel borders on the La Timpa nature reserve and is a short distance from the baroque center of Acireale. The structure was built in 1968 using the traditional farm building materials of the Etna region: lava stone details, ceramics and hand sculpted solid wood furnishings. The restaurant offers impeccable regional cuisine with a focus on genuine ingredients.
The structure has an agreement with the nearby Terme di Acireale. Beauty and health treatments are provided by a team of highly qualified practitioners. Essential oils of bergamot produced on site by organic farming methods are diffused in every room due to their considerable antiseptic, antioxidant and aromatic properties.
Treatments. Manipulative and therapeutic: massotherapy, lymphatic drainage. For health of mind and body: Bach flowers, aromatherapy, crystal healing. Beauty treatments: facials (cleansing, exfoliating and mini facials) body treatments (massages to eliminate cellulite,to regenerate tissue, to tone muscles). Spa treatments: inhalations, balneotherapy, fangotherapy, spa rehabilitation, entotympanic insufflations, physiokinesitherapy.

At night

La Caverna del Mastro Birraio
Via Colombo, tel.0958035019

"Brew pub", or rather a pub where real ale is brewed: the interior of the pub, which can hold up to 200 people, has a warm, cosy atmosphere. At the weekends, live music and, of course, rivers of beer.

Museums, Monuments and Churches

Pinacoteca Zelantea
Via Marchese di S. Giuliano 17,
tel.0957634516
www.comune.acireale.ct.it/zelant
ea/Default.htm
Opening times: Monday-
Thursday 9.00-13.00.

ADRANO

How to get there
BY CAR: exit Catania Est, A18 motorway Messina-Catania
BY TRAIN: Circumetnea Railway Station tel. 0957693015

AGRIGENTO

☑ **Azienda Autonoma Provinciale Incremento Turistico**
Viale della Vittoria 255,
tel. 0922401352
☑ **Azienda Autonoma Soggiorno e Turismo**
Via Empedocle 73,
tel. 092220391
☑ **Azienda Autonoma Soggiorno e Turismo**
Via Cesare Battisti 15,
tel. 092220454

How to get there
BY CAR: exit Imera, A19 motorway Palermo-Catania
BY TRAIN: FS Railway Station piazza Marconi

Hotels

Akragas ★★
San Leone, viale Emporium 16/18, tel. 0922414082
15 rooms. Restaurant, parking, air conditioned
Credit Cards: American Express, Diner's Club, Mastercard, Visa
A short distance from Valle dei Templi, a friendly hotel with immaculate rooms and bathrooms; regional cuisine with fresh fish.

Costazzurra ★★★
San Leone, via delle Viole 2,
tel. 0922411222
www.hotelcostazzurra.it
32 rooms. Restaurant, parking, air conditioned
Credit Cards: American Express, Mastercard, Visa
300 meters from the splendid

beach and 2 km from Valle dei Templi, modern structure with comfortable rooms; restaurant serves local cuisine.

G.H. Mosè ★★★
Viale L. Sciascia,
tel. 0922608388
www.iashotels.com
102 rooms. Restaurant, parking, air conditioned, swimming pool
Credit Cards: American Express, Diner's Club, Mastercard, Visa
In Valle dei Templi, elegant ambience, some suites, banqueting and conference rooms. Shuttle service to private beach.

Tre Torri ★★★ ★
Villaggio Mosè, tel. 0922606733
www.htretorri.com
118 rooms. Restaurant, parking, air conditioned, swimming pool, sauna, gym
Credit Cards: American Express, Diner's Club, Mastercard, Visa
At the entrance to Valle dei Templi, an unusually designed hotel built in the Eighties; good leisure and fitness facilities. Traditional Sicilian cuisine.

Villa Eos ★★★ ★
Villaggio Pirandello,
tel. 0922597170
www.villaeos.it
22 rooms. Restaurant, parking, air conditioned, swimming pool, tennis
Credit Cards: American Express, Diner's Club, Mastercard, Visa
In a peaceful position in the countryside with a sea view, comfortable rooms with balconies, in what was formerly an aristocratic villa.

Colleverde Park Hotel ★★★ ♿ ★
Strada Panoramica dei Templi,
tel. 0922229555
www.colleverdehotel.it
48 rooms. Restaurant, parking, air conditioned
Credit Cards: American Express, Diner's Club, Mastercard, Visa
Near the ruins, modern and friendly ambience; garden with beautiful terrace with a view of the temples.

Foresteria Baglio della Luna ★★★ ★
Maddalusa, tel. 0922511061
www.bagliodellaluna.com
24 rooms. Restaurant, parking, air conditioned
Credit Cards: American Express, Diner's Club, Mastercard, Visa
Ancient country seat, characterised by a genteel and charming ambience. Splendid view of Valle dei Templi from the terrace.

G.H. dei Templi ★★★
Villaggio Mosè, viale Leonardo

Sciascia, tel. 0922610175
www.grandhoteldeitempli.com
146 rooms. Restaurant, parking, air conditioned, swimming pool
Credit Cards: American Express, Diner's Club, Mastercard, Visa
In Valle dei templi, provides comfortable and quiet accommodation and a large choice of reception and conference rooms. Restaurant serves Sicilian and classic cuisine.

Jolly Hotel della Valle ★★★ ♿ ★
Via U. La Malfa 3,
tel. 092226966
www.jollyhotels.it
120 rooms. Restaurant, parking, air conditioned, swimming pool
Credit Cards: American Express, Mastercard, Visa
Comfortable rooms and some suites with jacuzzis. Congress facilities, garden with swimming pool and restaurant.

Villa Athena ★★★ ★
Via Passeggiata Archeologica 33,
tel. 0922596288
www.hotelvillaathena.com
40 rooms. Restaurant, parking, air conditioned, swimming pool
Credit Cards: American Express, Diner's Club, Mastercard, Visa
Charming late 18th century villa with a view of the Tempio della Concordia. Comfortable rooms with terraces; restaurant overlooking the citrus orchard serving Sicilian cuisine.

Bed & Breakfast

Casa Lerux
Via Callicratide 164,
tel. 092227203
Perfect for visiting the Valle dei Templi, this B&B is in a large, classic style apartment, in a renovated Seventies building, just a few minutes from the foot of the city center. Italian breakfast is served in the dining room. Dutch is spoken.

Restaurants

Dei Templi ❚❚ ♿ ★
Via Panoramica dei Templi 15,
tel. 0922403110
www.paginegialle.it/trattoriadei
templi
Closed Friday (Sunday in high season)
Cuisine: Sicilian
Credit Cards: American Express, Diner's Club, Mastercard, Visa
Vaulted ceilings, terracotta floors and brick arches all go to make up a warm ambience. Traditional fish cuisine; strictly Sicilian oils and cheeses.

Il Dèhor ❚❚ ★
Maddalusa, tel. 0922511061

www.bagliodellaluna.com
Closed Monday lunchtime
Cuisine: revisited regional
Credit Cards: American Express, Diner's Club, Mastercard, Visa
Immaculate, friendly restaurant, with a beautiful view of the Valle dei Templi. Sophisticated and impeccable cuisine offering dishes which are modern and creative in terms of their ingredients and presentation. Selection of local oils and cheeses.

Le Caprice ⅋ ⅋ ★
San Leone, via Cavaleri Magazzeni on the corner of vicolo Creta 2, tel. 0922411364
www.lecaprice.it
Closed Friday
Cuisine: of Agrigento
Credit Cards: American Express, Diner's Club, Mastercard, Visa
Rustic style restaurant surrounded by a lovely garden with tropical plants overlooked by one of the two dining rooms. Traditional menu.

Leon d'Oro ⅋
San Leone, viale Emporium 102, tel. 0922414400
Closed Monday
Cuisine: Sicilian
Credit Cards: American Express, Diner's Club, Mastercard, Visa
In the harbour area, large, professionally run restaurant. Sicilian cuisine based on fish, with some innovative touches. Cool garden for summer dining.

La Posata di Federico II ⅋ ⅋
Piazza Cavour 19, tel. 0922402953
www.oasi2000ag.it
Closed Monday (except from April to October)
Cuisine: Sicilian and classic
Credit Cards: American Express, Mastercard, Visa
Quiet restaurant with renovated furnishings. Space for al fresco dining. Serves Sicilian specialties and some Emilian dishes.

Ruga Reali ⅋ ★
Cortile Scribani 8, tel. 092220370
Closed Wednesday and Saturday lunchtime
Cuisine: Sicilian
Credit Cards: American Express, Diner's Club, Mastercard, Visa
In the heart of the old city center, a rustic style restaurant in what used to be the stables of a 15th century palace; traditional cuisine, especially fish; perfectly matched with local wines.

At night
Pix
Via Empedocle 63, tel. 0922594545
Open until 2: patronized by a young crowd who go there to eat, drink and meet friends. Charming summer terrace with a view of Valle dei Templi.

Museums, Monuments and Churches
Area archeologica
Strada panoramica dei Templi, tel. 0922621611
Opening times: Monday-Sunday 8.30-19.00 (8.30-17.00 for Tempio di Giove Olimpico and Greek- Roman Quarter).

Museo Archeologico Regionale
San Nicola, tel. 0922401565
www.regione.sicilia.it
Opening times: Monday, Sunday 9.00-13.30; Tuesday-Saturday 9.00-19.30.

ALCAMO

> ### How to get there
> **BY CAR:** exit Alcamo, A29 motorway Palermo-Mazara del Vallo
> **BY TRAIN:** FS Railway Station S.S. 113

At night
Alter Ego
Via Ten. De Blasi 2, tel. 3394048260
In the heart of the town, at the foot of the castle. This was the first Anglo-Saxon style pub in the town: beer, unique atmosphere and evenings with live music.

Pachà
Alcamo marina, via Magazzinazzi 809, tel. 3396985129
Trendy disco for crazy nights, house music and techno, performed by internationally and nationally famous artists. Open on Saturdays only.

Museums, Monuments and Churches
Castello
Piazza Castello
Opening times: Monday-Saturday 9.00-13.00, 16.00-20.00; Sunday 9.00-13.00.

Museo agricolo Pastorale e artigianale
Piazza Castello dei Conti di Modica, tel. 0924590287
Opening times: Monday-Sunday 8.00-13.00, 15.30-18.30.

ALÌ TERME

> ### How to get there
> **BY CAR:** exit Roccalumera, A18 motorway Messina-Catania
> **BY TRAIN:** FS Railway Station via Santoro

Hotels
La Magnolia ★★★ ★
Via Lungomare 18/A, tel. 0942716377
www.italiaabc.it/az/magnolia
26 rooms. Restaurant, parking, air conditioned
Credit Cards: Diner's Club, Mastercard, Visa
Only a road separates the beach from this hotel with its simple rooms, each of which has a small balcony with a view. Restaurant serves traditional cuisine.

AUGUSTA

Hotels
Europa Club ★★
Acquasanta, tel. 0931983080
www.megara.com/euroclub
Open May-September
35 rooms. Restaurant, parking, tennis
A terrace of simple rooms in a typically Mediterranean structure: panoramic view of the sea, leisure facilities.

Venus Sea Garden ★⅋★
Brucoli, contrada Monte Amara, tel. 0931998946
www.framonhotels.com
Open April-October
59 rooms. Restaurant, parking, air conditioned, swimming pool, tennis
Credit Cards: American Express, Diner's Club, Mastercard, Visa
On the rocks by the sea, an elegant and comfortable ambience, equipped with a swimming pool and tennis courts. Restaurant serves traditional specialties.

BAGHERIA

> ### ℹ **Uffcio Informazioni del Comune**
> *Corso Umberto I, tel. 091909020*
>
> ### How to get there
> **BY CAR:** exit Bagheria, A19 motorway Palermo-Catania
> **BY TRAIN:** Railway Station piazza Stazione

⅋⅋⅋ / ★ Hotels ⅀⅀⅀ / ⅋ Restaurants ⅋ Disabled ★ Special TCI Rates ⚖ Thermal spa 🏥 Health Center

Sicily, with almost 1500km of coastline, affords every kind of opportunity for water sports such as scuba diving and sailing.
Diving centers, sports clubs and associations are found all along the coast: from the promontories in the north and west part to the beaches in the west.
The numerous islands which surround Sicily, are a true paradise for scuba diving enthusiasts or simply for swimmers who love to dive into clear waters.

■ Diving

Catania
Acque Limpide
Viale Africa 186, tel. 095539947
www.acquelimpide.it

Egadi
Marettimo Diving Center
Marettimo, via Cuore di Gesù,
tel. 0923923083-3337994017
www.marettimodivingcenter.it

Voglia di Mare Diving Center
Marettimo, via Mazzini 50,
tel. 3394213845-3338755144
www.vogliadimare.com

Favignana
Progetto Atlantide
Punta Lunga harbour,
tel. 3475178338
www.progettoatlantide.com

Giardini Naxos
Nike Diving Center
Isola Bella, tel. 094247534-3391961559
www.divenike.com

Taormina Diving Center
Via Naxos 91, tel. 0942571071-3386545985
www.divingtaormina.it

Lampedusa e Linosa
Blue Dolphins
Lampedusa, via Volta 18,
tel. 0922971606
www.bluedolphins.net

Diving Lo Verde
Lampedusa, via Sbarcatoio,
tel. 0922971986

Lipari
La Gorgonia Diving
Salita S. Giuseppe,
tel. 0909812060-360863455
www.lagorgoniadiving.it

Sciacca
Omnia Maris
Via Cristoforo Colombo 16,
tel. 3474228136

Siracusa
Sport Oltre Mare
Viale Scala Greca 341,
tel. 0931756236

■ Sailing

Erice
Erice in Barca
Via Vito Carvini 80,
tel. 0923860132-3336970972
www.ericeinbarca.com

Marsala
Circolo Velico Marsala
Via Vito Falco 5,
tel. 0923951162
www.circolovelicomarsala.com

Pantelleria
Pantelleria Club
Scauri Basso 35,
tel. 0923916174

San Vito lo Capo
Circolo Velico San Vito
Via Faro 10, tel. 0923972888

At night
Il Barone di Münchausen
Via Palagonia 47, tel. 091900430
For a jolly evening, great nibbles, a cocktail, a beer or an online chat. Cosy atmosphere furnished with wooden tables and benches, imitating a typical Irish pub.

Museums, Monuments and Churches
Galleria comunale d'Arte moderna
S.S. 113, via Consolare,
tel. 091943902-091943903-091933315
www.museoguttuso.it
Opening times: Tuesday-Sunday 9.00-19.00.

Villa Palagonia
Piazza Garibaldi 3, tel. 091932088
www.villapalagonia.it
Opening times: April-October: Monday- Sunday 9.00-13.00, 16.00-19.00. November- March: Monday-Sunday 9.00-13.00, 15.30-17.30.

BELPASSO

How to get there
BY CAR: exit Catania Est, A18 motorway Messina-Catania
BY TRAIN: Circumetnea Railway Station via Nazionale

Bed & Breakfast
Etna ★
Via XII Traversa 116,
tel. 0957053048
www.etnabedandbreakfast.com
Located conveniently between Catania and Etna, an aristocratic house dating from the early 19th century with high ceilings and period furniture. Dining and living room.

Restaurants
Sala Incontro ⏹ & ★
Via XIX Traversa 62, tel. 095918646
www.comune.belpasso.ct.it/pubint.htm
Closed Saturday lunchtime and Monday evening
Cuisine: Sicilan
Credit Cards: American Express,

Diner's Club, Visa
Rustic ambience with brick vaults and exposed beams, lovely garden in an orange grove. Simple, regional cuisine with no lack of imaginative touches; extensive Sicilian wine list with focus on wines from Etna.

BIANCAVILLA

How to get there
BY CAR: exit Catania Est, A18 motorway Messina-Catania
BY TRAIN: Circumetnea Railway Station via Stazione

BOLOGNETTA

Restaurants
Mulinazzo ⏹⏹⏹ &
Mulinazzo, S.S. 121 al km 237,5
tel. 0918724870
www.mulinazzo.it
Closed Sunday evening and Monday
Cuisine: regional and refined

PRACTICAL INFO

Credit Cards: American Express, Diner's Club, Mastercard, Visa

This restaurant has, in a short space of time, managed to build up a reputation as one of the best in the entire region. Antonio Graziano, owner and chef, combined the experience he accumulated in France with great Sicilian products and his cuisine soon got itself noticed: full of local flavor, using the best ingredients, elaborated with artistry.

BRONTE

How to get there
BY CAR: exit Fiumefreddo, A18 motorway Messina-Catania

BY TRAIN: Circumetnea Railway Station piazza Stazione

Hotels
Parco dell'Etna ** ♿
Borgonovo, via Generale Dalla Chiesa 1, tel. 095691907
www.albergoparcoetna.3000.it
20 rooms. Restaurant, parking, air conditioned, swimming pool
Credit Cards: American Express, Mastercard, Visa
On the slopes of Etna, a recently renovated house serving elaborate local cuisine; conference and meeting rooms.

CALATAFIMI-SEGESTA

How to get there
BY CAR: exit Segesta, A29 motorway Trapani-Alcamo spur road

BY TRAIN: FS Railway Station station in Trapani

Health Centers
Terme Gorga ** 🐾
Gorga, tel. 092423842
www.termegorga.com
Open all year round
The structure is located inland, on the edge of the Alcamo region and a few kilometers from the temple and Greek theater of Segesta. The rooms have bathrooms with showers, TVs, telephones and air-conditioning.Guests may use the large thermal pool. The restaurant serves traditional Sicilian cuisine.

The center is small but well organised, offering a wellness program which, though limited, includes use of the solarium, sauna, Turkish bath and spa facilities. The waters well from the source of the (hot river) and their temperature constantly

hovers around 51 C. Treatments are always preceded by a medical check-up.

Treatments. Manipulative and therapeutic: thalassotherapy. Beauty treatments: spa beauty treatments.

CALTAGIRONE

> ☑ **Azienda Autonoma Soggiorno e Turismo**
> Via Volta Libertini 3, tel. 093353809
> ☑ **Ufficio Informazioni del Comune**
> Via Duomo 7, tel. 093334191-09333351073, www.comune.caltagirone.ct.it

How to get there
BY CAR: exit Catania Sud and exit Mulinello, A19 motorway Palermo-Catania

BY TRAIN: FS Railway Station piazza della Regione

Hotels
G.H. Villa San Mauro *** ♿
Via Porto Salvo 14, tel. 093326500
www.framon-hotels.com
91 rooms. Restaurant, parking, air conditioned, swimming pool
Credit Cards: American Express, Diner's Club, Mastercard, Visa
In a picturesque position, renovated and well-furnished rooms, with reproductions of the ancient majolicas of Caltagirone. Breakfast served in the garden and immaculate restaurant "Borgo dei Catalini".

Rural Lodgings
Colle San Mauro ♿
San Mauro Sotto, tel. 093353890
www.collesanmauro.it
Swimming pool
Credit Cards: Diner's Club, Visa, Mastercard
A few kilometers from Caltagirone, the ideal place for relaxing and hiking, mountain bike excursions or horse-riding. Accommodation in renovated cottages with plenty of room for socialising or quiet reading.

Il Casale delle Rose ♿ ★
Santo Stefano, tel. 093325064
www.casaledellerose.com
Swimming pool, availability of bikes
Credit Cards: American Express, CartaSi, Diner's Club, Visa
A short walk from Caltagirone, warm, family hospitality in a renovated 19th century farm, with an inner courtyard and a large restaurant.

La Casa degli Angeli ♿
Angeli, S.P. 39 al km 9, tel. 093325317

www.comune.caltagirone.ct.it/alberghi.htm
Bikes are available
Among vineyards and citrus orchards, a typical rural lodging on two floors, with a large terrace and a view of the Valle degli Angeli.

Bed & Breakfast
Antico Palmento
Via Gela 99, tel. 093323898
This 19th century house with a garden, 1km from the center of Caltagirone, takes its name from the room on the ground floor, in which you may still find an ancient device for squeezing grapes with a "screw-press" known as a "Palmento", one of the few left in Sicily.Here, a continental breakfast is served (English breakfast too, on request) with local fruit. Rooms are equipped with air-conditioning, a mini-bar and a TV. Guided tours of the area are also available. In addition, transport to and from Catania airport is provided on request.

Restaurants
La Scala ❚
Scala Santa Marìa del Monte 8, tel. 093357781
Closed Wednesday
Cuisine: Sicilian and classic
Credit Cards: American Express, Diner's Club, Mastercard, Visa
Two rooms that were once part of a noble 18th century palace and which, in summer, spill out into the inner courtyard. Classic Sicilian cuisine using whatever ingredients are in season.

At night
Giardino Spadaro
Via S. Giuseppe 5, tel. 093321331
In the daytime this summer-house hosts exhibitions and conferences and serves hearty, energising meals. Open until late in the evening with music and cocktails.

Museums, Monuments and Churches
Museo Civico e Pinacoteca "Luigi Sturzo"
Via Roma 10, tel. 093331590-093341812
www.turismo.catania.it/programmi/framericercaschede/htm
Opening times: Tuesday, Friday, Saturday 9.30-13.30, 16.00-19.00; Wednesday, Thursday 9.30-13.30; Sunday 9.30-12.30, 16.00-19.00.

Museo Regionale della Ceramica
Via Giardino Pubblico, tel. 093358418-093358423
Opening times: Monday-Sunday 9.00-18.30.

CALTANISSETTA

ℹ️ **Azienda Autonoma Provinciale Incremento Turismo**
Corso Vittorio Emanuele 109, tel. 0934530411, www.aapit.cl.it

ℹ️ **Azienda Autonoma Provinciale Incremento Turismo**
Viale Conte Testasecca 20, tel. 093421089
www.aapit.cl.it

How to get there

BY CAR: exit Imera, A19 motorway Palermo-Catania

BY TRAIN: FS Railway Station piazza Roma

Hotels

Plaza ★★★
Via B. Gaetani 5, tel. 0934583877
33 rooms. Air conditioned
Credit Cards: American Express, Diner's Club, Mastercard, Visa
In an excellent central location, recent hotel with bed and breakfast on four floors, with comfortable and modernly furnished rooms.

San Michele ★★★ ♿
Via Fasci Siciliani, tel. 0934553750
www.hotelsanmichelesicilia.it
136 rooms. Restaurant, parking, air conditioned, swimming pool
Credit Cards: American Express, Diner's Club, Visa
In a residential area, deep in a garden, elegantly furnished air-conditioned rooms and suites. Congress facilities and two restaurants serving Sicilian and classic cuisine.

Restaurants

Vicolo Duomo ⏣ ♿
Piazza Garibaldi 3, tel. 0934582331
Closed Sunday and Monday lunchtime
Cuisine: Mediterranean
Credit Cards: American Express, Diner's Club, Mastercard, Visa
Friendly restaurant situated in the most beautiful piazza of the city, next to the cathedral. The cuisine draws on ancient, local gastronomic traditions using genuine products.

Cortese ⏣ ♿
Viale Sicilia 166, tel. 0934591686
Closed Monday
Cuisine: Sicilian
Credit Cards: Diner's Club, Mastercard, Visa
Modern, friendly restaurant, with two large dining rooms bedecked with flowers and plants; do not miss the ricotta crema horns (cannoli).

At night

Hi Tech Cafè
Via Val d'Aosta 18, tel. 0934561343
Ideal for young people: modern pub furnished with steel and aluminum furniture, large choice of cocktails and internet point.

Museums, Monuments and Churches

Museo Archeologico
Via N. Colajanni 1, tel. 093425936
www.regione.sicilia.it
Opening times: Monday-Sunday 9.00-13.00, 15.30-19.00. Closed on the last Monday of every month.

Museo Mineralogico, Paleontologico della Zolfara
Viale della Regione 71, tel. 0934591280-0934592158
Opening times: Monday-Saturday 9.00-13.00. Visits can also be arranged.

CAMARINA

How to get there

BY CAR: exit Catania Est, A18 motorway Messina-Catania, and exit Catania Sud, A19 motorway Palermo-Catania

BY TRAIN: FS Railway Station station in Vittoria

CAMPOBELLO DI MAZARA

How to get there

BY CAR: exit Campobello di Mazara, A29 motorway Palermo-Mazara del Vallo

BY TRAIN: FS Railway Station piazza Stazione

Hotels

Club Ramuxara ★★★ ♿
Tre Fontane, Tonnara, tel. 0924945040
www.ventaglio.com
85 rooms. Restaurant, parking, air conditioned, swimming pool, tennis, gym
Credit Cards: Diner's Club, Visa
Very comfortable structure, suitable for relaxing holidays by the sea.

CAPO D'ORLANDO

ℹ️ **Azienda Autonoma Soggiorno e Turismo**
Via Volta on the corner of via Amendola, tel. 0941912784-0941903329
www.aastcapodorlando.it

How to get there

BY CAR: exit Brolo and exit Rocca Capri Leone, A20 motorway Messina-Palermo

BY TRAIN: FS Railway Station piazza Stazione

Hotels

Il Mulino ★★★ ♿
Via A. Doria 46, tel. 0941902431
www.agatirno.it/mulino
85 rooms. Restaurant, parking, air conditioned
Credit Cards: American Express, Diner's Club, Mastercard, Visa
A short walk from the sea and the center, furnished in Old America style, lovely terrace with a view; classic cuisine.

La Meridiana ★★★
Piana, tel. 0941957713
45 rooms. Restaurant, parking, air conditioned, swimming pool, sauna, gym
Credit Cards: American Express, Diner's Club, Mastercard, Visa
Recently built, 500 metres from the sea, with comfortable rooms and good leisure facilities.

La Tartaruga ★★★ ♿ ★
Lido San Gregorio, tel. 0941955012
www.hoteltartaruga.it
38 rooms. Restaurant, parking, air conditioned, swimming pool
Credit Cards: American Express, Diner's Club, Mastercard, Visa
Overlooking the bay of San Gregorio, complex with comfortable rooms set in a lemon grove.

Rural Lodgings

Milio
San Gregorio, tel. 0941955008
Restaurant, availability of bikes
On the bay of San Gregorio, 3km from the famous promontory, accommodation in small cottages in the peace and quiet of an olive grove 600 meters from the sea.

Restaurants

La Tartaruga ⏣ ♿ ★
San Gregorio, tel. 0941955012
www.hoteltartaruga.it
Closed Monday (from October to June)
Cuisine: of Messina

Credit Cards: American Express, Diner's Club, Mastercard, Visa
Located in the middle of an enchanting bay, immersed in the green of a lemon orchard, an elegant restaurant with a large veranda where fish is eaten in the summer.

Bontempo ¶ &
Fiumara di Naso, via Fiumara 38, tel. 0941961188
www.bontempoilristorante.com
Closed Monday
Cuisine: of Messina
Credit Cards: American Express, Diner's Club, Visa
A restaurant with three large, welcoming rooms, plus a large summer veranda; run by the same family since 1962. Their cuisine is characterised by regional flavors. They also make great pizzas.

At night
Lucky Luke
Via Crispi 45, tel. 3396946300
Live music, cabaret shows, cocktails and much more besides.

Museums, Monuments and Churches
Museo Parco di Villa Piccolo
S.S. 113 al km 109, tel. 0941957029
www.fondazionepiccolo.it
Opening times: Monday-Sunday 9.00-12.00, 16.00-18.30.
Summer: Monday-Sunday 9.00-12.00, 17.00-19.30.

CAPRI LEONE

Restaurants
L'Antica Filanda ¶
Raviola, tel. 0941919704
www.anticafilanda.it
Closed Monday
Cuisine: Sicilian
Credit Cards: American Express, Mastercard, Visa
Lovely, characteristic restaurant, with cherry wood furniture and some exquisite features. Dishes prepared with passion, imagination and excellent ingredients. Large selection of wines, including Sicilian labels.

CARLENTINI

How to get there
BY CAR: From Catania SS 114 towards Siracusa as far as the Lentini-Ragusa junction; detour for Carlentini at Lentini
BY TRAIN: FS Railway Station station in Lentini

Rural Lodgings
Tenuta di Roccadia & ★
Roccadia, tel. 095990362
www.roccadia.com
Swimming pool
Credit Cards: CartaSi
In the hills, fewer than 10km from the sea, you will find the lands belonging to the ancient estate of Roccadia: accommodation in large 19th century buildings complete with a lively restaurant.

CASTELBUONO

Pro Loco
Corso Umberto I 57, tel. 0921673467

How to get there
BY CAR: exit Castelbuono, A20 motorway Messina-Palermo
BY TRAIN: Railway Station station in Cefalù; bus connection

Restaurants
Nangalarruni ¶ &
Via Alberghi 5, tel. 0921671428
www.ristorantenangalarruni.it
Closed Wednesday (except in August)
Cuisine: Sicilian
Credit Cards: American Express, Diner's Club, Mastercard, Visa
In the old part of this small town in Madonie, fine cuisine with impeccably prepared dishes which contain the flavors and aromas of these parts. Large cheese selection.

Vecchio Palmento ¶ &
Via Failla 4, tel. 0921672099
Closed Monday
Cuisine: regional
Credit Cards: American Express, Visa
Intimate and characteristic restaurant with cuisine typical of Madonie, which reaches its apotheosis in the mushroom season. Also pizzeria.

CASTELLAMMARE DEL GOLFO

Ufficio Turistico del Comune
Viale Umberto I 3, tel. 092431320

How to get there
BY CAR: exit Castellammare del Golfo, A29 motorway Palermo-Mazara del Vallo
BY TRAIN: FS Railway Station contrada Magazzenazze

Hotels
Belvedere ★★ &
Belvedere, S.S. 187 al km 37, tel. 092433330
www.hotelbelvedere.net
11 rooms. Restaurant, parking, air conditioned
Credit Cards: American Express, Mastercard, Visa
On the slopes of Monte Inici, rooms with picturesque verandas with views and a large restaurant.

Al Madarig ★★★ ★
Piazza Petrolo 7, tel. 092433533
www.almadarig.com
33 rooms. Restaurant, air conditioned
Credit Cards: American Express, Diner's Club, Visa
Close to the sea, Mediterranean construction with large rooms and a restaurant with stone walls and a fireplace, serving fish specialties.

Cala Marina ★★★ &
Via Don Zangara 1, tel. 0924531841
www.hotelcalamarina.it
13 rooms. Air conditioned
Credit Cards: American Express, Diner's Club, Mastercard, Visa
In the old town center, modern hotel with bed and breakfast with a friendly ambience and comfortable rooms furnished in "arte povera".

Rural Lodgings
Camillo Finazzo ★
Baida, tel. 092438051
www.camillofinazzo.com
Availability of bikes
In a beautiful position with a wonderful view, close to the splendid Riserva dello Zingaro and not far from the Tempio di Segesta and Erice.

CASTELVETRANO

Hotels
Garzia ★★★ &
Marinella, via A. Pigafetta 2, tel. 092446660
www.hotelgarzia.com
37 rooms. Restaurant, parking, air conditioned
Credit Cards: Mastercard, Visa
A few steps from the sea, friendly, family run house; restaurant-pizzeria with panoramic views.

CASTIGLIONE DI SICILIA

How to get there
BY CAR: exit Giardini Naxos, A18 motorway Messina-Catania

CATANIA

🛈 *Azienda Autonoma Provinciale Incremento Turistico*
Via Domenico Cimarosa 10, tel. 0957306211-0957306222
www.apt.catania.it

🛈 *Azienda Provinciale per il Turismo*
Via Etnea 17, tel. 0957306233
www.apt.catania.it

🛈 *Azienda Provinciale per il Turismo*
Harbour, tel. 0957306209
www.apt.catania.it

🛈 *Azienda Provinciale per il Turismo*
F.S. Railway Station, tel. 0957306255
www.apt.catania.it

🛈 *Azienda Provinciale per il Turismo*
Fontanarossa airport, tel. 0957306266
www.apt.catania.it

How to get there

BY CAR: exit Catania Nord, A18 motorway Messina-Catania, exit Catania Sud, A19 motorway Palermo-Catania

BY TRAIN: FS Railway Station piazza Giovanni XXIII e Stazione Ferrovia Circumetnea, via Caronda 352/A, tel. 0955411

Hotels

Best Western Hotel Mediterraneo *** ♿ ★
Via Dottor Consoli 27, tel. 095325330
www.hotelmediterraneoct.it
64 rooms.Air conditioned
Credit Cards: American Express, Diner's Club, Mastercard, Visa
In the center, reception rooms decorated with paintings by contemporary artists. Spacious, comfortable rooms.

Jolly Hotel Ognina *** ★
Via Messina 628, tel. 0957528111
www.jollyhotels.it
56 rooms.Parking, air conditioned
Credit Cards: American Express, Diner's Club, Visa
Comfortable and functional hotel with bed and breakfast in Ognina, on the A-road to Acireale; well-furnished and comfortable rooms, meeting rooms.

La Vecchia Palma ***
Via Etnea 668, tel. 095432025
www.lavecchiapalma.com
12 rooms.Parking, air conditioned
Credit Cards: American Express, Diner's Club, Mastercard, Visa
Aristocratic, baroque building adorned with frescos and stuccos. Each room decorated differently and furnished with period pieces.

Poggio Ducale *** ♿
Via Paolo Gaifami 5, tel. 095330016
www.poggioducale.it
28 rooms. Restaurant, parking, air conditioned
Credit Cards: American Express, Diner's Club, Mastercard, Visa
On the ring road,conveniently located for the old city center and motorway access; provides modern rooms and meeting rooms. Large selection of vintage wines.

Jolly Hotel Bellini **** ★
Piazza Trento 13, tel. 095316933
www.jollyhotels.it
147 rooms. Restaurant, parking, air conditioned
Credit Cards: American Express, Mastercard, Visa
In the heart of the city. A good level of comfort. Rooms combine comfort and elegance. Functional meeting rooms.

Katane Palace Hotel **** ♿ ★
Via Finocchiaro Aprile 110, tel. 0957470702
www.katanepalace.it
58 rooms. Restaurant, air conditioned
Credit Cards: Diner's Club, Visa
In the old city center, an elegant building with a lovely patio full of flowers. Elegantly furnished rooms, romantic restaurant "Il Cuciniere".

Villa del Bosco **** ♿
Via del Bosco 62, tel. 0957335100
www.hotelvilladelbosco.it
52 rooms. Restaurant, parking, air conditioned, swimming pool
Credit Cards: American Express, Diner's Club, Mastercard, Visa
19th century villa with a professional staff and and every amenity. Elegant restaurant serves Sicilian and classic cuisine. Large congress rooms and wellness center.

Rural Lodgings

Bagnara ♿
Cardinale, tel. 095336407
www.agribagnara.it
Restaurant
Accommodation in renovated country cottages, with plenty of places for children and 50 hectares of countryside where you will find orange trees, grapevines, olive, peach and prickly pear trees.

Fondo 23 ♿ ★
Via San Giuseppe la Rena - fondo 23, tel. 095592521
www.fondo23.it
Restaurant, availability of bikes
19th century lava stone country house surrounded by bougainvillea and oleanders; accommodation in self-catering apartments, with a communal seating area.

Bed & Breakfast

Casamia
Via D'Annunzio 48, tel. 095445682
www.casamia48.cjb.net
A large apartment in an early Twentieth century building, in the center of Catania. Guests are provided with comfortable rooms furnished in "arte povera" and coordinated soft furnishings in bright colours. They may also use the communal sitting room equipped with hi-fi, television and library. Italian breakfast is served in the kitchen.

Restaurants

I Tre Bicchieri 🍷🍷🍷 ♿
Via S. Giuseppe al Duomo 31, tel. 0957153540
www.osteriaitrebicchieri.it
Open evenings only, closed Sunday
Cuisine: Creative mediterranean
Credit Cards: American Express, Diner's Club, Mastercard, Visa
In the heart of the old city center, behind the university, a sophisticated restaurant with many elegant flourishes. Elaborate cuisine offering innovative dishes without losing sight of local traditions.

Cugno Mezzano 🍷🍷 ♿
Via Museo Biscari 8, tel. 0957158710
www.cugnomezzano.it
Open evenings only
Cuisine: creative Sicilian
Credit Cards: American Express, Diner's Club, Mastercard, Visa
Located in Palazzo Biscari in the old city center, it combines a careful choice of organic raw ingredients with inventive recipes. Large selection of cheeses and hams. Excellent wine list.

Il Carato 🍷🍷 ♿
Via Vittorio Emanuele II 81, tel. 0957159247
www.ilcarato.it
Open evenings only, closed Sunday
Cuisine: Sicilian revisited
Credit Cards: American Express, Mastercard, Visa

In the heart of the old city, a small room lined by dressers stuffed with bottles and knick-knacks, appetising food bursting with traditional flavors.

La Siciliana ⅈⅈ ♿
Viale Marco Polo 52/A,
tel. 095376400
www.lasiciliana.it
Closed Sunday evenings and Monday
Cuisine: Sicilian
Credit Cards: American Express, Diner's Club, Mastercard, Visa
Warm ambience on the ground floor of a period villa offering regional cuisine.

Poggio Ducale ⅈⅈ ♿
Via Paolo Gaifami 5,
tel. 095330016
www.poggioducale.it
Closed Sunday evening
Cuisine: refined Sicilian
Credit Cards: American Express, Diner's Club, Visa
Simple but elegant, it offers a cuisine with Mediterranean flavors, rooted in tradition. Mainly fish specialties, excellent wine cellar and good selection of typically Sicilian oils and cheeses.

Metró ⅈ
Via dei Crociferi 76,
tel. 095322098
www.ristorantemetro.it
Closed Saturday lunchtime and Sunday
Cuisine: Sicilian
Credit Cards: American Express, Diner's Club, Mastercard, Visa
In a baroque building in the old city center, carefully prepared Mediterranean-inspired dishes and a well-stocked cellar with over 600 Italian and foreign wines.

Pagano ⅈ
Via De Roberto 37,
tel. 095537045
Closed Saturday lunchtime
Cuisine: Sicilan
Credit Cards: American Express, Mastercard, Visa
Classic restaurant in the old city center where you can try regional dishes and, above all, fish without fuss.

At night
Le Capannine
Viale Kennedy 172
The symbol of summer nights: a modernly furnished disco with a strict and exclusive door policy; the music ranges from hip-hop and dance to rap and techno.

Ma
Via Vela 6, tel. 095341153
Close to Castello Ursino, a new

pub which promises to become one of the most popular and lively pubs on the Catania scene.

The Other Place
Via E. Reina 18/20
One of the oldest and most historical pubs in the city on two levels, tables outside in the square in summer. Good wine list, excellent beer, fine choice of music.

Museums, Monuments and Churches
Anfiteatro
Piazza Stesicoro
Opening times: Monday-Sunday 9.00-13.30.

Monastero di S. Nicolò l'Arena
Piazza Dante
Opening times: Monday-Sunday 9.00-13.00, 16.00-20.00.

Museo Civico Belliniano
Piazza S. Francesco 3,
tel. 0957150535
www.comune.catania.it
Opening times: Monday-Saturday 9.00-13.00; Tuesday, Thursday also 15.00-18.00; Sundays and public holidays 9.00-13.00. Closed on January 1st, Easter, May 1st and December 25th.

Museo Civico Castello Ursino
Piazza Federico di Svevia,
tel. 095345830
www.comune.catania.it
Opening times: Tuesday-Saturday 9.00-13.00, 15.00-18.00; Sundays and public holidays 9.00-13.00. Times may vary for temporary exhibitions.

CAVA D'ISPICA

> **How to get there**
> **BY CAR:** exit Catania Sud, A19 motorway Palermo-Catania
> **BY TRAIN:** FS Railway Station station in Modica

CEFALÙ

> ℹ **Azienda Autonoma Soggiorno e Turismo**
> *Corso Ruggero 77,*
> *tel. 092142105*
> *www.cefalu-tour.pa.it*
> **How to get there**
> **BY CAR:** exit Gibilmanna, A20 motorway Messina-Palermo
> **BY TRAIN:** FS Railway Station piazza Stazione

Hotels
Carlton Hotel Riviera ★★★
Capo Plaia, tel. 0921420200

www.carltonhotelriviera.it
Open April-October
144 rooms. Restaurant, parking, air conditioned, swimming pool, tennis
Credit Cards: American Express, Visa
Lovely building with modern and elaborate furnishings. Some of the rooms, all with balconies, enjoy a view of the sea, which laps the garden and the seawater swimming pool.

Kalura ★★★
Caldura, via V. Cavallaro 13,
tel. 0921421354
www.hotel-kalura.com
75 rooms. Restaurant, parking, air conditioned, swimming pool, tennis
Credit Cards: American Express, Diner's Club, Mastercard, Visa
In a lovely location overlooking the sea. Comfortable and well-appointed rooms; good sports facilities (mountain bike and bicycle hire, sailing, surfing, canoeing).

Le Calette ★★★ ♿
Caldura, via V. Cavallaro 12,
tel. 0921424144
www.lecalette.it
50 rooms. Restaurant, parking, air conditioned, swimming pool, sauna, gym
Credit Cards: American Express, Diner's Club, Mastercard, Visa
Welcoming, well-appointed rooms with a view of the bay of Caldura. Excellent fish. Some accommodation available in apartments.

Bed & Breakfast
Ale Robi
Via Porpora 17, tel. 0921424020
www.alerobi.it
Between the old city center and the seafront, accommodation in two double rooms with en suite bathrooms and all amenities.

Restaurants
La Brace ⅈⅈ
Via XXV Novembre 10,
tel. 0921423570
www.ristorantelabrace.com
Closed Monday and Tuesday lunchtime
Cuisine: classic
Credit Cards: American Express, Diner's Club, Mastercard, Visa
Variously inspired dishes in this intimate restaurant rich in color and originality.

Ostaria del Duomo ⅈⅈ
Via Seminario 5,
tel. 0921421838
Open mid March-mid November, closed Monday in low season
Cuisine: Sicilian

Credit Cards: American Express, Diner's Club, Mastercard, Visa

A renovated and modernised dining room plus a spacious terrace in the shadow of the cathedral characterise this restaurant.

Gabbiano ⦁ ⛫ ★
Lungomare Giardina 17, tel. 0921421495
Closed Wednesday (except in the summer)
Cuisine: Sicilian and classic
Credit Cards: American Express, Diner's Club, Mastercard, Visa
Rustic restaurant, with a family atmosphere. Mainly fish; also pizzeria.

At night

Be Bop
Via N. Botta 4
Open until late in the night, a trendy pub where many young people congregate. A pleasant atmosphere with a small garden for summer evenings.

Lilie's Club
Piazza Bagno Cicerone, via Vittorio Emanuele
Always crowded and animated with young people: enormous choice of bottled and draught beers.

Villa dei Melograni
S.P. Cefalù-Gibilmanna 2, tel. 0921422517
In a beautiful villa, a cosy wine bar with an excellent choice of regional and other wines, accompanied by platters of local cheeses and cold meats, "Bruschette".

Museums, Monuments and Churches

Cattedrale
tel. 0921922021
Opening times: Monday- Sunday 8.00-12.00, 15.30-17.00.

Museo Mandralisca
Via Mandralisca 13, tel. 0921421547
www.museomandralisca.it
Opening times: August: Monday- Sunday 9.00-23.00. September-July: Monday-Sunday 9.00-19.00.

CENTURIPE

How to get there
BY CAR: exit Catania Est, A18 motorway Messina-Catania
BY TRAIN: FS Railway Station station in Catenanuova

Museums, Monuments and Churches

Museo archeologico
Via Giulio Cesare, tel. 093573079
Opening times: Tuesday-Sunday 9.00-19.00. Closed on public holidays. Open Easter Monday.

CONTESSA ENTELLINA

How to get there
BY CAR: exit Santa Ninfa, A29 motorway Palermo-Mazara del Vallo
BY TRAIN: FS Railway Station station in Palermo

CORLEONE

How to get there
BY CAR: exit Villabate, A19 motorway Palermo-Catania
BY TRAIN: FS Railway Station station in Palermo; bus connection

Restaurants

Antica Stazione Ferroviaria di Ficuzza ⦁ ⛫
Ficuzza, tel. 0918460000
www.anticastazione.it
Closed Monday
Cuisine: regional
Credit Cards: American Express, Diner's Club, Mastercard, Visa
A haven of peace in what was once the waiting room of the old railway station, now restored. Offers traditional cuisine from the island's interior, made up of simple but tasty dishes. Also pizzas in the evenings.

At night

Keystone
Piazza Falcone e Borsellino
Irish beer and loud music, but only until midnight.

ELORO

How to get there
BY CAR: exit Catania Est, A18 motorway Messina-Catania, exit Catania Sud, A19 motorway Palermo-Catania
BY TRAIN: FS Railway Station station in Noto

Museums, Monuments and Churches

Scavi
Opening times: Monday-Sunday 9.00-one hour before sundown.

Villa romana del Tellaro
tel. 0931573883
Opening times: Monday-Sunday 8.00-18.30.

ENNA

ℹ️ **Azienda Autonoma Provinciale Incremento Turistico**
Via Roma 411/413, tel. 0935528228-0935528288
www.apt-enna.com
ℹ️ **Azienda Autonoma Soggiorno e Turismo**
Piazza Colajanni 6, tel. 0935500875

How to get there
BY CAR: exit Enna, A19 motorway Palermo-Catania
BY TRAIN: FS Railway Station via Stazione

Hotels

G.A. Sicilia ★★★
Piazza Colaianni 7, tel. 0935500850
76 rooms.
Credit Cards: American Express, Diner's Club, Mastercard, Visa
Centrally located, comfortable hotel with bed and breakfast, with excellent congress facilities and some suites.

Riviera ★★★ ⦁
Pergusa, via Autodromo di Pergusa, tel. 0935541267
www.rivierahtl.it
26 rooms. Restaurant, parking, air conditioned, swimming pool
Credit Cards: American Express, Diner's Club, Mastercard, Visa
Modern, comfortable and friendly structure, surrounded by a pinewood, with a view of the lake. Restaurant serves Sicilian and classic cuisine.

Rural Lodgings

Il Mandorleto ⦁ ★
Gerace, tel. 0935541389
www.ilmandorleto.it
Restaurant
On Monte Gerace, a country house from which you can enjoy a beautiful view which stretches from Etna to Erice and from Nebrodi to Val di Noto. Excellent cuisine.

Restaurants

Ariston ⦁
Via Roma 353, tel. 093526038
Closed Sunday
Cuisine: Sicilian and classic
Credit Cards: American Express, Diner's Club, Mastercard, Visa
Centrally located, this restaurant serves mainly fish but also excellent grilled lamb, pork and

beef. Pleasant summer dining under a portico. Pizzeria too.

Liolà †
Via Duca d'Aosta 2,
tel. 093537706
Closed Tuesday
Cuisine: Sicilian
Credit Cards: American Express, Diner's Club, Mastercard, Visa
Pleasant, friendly restaurant, decorated with frescos and a gazebo for al fresco dining. Carefully prepared regional specialties. Also pizzas in the evenings.

At night
Caffè Italia
Via M. Chiaromonte 12,
tel. 0935501111
Overlooking Piazza Garibaldi: piano bar in summer; pastry-shop.

Museums, Monuments and Churches
Castello di Lombardia
Piazzale Lombardia
Opening times: Monday - Sunday 9.00-13.00, 16.00-19.00.

Museo "Alessi"
Via Roma 465, tel. 0935503165
Opening times: Monday-Sunday 8.00-20.00.

EOLIE

> ☑ **Ufficio Informazioni**
> *Porto Levante,*
> *tel. 0909852028*

At night
La Tartana Club
Ficogrande, tel. 090986025
Right by the sea, with many spaces to sit outside, where you can have something to eat or drink: snacks, salads or aperitifs. One of the most popular and trendy pubs with piano bar music.

Malupi Bar Ingrid
Via M. Bianchi 1
This spot boasts the most beautiful view from the island; you are sure to spend a pleasant evening here with cocktails, home-made water-ices, piano bar, pizza parlour. Charming terrace overlooking the sea.

ERACLEA MINOA

> **How to get there**
> **BY CAR:** exit, Castelvetrano A29 motorway Palermo-Mazara del Vallo
> **BY TRAIN:** FS Railway Station station in Agrigento

Museums, Monuments and Churches
Antiquarium di Eraclea Minoa
tel. 0922846005
www.regione.sicilia.it
Opening times: Monday-Sunday 9.00- one hour before sundown (summer 19.00).

ERICE

> ☑ **Azienda Autonoma Soggiorno e Turismo**
> *Via Tommaso Guarrasi 1,*
> *tel. 0923869388*

How to get there
BY CAR: exit Trapani, A29 motorway Trapani-Alcamo spur
BY TRAIN: FS Railway Station station in Trapani; bus connection

Hotels
Elimo ★★★
Via Vittorio Emanuele 73,
tel. 0923869377
www.charmerelax.com
21 rooms. Restaurant, parking, air conditioned
Credit Cards: American Express, Diner's Club, Mastercard, Visa
Immaculate rooms and elegant reception rooms guarantee

HORSE RIDING, TREKKING AND CYCLING

Whether it be hiking along trails, horse-riding through wild and uncontaminated natural scenery or pedaling in harmony with the surrounding environment, losing yourself in the countryside is something which enables people to get back to nature and to appreciate its loveliest forms. The network of marked footpaths Sicily offers is extensive, allowing hiking and pony-trekking at all levels, of difficulty suitable for both beginners and more expert enthusiasts.
Hiking, pony-trekking and cycling trails are to be found all over Sicily, especially in the nature reserves.
To climb to the summit of vulcanos you must apply to local authorized guides.

■ Horse riding

Agrigento
Centro Ippico Concordia Equitazione
Viale Cavaleri Magazzeni 44,
tel. 0922412903

Alcamo
Centro Ippico Lo Sperone Equitazione
Vallone di Nuccio,
tel. 092426638

Caltanissetta
Centro Ippico Le Fontanelle Equitazione
Via Pietro Leone 45,
tel. 0934592437

Catania
Centro Equitazione La Plaia Equitazione
Viale Kennedy 52,
tel. 095281826

Messina
Conca d'Oro Equitazione
Ciaramita, SS.Annunziata resort,
tel. 3479045453-3475545174
www.concadoro.vea.net

■ Trekking

Eolie
Associazione Guide Alpine Italiane Trekking
Stromboli, piazza S. Vincenzo,
tel. 090986263-090986211
www.stromboliguide.it

Magmatrek Trekking
Stromboli, via Vittorio Emanuele, tel. 0909865768
www.magmatrek.it

Linguaglossa
Gruppo Guide Alpine Etna Nord Trekking
Piazza Santa Caterina 24,
tel. 095647833-095643430

Nicolosi
Gruppo Guide Alpine Etna Sud Trekking
Via Etnea 49,
tel. 0957914755

■ Cycling

Bagheria
Siciclando Cicloturismo
Via M.te Cicerone 19,
tel. 091906086
www.siciclando.com

charming stays in a 17th century building with small inner courtyards and a veranda with a view; congress facilities. Restaurant serves Sicilian specialities.

L'Approdo ★★★
Pizzolungo, via Enea 3,
tel. 0923571555
www.hotelapprodotrapani.it
13 rooms. Restaurant, parking, air conditioned
Credit Cards: American Express, Diner's Club, Mastercard, Visa
Small structure providing rooms with a lovely sea view; large restaurant with spacious terrace for al fresco dining.

Moderno ★★★ ★
Via Vittorio Emanuele 63,
tel. 0923869300
www.pippocatalano.it
40 rooms. Restaurant, parking, air conditioned, swimming pool
Credit Cards: American Express, Diner's Club, Mastercard, Visa
Well-appointed 19th century building with a lovely terrace with a view for sunbathing.

Tirreno ★★★ ᵭ
Pizzolungo, via Enea 37,
tel. 0923571078
www.tirrenohotel.com
83 rooms. Restaurant, parking, air conditioned
Credit Cards: American Express, Diner's Club, Mastercard, Visa
On the sea, modern construction with mostly renovated and air-conditioned rooms; restaurant serves typically Sicilian cuisine and an assortment of regional wines.

Rural Lodgings
Pizzolungo Francesco Adragna
ᵭ ★
Pizzolungo-San Cusumano,
tel. 0923563710
www.pizzolungo.it
Restaurant
Between the sea and the mountains, a private villa with annexes dating from the early 20th century. Canoe hire and bathing in an ancient stone pool.

Restaurants
Moderno ⁇
Via Vittorio Emanuele 63,
tel. 0923869300
www.pippocatalano.it
Closed Monday not in the summer
Cuisine: Sicilian
Credit Cards: American Express, Diner's Club, Mastercard, Visa
In the heart of the small town, an intimate and characteristic restaurant, with a lovely terrace

with a view. Regional cuisine made with natural raw ingredients. Large selection of oils and mostly Sicilian cheeses.

Monte San Giuliano ⁇
Vicolo S. Rocco 7,
tel. 0923869595
www.montesangiuliano.it
Closed Monday
Cuisine: Sicilian
Credit Cards: American Express, Diner's Club, Mastercard, Visa
Pleasant restaurant with rustic decor offering flavorful regional cuisine.

Belvedere San Nicola ⁇ ᵭ
San Nicola, tel. 0923860124
www.pippocatalano.it
Closed Wednesday
Cuisine: Sicilian and classic
Credit Cards: American Express, Diner's Club, Mastercard, Visa
In a new building housed in a rural lodging, a warm ambience with a view of the gulf of Pizzolungo. Offers regional cuisine (excellent grilled meat) using fresh products.

At night
Bocadillo
Rigaletta Milo, via Begonia 21,
tel. 0923554218
An old stable turned into a jolly, friendly Mexican pub-restaurant, with live music and a range of snacks.

Boccaccio
Via dei Misteri
Disco pub for summer nights.

Museums, Monuments and Churches
Museo Civico "Antonio Cordici"
Piazza Umberto I,
tel. 0923860048-0923869172
www.kalat.org
Opening times: Monday, Thursday 8.00-14.00, 14.30-17.30; Tuesday, Wednesday, Friday 8.00-14.00.

FAVIGNANA

ⁱ Pro Loco
Piazza Matrice 8,
tel. 0923921647

How to get there
BY FERRY: From Naples and Ustica, seasonal hydrofoil with Ustica Lines

Hotels
Bouganville ★★ ᵭ
Via Cimabue 10,
tel. 0923922033
www.albergobouganville.it
13 rooms. Restaurant, air conditioned
Credit Cards: American Express,

Diner's Club, Mastercard, Visa
Centrally located. Basic comforts. Family management. Home cooking.

Aegusa ★★★ ᵭ
Via Garibaldi 11,
tel. 0923922430
www.egadi.com/aegusa
28 rooms. Restaurant, air conditioned
Credit Cards: American Express, Diner's Club, Mastercard, Visa
Genteel, end-of-the-19th century building with a pleasant atmosphere and every amenity; other rooms are available in the nearby annex "Tonnara di Favignana". Small, walled garden; restaurant serves Sicilian cuisine.

Egadi ★★★
Via Colombo 17,
tel. 0923921232
www.albergoegadi.it
Open Easter-September
12 rooms. Restaurant, air conditioned, sauna
Credit Cards: Mastercard, Visa
Classic style rooms, decorated in a mixture of relaxing pastel colors. Elegant restaurant serves fish and hearty breakfasts (home-baking, organic jams and honey).

L'Approdo di Ulisse ★★★
Calagrande, tel. 0923922525
www.apprododiulisse.it
Open June-September
126 rooms. Restaurant, parking, air conditioned, swimming pool, tennis
Credit Cards: American Express, Diner's Club, Visa
Like a resort, composed of white bungalows for people who like to holiday right by the sea; restaurant serves Sicilian and classic cuisine.

Restaurants
La Lampara ⁇
Via Vittorio Emanuele 2/4,
tel. 0923921220
Cuisine: regional
Credit Cards: American Express, Diner's Club, Mastercard, Visa
In an ex fisherman's cottage with exposed travertine vaults, elaborate cuisine offering fresh fish dishes cooked to traditional local recipes. Sicilian wines.

Trattoria El Pescador ⁇
Piazza Europa 43,
tel. 0923921035
Closed Wednesday lunchtime (except in high season)
Cuisine: Sicilian
Credit Cards: American Express, Diner's Club, Mastercard, Visa
Rustic interiors and nautical touches provided by the

furnishings, photos, and knick-knacks which celebrate tuna fishing. Simple and tasty fish dishes. On summer evenings you can dine outside in the small square.

At night
Alternative Pub
Piazza Europa 4,
tel. 3381373127
Small rooms in wood and tuff, beer, music and, in summer, tables outside.

L'Approdo di Ulisse
Calagrande, tel. 0923922525
www.apprododiulisse.com
In a small bay on the South West coast, an open-air disco inside a holiday village which bears the same name.

FILICUDI

Restaurants
Villa La Rosa ⁛ ⎣ ★
Via Rosa 24, tel. 0909889965
www.villalarosa.it
Cuisine: Aeolian
Credit Cards: Mastercard, Visa
Modern hilltop villa, with large terrace and garden for summer eating. Elegant cuisine, beginning with home-made bread and fish specialties. Pizzas too. Some accommodation is available.

GELA

📋 **Azienda Autonoma Soggiorno e Turismo**
Via Pisa 75,
tel. 0933913788
How to get there
BY CAR: exit Mulinello, A19 motorway Palermo-Catania
BY TRAIN: FS Railway Station via S. Cristoforo

Restaurants
Casanova ⁛
Via Venezia 89/91,
tel. 0933918580
Closed Monday in winter,
Sunday in summer
Cuisine: Sicilian
Credit Cards: American Express, Diner's Club, Mastercard, Visa
Warm, elegant ambience and cuisine. Specialties include fresh pasta stuffed with fish and delicious home-made fruit sorbets. Good selection of wines. Wine-tasting evenings.

Museums, Monuments and Churches
Acropoli
Molino a Vento

Opening times: Monday-Sunday 9.00-one hour before sundown.

Fortificazioni di Capo Soprano
Viale Indipendenza,
tel. 0933930975
Opening times: Monday-Sunday 9.00-17.00.

Museo Archeologico Regionale
Corso Vittorio Emanuele 1,
tel. 0933912626
Opening times: Monday-Sunday 9.00-13.30, 14.00-19.00.
Closed on the last Monday of every month.

GIARDINI NAXOS

📋 **Azienda Autonoma Soggiorno e Turismo**
Lungomare Tysandros 54,
tel. 094251010,
www.aastgiardininaxos.it
📋 **Punto Blu Ufficio Informazioni**
A18 motorway tollbooth,
tel. 094250371
www.aastgiardininaxos.it

How to get there
BY CAR: exit Giardini Naxos, A18 motorway Messina-Catania
BY TRAIN: FS Railway Station via Nazionale

Hotels
Palladio ★★ ★
Via IV Novembre 269,
tel. 094252267
www.palladiohotel.com
16 rooms. Parking
Credit Cards: American Express, Diner's Club, Mastercard, Visa
On the seafront, it retains the warmth of an old family house; rooms are painted in different colours and have different furniture while all have balconies; hearty breakfast.

Arathena Rocks ★★★
Via Calcide Eubea 55,
tel. 094251349
www.hotelarathena.com
Open Easter-October
49 rooms. Restaurant, parking, air conditioned, swimming pool
Credit Cards: American Express, Diner's Club, Mastercard, Visa
Large building on three floors, furnished with antiques, situated in a haven of peace, surrounded by palm trees and gardens which slope down towards the beach. Picturesque restaurant serves Sicilian specialities.

Nike Hotel ★★★ ⎣ ★
Via Calcide Eubea 27,
tel. 094251207
www.hotelnike.it

58 rooms. Restaurant, parking, air conditioned
Credit Cards: American Express, Diner's Club, Mastercard, Visa
In a lovely, secluded spot. Pleasant atmosphere, with a large terrace overlooking the sea. Simple, pretty rooms, with terracotta floors and iron beds. Piano bar in summer.

Atahotel Naxos Beach Club Parco ★★★ ★
Via Recanati 26, tel. 09426611
www.naxosbeachclubparco.com
Open March-October
261 rooms. Restaurant, parking, air conditioned, swimming pool, tennis, gym
Credit Cards: American Express, Diner's Club, Mastercard, Visa
Annex of Naxos Beach Resort, sharing sports and congress facilities. Guests are accommodated in small, pleasant and comfortable cottages.

Atahotel Naxos Beach Hotel ★★★ ★
Via Recanati 26, tel. 09426611
www.hotelnaxosbeach.com
Open March-October
189 rooms. Restaurant, parking, air conditioned, swimming pool, tennis, gym
Credit Cards: American Express, Diner's Club, Mastercard, Visa
Part of the Naxos Beach Resort complex, surrounded by orange and olive groves. Many congress facilities (outstanding plenary room with over 1000 seats), welcoming rooms and suites.

Atahotel Naxos Beach Mare ★★★ ★
Via Recanati 26, tel. 09426611
www.hotelnaxosbeach.com
Open March-October
192 rooms. Restaurant, parking, swimming pool, tennis, gym
Credit Cards: American Express, Diner's Club, Mastercard, Visa
In a luxuriant nature reserve close to the sea. Small, well-appointed two storey cottages. Part of the Naxos Beach Resort (see also Naxos Beach Hotel).

Hellenia Yachting ★★★ ★
Via Jannuzzo 41, tel. 094251737
www.hotel-hellenia.it
112 rooms. Restaurant, parking, air conditioned, swimming pool, gym
Credit Cards: American Express, Diner's Club, Mastercard, Visa
Facing the sea, rooms and suites with marble floors, classic furnishings, elegant upholstery and spacious bathrooms; large reception rooms. Restaurant "Il Veliero".

⁛ / ✦ Hotels ▦ / ⁛ Restaurants ⎣ Disabled ★ Special TCI Rates ⚕ Thermal spa ⚕ Health Center

Ramada Hotel ★☆★ ♿ ★
Via Jannuzzo 47, tel. 094251931
www.holidayclubnaxos.com/ram
adanaxos

298 rooms. Restaurant, parking, air conditioned, swimming pool, tennis

Credit Cards: American Express, Diner's Club, Mastercard, Visa

Right on the beach; an exclusive structure surrounded by a tropical garden, fabulous suites. Rooms with terraces; grand hall furnished American style, with local flourishes; two restaurants serve Mediterranean cuisine.

Museums, Monuments and Churches

Scavi
Lungomare Schisò,
tel. 094251001
www.regione.sicilia.it
Opening times: Monday-Sunday 9.00- two hours before sundown.

GIBELLINA

📄 **Azienda Provinciale per il Turismo**
Piazza 15 Gennaio 1968,
tel. 092467877,
www.apt.trapani.it

How to get there
BY CAR: exit in Salemi, A29 Palermo-Mazara del Vallo
BY TRAIN: FS Railway Station station in Salemi

GOLA DELL'ALCANTARA

How to get there
BY CAR: exit Giardini Naxos, A18 motorway Messina-Catania

ISOLA DELLE FEMMINE

How to get there
BY CAR: exit Capaci, A29 motorway Palermo-Mazara del Vallo

Restaurants

Cutino ❘
Via Palermo 10, tel. 0918677062
Closed Tuesday
Cuisine: Sicilian
Credit Cards: American Express, Diner's Club, Mastercard, Visa
Rustic-modern restaurant with two dining rooms as well as a summer veranda overlooking a small garden; set menu, mainly fish, regional wines.

LAMPEDUSA

How to get there
BY FERRY: From Porto Empedocle, Si.Re.Mar ferry

Hotels

Guitgia Tommasino ★★★ ★
Via Lido Azzurro 13,
tel. 0922970879
www.guitgia.com
Open March-October
36 rooms. Restaurant, parking, air conditioned, gym
Credit Cards: American Express, Diner's Club, Mastercard, Visa
Two Mediterranean style structures right on the beach, comfortable rooms, almost every one with a small terrace. Large restaurant serves Sicilian cuisine.

Medusa ★★★
Piazza Medusa 3,
tel. 0922970126
www.medusahotels.it
20 rooms. Restaurant, air conditioned
Credit Cards: American Express, Visa
In a Moorish building, a hotel tailored to the needs of guests; impeccable fish dishes. Terrace for dining out in summer.

Restaurants

Gemelli ❘❘❘ ♿
Via Cala Pisana 2,
tel. 0922970699
www.ristorantegemelli.it
Open Easter-October; evenings only
Cuisine: Sicilian
Credit Cards: American Express, Diner's Club, Visa
Pleasant restaurant with Moorish touches: Serves fish dishes based on Sicilian tradition, reminiscent of Arabic cuisine; large, pleasant terrace for al fresco dining.

Il Saraceno ❘❘
Via Belvedere 7, tel. 0922971641
Open April-October; evenings only
Cuisine: regional
Credit Cards: American Express, Diner's Club, Mastercard, Visa
You will be welcomed onto a beautiful terrace overlooking the harbour, where you can try excellent fish cuisine. Fresh pasta and home-made desserts; targeted choice of wines.

At night

Bar 13.5
Via Roma 45/47,
tel. 0922971798
Nautical ambience, cane furniture and, above all, an enormous choice of ice-creams and water-ices, cocktails and evenings with live music. Open in high season until 4am.

Mughara
Lungomare L. Rizzo,
tel. 3392130559
In the heart of the Old Harbour, an alternative pub built in an old cave turned into a cellar with a chimney, an ancient Eastern method of ventilation. Oriental music and belly dancing. The atmosphere is warm and welcoming and, above all, you can try out various Sicilian liqueurs such as bay-leaf, fennel or prickly pear.

LINOSA

How to get there
BY FERRY: From Porto Empedocle, Si.Re.Mar ferry

LENI

How to get there
BY FERRY: From Milazzo, links with Ustica Lines, Si.Re.Mar and N.G.I.; from Palermo, seasonal hydrofoil with Ustica Lines

LENTINI

How to get there
BY CAR: exit Catania Est, A18 motorway, Messina-Catania, exit Catania Sud, A19 motorway Palermo-Catania
BY TRAIN: FS Railway Station via Stazione

Museums, Monuments and Churches

Museo Archeologico
Via del Museo 1,
tel. 0957832962
www.regione.sicilia.it
Opening times: Tuesday-Sunday 9.00-18.00.

LETOJANNI

Restaurants

Da Nino ❘❘
Via L. Rizzo 29, tel. 094236147
Closed Tuesday (except from June to September)
Cuisine: Sicilian
Credit Cards: American Express, Diner's Club, Mastercard, Visa
Nautical style ambience, in a splendid position on the seafront, with a beautiful terrace. First-rate fish cuisine; kitchen open until midnight;

take a look at the lovely cellar with exposed bricks, wood panelling and about 700 wine labels.

LINGUAGLOSSA

🛈 **Pro Loco**
*Piazza Annunziata 7,
tel. 095643094*

How to get there

BY CAR: exit Fiumefreddo, A18 motorway Messina-Catania

BY TRAIN: Circumetnea Railway Station
tel. 095647648

Rural Lodgings
Arrigo &
*Arrigo Soprano, tel. 095643612
www.arrigo.it
Open on request*
Restaurant
In a country house dating from the early 19th century which has been beautifully renovated using lava stone, Sicilian terracotta, wrought iron and chestnut wood.

LIPARI

🛈 **Ufficio Informazioni**
Corso Vittorio Emanuele 202, tel. 0909880095

How to get there

BY FERRY: From Milazzo, links with Ustica Lines, Si.Re.Mar and N.G.I.; from Palermo, seasonal hydrofoil with Ustica Lines

Hotels
Augustus ★★★ ★
*Vico Ausonia 16,
tel. 0909811232
www.villaaugustus.it
Open March-October*
34 rooms. Parking, air conditioned, gym
Credit Cards: American Express, Diner's Club, Mastercard, Visa
Ancient renovated private villa. Rooms with tiled floors and pleasant reception rooms. Pretty Moorish style courtyard and terrace-solarium.

Casajanca ★★★ &
*Canneto, vicolo G. Galilei 3,
tel. 0909880222
www.casajanca.it*
10 rooms.
Credit Cards: American Express, Mastercard, Visa
Ten comfortable, tastefully furnished rooms, a short walk from the beach. Breakfast served in the large sitting room overlooking the sea.

Gattopardo Park Hotel ★★★ ★
*Via Diana, tel. 0909811035
www.netnet.it/hotel/gattopardo/index.html
Open March-October*
53 rooms. Restaurant, air conditioned, swimming pool
Credit Cards: American Express, Mastercard, Visa
Accommodation in a 19th century villa and a few Aeolian style buildings, set in a garden with a beautiful view from the terraces bedecked with flowers. Minibus to the beach, fish cuisine.

Giardino sul Mare ★★★ & ★
*Via Maddalena 65,
tel. 0909811004
www.netnet.it/conti
Open April-October*
40 rooms. Restaurant, air conditioned, swimming pool
Credit Cards: American Express, Diner's Club, Mastercard, Visa
Welcoming Mediterranean building, a few minutes from the small picturesque harbour of Marina Corta. Comfortable rooms with direct access to the beach. Sicilian cuisine.

Tritone ★⁂★ & ★
*Via Mendolita, tel. 0909811595
www.bernardigroup.it*
10 rooms. Restaurant, parking, air conditioned, swimming pool
Credit Cards: Diner's Club, Mastercard, Visa
Point of reference for relaxing holidays in the countryside, but also for congresses; soundproof, comfortable rooms with a sea view. Piano bar on summer evenings.

Villa Meligunis ★⁂★ &
*Via Marte 7, tel. 0909812426
www.villameligunis.it*
37 rooms. Restaurant, air conditioned, swimming pool
Credit Cards: American Express, Diner's Club, Mastercard, Visa
A few meters from the small square of Marina Corta and the little harbour, an elegant 18th century villa; restaurant (open from April to October) serves Aeolian cuisine.

Rural Lodgings
U Zu Peppino & ★
*Pianoconto, via Quattropani 21,
tel. 0909822330
www.uzupeppino.com*
Credit Cards: American Express, CartaSi, Diner's Club, Visa
A few kilometers from the sea, with an enchanting panoramic view. Provides cosy, comfortable rooms; flavorful cuisine.

Bed & Breakfast

Saltamacchia Marcello ★
*Via Munciarda, tel. 0909811692
www.lamunciarda.com*
Surrounded by a garden and with a splendid view of the sea, a typical Aeolian construction with 11 rooms equipped with all mod cons.

Restaurants
E Pulera ⫪ & ★
*Via Isabella Conti Vainicher,
tel. 0909811158
www.filippino.it
Open May-October, evenings only*
Cuisine: Aeolian
Credit Cards: Diner's Club, Mastercard, Visa
Characteristic, pleasant restaurant with a cool pergola surrounded by a lovely orange and lemon grove where you can dine at tables with tiled tops. Excellent local ingredients.

Filippino ⫪ & ★
*Piazza Municipio,
tel. 0909811002
www.filippino.it
Closed Monday in low season*
Cuisine: Aeolian
Credit Cards: Diner's Club, Mastercard, Visa
Rustic-modern ambience, with terracotta floors and tiled walls. Fish cuisine using the flavors and aromas of island produce. The menu changes every day, depending on the fish catch.

La Nassa ⫪ &
*Via G. Franza 36,
tel. 0909811319
www.lanassa.it
Open mid March-mid November, evenings only (except July and August)*
Cuisine: Aeolian and Sicilian
Credit Cards: American Express, Diner's Club, Mastercard, Visa
Close to the old city center, a charming restaurant with a beautiful and characteristic terrace for al fresco dining. Strictly traditional cuisine.

At night
Cantine Stevenson
Vulcano, tel. 0909852643
A stop recommended to night owls, in the Porto di Levante neighborhood: the ambience is elegant and sophisticated and there is a large choice of cocktails and snacks. Pleasant undertone with live music.

Chitarra Bar
*Marina Corta, salita S. Giuseppe 5,
tel. 0909811554*
Here, between 8am and 2am, you can make the acquaintance of Lucio Dalla, get carried away

🏃 / ★ Hotels ⫿⫿ / ⫪ Restaurants & Disabled ★ Special TCI Rates ♨ Thermal spa 🏃 Health Center

on the notes of the Merlo brothers or the rhythm of Zio Guy's Band but, mainly, meet many fine people.

Kasbah Cafè
Via Maurolico, tel. 0909811075
In the center, the ideal place to have a drink and relax in a truly pleasant atmosphere: splendid open-air garden. Also restaurant and pizza parlour.

La Precchia
Via Vittorio Emanuele 191, tel. 0909811303
This immediately became one of the trendy pubs, popular with people of all ages due to the excellent snacks and cocktails, live music and, above all, the friendly atmosphere you breathe.

Lisca Bianca
Panarea, via Lani 1, tel. 090983004
Inside the hotel of the same name, a pub with an unusual but genuinely friendly atmosphere: a mixture of Arabic and Sicilian music and colors, part bar and part rotisserie. Here you will find night owls having breakfast or an aperitif or after dinner drink.

Raya
Panarea, via S. Pietro, tel. 090983013
www.hotelraya.it
Hotel disco: you dance outside on a terrace overlooking the rocks, with a breath-taking view of the sea. Very elegant, patronized by celebrities: it is open in summer from 10pm to 5am.

MALETTO

How to get there
BY CAR: exit Fiumefreddo, A18 motorway Messina-Catania

MALFA

How to get there
BY FERRY: From Milazzo, links with Ustica Lines, Si.Re.Mar and N.G.I.; from Palermo, seasonal hydrofoil with Ustica Lines

MARETTIMO

Restaurants
Il Veliero ⁐
Via Umberto 22, tel. 0923923274
Cuisine: Sicilian

Friendly trattoria, by the sea, cheerful family management; strictly fish.

MARINA DI RAGUSA

Hotels
Terraqua ★★★ ♿
Via delle Sirene 35, tel. 0932615600
www.shr.it
Open April-October
77 rooms. Restaurant, parking, air conditioned, swimming pool, tennis
Credit Cards: American Express, Diner's Club, Visa
Lovely hotel with well-appointed rooms; restaurant "Baia d'Ulisse" overlooking the swimming pool. Week-long stays.

MARINELLA

How to get there
BY CAR: exit Castelvetrano, A29 motorway Palermo-Mazara del Vallo
BY TRAIN: FS Railway Station station in Castelvetrano

MARSALA

ℹ️ **Azienda Provinciale per il Turismo**
Via XI Maggio 100, tel. 0923714097
www.apt.trapani.it

How to get there
BY CAR: exit Marsala, A29 motorway, spur road to Birgi or exit Mazara del Vallo, A29 motorway Palermo-Mazara del Vallo
BY TRAIN: FS Railway Station viale A. Fazio

Hotels
Delfino Beach ★★★ ♿ ⭐
Lungomare Mediterraneo 672, tel. 0923751076
www.delfinobeach.com
91 rooms. Restaurant, parking, air conditioned, swimming pool, tennis
Credit Cards: American Express, Diner's Club, Mastercard, Visa
On the beach, a recent complex composed of a modern building and a small, elegant art nouveau style building; also cosy apartments with kitchenettes.

Villa Favorita ★★★ ♿
Via Favorita 27, tel. 0923989100
www.villafavorita.com
29 rooms. Restaurant, parking, air conditioned, swimming pool, tennis

---

Credit Cards: American Express, Diner's Club, Mastercard, Visa
A late 19th century wine-producing "baglio" offers accommodation in well-appointed, comfortable bungalows. Conference room and elegant restaurant. Lovely garden with tennis court and swimming pool.

New Hotel Palace ★★★
Lungomare Mediterraneo 57, tel. 0923719492
www.newhotelpalace.com
8 rooms. Restaurant, parking, air conditioned
Credit Cards: American Express, Diner's Club, Visa
On the harbour, 19th century English style villa with garden. Elegant, refined rooms with frescos and paintings; restaurant serves typical cuisine.

Resort Baglio Oneto ★★★ ♿
Baronazzo Amafi 55, tel. 0923746222
Open March-October
48 rooms. Restaurant, parking, air conditioned, swimming pool
Credit Cards: American Express, Diner's Club, Visa
18th century "baglio". Provides rooms with a patio or small terrace with panoramic views; swimming pool and area for functions and congresses. The restaurant serves Sicilian cuisine in a romantic atmosphere.

Rural Lodgings
Baglio Vajarassa
Spagnola, via Vajarassa 176, tel. 0923968628
Availability of bikes
Pleasant late 19th century house with an art nouveau atmosphere and an annexed farm museum.

Bed & Breakfast
Villa Rallo
Via Trapani 251, tel. 0923736351
www.villarallo.it
A 1930s villa close to the old city center. It provides accommodation in two double rooms with a shared bathroom.

Restaurants
Delfino ⁐ ♿ ⭐
Lungomare Mediterraneo 672, tel. 0923998188
www.delfinobeach.com
Closed Tuesday from November to March
Cuisine: Sicilian and classic
Credit Cards: American Express, Diner's Club, Mastercard, Visa
Restaurant with a beautiful terrace from where you can admire the sea. Traditional, freshly cooked, unpretentious cuisine. Home-made desserts

and bread; good selection of wines, focussing on wines from Marsala.

Il Gallo e l'Innamorata ⸚
Via S. Bilardello 18,
tel. 3292918503
Open evenings only, closed Tuesday
Cuisine: regional
Credit Cards: American Express, Diner's Club, Mastercard, Visa
Osteria with few place-settings so it is best to book to avoid disappointment. Elaborate fish and meat dishes. A professional sommelier advises on wines.

Tenuta Volpara ⸚ &
Volpara Digerbato,
tel. 0923984588
www.delfinobeach.com
Closed Monday (except in summer)
Cuisine: Sicilian
Credit Cards: American Express, Diner's Club, Mastercard, Visa
In what was once a farm, a classic ambience with good regional cuisine; strictly home made bread and pasta. Pizzas too in the evenings.

Trattoria Garibaldi ⸚ &
Piazza dell'Addolorata 35,
tel. 0923953006
Closed Saturday lunchtime and Sunday evening in winter
Cuisine: Sicilian
Credit Cards: American Express, Diner's Club, Mastercard, Visa
In the heart of the old city center with many place settings, regional cuisine; oil from the Belice valley and local cheeses.

At night
Di Vino Rosso
Largo A. Di Girolamo 13/V,
tel. 0923711770
Wine bar but also disco-pub in the heart of the old city center; extensive wine list, live music and a young crowd, above all on Friday and Saturday.

Irish Pub O'Mahenran's
Via F. Crispi 98, tel. 0923952275
www.irishpubsicilia.com
Typical Irish pub, created by the Irish Pub Company of Dublin: open all day, mixed clientele (the older crowd are there on Friday evening). Beer, especially Guiness, reigns, but you will also find local wines to accompany some of the typical Irish dishes on the menu. Numerous themed evenings, with live music and eminent guests. The ideal place to spend a jolly evening.

Museums, Monuments and Churches
Associazione Amici del Museo della Matrice
Via G. Garaffa 57,
tel. 3201860115-0923712903
Opening times: Tuesday-Saturday 9.00-13.00, 16.00-18.00; Sunday 9.00-13.00.

Ente Mostra Nazionale di Pittura Contemporanea Città di Marsala
Piazza Carmine 1,
tel. 0923711631-0923713822
www.pinacotecamarsala.it
Opening times: April-September: Tuesday-Sunday 10.00-13.00, 18.00-20.00. October-March: Tuesday-Sunday 10.00-13.00, 17.00-19.00.

Museo Archeologico "Baglio Anselmi"
Lungomare Boeo 30,
tel. 0923952535
www.regione.sicilia.it
Opening times: Monday-Sunday 9.00-14.00; Wednesday, Friday, Saturday, Sunday also 16.00-19.00.

MAZARA DEL VALLO

> ℹ **Azienda Provinciale per il Turismo**
> Piazza S. Veneranda 2,
> tel. 0923941727
> www.apt.trapani.it
>
> ### How to get there
> **BY CAR:** exit, Mazara del Vallo A29 motorway Palermo-Mazara del Vallo
> **BY TRAIN:** FS Railway Station piazza De Gasperi

Hotels
Hopps Hotel ★★★
Via Hopps 29, tel. 0923946133
188 rooms. Restaurant, parking, air conditioned, swimming pool
Credit Cards: American Express, Diner's Club, Mastercard, Visa
On the seafront, surrounded by palm trees, a vast, recently renovated, Mediterranean style complex; open air bar and restaurant.

Restaurants
Pescatore ⸚ &
Via Castelvetrano 191,
tel. 0923947580
www.ristorantedelpescatore.com
Closed Monday
Cuisine: Revisited and classic Sicilian
Credit Cards: American Express, Diner's Club, Mastercard, Visa
On the outskirts of the town, large, bright restaurant with furnishings which evoke the Art

Nouveau style ; mainly fish, meditated choice of wines.

Museums, Monuments and Churches
Museo Civico
Piazza Plebiscito 2,
tel. 0923949593
www.comune.mazara-del-vallo.tp.it
Opening times: Monday-Sunday 9.00-13.00; Tuesday, Thursday also 15.00-18.00.

Museo Diocesano
Via dell'Orologio 7,
tel. 0923909431-0923941665
www.comune.mazara-del-vallo.tp.it
Opening times: Monday-Friday 9.00-12.00.

MEGARA HYBLAEA

> ### How to get there
> **BY CAR:** exit Catania Sud, A19 motorway Palermo-Catania

Museums, Monuments and Churches
Rovine
tel. 0931512364
Opening times: Monday-Sunday 8.00 - one hour before sundown.

MESSINA

> ℹ **Azienda Autonoma Provinciale Incremento Turistico**
> Via Calabria is. 301 bis,
> tel. 090674271-090674236
> ℹ **Azienda Autonoma Soggiorno e Turismo**
> Piazza Cairoli 45,
> tel. 0902935292,
> www.azienturismomessina.it
>
> ### How to get there
> **BY CAR:** exit Messina Centro, A18 motorway Messina-Catania, exit Messina Boccetta, A20 motorway Messina-Palermo
> **BY TRAIN:** FS Railway Station piazza Repubblica
> **BY FERRY:** From Reggio di Calabria Meridiano Lines ferry connects travelers with FS trains; from Villa San Giovanni take the Tourist Ferry Boat.

Hotels
Giardino delle Palme ★★★
Lido di Mortelle, S.S. 113,
tel. 090321017
www.giardinodellepalme.it
25 rooms. Restaurant, parking, air conditioned, swimming pool

‡‡‡ / ★ Hotels ⌂⌂ / ⸚ Restaurants & Disabled ★ Special TCI Rates ♨ Thermal spa ⚕ Health Center

Credit Cards: American Express, Diner's Club, Mastercard, Visa
Conveniently located, provides direct access to a sandy beach; alternatively, there is accommodation in cabins which overlook a swimming pool with a restaurant in the center.

Best Western Europa Palace Hotel ★★★ ♿ ★
Pistunina, S.S. 114 al km 5,4
tel. 090621601
www.europalacehotel.it
115 rooms. Restaurant, parking, air conditioned
Credit Cards: American Express, Diner's Club, Mastercard, Visa
Renovated complex, with comfortable rooms and two junior suites; sweet buffet breakfast and restaurant "I Vespri" serving classic and Sicilian cuisine.

Jolly Hotel ★★★ ★
Via Garibaldi 126,
tel. 090363860
www.jollyhotels.it
96 rooms. Restaurant, parking, air conditioned
Credit Cards: American Express, Visa
Functional Fifties building provides roooms with a view of the strait or the theatre; restaurant "Dello Stretto" serves specialities of Messina; sweet and savoury buffet breakfast.

Bed & Breakfast

Scilla e Cariddi
Citola, viale Annunziata,
tel. 090357849
www.scillaecariddi.com
Surrounded by a luxuriant garden with eucalyptus, orange and almond trees, this B&B provides two large rooms inspired by the Odyssey, furnished with antiques and supplied with air-conditioning. Italian breakfast is served on the splendid terrace overlooking the strait. Six mini apartments are also available.

Restaurants

Casa Savoia ⑪ ♿
Via XXVII Luglio 36/38,
tel. 0902934865
www.ristorantecasasavoia.it
Closed Sunday evening
Cuisine: of Messina and creative
Credit Cards: American Express, Diner's Club, Mastercard, Visa
Comfortable, welcoming restaurant which preserves some souvenirs of the Regio Teatro Savoia, such as pier glasses, decorative stuccoes and portraits. Local, mainly fish, specialties, impeccable wine

selection. The kitchen is open until midnight.

Piero ⑪
Via Ghibellina 119,
tel. 0906409354
www.paginegialle.it/ristorante piero
Closed Sunday
Cuisine: of Messina
Credit Cards: American Express, Diner's Club, Mastercard, Visa
Restaurant with three comfortable dining rooms and menu of local dishes, inspired by the day's fish catch and carefully selected meats.

Le Due Sorelle ⑪
Piazza Municipio 4,
tel. 09044720
Closed Saturday and Sunday lunchtime
Cuisine: innovative Sicilian
Credit Cards: Mastercard, Visa
In the town square, a small restaurant offering an impeccable wine menu and a mixture of meat and fish dishes, based on whatever fresh ingredients are available.

At night

Tortuga
Via M.Giurba 27
www.tortugapubmessina.it
Tortuga (tortoise) is the "hideout" for the folks of Messina who come here to spend jolly, entertaining evenings listening to live music from both well-known and emerging bands.

Museums, Monuments and Churches

Museo Regionale
Viale della Libertà 465,
tel. 090361292-090361293
www.regione.sicilia.it
Opening times: Monday-Friday 9.00-13.30; Tuesday, Thursday and Saturday also 16.00-18.30; Sundays and public holidays 9.00-12.30. Closed on Wednesday.

MILAZZO

Hotels

Petit Hotel ★★★ ♿
Via dei Mille 37,
tel. 0909286784
www.petithotel.it
9 rooms. Restaurant, air conditioned
Credit Cards: American Express, Diner's Club, Mastercard, Visa
Elegant mid 19th century building renovated in deference to the principles of bioarchitecture; welcoming rooms; Sicilian cuisine with organic produce.

Riviera Lido ★★★
Strada Panoramica,
tel. 0909283456
www.milazzonline.it/rivieralido
38 rooms. Restaurant, parking, air conditioned
Credit Cards: American Express, Diner's Club, Visa
White building with small balconies in a peaceful spot right by the sea; classic furnishings, professional management.

Restaurants

Covo del Pirata ⑪ ♿
Via Marina Garibaldi 2,
tel. 0909284437
www.paginegialle.it/ilcovodel pirata
Closed Wednesday (not holidays)
Cuisine: of Messina
Credit Cards: American Express, Diner's Club, Mastercard, Visa
Elegant ambience with nautical furnishings and large windows overlooking the sea. Good traditional Messina cooking. Pizzas too.

Piccolo Casale ⑪ ♿
Via R. D'Amico 12,
tel. 0909224479
www.piccolocasale.it
Closed Monday
Cuisine: refined
Credit Cards: American Express, Diner's Club, Mastercard, Visa
Pleasant restaurant on several levels, in an aristocratic villa with a beautiful summer terrace and a cellar, which may be visited, containing about 900 wines.

Salamone a Mare ⑪ ♿ ★
Strada Panoramica 36,
tel. 0909281233
Closed Monday
Cuisine: Sicilian and classic
Credit Cards: American Express, Diner's Club, Mastercard, Visa
Spacious, consisting of two dining rooms with a nautical theme, and a terrace

overlooking the sea. Cuisine based on the daily fish catch; extensive wine list.

At night

Babylon Cafè
Via Tonnara 39,
tel. 3384928449
For years the most popular place in Messina for Latin American dancing.

Museums, Monuments and Churches

Castello
Salita Castello,
tel. 0909221291
Opening times: March-May and September: Monday-Sunday 10.00-13.00, 15.00-18.00. June-August:10.00-13.00, 17.00-19.00. October-February: Monday-Sunday 9.00-12.00, 14.30-16.30.

MILO

How to get there
BY CAR: exit Giarre, A18 motorway Messina-Catania

MODICA

How to get there
BY CAR: exit Catania Sud, A19 motorway Palermo-Catania
BY TRAIN: FS Railway Station via Stazione

Rural Lodgings

Case Brizza ★
Via Aurnia Brizza Gisana 6,
tel. 3381895842
www.agriturismocasebrizza.com
Among carob, olive and almond trees, a 19th century stone farm with simple but functional interiors; meals cooked on the farm to traditional recipes.

Villa Teresa ఉ ★
Bugilfezza, via Crocevia Cava d'Ispica, tel. 0932771690
www.villateresaweb.it
Bikes are available
Credit Cards: CartaSi
Lovely 17th century farm surrounded by centuries old carob trees; simple and functional rooms open onto small verandas which face a treelined lawn.

Bed & Breakfast

Giogaia
Via Modica Giarratana 83/a,
tel. 0932751769
www.giogaia.it

On the slopes of the Sicilian mountains, a few kilometres from the center of Modica and the sea, this B&B is housed in a recently built country house, where guests sleep in a large air-conditioned loft, with a small sunny terrace and a sitting room with a kitchenette. A breakfast of local specialties and organic produce is served in the family living room or on the terrace. In the garden and orchard there is a play area for children.

Restaurants

Fattoria delle Torri ⅲ ఉ
Vico Napolitano 14,
tel. 0932751928
Closed Monday
Cuisine: revisited regional
Credit Cards: American Express, Diner's Club, Mastercard, Visa
In a baroque building in the old city center, a little door, a flight of steps, a small garden, and, finally, the surprise!: a gorgeous restaurant of modern architectural design. Traditional cuisine, often elaborated to make it even more tempting; small room for wine tasting.

Le Magnolie ⅋ ఉ ★
Frigintini, via Gianforma P.M. 179,
tel. 0932908136
www.ristorantelemagnolie.it
Closed Tuesday
Cuisine: regional
Credit Cards: Mastercard, Visa
In an old oil-mill, large, welcoming, thoughtfully furnished dining rooms; good regional cuisine.

Taverna Nicastro ⅋
Via S. Antonino 28,
tel. 0932945884
Open evenings only, closed Sunday and Monday
Cuisine: regional
At the top of a picturesque flight of steps (where there are a few tables for dining out in the summer) in the heart of the upper town. Cuisine based on local flavors and aromas, home-made salamis and pastas. Large selection of, mostly regional, wines.

At night

Bar Sicilia
Corso Umberto I 6,
tel. 0932943651
www.barsicilia.it
In the heart of the town; since the beginning of the last century citizens of Modica have enjoyed the home-made water-ices and ice-creams, croissants and

cream horns. A few years ago it also became a wine bar, open until late at night. Opens at 5am every day. Do not miss the Modican hot drinking chocolate.

Museums, Monuments and Churches

Museo Civico "F.L. Belgiorno"
Via Mercè, tel. 0932945081
Opening times: Monday-Saturday 9.00-13.00; Tuesday and Thursday also 15.30-17.30.

MONREALE

How to get there
BY CAR: exit Palermo, A19 motorway Palermo-Catania
BY TRAIN: FS Railway Station station in Palermo: bus connection

Restaurants

La Botte 1962 ⅋
Lenzitti 20, S.S. 186 al km 10,
tel. 091414051
www.mauriziocascino.it
Open Sunday lunchtime and holidays
Cuisine: Sicilian and classic
Credit Cards: American Express, Diner's Club, Mastercard, Visa
Ancient wine store with large fireplace and garden for al fresco dining; experienced family management.

Taverna del Pavone ⅋ ఉ ★
Vicolo Pensato 18,
tel. 0916406209
www.tavernadelpavone.it
Closed Monday
Cuisine: Sicilian
Credit Cards: American Express, Diner's Club, Mastercard, Visa
Rustic trattoria in a lovely period building a few steps from the cathedral. Offers traditional cuisine with modern, imaginative flourishes.

Museums, Monuments and Churches

Chiostro
tel. 0916404403
Opening times: Monday-Saturday: 9.00-19.00; public holidays 9.00-13.00.

Duomo
tel. 0916404413
Opening times: May-September: Monday-Sunday 8.00-18.00; October-April: Monday-Sunday 8.00-12.30, 15.30-18.00

★☆☆ / ★ Hotels ⅲ / ⅋ Restaurants ఉ Disabled ★ Special TCI Rates ⚱ Thermal spa ⚕ Health Center

MONTEVAGO

How to get there
BY CAR: exit Santa Ninfa,
A29 motorway Palermo-
Mazara del Vallo
BY TRAIN: FS Railway
Station station in
Castelvetrano

MORGANTINA

How to get there
BY CAR: exit Agira, A19
motorway Palermo-Catania
BY TRAIN: FS Railway
Station station in Aidone

Museums, Monuments and Churches

Scavi
tel. 093587955
Opening times: Winter: Monday-
Sunday 9.00-17.00. Summer:
Monday-Sunday 9.00 - one hour
before sundown.

MOZIA

How to get there
BY CAR: exit Marsala, A29
motorway Spur road to Birgi

GOLF & TENNIS

Another way to holiday in
Sicily is to partake of some
the traditional sports
activities on offer, from
tennis to golf.

Golf

Castiglione di Sicilia
Il Picciolo Golf Club Golf
Via Picciolo 1, tel. 0942986252
www.ilppicciologolf.com

Tennis

Palermo
Mediterraneo Club Tennis
Via Imperatore Federico 74,
tel. 0916372444

Siracusa
Tennis Club Match Ball Tennis
Via Agnello 26, tel. 093169675

Trapani
Circolo Tennis Tennis
Milo 49, tel. 0923532488

Museums, Monuments and Churches

Scavi
tel. 0923712598
Opening times: Monday-Sunday
9.00-13.00, 15.00-18.30.

NARO

How to get there
BY CAR: exit Imera, A19
motorway Palermo-Catania
BY TRAIN: FS Railway
Station station in Canicattì;
bus connection

At night

David Barry
Largo Milazzo 12,
tel. 3209296393
New management, friendly pub
with wooden furniture and a
small room where you can
dance until dawn. Live music
only on special occasions.
Sandwiches and spaghetti for
the very greedy.

NICOLOSI

🛈 **Azienda Autonoma
Soggiorno e Turismo**
Via Garibaldi 63,
tel. 095911505-095911784
www.aast-nicolosi.it

How to get there
BY CAR: exit Acireale, A18
motorway Messina-Catania
BY TRAIN: FS Railway
Station station in Catania

Hotels

Biancaneve ★★★
Via Etnea 163, tel. 095914139
www.hotel.biancaneve.com
83 rooms. Restaurant, parking,
air conditioned, swimming pool
Credit Cards: American Express,
Diner's Club, Mastercard, Visa
Modern Mediterranean style
construction with a view of
Etna. Provides renovated,
comfortable rooms, well-
appointed reception rooms and
an immaculate restaurant.

Gemmellaro ★★★ &
Via Etnea 160, tel. 095911060
www.hotelgemmellaro.it
56 rooms. Restaurant, parking
Credit Cards: American Express,
Diner's Club, Mastercard, Visa
A few kilometers from the
central crater of Etna and the
cable cars, a modern and
comfortable building on four
floors. Restaurant serves
regional food.

Restaurants

Corsaro ⑪ & ★
Cantoniera Etnea, piazza
Cantoniera, tel. 095914122
www.hotelcorsaro.it
Cuisine: Sicilian
Credit Cards: American Express,
Mastercard, Visa
In a picturesque position, about
three kilometers from the
craters of Etna and 200 metres
from the cable cars, it offers
well-prepared traditional cuisine.
Huge choice of regional wines
and wines from Etna, selection
of sheep's cheeses.

Villa Michelangelo ⑪ & ★
Via Oasi S. Bernardo 8,
tel. 095910176
Cuisine: Sicilian
Credit Cards: Diner's Club,
Mastercard, Visa
On the slopes of Etna, in a
recently renovated villa, a large
restaurant, with red velvet and
steel furnishings and some walls
clad in Ragusa white stone.
Splendid garden with luxuriant
palm and olive trees, swimming
pool and terrace. Excellent
Sicilian cuisine with fresh pasta
and fish.

NOTO

🛈 **Azienda Autonoma
Provinciale Incremento
Turistico**
Piazza XVI Maggio,
tel. 0931573779
apt-siracusa.it

How to get there
BY CAR: exit Catania Est,
A18 motorway Messina-
Catania, exit Catania Sud,
A19 motorway Palermo-
Catania
BY TRAIN: FS Railway
Station piazzale Stazione

Hotels

Villa Mediterranea ★★ &
Lido di Noto, viale Lido,
tel. 0931812330
www.villamediterranea.it
15 rooms. Parking, swimming
pool
Credit Cards: American Express,
Diner's Club, Mastercard, Visa
In a Mediterranean style villa,
direct access to the beach from
the garden: comfortable, air-
conditioned rooms; sweet buffet
breakfast.

Eloro Hotel Club ★★★
Lido di Noto, tel. 0931812244
Open March-September
222 rooms. Restaurant, parking,
air conditioned, swimming pool,
sauna, tennis, gym

Credit Cards: American Express, Visa

Modern building on four floors, with numerous sports facilities: canoeing, sailing, tennis. Amphitheatre for summer entertainment.

Masseria degli Ulivi ★★★ &
Porcari, tel. 0931813019
www.masseriadegliulivi.com
16 rooms. Restaurant, air conditioned, swimming pool, tennis

Credit Cards: American Express, Diner's Club, Mastercard, Visa

Old late 19th century private house, converted into a welcoming hotel. Ceilings with exposed beams and terracotta floors have been tastefully preserved; simple, quiet rooms.

Monteluce
Vaddeddi, tel. 3356901871
www.monteluce.com
3 rooms. Parking
Credit Cards: American Express, Mastercard, Visa

Early 20th century country dwelling, set amongst olive, orange and prickly pear trees; large,elegant rooms with plenty of atmosphere. Buffet breakfast with home-baked products.

Rural Lodgings

Terra di Solimano &
Busulmone, S.P. 24 al km 1,8 tel. 0931836606
www.terradisolimano.it
Bikes are available

19th century villa on a large organic farm, against the splendid backdrop of the Val di Noto.

Bed & Breakfast

Centro Storico
Corso Vittorio Emanuele 64, tel. 0931573967
www.centro-storico.com
The B&B is situated on the first floor of a renovated Eighteenth century building, on Noto's principal thoroughfare, in the heart of the old city center, in a partly pedestrian only area. Guests are provided with a room equipped with fridge and television, or a suite equipped with a kitchenette and washing machine. Italian breakfast is served in your room. Noto, capital of the Sicilian Baroque, famous for its churches and buildings fancifully decorated in travertine, is 30km from Siracusa and just 5km from the sea.

Liberty
Via Ferruccio 2, tel. 0931839548
www.villacatera.com
In the center of Noto, an apartment which sleeps four in a renovated art nouveau building.

Noto B&B ★
Via Angelo Cavarra 70, tel. 0931838299
www.notob-b.com
Situated in the old city center, it provides spacious rooms overlooking the park and main thoroughfare.

Restaurants

Masseria degli Ulivi ¶¶¶ &
Porcari, tel. 0931813019
www.masseriadegliulivi.com
Open evenings only (Sunday lunchtime too)
Cuisine: revisited regional
Credit Cards: American Express, Diner's Club, Mastercard, Visa

Deep in the countryside, a beautiful 19th century farmhouse with a pleasant restaurant. Characteristic indoor dining rooms and "baglio" (typical courtyard) for summer dining. Cuisine revives traditional recipes, based on local products, using what is in season.

At night

Alla Vecchia Fontana
Corso Vittorio Emanuele III 150, tel. 0931839412
Excellent café for desserts, ice-creams or coffee in a lovely setting, at the foot of the church of San Francesco. Courteous hospitality.

Museums, Monuments and Churches

Museo Civico Archeologico
Corso Vittorio Emanuele, tel. 0931836462
Opening times: Temporarily closed.

PACHINO

Restaurants

Taverna La Cialoma ¶¶
Marzamemi, piazza Regina Margherita 23, tel. 0931841772
Closed Tuesday (except July-September)
Cuisine: regional
Credit Cards: American Express, Diner's Club, Mastercard, Visa

The "cialoma" is the ancient song sung by tuna fisherman.It is now the name of this charming restaurant, a former 18th century tuna fishery, where you can try traditional, tasty and flavorful cuisine.

PALAZZOLO ACREIDE

☑ Pro Loco
Via Carceri 4, tel. 3338213589

How to get there
BY CAR: exit Catania Est, A18 motorway Messina-Catania, exit Catania Sud, A19 motorway Palermo-Catania
BY TRAIN: FS Railway Station station in Siracusa; bus connection on week days

Hotels

Santoro ★ &
Via S. Sebastiano 21, tel. 0931883855
www.hotelsantoro.com
8 rooms.Parking
Credit Cards: Mastercard, Visa

In the old town center, a renovated Thirties house, provides a base for a visit to the town. Air-conditioned rooms; restaurant "La Sfiziosa" with different management.

Senatore ★★★
Largo Senatore Italia 5, tel. 0931883443
www.hotelsenatore.it
21 rooms. Restaurant, parking, air conditioned
Credit Cards: American Express, Diner's Club, Mastercard, Visa

Well-equipped, comfortable structure; sweet and savoury buffet breakfast; restaurant "Il Senatore" serves regional and classic cuisine.

Restaurants

Il Camino ¶ ★
Via Martiri di via Fani 13, tel. 0931881860
Closed Tuesday
Cuisine: Sicilian
Credit Cards: American Express, Diner's Club, Visa

Rustic restaurant, with terrace for eating outside in the summer ; island specialties and, when in season, mushrooms, game and snails. Large selection of oils, cheese and salami. Pizzeria too.

La Trota ¶ & ★
Pianette, on the S.S. 287, tel. 0931883433
www.latrota.it
Closed Monday
Cuisine: Sicilian
Credit Cards: American Express, Diner's Club, Mastercard, Visa

Restaurant consisting of a room built into a rock and a second room which is larger and more modern, for banquets; cuisine is mainly trout, eels and sturgeon from the annexed fish farms.

At night

La Corte di Eolo
Via A. Uccello 1, tel. 0931883185
www.lacortedieolo.it
Rustic style pub built in an old
munitions depot. Also restaurant
and disco with live music.

Museums, Monuments and Churches

Area archeologica
tel. 0931881499
Opening times: Monday-Sunday
9.00-one hour before sundown.

PALERMO

ℹ Azienda Autonoma Provinciale Incremento Turistico
F.S. Railway Station,
piazza Giulio Cesare,
tel. 0916165914
www.palermotourism.com

ℹ Azienda Autonoma Provinciale Incremento Turistico
Falcone e Borsellino
airport,
tel. 091591698
www.palermotourism.com

ℹ Azienda Autonoma Provinciale Incremento Turistico
Piazza Castelnuovo 35,
tel. 091583847-
0916058351
www.palermotourism.com

ℹ Azienda Autonoma Soggiorno e Turismo
Salita Belmonte 43,
tel. 0916398011
www.aziendautonomaturis
mopalermo.it

How to get there

BY CAR: exit Palermo, A19
motorway from Catania
and A20 motorway from
Messina, exit Palermo-Via
Belgio, A29 Palermo-
Mazara del Vallo motorway
BY TRAIN: FS Railway
Station piazza G. Cesare
BY FERRY: From Cagliari,
Tirrenia ferries; from
Genova, Grandi Navi Veloci
ferries; from Naples SNAV
and Tirrenia ferries; from
Salerno, Grimaldi Ferries;
also from Ustica with
Si.Re.Mar ferries and from
Lipari with Ustica Lines

Hotels

Villa Archirafi ** ★
Via Lincoln 30, tel. 0916168827
40 rooms. Parking, air
conditioned
Credit Cards: American Express,
Mastercard, Visa
Small art nouveau villa, close to
the Botanical Garden, with a
pergola in the garden where
breakfast is served. Rooms
provide a good level of comfort.

Addáura Hotel Residence Congressi ★★★ ♿ ★
Addaura, lungomare Cristoforo
Colombo 4452, tel. 0916842222
www.addaura.it
50 rooms. Restaurant, parking,
air conditioned, swimming pool
Credit Cards: American Express,
Diner's Club, Mastercard, Visa
In the neighborhood of Addaura,
a new construction overlooking
the sea which caters for summer
tourists and business guests.
The lively restaurant "Graffiti"
serves food inspired by various
sources.

Bel 3 ★★★
Via Ruffo di Calabria 20,
tel. 091223560
www.bel3.com
67 rooms. Restaurant, parking,
air conditioned
Credit Cards: American Express,
Diner's Club, Mastercard, Visa
Modern construction up in the
hills, on different levels,which
means that the rooms have
views of the city and the sea.
Courteous hospitality.

Europa ★★★
Via Agrigento 3,
tel. 0916256323
www.abeuropa.com
73 rooms. Restaurant, air
conditioned
Credit Cards: American Express,
Diner's Club, Mastercard, Visa
Close to Piazza Politeama,
it provides comfortable, air-
conditioned rooms. Continental
breakfast. Small meeting room.

Massimo Plaza ★★★ ★
Via Maqueda 437,
tel. 091325657
www.massimoplazahotel.com
15 rooms. Air conditioned
Credit Cards: American Express,
Diner's Club, Mastercard, Visa
Art nouveau building opposite
Teatro Massimo, provides
modern facilities, large rooms
and a pleasant reading room.

Posta ★★★ ★
Via A. Gagini 77, tel. 091587338
www.hotelpostapalermo.it
30 rooms. Air conditioned
Credit Cards: American Express,
Diner's Club, Mastercard, Visa
This hotel has been in the
business for over eighty years
and once catered to theatrical
actors. Suitable for both
business people and tourists;
buffet breakfast.

Astoria Palace ★★★ ★
Via Monte Pellegrino 62,
tel. 0916281111
www.ghshotels.it
315 rooms. Restaurant, parking,
air conditioned
Credit Cards: American Express,
Diner's Club, Mastercard, Visa
Hotel on fourteen floors with
every amenity; well-organised
conference center equipped with
an elegant American bar and
restaurant. Shuttle service to
the old city center.

Baglio Conca d'Oro ★★★ ♿ ★
Sobborgo Molara,
via Aquino 19/C-D,
tel. 0916406286
www.paginegialle.it/baglioconca
doro
27 rooms. Restaurant, parking,
air conditioned
Credit Cards: American Express,
Diner's Club, Mastercard, Visa
Formerly the 18th century
"Cartiera Grande", this
renovated hotel has a large
courtyard (baglio) with a
pleasant atmosphere.
Sophisticated restaurant with
Moorish touches.

Centrale Palace Hotel ★★★ ♿
Corso Vittorio Emanuele 327,
tel. 091336666
www.centralepalacehotel.it
103 rooms. Restaurant, parking,
air conditioned
Credit Cards: American Express,
Diner's Club, Mastercard, Visa
19th century patrician dwelling
which combines old-fashioned
charm with modern comfort.
Well-equipped congress rooms.
Restaurant with sophisticated
cuisine and terrace with a view.

Jolly Hotel ★★★ ★
Foro Italico 22, tel. 0916165090
www.jollyhotels.it
237 rooms. Restaurant, parking,
air conditioned, swimming pool
Credit Cards: American Express,
Mastercard, Visa
Surrounded by the gardens of
Villa Giulia and close to the
Botanical Graden, an elegant
and well-kept building. Lively
restaurant "Sala Paladini".

Principe di Villafranca ★★★
Via G. Turrisi Colonna 4,
tel. 0916118523
www.principedivillafranca.it
34 rooms. Restaurant, parking,
air conditioned, gym
Credit Cards: American Express,
Diner's Club, Mastercard, Visa
The atmosphere is that of a
private home, though it is
professionally managed, inside
a shopping mall. Restaurant
serves regional cuisine.

Splendid Hotel la Torre ★★★ ♿ ★
Mondello, via Piano Gallo 11,
tel. 091450222

www.latorre.com

168 rooms. Restaurant, parking, air conditioned, swimming pool, tennis

Credit Cards: American Express, Diner's Club, Visa

Surrounded by a cool garden, a modern hotel built on the rocks. Internet point; restaurant serves Sicilian and classic cuisine.

Bed & Breakfast

B&B Castiglione
Piazza Stazione Lolli 3, tel. 091335300

Overlooking a tree-lined square in the center of Palermo, this apartment, on the first floor of a late 19th century building, has three large rooms, including one decorated with precious friezes and frescos for guests. The hearty breakfast includes fresh baked products with fruit and yoghurt and is usually served in your room. The landlady is an expert on the artistic treasures of the city and outlying areas and is happy to act as your guide.

Il Glicine La Piana dei Colli
Mondello, tel. 091454565-3283188027

www.ilglicine.net

Il Glicine is a large 18th century villa in the shape of a typical Sicilian "baglio", situated near Mondello beach, a few minutes from the center of Palermo. Guests are accommodated in three rooms in a large apartment in the building, whose interior preserves its ancient charm, with terracotta floors, precious woods and a large fireplace. Breakfast includes fruit from the garden, personally tended by the owner who is a gardening expert.

Il Glicine Palermo Sul Golfo
Mondello, tel. 091453260-3402803437

www.ilglicine.net

With an enviable picturesque position on the gulf of Mondello, the villa is situated under the lee of the town, a few steps from the famous beach. It is a lovely house with a Mediterranean flavor, clad in an enormous wisteria and encircled by pine trees. The interiors have cosy furnishings and family pieces. Guests may choose from a double room and an independent mini-apartment sleeping four people, with a kitchenette. Breakfast, made with loving care, is served outside or in the dining room.

Restaurants

Gourmet Bar ¶¶¶ ⅋ ★
Viale Strasburgo 235,

tel. 091589797

www.enotecapicone.it

Closed Sunday

Cuisine: classic

Credit Cards: American Express, Diner's Club, Mastercard, Visa

Elegant restaurant with ambience, lined with shelves overflowing with bottles. Excellent fresh fish, cooked in sundry, clever ways, with a modern slant.

Il Ristorantino ¶¶¶ ⅋
Piazzale A. De Gasperi 19, tel. 091512861

Closed Monday

Cuisine: Sicilian

Credit Cards: American Express, Diner's Club, Mastercard, Visa

Situated in a residential area, this is an elegant and welcoming restaurant. Impeccable cuisine based on solid traditions using whatever ingredients are in season.

'A Cuccagna ¶¶ ⅋ ★
Via Principe Granatelli 21/A, tel. 091587267

www.acuccagna.com

Cuisine: Sicilian and classic

Credit Cards: American Express, Diner's Club, Mastercard, Visa

Elegant trattoria, situated in the heart of the city and characterised by a large dining room with rustic furniture. Elaborately prepared traditional specialties.

Bye Bye Blues ¶¶
Mondello, via del Garofalo 23, tel. 0916841415

www.byebyeblues.it

Open evenings only, closed Tuesday

Cuisine: refined Sicilian

Credit Cards: American Express, Diner's Club, Mastercard, Visa

This friendly restaurant has a cool garden where you can eat out in the summer. The food is tasty and appealing and able to satisfy the most demanding of palates.

Cucina Papoff ¶¶
Via Isidoro la Lumia 32, tel. 091586460

www.regalis.com/papoff

Closed Saturday lunchtime and Sunday

Cuisine: Sicilian

Credit Cards: American Express, Diner's Club, Mastercard, Visa

In the heart of the city, divided into rooms with wooden coffered ceilings, bare stone walls and arches. Traditional food with a large selection of local cheeses and salamis.

Friend's Bar ¶¶ ⅋
Via Brunelleschi 138,

tel. 091201401

Closed Monday

Cuisine: Sicilian and classic

Credit Cards: American Express, Diner's Club, Visa

Restaurant composed of two dining rooms, with an abundance of mirrors and lacquered furniture, as well as a gazebo for dining outside in the summer. Pizza to go.

Osteria dei Vespri ¶¶
Piazza Croce dei Vespri, tel. 0916171631

www.osteriadeivespri.it

Closed Sunday

Cuisine: revisited Sicilian

Credit Cards: American Express, Diner's Club, Mastercard, Visa

Once the carriage shed of Palazzo Ganghi, now a small and intimate restaurant with al fresco dining in the summer; it has a good selection of wines and an interesting seasonal menu, cooked imaginatively and intuitively.

Palazzo Trabucco ¶¶ ⅋ ★
Via dei Bottai 24/28, tel. 091326123

www.palazzotrabucco.com

Closed Monday

Cuisine: Sicilian

Credit Cards: American Express, Mastercard, Visa

In an aristocratic building dating from the late 17th century, with beautiful exposed beams, tiled floors and straw-bottomed chairs; the kitchen is open until 22 serving typical and traditional Sicilian dishes.

Regine ¶¶
Via Trapani 4/A, tel. 091586566

www.ristoranteregine.it

Closed Sunday

Cuisine: Sicilian and classic

Credit Cards: American Express, Diner's Club, Visa

A short walk from the Politeama theatre, classic "display" of fish at the entrance to a warm and elegantly furnished dining room.

Santandrea ¶¶ ⅋
Piazza S. Andrea 4, tel. 091334999

Closed Tuesday and Wednesday lunchtime (in summer, Sunday and Monday lunchtime)

Cuisine: Sicilian

Credit Cards: American Express, Mastercard, Visa

Right behind the famous "Vucciria" market, a pleasant restaurant which offers home cooking based on whatever is in season and whose congenial style and careful presentation of the food is immediately winning.

Dal Maestro del Brodo ⏐
Via Pannieri 7, tel. 091329523
www.ilmaestrodelbrodo.it
Open lunchtimes (Oct-mid June Fri and Sat evenings. Sunday lunchtime), closed Sunday in summer and Monday in winter
Cuisine: regional
Credit Cards: American Express, Mastercard, Visa
What were originally 19th century rooms have been renovated to create a comfortable and suitable space for dining. The cuisine is inspired by the traditions of the well-known neighbourhood of Vucciria.

Kursaal Kalhesa ⏐ ♿
Foro Umberto I 21,
tel. 0916162282
www.kursaalkalhesa.it
Closed Monday and Sunday evening
Cuisine: Mediterranean
Credit Cards: American Express, Diner's Club, Mastercard, Visa
This splendid venue in the old city center, inside the 16th century Bastione Vega and facing the sea, is now one of the city's main points of reference,not only because of the facilities it offers but also, and above all, because of the cultural events it promotes. It is, at one and the same time, a literary café, wine bar, bookshop, travel agency and internet point. Upstairs there is also a restaurant with an open air garden.

Mi Manda Picone ⏐ ♿
Via A. Paternostro 59,
tel. 0916160660
Open evenings only, closed Sunday
Cuisine: classic
Credit Cards: American Express, Mastercard, Visa
In a 14th century building situated in the old city center, picturesque wine-bar: wine and cheese tasting at the counter, meat and fish served in the dining rooms on the first floor.

At night
Berlin Café
Via I. La Lumia 21
Trendy pub inspired by London fashions: post modern look with mirrors and glass and music, music, music. A place to meet friends either inside or outside for an aperitif or, later, for a cocktail or a goblet of wine. For people who enjoy dressing up and following fashion. Chic.

Cuba
Via Scaduto 12, tel. 091309201
Trendy pub inside Villa

Sperlinga: Arabic atmosphere with pink turrets and domes and a winter garden where you can eat, drink and dance.

I Candelai
Via dei Candelai 65,
tel. 091327151
In the heart of the old city center, the place for thrills and sheer entertainment: live music, exhibitions, cabaret and much more besides.

Kursaal Kalesa
Foro Umberto I 21,
tel. 0916162111
www.kursaalkalhesa.it
Situated on the ancient ramparts of the city, a short walk from the sea, atmospheric pub with high vaulted ceiling, terracotta floors and exposed brick tuff walls. Many cultural events on offer; elegant restaurant, wine bar with live music for the younger crowd, internet point, bookshop and travel agency.

Mi Manda Picone
Via A. Paternostro 59,
tel. 0916160660
In the heart of Palermo, the first wine bar in the city: an agreable place where, from 19 into the small hours, you can nibble on an elaborate selection of cold meats and cheeses accompanied by a remarkable number and variey of wines. Another bar with a small restaurant was opened a few years ago in the ancient stores of an aristocratic 14th century palace in Piazza di San Francesco.

Museums, Monuments and Churches
Cappella Palatina
Piazza Indipendenza,
tel. 0917054879
Opening times: Monday-Friday 9.00-11.45, 15.00-16.45; Saturday 9.00-11.45; Sunday 9.00-9.45, 12.00-12.45.

Galleria Regionale della Sicilia Palazzo Abatellis
Via Alloro 4, tel. 0916230033
www.regione.sicilia.it
Opening times: Monday, Saturday, Sunday 9.00-13.30; Tuesday, Wednesday, Thursday, Friday 9.00-13.30, 14.30-19.30; Sundays and public holidays 9.00-13.00.

Museo Archeologico Regionale "Antonino Salinas"
Piazza Olivella, tel. 0916116805
www.regione.sicilia.it/benicultura li/dirbenicult/salinas/index.htm
Opening times: Monday-Friday 9.00-18.00; Saturdays, Sundays and public holidays 9.00-13.00.

Oratorio del Rosario di S. Domenico
Via dei Bambinai
Opening times: Monday-Friday 9.00-13.00, 14.00-17.30; Saturday 9.00-13.00.

Oratorio di S. Cita
Via Valverde 3, tel. 091332779
Opening times: Monday-Friday 9.00-11.00.

Palazzo dei Normanni
Piazza Indipendenza,
tel. 0917057003
Opening times: Guided tours: Monday, Friday and Saturday 9.00-12.00; other days by arrangement.

Parco della Favorita
tel. 0916961319
Opening times: Visits by arrangement.

Zisa
Piazza Guglielmo il Buono,
tel. 0916520269
Opening times: Monday-Saturday 9.00-18.30; Sundays and public holidays 9.00-13.00.

PANAREA

Hotels
Hycesia ⋆⋆
Via S. Pietro, tel. 090983041
www.hycesia.it
Open Easter-October
8 rooms. Restaurant, air conditioned
Credit Cards: American Express, Diner's Club, Mastercard, Visa
A few minutes from the small tourist harbour, it provides comfortable rooms. Restaurant beneath a cool pergola with a menu based on the day's fish catch and whatever ingredients are in season.

Raya ⋆⋆
Via S. Pietro, tel. 090983013
www.hotelraya.it
Open April-mid October
36 rooms. Restaurant
Credit Cards: American Express, Diner's Club, Mastercard, Visa
Pyramid shaped hotel composed of three buildings. Provides rooms with a sea view, furnished in a minimalist style. Mediterranean inspired cuisine.

La Piazza ⋆⋆⋆ ★
Via S. Pietro, tel. 090983154
Open April-October
31 rooms. Restaurant, air conditioned, swimming pool
Credit Cards: American Express, Diner's Club, Visa
Overhanging the sea, recently renovated, Aeolian architecture; seawater swimming pool, garden and jetty. Buffet

breakfast and typical Sicilian cuisine.

Lisca Bianca ★★★ ★
Via Lani 1, tel. 090983004
www.liscabianca.it
Open April-October
38 rooms. Air conditioned
Credit Cards: American Express, Diner's Club, Mastercard, Visa
Opposite the small tourist harbour, in a garden full of bougainvillea and hibiscus. Moorish style rooms, with sea views. Connected to the restaurant "Cusiritati".

Quartara ★★★
Via S. Pietro, tel. 090983027
www.quartarahotel.com
Open April-October
13 rooms. Restaurant, air conditioned
Credit Cards: American Express, Diner's Club, Mastercard, Visa
Central but peaceful, it provides accommodation in air-conditioned rooms with lava stone or hand-decorated tile floors. Panoramic terrace, internet point.

PANTALICA

How to get there
BY CAR: exit Catania Est, A18 motorway to Messina, exit Catania Sud, A19 motorway to Palermo

PANTELLERIA

ℹ️ Pro Loco
Piazza Cavour 1, tel. 0923911838

How to get there
BY FERRY: From Trapani, hydrofoil with Ustica Lines and Si.Re.Mar ferries

Hotels

Miryam ★★ ★
Corso Umberto I 1, tel. 0923911374
www.miryamhotel.it
28 rooms. Air conditioned
Credit Cards: American Express, Diner's Club, Mastercard, Visa
Unpretentious hotel with bed and breakfast overlooking the tourist harbour: two kilometres away there are holiday homes and a rooming-house.

Papuscia ★★ ★
Sopra Portella 46/48, tel. 0923915463
www.papuscia.it
11 rooms. Restaurant, parking
Credit Cards: American Express,

Mastercard, Visa
A typical 18th century "dammuso" (stone building with a domed roof), not far from the sea, divided into four buildings with terraces with views.

Cossyra ★★★
Mursia, tel. 0923911154
www.cossyrahotel.it
Open April-October
80 rooms. Restaurant, parking, air conditioned, swimming pool, tennis
Credit Cards: American Express, Diner's Club, Mastercard, Visa
White Mediterranean style structure, balconies with sea views, good facilities; scuba diving and sailing lessons; excursions. Restaurant serves Sicilian and Arabic specialties.

Mursia ★★★ ♿
Mursia, tel. 0923911217
www.mursiahotel.it
Open April-October
74 rooms. Restaurant, parking, air conditioned, swimming pool, tennis
Credit Cards: American Express, Diner's Club, Mastercard, Visa
Vaulted roof, terraces and steps; restaurant serves local, classic and Arabic specialities. Free shuttle service to Pantelleria; diving center and sailing school.

Restaurants

I Mulini ⅋⅋⅋
Tracino, tel. 0923915398
Open evenings only
Cuisine: Mediterranean
Credit Cards: American Express, Diner's Club, Mastercard, Visa
In an ancient mill (built from typical " dammusi"), the most elegant restaurant on the island. Light, tasty cuisine of mainly vegetables combined with fish and meat.

Favarotta ⅋
Khamma Fuori, tel. 0923915347
Closed Wednesday
Cuisine: Sicilian
Credit Cards: Diner's Club, Mastercard, Visa
In a nature reserve, a restaurant built in lava stone which recalls the shape of the "dammuso" and a lovely outside eating area with an enormous towering carob tree. The chef uses many vegetables from the garden to go with the fish; excellent local desserts.

La Nicchia ⅋ ♿
Scauri Basso, tel. 0923916342
Open evenings only, closed Wednesday (except in the summer)

Cuisine: fish
Credit Cards: American Express, Diner's Club, Mastercard, Visa
Cosy, rustic style restaurant (typical "dammuso") providing al fresco dining in a cool garden with interesting flavorful cuisine. Pizzeria too.

At night

Cicci's
Via Cagliari
In the center, small, quiet pub popular with youngsters: live local bands.

Alta Marea
Scauri
Recently opened pub with live music in the evenings.

PATTI

Hotels

Park Philip Hotel ★★★
Marina di Patti, via Lungomare 57, tel. 0941361332
www.parkphiliphotel.it
Open March-October
43 rooms. Restaurant, swimming pool
Credit Cards: American Express, Diner's Club, Mastercard, Visa
A few meters from the sea, for restorative, peaceful holidays; restaurant serves Sicilian cuisine.

PEDARA

How to get there
BY CAR: exit Acireale, A18 motorway Messina-Catania

Hotels

G.H. Bonaccorsi ★⅋★ ♿
Via Pirandello 2, tel. 0957928529
www.classicahotels.com
91 rooms. Restaurant, parking, air conditioned, swimming pool, gym
Credit Cards: American Express, Diner's Club, Mastercard, Visa
An excellent point of reference both for business people and tourists. Some suites available; restaurant with terrace serves innovative cuisine.

PETRALIA SOPRANA

How to get there
BY CAR: exit Tre Monzelli, A19 motorway Palermo-Catania
BY TRAIN: FS Railway Station station in Castelbuono

‡‡‡ / ★ Hotels ⅋⅋⅋⅋ / ⅋ Restaurants ♿ Disabled ★ Special TCI Rates ♨ Thermal spa 🏋 Health Center

PETRALIA SOTTANA

How to get there

BY CAR: exit Tre Monzelli, A1 motorway Palermo-Catania

BY TRAIN: FS Railway Station station in Palermo; bus connection

Rural Lodgings

Monaco di Mezzo &
Monaco, tel. 0934673949
www.monacodimezzo.com
Open on request
Swimming pool, tennis, availability of bikes
Credit Cards: CartaSi, Visa
In Parco delle Madonie, a large farm characterised by warm wood and local tradition. Surrounded by wheat fields as far as the eye can see.

PIAZZA ARMERINA

ℹ️ **Azienda Autonoma Soggiorno e Turismo**
Viale Generale Muscarà, tel. 0935680201
www.aziendaautonomapiazza.com

How to get there

BY CAR: exit Mulinello, A19 motorway Palermo-Catania

BY TRAIN: FS Railway Station station in Catania or Dittaino Stazione; bus connections

Hotels

Park Hotel Paradiso ★★★
Ramalda, tel. 0935680841
95 rooms. Restaurant, parking, air conditioned, swimming pool, sauna, tennis, gym
Credit Cards: American Express, Diner's Club, Mastercard, Visa
Very comfortable, recently renovated, for peaceful stays in the countryside. Will soon be 4 star.

Rural Lodgings

Gigliotto & ★
Gigliotto, tel. 0933970898
www.gigliotto.com
Swimming pool, bikes are available
Credit Cards: American Express, Visa, Mastercard
Old-fashioned atmosphere in an ancient monastery in the middle of an organic farm where cereals, prickly pears, grapes and olive trees are grown.

Il Glicine &
Vallegrande C.P. 187, tel. 0935684119

Swimming pool, bikes are available
Art and organic farming: this sums up the atmosphere of this small structure which welcomes guests in a context of rustic simplicity. Vegetarian cuisine.

Restaurants

Al Fogher ⁛ &
Bellia 1, S.S. 117 Bis, tel. 0935684123
www.alfogher.net
Closed Sunday evening and Monday
Cuisine: Sicilian and experimental
Credit Cards: American Express, Visa
Just outside the village, an old railway gateman's box made into a restaurant. Traditional cuisine using natural local ingredients, revisited with skill and imagination.

Trattoria La Ruota ⁛ &
Paratore Casale, tel. 0935680542
www.trattorialaruota.it
Open lunchtime only (in the summer evenings too, bookings only)
Cuisine: Sicilian and classic
Credit Cards: American Express, Mastercard, Visa
Former water-mill, not far from the Roman villa of Casale, a rustic style, family run restaurant. Home-made pasta, almond sweets.

At night

Pub Sesterzio
Via Padova 13, tel. 3476602601
For a simple, informal evening: pub, creperie and "bruschetteria".

Museums, Monuments and Churches

Villa romana del Casale
Casale 1, tel. 0935680036
Opening times: Monday-Sunday 8.00-16.00.

PIEDIMONTE ETNEO

How to get there

BY CAR: exit Fiumefreddo, A18 motorway Messina-Catania

RAGALNA

How to get there

BY CAR: exit Acireale, A18 motorway Messina-Catania

RAGUSA

ℹ️ **Azienda Autonoma Provinciale Incremento Turistico**
Via Capitano Bocchieri 33, tel. 093222151
www.ragusaturismo.it

ℹ️ **Pro Loco**
Largo Camerina 5
tel. 0932244473
www.prolocoragusa.it

How to get there

BY CAR: exit Catania Est, A18 motorway Messina-Catania, exit Catania Sud, A19 motorway Palermo-Catania

BY TRAIN: FS Railway Station piazza del Popolo

Hotels

Il Barocco ★★★
Via S. Maria la Nuova 1, tel. 0932663105
www.ilbarocco.it
14 rooms. Restaurant, air conditioned
Credit Cards: American Express, Diner's Club, Mastercard, Visa
Renovated, aristocratic baroque building, ideal for peaceful stays with all amenities. Also has a small conference room.

Kroma ★★★
Via D'Annunzio 60, tel. 0932622800
www.hotelkroma.it
26 rooms. Restaurant, air conditioned
Credit Cards: American Express, Diner's Club, Mastercard, Visa
Classy modern building. Sweet buffet breakfast, restaurant-pizzeria and meeting room.

Montreal ★★★ & ★
Corso Italia 70, tel. 0932621133
www.hotelmontreal.sicily-hotels.net
50 rooms. Restaurant, air conditioned
Credit Cards: American Express, Diner's Club, Mastercard, Visa
The main part of the hotel has a classic ambience; comfortable rooms and conference facilities.

Mediterraneo Palace ★⁛★ & ★
Via Roma 189, tel. 0932621944
www.mediterraneopalace.it
92 rooms. Restaurant, air conditioned
Credit Cards: American Express, Diner's Club, Visa
Renovated building, centrally located, offers a high level of comfort. Restaurant and typical "churrascheria" with different management. Good congress facilities.

Eremo Giubiliana ✻✻✻ ♿ ★
Giubiliana, S.P. 25 al km 9,
tel. 0932669119
www.eremodellagiubiliana.it
18 rooms. Restaurant, parking,
swimming pool
Credit Cards: American Express,
Diner's Club, Mastercard, Visa
An extremely charming hotel
which was formerly a 15th
century convent; private beach.
Private landing strip for
excursions and a cruiser for
cruises along the coast.

Restaurants
Duomo ▯▯▯ ★
Via Capitano Boccheri 31,
tel. 0932651265
www.ristoranteduomo.it
Closed Monday and Sunday
evening (from May to
September, Sunday and
Monday lunchtime)
Cuisine: revisited Sicilian
Credit Cards: American Express,
Diner's Club, Mastercard, Visa
An aristocratic and elegant
restaurant serving excellent
food with island flavors and an
ever-changing menu. Home-
made fresh pasta, bread and
desserts.

Eremo Giubiliana ▯▯▯ ★
Giubiliana, tel. 0932669119
www.eremodellagiubiliana.it
Closed Monday lunchtime
Cuisine: regional
Credit Cards: American Express,
Diner's Club, Mastercard, Visa
In a 15th century hermitage;
traditional meat and fish based
cuisine, using mainly their own
organic produce.

Da Nino "Titos" ▯▯ ♿
Via Porta Modica 21-31/a,
tel. 0932651449
www.ristorantetitos.com
Closed Monday
Cuisine: regional
Credit Cards: American Express,
Diner's Club, Mastercard, Visa
Elegant ambience Extremely
fresh fish and meat,
accompanied by a pondered
selection of wines; à la carte
desserts and oils.

La Fenice ▯▯ ♿
Via Gandhi 3, tel. 0932252070
www.al318.com
Open evenings only and Sunday
lunchtime, closed Monday
Cuisine: revisited regional
Credit Cards: American Express,
Diner's Club, Mastercard, Visa
A modern restaurant with a
large dining room for banquets
and a smaller one providing
first-rate catering. Elaborate
choice of wines and Sicilian
products; polite, professional
service.

MONASTERIES AND CONVENTS

Abbeys, monasteries, convents and sanctuaries are dotted
all over Italy's and Sicily's beautiful landscape, and are
usually built in superb locations. They include ancient
Benedictine foundations, Franciscan monasteries and
Cistercian abbeys, and they have been fundamental to
Italian art and culture for over a thousand years of history.
Accommodation is available in many of these spiritual
places. They provide the perfect solution if you want silence,
and if you wish to treat yourself to a time of meditation, as
well as psychological and physical regeneration.

Acireale
Convento di San Biagio
Piazza San Biagio 20,
tel. 095601377
digilander.libero.it/conventosan
biagio
Acireale, born from the ashes
of two earthquakes, the shore
of Cyclops and and the
immense form of Etna are
loaded with history and
legend: the convent, on the
other, hand is a more modern
and vital concern.

Alessandria della Rocca
Eremo-Santuario Madonna della Rocca
Via Santuario, tel. 0922981077
You can get there from

Agrigento or Sciacca and
Ribera; or from Palermo,
via Corleone or Lercara
Friddi; in the hills of the
Agrigento hinterland a
hermitage and a town are
linked under the banner of a
long ago event.

Cefalù
Convento-Santuario di Maria Santissima di Gibilmanna
Gibilmanna, tel. 0921421835
At an altitude of 800m, in the
woods which cover the slopes
of pizzo Sant'Angelo, one of
the most important places of
pilgrimage in the whole of
Sicily; tremendous panoramic
views of the Madonie and sea
of Cefalù.

Villa Fortugno ▯▯
tel. 0932667134
Closed Monday
Cuisine: Sicilian and classic
Credit Cards: American Express,
Mastercard, Visa
In a late 18th century villa, two
elegantly decorated dining
rooms and a large garden for
dining out in the summer.

Il Barocco ▯
Via Orfanotrofio 29,
tel. 0932652397
www.ilbarocco.it
Closed Wednesday
Cuisine: Sicilian
Credit Cards: American Express,
Diner's Club, Mastercard, Visa
18th century building, typical
regional cooking with a variety
of starters and specialties from
the land.

Il Calesse ▯ ♿
Magazzinazzi, S.P. to Marina di
Ragusa, tel. 0932667511
Closed Tuesday
Cuisine: regional and classic
Credit Cards: American Express,
Diner's Club, Mastercard, Visa
Former mid 19th century country
house. Cuisine ranges from

ingredients grown on the land to
fish specialties. Pizzas too.

Monna Lisa ▯ ♿ ★
Via Ettore Fieramosca,
tel. 0932642250
Closed Monday
Cuisine: Sicilian and classic
Credit Cards: American Express,
Diner's Club, Mastercard, Visa
Large late 19th century
restaurant with modern decor.
Kitchen open after 10pm.
A mixture of meat and fish;
pizzas too.

Orfeo ▯
Via S. Anna 117,
tel. 0932621035
Closed Sunday
Cuisine: Sicilian
Credit Cards: American Express,
Diner's Club, Mastercard, Visa
Traditional, informal restaurant,
serving typical regional cuisine.

At night
La Bella Vita
Marina di Ragusa, S.P Marina di
Ragusa al km 1.4,
tel. 0932825249
www.koalamaxi.com
One of the largest discos in
Sicily, open 12 months of the

Erice

Eremo "La Casa del Sorriso"
Cappuccini, tel. 0923869136
The site, on the slope of Monte San Giuliano, just below the walls of Erice, is most picturesque, as is the view; the hermitage is peaceful and an ideal place for religious holidays, spiritual retreats and cultural exchanges.

Ispica

Convento di Santa Maria di Gesù
Via Roma 116, tel. 0932951020
The convent rises on the brow of the picturesque plateau of Ispica, from which you can see the nearby sea and Cape Passero; the convent, which survived the earthquake of 1693, is one of the most ancient buildings in the town.

Mascalucia

Convento-Santuario dell'Addolorata
Via del Bosco 1, tel. 0957274006-0957274309
On the road between Etna and Catania, the two principal places of interest in this part of Sicily, a large house of worship, run by the Passionisti fathers; open in August to single travelers and families.

Modica

Monastero di San Benedetto
Via San Benedetto da Norcia 11, tel. 0932941033
On the hill of Itria, next to Modica, this monastery keeps the ancient Benedictine traditions of spirituality and hospitality alive in the town; as ordained by the rule of Saint Benedict.

Monreale

Abbazia di San Martino delle Scale
San Martino delle Scale, piazza Platani 11, tel. 091418104
www.abbaziadisanmartino.it
The only Benedictine abbey remaining in Sicily, it conserves a wealth of art and cultural treasures in the pinewoods on the slopes of Serra dell'Occhio, not far from the wonders of the cathedral of Monreale.

Palermo

Convento San Giovanni Battista
Baida, via al Convento di Baida 43, tel. 091223595
In an enchanting position with a view, amidst olive groves and citrus orchards, on the foothills which rise behind Palermo towards Monte Cuccio, the convent is a haven of peace and Franciscan spirituality.

---

year: myriad dance floors, both inside and out, each offering a different musical genre; from funky to '70s and '80s music, from dance to house music or Latin-American. Who goes? Everyone from teenagers to forty-somethings.

Sherwood Pub
Via Archimede 17/S, tel. 0932227980
Snacks, beer, live music, cabaret shows and themed evenings.

Museums, Monuments and Churches

Museo Archeologico Ibleo
Via Natalelli, tel. 0932622963
www.regione.sicilia.it
Opening times: Monday-Sunday 9.00-13.00, 16-19.30. Visits can also be arranged.

RANDAZZO

How to get there
BY CAR: exit Fiumefreddo, A18 motorway Messina-Catania

BY TRAIN: Circumetnea Railway Station tel. 095921156

Hotels

Scrivano ★★★ &
Via Bonaventura 2, tel. 095921126
www.hotelscrivano.com
30 rooms. Restaurant, parking, air conditioned
Credit Cards: American Express, Diner's Club, Mastercard, Visa
Recently renovated and extended hotel; restaurant "Le Delizie" serves Sicilian and classic cuisine. New terrace for sunbathing.

Rural Lodgings

L'Antica Vigna & ★
Montelaguardia, tel. 095924003
Tennis, availability of bikes
The farm is on the edge of Parco dell'Etna, close to Parco dei Nebrodi and the Valle dell'Alcantara nature reserve. Local cuisine.

Restaurants

Trattoria Veneziano ❚❚ ★
Via dei Romano 8, tel. 0957991353
www.ristoranteveneziano.it

Closed Monday and Sunday evening
Cuisine: Sicilian
Credit Cards: American Express, Diner's Club, Mastercard, Visa
Family-run restaurant, centrally located: traditional local cuisine, with mushrooms very much in evidence; own oil production.

Museums, Monuments and Churches

Museo Archeologico "Paolo Vagliasindi"
tel. 09579921861
www.comune.randazzo.ct.it
Opening times: Monday-Sunday 10.00-13.00, 15.00-20.00.

Museo dei Pupi Siciliani
tel. 0957991214
Opening times: Monday-Sunday 9.00-13.00, 16.00-19.00.

SALINA

Hotels

Punta Scario ★★ & ★
Scario, Malfa, via Scalo 8, tel. 0909844139
www.hotelpuntascario.it
Open April-October
17 rooms. Restaurant
Credit Cards: American Express, Diner's Club, Mastercard, Visa
Simple and essential with large rooms with views overhanging the sea; ideal for beach holidays. Fish and vegetable specialties served in the immaculately kept restaurant.

Signum ★★★
Malfa, via Scalo 15, tel. 0909844222
www.hotelsignum.it
Open mid March-October
30 rooms. Restaurant, swimming pool
Credit Cards: Diner's Club, Mastercard, Visa
Charming hotel built on the site of a farming hamlet. The rooms are in small houses set deep in the countryside. Local cuisine based on fresh fish from the day's catch.

Restaurants

Da Franco ❚❚
Santa Marina Salina, via Belvedere 8, tel. 0909843287
www.ristorantedafranco.com
Cuisine: Aeolian
Credit Cards: American Express, Diner's Club, Mastercard, Visa
A safe bet where you can try authentic cuisine with all kinds of seafood, surrounded by wonderful nature.

Porto Bello ⁙ ★
*Santa Marina Salina, via Bianchi 1,
tel. 0909843125*
Closed Wednesday (in winter)
Cuisine: Aeolian
Credit Cards: American Express,
Diner's Club, Mastercard, Visa
A pleasant dining room with
nautical decor and terraces with
a breath-taking view of the sea,
mainly fish specialties.

SAMBUCA DI SICILIA

How to get there
BY CAR: exit Santa Ninfa,
A29 motorway Palermo-
Mazara del Vallo
BY TRAIN: FS Railway Station
station in Castelvetrano

SAN VITO LO CAPO

🗓 *Azienda Autonoma
Provinciale Incremento
Turistico*
*Via Savoia, tel. 0923972464
www.apt.trapani.it*
🗓 *Azienda Autonoma
Provinciale Incremento
Turistico*
*Via Savoia, tel. 0923972464
www.apt.trapani.it*

How to get there
BY CAR: exit Castellammare
del Golfo, A29 motorway
Palermo-Mazara del Vallo
BY TRAIN: FS Railway
Station stations in Trapani
or Palermo; bus connections

Hotels
Miraspiaggia ★★ ♿
*Via Lungomare 44,
tel. 0923972355
www.miraspiaggia.it*
27 rooms. Restaurant, air
conditioned
Credit Cards: American Express,
Diner's Club, Mastercard, Visa
Built on the sea, bright rooms;
restaurant serves fish and local
produce.

Piccolo Mondo ★★
*Via Nino Bixio, tel. 0923972032
www.piccolomondohotel.net*
10 rooms. Restaurant, air
conditioned
Credit Cards: American Express,
Diner's Club, Mastercard, Visa
It's all in the name: just ten
rooms in a Mediterranen style
building. Immaculate furnishings
and facilities.

Riva del Sole ★★
*Via G. Arimondi 11,
tel. 0923972629
www.hotelrivadelsole.it*
9 rooms. Restaurant, air
conditioned
Credit Cards: American Express,
Diner's Club, Mastercard, Visa

Close to the sea, modern
Mediterranean style building,
with comfortable rooms, most of
which have large verandas.
Restaurant serves Sicilian and
classic cuisine.

Egitarso ★★★ ♿
*Via Lungomare 54,
tel. 0923972111
www.hotelegitarso.it*
42 rooms. Restaurant, parking,
air conditioned
Right on the beach, family
managed hotel; terrace with a
view for sunbathing and restaurant
serving typical Sicilian cuisine; al
fresco dining in summer.

Bed & Breakfast
Baglio La Luna
*Sauci Grande, on the road to
Riserva dello Zingaro,
tel. 3358362856
www.bagliolaluna.com*
The B&B is housed in an ancient
"baglio", on a bluff, with a view
of the cape, in the countryside.
Guests are accommodated in
three rooms furnished with
modern wooden furniture and
local crafts and have the use of
a sitting room and a garden with
a barbecue. Italian breakfast,
with local produce, is served
beneath the almond trees. On
request the landlords will
organise hiking expeditions and
cookery classes.

Da Pina
*Via Santuario 19,
tel. 0923972568
www.bed-breakfast-sanvito.it*
Not far from the sea, three
comfortable double rooms,
guests have access to the
beautiful terrace where Signora
Pina serves breakfast.

Restaurants
Alfredo ⁙ ♿
Valanga, tel. 0923972366
Closed Monday in low season
Cuisine: seafood
Credit Cards: American Express,
Diner's Club, Mastercard, Visa
Ancient 18th century building,
deep in the countryside; terrace
with seaview, Fish based cuisine,
fresh pasta first courses.

Pocho ⁙
*Isulidda Macari, S.P. Custonaci-
S. Vito, tel. 0923972525*
*Open March-November,
evenings only, closed Tuesday in
low season and Sunday
lunchtime in summer*
Cuisine: Sicilian and refined
cuisine
Credit Cards: American Express,
Diner's Club, Mastercard, Visa
Looking out onto the gulf of
Maccari, a welcoming and
elegant restaurant, with a
terrace overhanging the sea.

Varied fish-based cuisine;
couscous only on Sundays.

Health Centers
Capo San Vito ★★ 🏊 🏥
*Via S. Vito 1, tel. 0923972122
www.caposanvito.it*
Closed January-February
With its own private beach, on
the most beautiful stretch of the
Sicilian coast. Rooms are well-
appointed. The restaurant
serves Mediterranean food with
immaculately prepared Sicilian
dishes.
The Wellness Center is located
on the top floor of the structure
and is equipped with a jacuzzi,
mini pool, Finnish sauna and
Turkish bath, gym equipment
and a chill-out zone. You may
book the center for your own
exclusive use in complete
privacy from 9pm to 11pm.
Treatments. Manipulative and
therapeutic: thalassotherapy,
Chinese medicine,Tibetan
medicine, connective massage,
ayurvedic, Tuina and Trager
massage, Rolfing, lymphatic
drainage. For health of body and
mind: color therapy, aromatherapy.

At night
Gambrinus
Via Savoia 10, tel. 0923972225
Restaurant-pub 5 meters from
the beach: rustic furniture, cosy
atmosphere, low music,
excellent crepes.

The Murphy's Pub
Via Savoia 7
On the main street, typical
English style pub where you can
drink great beer and spend
a pleasant evening.

SANTA FLAVIA

Hotels
Kafara ★★★
*Sant'Elia, litoranea Mongerbino,
tel. 091957377
www.kafarahotel.it*
63 rooms. Restaurant, parking,
air conditioned, swimming pool,
sauna, tennis
Credit Cards: American Express,
Diner's Club, Mastercard, Visa
Built on the rocks overhanging
the sea, rooms with jacuzzis,
seawater swimming pool, piano
bar and entertainment.
Restaurant serves Sicilian and
international cuisine.

SANTA MARIA DI LICODIA

How to get there
BY CAR: exit Catania Est,
A18 motorway Messina-
Catania

SANTA MARINA SALINA

How to get there
BY FERRY: From Milazzo, links with Ustica Lines, Si.Re.Mar and N.G.I.; from Palermo, seasonal hydrofoil with Ustica Lines

SANT'ALFIO

How to get there
BY CAR: exit Giarre, A18 motorway Messina-Catania
BY TRAIN: FS Railway Station station in Riposto

Rural Lodgings
La Cirasella &
Petralia Finaita, via Trisciala 13, tel. 095968000
www.cirasella.com
Bikes are available.
Farm characterised by its concern for the environment. Accommodation in ancient renovated lava stone cottages with large terraces full of flowers.

Restaurants
Case Perrotta ⌑ &
Perrotta, via Andronico 2, tel. 095968928
www.caseperrotta.it
Closed Tuesday
Cuisine: Sicilian
Credit Cards: Mastercard, Visa
Former 17th century convent in the middle of a farmstead. Accommodation is available. You may also eat outside. Traditional dishes are offered with wine included.

SCIACCA

ⓘ Azienda Autonoma delle Terme
Via Agatocle 2, tel. 0925961111-800881079
www.termesciacca.it
ⓘ Azienda Autonoma di Cura Soggiorno e Turismo
Corso Vittorio Emanuele 84, tel. 092522744,
www.aziendaturismosciacca.it
ⓘ Ufficio Informazioni
G.H. Terme, via delle Terme 1, tel. 092523133
ⓘ Ufficio Informazioni del Comune
Corso Vittorio Emanuele 94, tel. 092586247

How to get there
BY CAR: exit Castelvetrano, A29 motorway Palermo-Mazara del Vallo
BY TRAIN: FS Railway Station station in Palermo; bus connection

Hotels
Villa Palocla *⁂*
Raganella, tel. 0925902812
www.villapalocla.it
8 rooms. Restaurant, parking, air conditioned, swimming pool
Credit Cards: American Express, Diner's Club, Mastercard, Visa
18th century country seat; charming and modern rooms; elegant restaurant, swimming pool and garden.

Rural Lodgings
Montalbano ★
Scunchipani, via Montagna Ferraro 6, tel. 092580154
montalb.supereva.it
Restaurant, swimming pool, availability of bikes
Among citrus orchards and olive groves, a pretty, modern rural lodging; with a view of the sea and the mountains.

Bed & Breakfast
Aliai
Via Gaie di Garaffe 60, tel. 0925905388
www.aliai.com
This comfortable hotel was formerly a fisherman's dwelling. Sicilian style rooms with a sea view. Gracious hospitality from the Cavataio family.

Restaurants
Badia Grande ⍾
Piazza Noceto 11, tel. 092583766
Cuisine: Sicilian
Credit Cards: American Express, Diner's Club, Mastercard, Visa
Inside a beautifully conserved monastery, in the high part of the town, an immaculate restaurant offering traditional food.

Hostaria del Vicolo ⍾ &
Vicolo Sammaritano 10, tel. 092523071
www.hostariadelvicolo.com
Closed Monday
Cuisine: Mediterranean
Credit Cards: American Express, Diner's Club, Mastercard, Visa
In the old town center, a pleasant, gourmet restaurant. Here the Sicilian passion for food can be appreciated to the full. Beautiful cellar only stocks island labels.

Porto San Paolo ⍾
Largo S. Paolo 1, tel. 092527982
Closed Wednesday
Cuisine: Sicilian
Credit Cards: American Express, Diner's Club, Mastercard, Visa
On the harbour, with a terrace

overlooking the sea; you can dine in elegant late 18th century dining rooms.A variety of fish and a large selection of wines, including some from Spain and Chile.

Amadeus ⌑ & ★
Corso Vittorio Emanuele II 186, tel. 092523203
Closed Thursday in winter
Cuisine: Sicilian
Credit Cards: American Express, Diner's Club, Mastercard, Visa
In a period building in the old town center; regional cuisine. Kitchen open after 10pm. Wine list with Sicilian labels.

La Vecchia Conza ⌑
Via Gerardi 39, tel. 092525385
www.vecchiaconza.it
Closed Monday
Cuisine: regional
Credit Cards: Mastercard, Visa
Large rustic style restaurant adorned with a red brick arch; strictly fish cuisine; mostly Sicilan wines.

Health Centers
G.H. delle Terme *⁂* ⚘
Viale Nuove Terme 1092523133
www.termehotel.com
With magnificent views this is a modern and functional hotel on three floors The structure offers numerous spa treatments, especially fangotherapy, balneotherapy and physiotherapy. The spa pools are located inside the complex and filled with sulphurous water. There are two restaurants: La Buvette and Sala Ferdinandea. Both have special menus and a large selection of wines.

At night
Armagnac
Via Lido Esperando
Now one of the most popular pubs with all age-groups, who have chosen the beach of Stazzone as a place to hang out, in summer and in winter. The atmosphere is warm and friendly with an enormous choice of cocktails and snacks. In summer there are tables outside where you can also take a stroll along the seafront.

Vittorio Emanuele
Corso Vittorio Emanuele 230, tel. 092585080
In the old town center, the place to be seen in Sciacca: ideal for a drink or a snack in a friendly, pleasant atmosphere, with a great deal of music and merriment. Tables outside in summer.

SCICLI

ℹ Pro Loco
Via Castellana 2,
tel. 0932932782

How to get there

BY CAR: exit Catania Est,
A18 motorway Messina-
Catania, exit Catania Sud,
A19 motorway Palermo-
Catania

BY TRAIN: FS Railway
Station corso Mazzini

Hotels

Baia Samuele ★★★ ♿
Sampieri, tel. 0932848111
www.baiasamuele.it
244 rooms. Restaurant, parking,
air conditioned, swimming pool,
tennis, gym
Credit Cards: American Express,
Diner's Club, Mastercard, Visa
On a gentle slope close to the
beach, a hotel-village with well-
appointed rooms and a
restaurant with a view. Congress
center also suitable for small
functions.

Bed & Breakfast

Loggia dell'Acanto
Balata, tel. 0932932701
www.loggiadellacanto.it
Lovely villa in a picturesque and
peaceful position in the heart of
the Sicilian baroque area: two
tastefully furnished double
rooms and a triple. The sea is
7km away.

Restaurants

Al Molo ⑂
Donnalucata, via Perello 90,
tel. 0932937710
Closed Monday
Cuisine: fish
Credit Cards: American Express,
Diner's Club, Mastercard, Visa
Halfway round the harbour, a
small restaurant with al fresco
dining on a veranda overlooking
the sea. Simple seafood dishes.

SCOPELLO

How to get there

BY CAR: exit Castellammare
del Golfo, A29 motorway
Palermo-Mazara del Vallo

BY TRAIN: FS Railway
Station station in
Castellammare del Golfo

Rural Lodgings

Tenute Plaia ♿
Scopello 3, tel. 0924541476
www.plaiavini.com
Swimming pool
Credit Cards: American Express,
Visa, Mastercard

A structure typical of the "bagli"
of Trapani with a large courtyard
surrounded by different types of
accommodation, from which you
can enjoy a beautiful view of the
sea and the garden.

At night

Bar La Palma
Baglio Isonzo, tel. 0924541116
In the courtyard of an 18th
century "baglio" with a slender
eucalyptus tree: the ideal place
for relaxing with friends.

SEGESTA

How to get there

BY CAR: exit Segesta, A29
motorway Palermo-Mazara
del Vallo

BY TRAIN: FS Railway
Station station in Trapani

Museums, Monuments and Churches

Tempio
tel. 0924952356
Opening times: October-March:
Monday-Sunday 9.00 16.00,
April-September: Monday-
Sunday 9.00-18.00.

SELINUNTE

**ℹ Azienda Autonoma
Provinciale Incremento
Turistico**
Archeological site,
tel. 092446251
www.apt.trapani.it

How to get there

BY CAR: exit Castelvetrano,
A29 motorway Palermo-
Mazara del Vallo

BY TRAIN: FS Railway
Station station in
Castelvetrano; bus
connection

Hotels

Alceste ★★★ ★
Marinella, via Alceste 21,
tel. 092446184
www.hotelalceste.it
26 rooms. Restaurant, parking,
air conditioned
Credit Cards: American Express,
Diner's Club, Mastercard, Visa
In the high part of the village, a
hotel with modern and well-
appointed rooms. Buffet
breakfast with a terrace
overlooking the sea: restaurant
serves traditional cuisine.

Restaurants

Pierrot ⑂ ★
Marinella, via Marco Polo 108,
tel. 092446205
www.ristorantepierrotselinunte.it
Closed Tuesday in winter
Cuisine: Mediterranean

Credit Cards: American Express,
Diner's Club, Mastercard, Visa
With a view of the sea and the
famous Acropoli, this restaurant
has a pleasant feel. The kitchen
is open after 22 and serves
traditional Mediterranean food;
pizzas too.

Museums, Monuments and Churches

Parco archeologico
tel. 092446251
Opening times: April-October:
Monday-Sunday 9.00-18.00,
November-March: Monday-
Sunday 9.00-16.00.

SICULIANA

How to get there

BY CAR: exit Imera, A19
motorway Palermo-Catania

BY TRAIN: FS Railway
Station station in
Agrigento

Hotels

Villa Sikania Park Hotel ★★★ ♿
S.S. 115 al km 169,3,
tel. 0922817818
www.villasikania.com
42 rooms. Restaurant, parking,
air conditioned, swimming pool
Credit Cards: American Express,
Diner's Club, Visa
Hotel with glassed pillars and
arches; large, modern rooms.
Conceived for relaxing holidays
or as a base for cultural trips.

SIRACUSA

**ℹ Azienda Autonoma
Provinciale Incremento
Turistico**
Via S. Sebastiano 43,
tel. 093167710-0931481200
www.apt-siracusa.it
**ℹ Azienda Autonoma
Soggiorno e Turismo**
Via Maestranza 33,
tel. 0931464255
www.aatsr.it

How to get there

BY CAR: exit Catania Est,
A18 motorway to Messina,
exit Catania Sud, A19
motorway to Palermo

BY TRAIN: FS Railway
Station piazza Stazione

Hotels

Domus Mariae ★★★
Via Vittorio Veneto 76,
tel. 093124854
www.sistemia.it/domusmariae
12 rooms. Restaurant, air
conditioned
Credit Cards: American Express,
Diner's Club, Mastercard, Visa

In the heart of the old city center, a house with large, comfortable rooms, run by Orsoline nuns; regional cooking.

Gran Bretagna ★★★ &
Via Savoia 21, tel. 093168765
www.hotelgranbretagna.it
17 rooms. Parking, air conditioned
Credit Cards: American Express, Diner's Club, Mastercard, Visa
On the island of Ortigia, renovated 18th century building; spacious rooms, some of which have ancient frescoed ceilings. You can see the ancient fortifications beneath the floor in the breakfast room.

Gutkowski ★★★ & ★
Via Lungomare di Levante 26, tel. 0931465861
www.guthotel.it
26 rooms. Air conditioned
Credit Cards: American Express, Diner's Club, Mastercard, Visa
Small hotel with a warm ambience; sitting room with fireplace, comfortable rooms, internet point. Breakfast includes organic products.

Relax ★★★ & ★
Viale Epipoli 159, tel. 0931740122
www.hotelrelax.it
57 rooms. Restaurant, parking, air conditioned, swimming pool
Credit Cards: American Express, Diner's Club, Mastercard, Visa
In the Neapolis park, a small Mediterranean style building; comfortable rooms with a view of the harbour or the old city center; buffet breakfast, restaurant.

Caiammari ★☆★ &
Isola Fanusa, via D. Impellizzeri, tel. 0931721217
www.caiammari.sr.it
18 rooms. Restaurant, parking, air conditioned, swimming pool
Credit Cards: American Express, Diner's Club, Mastercard, Visa
Close to the beach of Lido Arenella, a renovated 18th century villa; elegant hospitality in well-appointed rooms; some suites.

Grand Hotel ★☆★ & ★
Viale Mazzini 12, tel. 0931464600
www.grandhotelsr.it
58 rooms. Restaurant, parking, air conditioned
Credit Cards: American Express, Diner's Club, Mastercard, Visa
On the island of Ortigia, overlooking the sea, an art nouveau style hotel with modern rooms and pleasant reception rooms. Internet point, roof garden restaurant facing the sea.

Lady Lusya ★☆★ & ★
Cassibile, feudo Spinagallo, tel. 0931710277
www.ladylusya.it
17 rooms. Restaurant, parking, air conditioned, swimming pool
Credit Cards: American Express, Mastercard, Visa
A charming hotel which is the result of the practical and conservative restoration of an aristocratic 17th-18th century villa. Comfortable rooms, impeccable cuisine, sun-roof, country walks in the lemon orchard which belongs to the estate.

Rural Lodgings
Case Damma & ★
Damma, S.P. 14 al km 9, tel. 0931717405
www.casedamma.it
Bikes are available
Ancient farm with 19th century architecture. Modern comfortable rooms in the renovated hay-loft and stores.

La Perciata &
Via Spinagallo 77, tel. 0931717366
www.perciata.it
Swimming pool, tennis
Credit Cards: American Express, Visa
On the Mare Monti road, a farm well-equipped with sports facilities and home comforts. 10km from Siracusa.

Limoneto &
Via del Platano 3, tel. 0931717352
www.emmeti.it/limoneto
Credit Cards: Bancomat
Beautiful farm between the sea and the mountains, Siracusa, the Fiume Ciane nature reserve and the agricultural and sheep-rearing interior, all just waiting to be explored. Fruit-picking on the farm.

Terrauzza sul Mare & ★
Via Blanco 8, tel. 0931714362
www.terramar.it
Restaurant, availability of bikes
Credit Cards: American Express, CartaSi, Diner's Club, Visa
Farm with direct accesss to the sea, accommodation provided in small air-conditioned apartments. Pottery studio with lessons in traditional Sicilian pottery decoration.

Villa Lucia & ★
Isola, traversa Mondello 1, tel. 0931721007
Restaurant, swimming pool
Credit Cards: American Express, CartaSi, Diner's Club, Visa
Farm set in the heart of centuries old parkland: a private home built in the early 20th

century in the style of a hotel and a rustic annex, with self-catering rooms and mini-apartments.

Bed & Breakfast
Archè
Via Faro Massoliveri 24, tel. 0931721094
www.bandbarche.it
A beautiful stone villa dating from the Fifties, positioned by the sea, opposite the island of Ortigia. Guests are welcomed into a warm atmosphere created by period and art nouveau furnishings. A breakfast of organic products and home-produce, is served in a gazebo in the garden or in the kitchen. Guests may also use a sitting room with a fireplace and large windows overlooking the rocks and a private path down to the sea.

Dolce Casa
Isola, via Lido Sacramento 4, tel. 0931721135
www.bbdolcecasa.it
Situated in the environs of lido Arenella, in a residential area just a few minutes from the center of Siracusa, Dolce Casa is a large villa surrounded by a blooming garden with palm trees, pines and a terrace. Guests are given the choice of six double rooms on the top floor and four on the ground floor, equipped with air conditioning and decorated in country style. They may also use the sitting room. Breakfast, made by the landlady, includes home-baking such as doughnuts and jam tarts and fresh fruit juice. The archaeological site is a short distance away.

Dolce Silenzio
Via Mirabella 18, tel. 093164201
www.dolcesilenzio.too.it
Situated on the island of Ortigia, in the most picturesque part of the city, this B&B, housed in a building dating from the 1600s, offers guests a double room (eventually 2 more beds may be added) in the attic, furnished with period pieces and modern furniture. Italian breakfast is served on the terrace or in the kitchen.

Oikos
Via delle Carceri Vecchie 21/23, tel. 0931483073, www.bboikos.it
Very central, behind Piazza Duomo, eleven rooms of various sizes, all furnished with reproduction furniture, some with balconies overlooking the sea.

Restaurants

Archimede ⅱ
Via Gemmellaro 8,
tel. 093169701
www.trattoriaarchimede.it
Closed Sunday
Cuisine: Sicilian
Credit Cards: American Express,
Diner's Club, Mastercard, Visa
Three welcoming dining rooms
separated by 14th century
arches, open since 1938; fish
specialties. On the other side of
the street, there is a pizza parlor
owned by the same
management.

Darsena-da Ianuzzo ⅱ &
Riva Garibaldi 6,
tel. 093161522
Closed Wednesday
Cuisine: Sicilian
Credit Cards: American Express,
Diner's Club, Mastercard, Visa
Welcoming and functional,
thanks too to the summer
veranda overlooking the sea;
the kitchen is open until 23.
Mainly fish specialties.

Don Camillo ⅱ
Via Maestranza 92/100,
tel. 093167133
www.ristorantedoncamillo
siracusa.it
Closed Sunday
Cuisine: Sicilian
Credit Cards: American Express,
Diner's Club, Mastercard, Visa
On the island of Ortigia, in a
fifteenth century building, fresh
cuisine consisting of light, tasty
dishes, prepared with excellent
quality ingredients.

La Spiaggetta ⅱ &
Fontane Bianche,
viale dei Lidi 473,
tel. 0931790334
Closed Tuesday in winter
Cuisine: Sicilian
Credit Cards: American Express,
Diner's Club, Mastercard, Visa
Restaurant with large windows
overlooking a natural cove. Tasty
local dishes and pizzas.

Cantinaccia ⅰ
Via XX Settembre 13,
tel. 093165945
www.trattorialacantinaccia.it
Closed Tuesday
Cuisine: Sicilian
Credit Cards: Diner's Club,
Mastercard, Visa
Centrally located, rustic style
restaurant, with a veranda
facing the sea and a garden; the
menu is influenced by the daily
fish catch.

Il Cenacolo ⅰ ★
Via del Consiglio Reginale 10,
tel. 093165099

www.trattoriailcenacolo.it
Closed Wednesday (except in
summer)
Cuisine: Mediterranean
Credit Cards: American Express,
Diner's Club, Mastercard, Visa
In an ancient building in the old
city center, fish specialties
inspired by Mediterranean
traditions. Themed evenings and
singing staff.

Jonico-'a Rutta 'e Ciauli ⅰ
Riviera Dionisio il Grande 194,
tel. 093165540
Closed Tuesday
Cuisine: Sicilian
Credit Cards: American Express,
Diner's Club, Mastercard, Visa
On the clifftop in an art nouveau
villa dating from the beginning
of the 20th century. A rustic
ambience with an ancient stone
fireplace and terrace with a
view. Traditional dishes, pizza
too.

Osteria da Mariano ⅰ
Vicolo Zuccalà 9,
tel. 093167444
Closed Tuesday
Cuisine: Sicilian
Credit Cards: American Express,
Diner's Club, Mastercard, Visa
Informal restaurant with a
friendly atmosphere, benefited
by the courtesy of the manager.
Simple cuisine with recipes from
the hinterland of Siracusa.

At night

Nuovo Caffè Centrale
Ortigia, piazza Archimede 22
There's rooms to sit outside,
facing a gorgeous fountain.

Museums, Monuments and Churches

Castello Eurìalo
tel. 0931711773
Opening times: Monday-Sunday
9.00-16.00 an hour and a half
before sundown.

Castello Maniace
Piazza Federico II,
tel. 0931464420
Opening times: 8.30-13.00.

Galleria Regionale di Palazzo Bellomo
Via Capodieci 14/16,
tel. 093169511
Opening times: Tuesday-
Saturday 9.00-19.00; Sundays
and public holidays 9.00-14.00.

Museo Archeologico Regionale "Paolo Orsi"
Viale Teocrito 66,
tel. 0931464022
www.ibmsnet.it/siracusa/paolo
ors.html
Opening times: Monday 15.00-
17.00; Tuesday-Saturday 9.00-

13.00, 15.00-17.00; Sundays and
public holidays 9.00-13.00.

Parco archeologico della Neàpolis
Viale Paradiso,
tel. 093166206
Opening times: Monday-Sunday
9.00-two hours before sundown.

SOLUNTO

How to get there
BY CAR: exit Bagheria, A19
motorway Palermo-Catania
BY TRAIN: FS Railway
Station station in Palermo

STRÒMBOLI

Hotels

La Sciara Residence ★★★
Piscità, via Barnao 5,
tel. 090986004
www.lasciara.it
Open April-October
62 rooms. Restaurant, parking,
swimming pool, tennis
Credit Cards: American Express,
Diner's Club, Mastercard, Visa
Set in a nature reserve,
consisting of a central body and
pretty little houses. The terrace
overlooking the sea and the
stylish furnishings lend a warm
atmosphere.

La Sirenetta Park Hotel ★★★ &
Ficogrande, via Marina 33,
tel. 090986025
www.lasirenetta.it
Open April-October
55 rooms. Restaurant, air
conditioned, swimming pool,
tennis, gym
Credit Cards: American Express,
Diner's Club, Mastercard, Visa
Aeolian style building with
rooms aranged around the crest
of the vulcano. Seawater
swimming pool and jacuzzi,
scuba diving center and
amphitheatre; piano bar and
buffet on the sea shore.

La Locanda del Barbablù
San Vincenzo, via Vittorio
Emanuele 17/19,
tel. 090986118
www.barbablu.it
Open March-October
6 rooms. Restaurant, air
conditioned
Credit Cards: American Express,
Diner's Club, Mastercard, Visa
Preserves the charm of what
was once a "maritime hostel".
Redolent atmosphere in the six
roooms which overlook the sea
or the vulcano. Terrace for
sunbathing.

Restaurants

Ai Gechi ⍥
Via Salina 12, tel. 090986213
Open evenings only (lunchtime bookings only)
Cuisine: Aeolian
Credit Cards: American Express, Mastercard, Visa
Romantic ambience which spills out onto a terrace with a view. Seafood. "Fusion" and Burmese cuisine on request.

TAORMINA

ℹ Azienda Autonoma Soggiorno e Turismo
Piazza S. Caterina,
tel. 094223243
www.gate2taormina.com

How to get there
BY CAR: exit Taormina, A18 motorway Messina-Catania
BY TRAIN: FS Railway Station station in Giardini Naxos; bus connection

Hotels

Condor ⋆⋆ ⭐
Via Dietro Cappuccini 25,
tel. 094223124
www.condorhotel.com
Open March-mid November
12 rooms. Parking, air conditioned
Credit Cards: American Express, Diner's Club, Mastercard, Visa
Small Mediterranean style building on four floors. Breakfast served on the panoramic terrace, also used as a solarium. Courteous family hospitality.

La Campanella ⋆⋆ ⭐
Via Circonvallazione 3,
tel. 094223381
12 rooms.
Sixties villa in the middle of a garden with bright, soundproof rooms. The collection of rare Sicilian carts is something to see; family hospitality.

Villa Ducale ⋆⋆ ⭐
Via L. da Vinci 60,
tel. 094228153
www.villaducale.com
18 rooms. Parking, air conditioned
Credit Cards: American Express, Diner's Club, Mastercard, Visa
Elegant late 19th century villa which maintains intact the atmosphere of the age. Romantic and well-appointed rooms; hall with internet point.

Bel Soggiorno ⋆⋆⋆
Via Pirandello 60,
tel. 094223342
30 rooms. Parking

Credit Cards: American Express, Diner's Club, Mastercard, Visa
Peaceful and charming early 20th century hotel with bed and breakfast; rooms with fireplaces and wrought iron beds.
Breakfast served on the veranda or on the terrace.

Isabella ⋆⋆⋆
Corso Umberto 58,
tel. 094223153
www.gaishotels.com
32 rooms. Restaurant, air conditioned
Credit Cards: American Express, Diner's Club, Mastercard, Visa
Charming hotel in the old city center, with bright rooms, terrace with a view and summer roof restaurant. Shuttle service to the private beach in the summer.

Vello d'Oro ⋆⋆⋆
Via Fazzello 2, tel. 094223788
www.hotelvellodoro.com
Open March-October
50 rooms. Restaurant, parking, air conditioned
Credit Cards: American Express, Diner's Club, Mastercard, Visa
Between the white of the walls and the red of the roofs, the building is embellished with Moorish flourishes; restaurant is also open to non hotel guests.

Villa Belvedere ⋆⋆⋆ ⭐
Via Bagnoli Croce 79,
tel. 094223791
www.villabelvedere.it
Open mid-March-mid-November and Christmas
49 rooms. Restaurant, parking, air conditioned, swimming pool
Credit Cards: Mastercard, Visa
Villa dating from the early nineteen hundreds, with panoramic views; centrally located. Air-conditioned rooms, pool side restaurant, supervised pay car park.

Villa Fiorita ⋆⋆⋆
Via Pirandello 39,
tel. 094224122
www.villafioritahotel.com
25 rooms.Air conditioned, swimming pool
Credit Cards: American Express, Mastercard, Visa
A renovated and extended villa dating from the early nineteen hundreds. A happy marriage of ancient and modern. Continental breakfast.

Villa Schuler ⋆⋆⋆
Piazzetta Bastione on the corner of via Roma, tel. 094223481
www.villaschuler.com
Open March-mid November
25 rooms. Parking, air conditioned, tennis

Credit Cards: American Express, Diner's Club, Mastercard, Visa
Early 20th century renovated villa deep in parkland. Extremely comfortable rooms, plus three junior suites; "à la carte" breakfast, mountain bikes available.

Villa Sirina ⋆⋆⋆
Contrada Sirina, tel. 094251776
www.villasirina.tao.it
Open March-October
15 rooms. Restaurant, parking, air conditioned, swimming pool
Credit Cards: American Express, Diner's Club, Mastercard, Visa
Pretty villa surrounded by countryside, furnished with local ancient handicrafts. Large rooms with balconies or terraces, sweet and savoury buffet breakfast.

Atahotel Capotaormina ⋆⋆⋆ ♿ ⭐
Capo Taormina,
via Nazionale 105,
tel. 0942572111
www.capotaorminahotel.com
Open March
200 rooms. Restaurant, parking, air conditioned, swimming pool, sauna, gym
Credit Cards: American Express, Diner's Club, Mastercard, Visa
On a short promontory, with an elevator which takes you down to the beach; seawater swimming pool and jacuzzi. Elegant and well-appointed structure, with its own beauty center and restaurant.

Excelsior Palace ⋆⋆⋆ ⭐
Via Toselli 8, tel. 094223975
www.excelsiorpalacetaormina.it
88 rooms. Restaurant, parking, air conditioned, swimming pool
Credit Cards: American Express, Diner's Club, Mastercard, Visa
Building with characteristic Moorish facade, provides renovated rooms with carpets and functional bathrooms; restaurant serves classic cuisine. Courteous hospitality.

Méditerranée ⋆⋆⋆ ⭐
Via Circonvallazione 61,
tel. 094223901
www.taorminahotels.com
Open mid March-October
50 rooms. Restaurant, parking, air conditioned, swimming pool
Credit Cards: American Express, Diner's Club, Mastercard, Visa
In an enviable position, amidst the scents and colors of Mediterranean flora; comfortable, welcoming and professionally managed.

Villa Fabbiano ⋆⋆⋆
Via Pirandello 81 on the corner of via Bagnoli Croci,

tel. 0942626058
www.villafabbiano.com
Open March-October
27 rooms. Parking, air
conditioned, swimming pool
Credit Cards: Mastercard, Visa
Original, renovated late 19th
century building, provides a
mixture of warmth and
efficiency. Comfortable suites
and rooms, terrace with winter
garden and view.

Villa Paradiso *∗* ★
Via Roma 2, tel. 094223922
37 rooms. Restaurant, air
conditioned
Credit Cards: American Express,
Diner's Club, Mastercard, Visa
Comfortable, genteel ambience;
bar and garden with a sea view,
restaurant with terrace, library.
Shuttle service to private beach,
with seawater swimming pool
and jacuzzi.

Villa Sant'Andrea *∗* &
Mazzarò, via Nazionale 137,
tel. 094223125
www.framonhotels.com
Open March-mid October
78 rooms. Restaurant, air
conditioned
Credit Cards: American Express,
Diner's Club, Mastercard, Visa
19th century villa overlooking
the sea, deep in subtropical
vegetation; buffet breakfast,
restaurant serving regional and
classic cuisine.

Bed & Breakfast
Arca
Via Leonardo da Vinci 18,
tel. 094228611
www.arcataormina.com
In a picturesque spot with a
view of the sea and Etna, a
beautiful 1950s house
surrounded by a citrus orchard.
Three pleasant triple rooms
(only one has its own bathroom)
and a lovely garden. The old city
center and sea are a few
minutes away.

Restaurants
Casa Grugno ⅢⅢ
Via S. Maria de' Greci,
tel. 094221208
www.casagrugno.it
Open evenings only, closed
Wednesday
Cuisine: classic
Credit Cards: American Express,
Diner's Club, Mastercard, Visa
A restaurant inside an ancient
building, with a dining room
brightened by trompe l'oeils
which take up the yellow-orange
motifs of the period drapery.
The cuisine is a light and
elegant version of regional
dishes which may sometimes be
a little on the rich side.

'A Zammàra ⅢⅢ
Via F.lli Bandiera 15,
tel. 094224408
www.zammara.it
Closed Wednesday in August
Cuisine: of Messina and Sicilian
Credit Cards: Diner's Club,
Mastercard, Visa
The name of this restaurant, set
deep in an orange and lemon
grove, means agave in Sicilian.
Regional cuisine. Excellent
selection of wines, liqueurs and
distillates.

Al Duomo ⅢⅢ
Vico Ebrei 11, tel. 0942625656
www.ristorantealduomo.it
Closed Monday (in low season)
Cuisine: Sicilian
Credit Cards: American Express,
Diner's Club, Mastercard, Visa
Friendly restaurant in the center,
with bright colours and pleasant
al fresco dining. Well-prepared,
elegant cuisine serving
specialties based on the best of
local traditions.

Delfino-da Angelo ⅢⅢ ★
Mazzarò, via Nazionale,
tel. 094223004
Open mid April-October
Cuisine: of Messina
Credit Cards: American Express,
Diner's Club, Mastercard, Visa
Immaculate ambience, with a
pleasant terrace with a view;
seafood.

Griglia ⅢⅢ &
Corso Umberto 54,
tel. 094223980
www.hotelvillasonia.com
Closed Tuesday
Cuisine: of Messina
Credit Cards: American Express,
Diner's Club, Visa
Excellent grills, but also good
first courses. Do not miss the
typical "cassata" at the end of
the meal.

Il Ciclope Ⅰ & ★
Corso Umberto,
tel. 094223263
Closed Wednesday
Cuisine: Messina
Credit Cards: American Express,
Diner's Club, Mastercard, Visa
In the heart of the old town
center, with a summer terrace;
elegant service and impeccable
family management since 1970.
Good value for money.

At night
Marrakech
Piazza S. Domenico
Arabic atmosphere with
cushions, mosaics, wrought iron
ornaments and oriental music;
we recommend the mint tea,
although all kinds of drinks and
cocktails are served.

Tout Va
Via Pirandello 70,
tel. 094223824
One of the most popular discos
in the area: many dance floors,
good music and a great deal of
fun to be had.

Ziggy Bar
Piazza S. Domenico 2/A,
tel. 3336565978
In an 18th century villa in the
heart of Taormina, a cocktail bar
with some outrageous furnishings,
open until late at night, popular
with all age-groups.

Museums, Monuments and Churches
Palazzo Corvaja
Piazza Vittorio Emanuele II,
tel. 094223243
Opening times: Monday-
Saturday 9.00-14, 16.00-19.00.

Teatro greco
Via Teatro Greco 40,
tel. 094223220
Opening times: Monday-Sunday
9am-an hour before sundown.

TERME VIGLIATORE

> **How to get there**
> **BY CAR:** exit Falcone or exit
> di Patti, A20 motorway
> Messina-Palermo
> **BY TRAIN:** FS Railway
> Station largo Stazione

Hotels
Il Gabbiano ★★★ & ★
Marchesana, lungomare
Marchesana 4, tel. 0909782343
www.hotelgabbiano.org
40 rooms. Restaurant, parking,
air conditioned, swimming pool
Credit Cards: American Express,
Diner's Club, Mastercard, Visa
Small building with well-
equipped beach, 1km from
Castroreale. Large rooms,
panoramic restaurant, swimming
pool with jacuzzi, reception and
conference rooms, internet point.

Health Centers
G.H. Terme ★★★ ★
Viale delle Terme 85,
tel. 0909781078
Open May-mid October
A modern structure, surrounded
by a large park, opposite the
Isole Eolie. This is one of the
most well- equipped spas in
Sicily, offering every major spa
and beauty treatment. The
restaurant serves Mediterranean
dishes and international cuisine.

Museums, Monuments and Churches
Villa romana
tel. 0909740488
Opening times: Monday-Sunday
9.00-one hour before sundown.

‡‡‡ / ∗ Hotels ⅢⅢⅢ / Ⅰ Restaurants & Disabled ★ Special TCI Rates ⚕ Thermal spa 🐾 Health Center

TERMINI IMERESE

How to get there
BY CAR: exit Termini Imerese, A19 motorway Palermo-Catania

BY TRAIN: FS Railway Station piazza Europa

Hotels

Himera Polis Hotel *⚹*
S.S. 113 - zona Buonfornello, tel. 0918140566
55 rooms. Restaurant, parking, air conditioned, sauna, gym
Credit Cards: American Express, Diner's Club, Mastercard, Visa
Mediterranean style building, with large rooms and rustic furnishings, comfortable hall and restaurant. Courteous and helpful staff.

Health Centers

G.H. delle Terme *⚹* ♨
Piazza delle Terme 2, tel. 0918113557
www.grandhoteldelleterme.it
Housed in a late 19th century building, guests may use the facilities for traditional health treatments and leisure time activities; in addition, a gym, thermal pool, private beach, three restaurants, piano bar, large reception rooms and a park make this an ideal place for an amusing and relaxing holiday. A medical check-up is offered in the spa center. The complex also has a beauty center and a center for physiokinesitherapy.

Museums, Monuments and Churches

Museo Civico "Baldassare Romano"
Via M.tel. Cicerone, tel. 0918128550
www.comune.termini-imerese.pa.it
Opening times: Tuesday-Saturday 9.00-13.00, 16.00-19.00; Sunday 9.00-13.00.

TINDARI

ℹ Azienda Autonoma Soggiorno e Turismo
Via del Teatro Greco 15, tel. 0941369184, www.pattietindari.it

How to get there
BY CAR: Falcone, A20 motorway Messina-Palermo

BY TRAIN: FS Railway Station station in Patti; bus connection

Museums, Monuments and Churches

Scavi di Tindari
Via Teatro Greco, tel. 0941369023
Opening times: October-May: Monday-Sunday 9.00- an hour before sundown, June-September: Monday-Sunday 9.00-19.00.

TRAPANI

ℹ Azienda Provinciale per il Turismo
Via Francesco d'Assisi 27, tel. 0923545511
www.apt.trapani.it

ℹ Ufficio Informazioni Azienda Provinciale per il Turismo
Piazzetta Scarlatti, tel. 092329000
www.apt.trapani.it

How to get there
BY CAR: exit Trapani, A29 motorway Trapani-Alcamo spur

BY TRAIN: FS Railway Station piazza Umberto I

BY FERRY: From Cagliari, Tirrenia Navigazione ferries; from Naples, Ustica and Favignana, seasonal hydrofoil with Ustica Lines; links to Pantelleria with Si.Re.Mar ferries and Ustica Lines

Hotels

Nuovo Albergo Russo *** ⭐
Via Tintori 4, tel. 092322166
35 rooms. Parking, air conditioned
Credit Cards: Mastercard, Visa
A renovated structure located near the S. Lorenzo cathedral; it has an arrangement with restaurant "Picolit" and tavern "Al Lumi", two minutes away.

Vittoria ***
Via Crispi 4, tel. 0923873044
www.hotelvittoriatrapani.it
65 rooms. Air conditioned
Credit Cards: American Express, Diner's Club, Mastercard, Visa
Comfortable hotel wih bed and breakfast on six floors not far from the sea; air-conditioned rooms, multi-purpose conference room. Buffet breakfast.

Baia dei Mulini *⚹*
San Cusumano, lungomare Alighieri, tel. 0923562400
www.baiadeimulini.it
93 rooms. Restaurant, parking, air conditioned, swimming pool, tennis
Credit Cards: American Express, Diner's Club, Mastercard, Visa
Modern and comfortable, recently renovated house with Mediterranean style furniture and good sports facilities.

Crystal *⚹* ♿
Via S. Giovanni Bosco 12, tel. 092320000
www.framon-hotels.com
70 rooms. Restaurant, air conditioned
Credit Cards: American Express, Diner's Club, Mastercard, Visa
A short walk from the shopping district, this structure provides a good level of accommodation. Large, well-appointed rooms; restaurant "Cycas" with pretty garden.

Rural Lodgings

Duca di Castelmonte ♿
Xitta, via S. Motisi 3, tel. 0923526139
www.ducadicastelmonte.it
Swimming pool, availability of bikes
Credit Cards: American Express, CartaSi
An early 19th century renovated "Baglio" with accommodation in the stables, barn and stores; beautiful collection of historical farming implements, kept in the ancient oil-mill.

Restaurants

Taverna Paradiso 🍴 ♿
Lungomare D. Alighieri 22, tel. 092322303
Closed Sunday
Cuisine: seafood
Credit Cards: American Express, Diner's Club, Mastercard, Visa
Close to the fish market, a friendly ambience, with space for al fresco dining outside, mainly fish menu.

Ai Lumi 🍴 ♿
Corso Vittorio Emanuele 75, tel. 0923872418, www.ailumi.it
Closed Sunday
Cuisine: Sicilian
Credit Cards: American Express, Diner's Club, Mastercard, Visa
Restaurant in the old city center with a good choice of wines, oils, cheeses and home-made desserts. The specialties on the menu reflect the flavors of the sea and the countryside around Trapani.

Trattoria Cantina Siciliana 🍴
Via Giudecca 32, tel. 092328673
www.cantinasiciliana.it
Cuisine: Sicilian
Credit Cards: Visa
Restaurant characterised by typical Sicilian cuisine (fish couscous); wonderful regional wine list and sale of typical products.

At night

Irish Pub
Via Palermo 94, tel. 0923552424
One of the best-known pubs in the city: the atmosphere and ambience are typical of an Irish

pub with wooden tables and chairs and rivers of draught beer to drink with "bruschette", grilled sandwiches and fries. Live music sometimes.

Per...Bacco
Via G. B. Fardella 346,
tel. 092322062

Not just a wine bar: as well as a well-stocked cellar with mainly Sicilian wines, you can have meals and quick snacks with platters of local cold meats and cheeses, hearty salads and much more besides. Wood and stone furniture, low music, friendly and lively atmosphere, open until 5. One of the most popular and well-loved pubs with all age-groups.

Museums, Monuments and Churches

Museo Regionale "Conte Agostino Pepoli"
Via Conte Agostino Pepoli 180,
tel. 0923553269-0923531242
www.regione.sicilia.it
Opening times: Monday-Saturday 9.00-13.30; Sundays and public holidays 9.00-12.30.

TRECASTAGNI

> **How to get there**
> **BY CAR:** exit Acireale, A18 motorway Messina-Catania

Bed & Breakfast

Casa Billotta
Via Galileo Galilei 3,
tel. 0957806390
www.casabillotta.it

In a picturesque position on the slopes of Etna, this pretty 19th century house has a wine- cellar open to the public and two apartments with kitchens and private bathrooms. Hearty breakfast with home-made jams and fruit pies.

Restaurants

Villa Taverna ⌑ &
Corso Colombo 42,
tel. 0957806458
Open evenings only
Cuisine: Sicilian
Credit Cards: Visa
Restaurant typical of the old working class district of Catania. Typical regional dishes lovingly prepared.

USTICA

> **How to get there**
> **BY FERRY:** From Favignana, Naples and Trapani, seasonal hydrofoil with Ustica Lines; from Palermo, Si.Re.Mar hydrofoil and ferries

Hotels

Grotta Azzurra *⌑*
San Ferlicchio, tel. 0918449048
www.framonhotels.com
Open June-September
51 rooms. Restaurant, air conditioned, swimming pool
Credit Cards: American Express, Diner's Club, Mastercard, Visa
Sheltering in the most picturesque part of the island, sloping down towards the sea and deep in the maquis. Well-appointed rooms, summer piano bar and restaurant serving local specialties.

Restaurants

Da Umberto ⌑ ★
Piazza della Vittoria 7,
tel. 0918449542
www.isoladiustica.com
Open Easter-September
Cuisine: fish
Credit Cards: American Express, Mastercard, Visa
Nautical style trattoria with a pleasant terrace for al fresco dining. Excellent fresh fish.

At night

L'Isolotto
Via Petriera, tel. 0918449012
One of the pubs patronized by youngsters who live on the island: rustic ambience, beer, cocktails, some snacks and music. Open all year round (only on Saturday and Sunday in winter).

VULCANO

Hotels

Conti *** &
Porto Ponente, tel. 0909852012
www.netnet.it/conti
Open mid April-mid October
67 rooms. Restaurant
Credit Cards: American Express, Diner's Club, Mastercard, Visa
On the sea, rooms with independent entrances from the garden, run by the same family for forty years; regional cuisine.

Eolian *** ★
Porto Ponente, tel. 0909852151
www.eolianhotel.com
Open April-September
88 rooms. Restaurant, parking, swimming pool, tennis
Credit Cards: American Express, Diner's Club, Mastercard, Visa
Aeolian style building; comfortable rooms, restaurant on the terrace and swimming pool filled with spa and sea water. A flight of steps leads down to the beach.

Les Sables Noirs *⌑*
Porto Ponente, tel. 0909850
www.framonhotels.com
Open May- mid October
48 rooms. Restaurant, parking, air conditioned, swimming pool
Credit Cards: American Express, Diner's Club, Mastercard, Visa
Typical Mediterranean style

construction on the sea. Comfortable furnishings and infrastructures; restaurant "Baia di Ponente", for hotel guests only.

Restaurants

Maria Tindara ⌑ & ★
Via Provinciale 38,
tel. 0909853004
Cuisine: Aeolian
Credit Cards: American Express, Diner's Club, Mastercard, Visa
A few kilometers from the sea, this restaurant serves regional cuisine based on fish and meat specialties; do not miss the home-made pasta and desserts.

ZAFFERANA ETNEA

> **ℹ Pro Loco**
> *Piazza Luigi Sturzo 1,*
> *tel. 0957082825*
> *www.prolocozafferanaetnea.it*
>
> **How to get there**
> **BY CAR:** exit Giarre, A18 motorway Messina-Catania
> **BY TRAIN:** FS Railway Station station in Catania; bus connection

Hotels

Airone *** &
Airone, via Cassone 67,
tel. 0957081819
www.hotel-airone.it
60 rooms. Restaurant, parking, air conditioned, swimming pool, sauna, gym
Credit Cards: American Express, Diner's Club, Mastercard, Visa
Thirties construction, renovated in keeping with the surrounding countryside. Rustic-elegant ambience, meeting rooms and wellness center.

Primavera dell'Etna *** & ★
Airone, via Cassone 86,
tel. 0957082348
www.hotel-primavera.it
57 rooms. Restaurant, parking, air conditioned, tennis
Credit Cards: American Express, Diner's Club, Mastercard, Visa
Located on the road to Etna, a building with a panoramic view all the way to the sea. Large, bright rooms; restaurant serves Sicilian specialties.

Restaurants

Parco dei Principi ⌑⌑ &
Via delle Ginestre 1,
tel. 0957082335
www.paginegialle.it/pdprincipi
Closed Tuesday
Cuisine: Sicilian and classic
Credit Cards: American Express, Diner's Club, Mastercard, Visa
In a 19th century villa surrounded by a park, an elegant restaurant with conference and banqueting rooms. Not to be missed, especially during the Etna mushroom season.

⁑⁑⁑ / ★ Hotels ▥ / ⌑ Restaurants & Disabled ★ Special TCI Rates ♨ Thermal spa ⚕ Health Center

METRIC CONVERTIONS

DISTANCE

Kilometres/Miles

km to mi	mi to km
1 = 0.62	1 = 1.6
2 = 1.2	2 = 3.2
3 = 1.9	3 = 4.8
4 = 2.5	4 = 6.4
5 = 3.1	5 = 8.1
6 = 3.7	6 = 9.7
7 = 4.3	7 = 11.3
8 = 5.0	8 = 12.9

Meters/Feet

m to ft	ft to m
1 = 3.3	1 = 0.30
2 = 6.6	2 = 0.61
3 = 9.8	3 = 0.91
4 = 13.1	4 = 1.2
5 = 16.4	5 = 1.5
6 = 19.7	6 = 1.8
7 = 23.0	7 = 2.1
8 = 26.2	8 = 2.4

WEIGHT

Kilograms/Pounds

kg to lb	lb to kg
1 = 2.2	1 = 0.45
2 = 4.4	2 = 0.91
3 = 6.6	3 = 1.4
4 = 8.8	4 = 1.8
5 = 11.0	5 = 2.3
6 = 13.2	6 = 2.7
7 = 15.4	7 = 3.2
8 = 17.6	8 = 3.6

Grams/Ounces

g to oz	oz to g
1 = 0.04	1 = 28
2 = 0.07	2 = 57
3 = 0.11	3 = 85
4 = 0.14	4 = 114
5 = 0.18	5 = 142
6 = 0.21	6 = 170
7 = 0.25	7 = 199
8 = 0.28	8 = 227

TEMPERATURE

Celsius/Fahrenheit

C	F
-25	-13
-20	-4
-15	5
-10	14
-5	23
0	32
5	41
10	50
15	59
20	68
25	77
30	86
35	95
40	104
45	113
50	122
55	131
60	140

LIQUID VOLUME

Liters/U.S. Gallons

L to gal	gal to L
1 = 0.26	1 = 3.8
2 = 0.53	2 = 7.6
3 = 0.79	3 = 11.4
4 = 1.1	4 = 15.1

Liters/U.S. Gallons

L to gal	gal to L
5 = 1.3	5 = 18.9
6 = 1.6	6 = 22.7
7 = 1.8	7 = 26.5
8 = 2.1	8 = 30.3

GENERAL INDEX

GLOSSARY

Aedicule
Small, classical structure, containing a sacred image, either inside a church or building or standing on its own.

Altar-frontal
Decorative panel covering the front, lower part of an altar.

Altar-piece
Painting or sculpture, placed behind or above an altar

Ambulatory
Open-air walkway flanked by columns or trees; also corridor or passageway in theater, amphitheatre, or catacombs.

Anta (pl. Antae)
Pilaster forming the ends of the lateral walls of a temple cella; when the facade consists of columns set between two antae, the columns are said to be in antis.

Apse
Part of a church at the end of the nave; generally semi-cylindrical in shape, with a semi-spherical roof.

Architrave
Horizontal frame above a door or opening.

Archivolt
Molded architrave carried round an arch

Ashlar
Type of external wall covering, made of protruding, roughly-hewn stones

Barrel vault
Vault which has a rectangular ground-plan and semicircular cross-section.

Bas relief
Type of sculpture (in marble, ivory, bronze or other material) where the carved figures stand out on a flat background to a lesser extent than in a high-relief

Calidarium see **Terme**

Candelabra
Bas relief or painting consisting of fruit, flowers, leaves, or other decorative motifs, used to ornament columns, vaults, walls, etc.

Capital
Part which links a column to the structure above. In classical architecture, capitals were Doric, Ionian, or Corinthian.

Cartoon
Full-size, preparatory drawing for a painting, fresco or tapestry

Choir
Area for choir members, either in front of or behind the high altar in a church presbytery.

Ciborium
Square structure with four columns supporting an overhead cover; usually containing an altar or tomb; or casket or tabernacle containing the host.

Comacine masters
Skilled Lombard stone-masons

Counter-facade
Internal wall of the facade of a building

Cross vault
Vault consisting of two intersecting barrel vaults, with a square ground-plan

Depressed Arch
Arch where the curved part consists of a short segment of a circumference

Drum
Part of a cupola, with vertical walls, which the dome extends from.

Frigidarium see **Terme**

Greek cross
Cross with arms of equal length

High relief
Type of sculpture where the carved figures protrude substantially from the flat background

Hypogeum
Subterranean excavation for burial of the dead (usually Etruscan)

Krater
Ancient Greek and Roman mixing bowl, conical in shape with rounded base.

Lacunar ceiling
Ceiling decorated with symmetrically-arranged, embedded panels, usually made of richly-ornamented stucco or wood.

Lantern
Topmost part of a cupola, either open or with windows, to allow light inside. It generally resembles a circular temple.

Latin cross
Cross with a long vertical arm

Lavabo
Hand-basin usually outside a refectory or sacristy.

Lunette
Semi-circular space on a wall, vault or ceiling, often decorated with a painting or relief.

Oeil-de-boeuf
Small, round or oval window

Ogival arch
Arch which is pointed at the top, typical of Gothic architecture

Oratory
Place of worship, reserved for certain people or communities

Palestra (pl. Palestrae) see **Terme**

Pediment
Structure crowning the facade of a building, usually triangular in shape.

Pendentive
Concave surface between arches beneath a dome

Polyptych
Altar-piece consisting of a number of panels. A diptych has two panels; a triptych has three.

Predella
Small painting or panel, usually in sections, attached below a large altar-piece Presbytery Part of a church where the main altar is situated; generally raised or separated from the rest of the nave by a balustrade or such like.

Pronaos
Front part or entrance area to a building, with columns.

Putto
Figure of a child sculpted or painted; usually nude

Sacristy
Part of church where furnishings and vestments are kept, and where clergy prepare for services.

Splayed portal
Portal set into diagonally-sloped wall facings

Stall
Wide, wooden seat with arm-rests and back, placed in a row with others.

Stoup
Vessel for holy water, generally placed near church entrance

Tabernacle
Aedicule or niche containing sacred image, inside or outside a church, or standing on its own; also a small, enclosed aedicule placed on the altar, containing the host.

Tepidarium see **Terme**

Terme
In Ancient Rome, usually public building complexes for hot and cold baths. Already common by the 2nd century BC, the popularity of bath complexes reached its height in the Imperial period, when swimming-pools, massage rooms, gymnasiums (palestrae), gardens and libraries were added. The actual bath complex (Terme) consisted of a changing room, a warm room with a warm pool (tepidarium), a hot room with a hot pool (calidarium), a sauna and a room with pools of cold water for cold baths (frigidarium).

Tondo
Round painting or bas relief

Transept
Area perpendicular to the nave, often extending out at the sides and giving the building a cross-shaped ground-plan.

Tribune
Area including the presbytery, choir and apse, in early-Christian basilicas; in churches generally, any loggia set into or protruding from the walls.

Triptych
see Polyptych

THE ANCIENT PANTHEON

The ancient Greeks believed there was a large family of gods and goddesses, which they called the Pantheon. The first race of gods, called the Titans, was overthrown by the Olympian gods, who took their name from Mount Olympus in Greece, where they lived.

The Ancient Romans incorporated much of the mythology of Ancient Greece into their own and many of the Greek gods have matching Roman gods. There follows a list of the main deities of the Greek/Roman pantheon.

THE TWELVE PRINCIPAL DEITIES:

Greek Name	Roman name	Description
Aphrodite	Venus	Goddess of love and beauty. Daughter of Zeus. Symbols: myrtle tree, dove, sparrow, swan, mirror.
Apollo	Apollo	God of the sun, music, poetry and medicine. Symbols: laurel tree, dolphin, crow.
Ares	Mars	God of war, son of Zeus and Hera. Usually depicted wearing helmet and shield.
Artemis	Diana	Goddess of the moon and hunting. Symbols: bow and quiver or spear, chariot drawn by stags.
Athena	Minerva	Goddess of wisdom. Symbols: olive, owl.
Hades	Pluto	God of the Underworld. Brother of Zeus. Had a helmet which rendered its wearer invisible.
Hephaistos	Vulcan	Son of Hera. God of fire and blacksmiths. Usually depicted in a forge, at the anvil, holding a hammer.
Hera	Juno	Queen of the gods, goddess of the atmosphere, wife of Zeus. Symbols: cow, peacock.
Hermes	Mercury	Son of Zeus, messenger of the gods. Symbols: winged sandals, winged hat.
Hestia	Vesta	A virgin goddess and sister of Zeus. Goddess of the hearth and symbol of the home.
Poseidon	Neptune	Ruler of the sea, brother of Zeus. Usually depicted with a crown and a three-pronged spear known as a trident.
Zeus	Jupiter	Lord of the sky and supreme ruler of the gods of Olympus, husband of Hera. Known for throwing thunder- bolts when angry. Symbols: eagle, thunderbolt, sceptre.

OTHER DEITIES MENTIONED IN THE GUIDE:

Greek Name	Roman name	Description
Demeter	Ceres	Goddess of the earth, farming and fertility. Symbols: corn-sheaf, cornucopia flowing with fruit and vegetables, or sickle.
Dionysus	Bacchus	God of wine and the theater. Often depicted naked with a crown of vine-leaves and grapes.
Herakles	Hercules	The most popular of all the gods, son of Zeus and Alcmene. Famous for his "Twelve Labors", in which he triumphs over evil. Often depicted wearing a lion's skin. Symbols: club, snakes.
Pesephone/ Kore	Proserpina	Daughter of Zeus and Demeter, queen of the Underworld. Symbol: pomegranite symbolizing her return to earth each spring to regenerate the earth.

Tradition and Modernity

COMUNE DI TRAPANI
ASSESSORATO TURISMO
E SVILUPPO ECONOMICO

Trapani sailing φ5

Portorosa

APT
Azienda Autonoma Provinciale
per l'Incremento Turistico
MESSINA

The Province of Messina:
from Taormina to the Aeolian Islands

Taormina - Il Teatro greco

Lipari - I Faraglioni

Taormina - Palazzo Duchi di Santo Stefano

Nebrodi - Escursione

Messina - Duomo

**Aapit - Azienda Autonoma Provinciale
per l'Incremento Turistico**
Via Calabria, is. 301 bis - 98122 Messina
tel. 090640221, fax 0906411047
telex 980112 APT ME - I - e-mail: aptme@tiscalinet.it

Uffici informazioni turistiche
Messina - via Calabria, is.301 bis,
ang. via T. Capra - Cap 98122 - tel. 090674236
Roma - via Vittorio Veneto, 96 - cap 00187 - tel. 064814903